CCNA Complete Guide 2nd Edition

Copyright © 2008 Yap Chin Hoong

www.yapchinhoong.com

About the Author

Yap Chin Hoong is a senior network engineer with a computer network consulting firm at Malaysia. He found great satisfaction when conveyed complex networking concepts to his peers. Yap holds a bachelor's degree in Information Technology from Universiti Tenaga Nasional.

When not sitting in front of computers, Yap enjoying playing various types of musical instruments. Visit his YouTube channel during your study breaks. :-)

Facebook: http://www.facebook.com/yapchinhoong
Website: http://www.itcertguides.com/
YouTube: http://www.youtube.com/user/yapchinhoong

Dear valued customer,

Your investment of the CCNA Complete Guide 2nd Edition Companion CD will really worth it because it contains much valuable information that can enhance your CCNA studies. ☺ Kindly download the Companion CD by following the instructions at *http://tinyurl.com/CD36791*.

The **Dynamips** folder contains a FREE software that provides a tool to simulate real Cisco routers (and switches) for your CCNA practices. It is so powerful that can simulate any real Cisco IOS commands because it actually loads and runs real Cisco IOS software. ☺

Setup the Dynamips/Dynagen using a tutorial file included in the folder. However, you may face some issues with Telnet in Windows Vista and Windows 7. Try to Google around to solve that, it isn't that difficult. ☺

The **MISC Tools and Guides** folder contains some extra info regarding Dynamips. Actually you don't really need to look into it. It contains the tools and guides when you wanted to use other IOS files other than those provided in the **IOS** folder in the CD. The **VBUnzip** is actually a tool used to extract Cisco IOS files. So when Dynamips load an extracted IOS image file, it doesn't need to extract it because it is already extracted. This will speed up the boot up time of the IOS. If you managed to see how real Cisco routers boot, you will see "extracting images.......". Basically we want to skip that step in the simulation. ☺

The **Lab Setups** folder contains all the labs setup using Dynamips according to the CCNA Guide. Whenever you saw a network diagram with some routers and IP addresses, and feel like wanted to see how it works yourself. You may first look at the page number in the CCNA guide, then heads towards the **Lab Setups** folder, most likely that there is a lab for it. Copy it out to your desktop, extract it, launch the Dynamips engine, and run the Network.net file for the lab, the lab should be loaded in 10 seconds. Console into every routers, copy and paste the basic configuration into the routers (the config files are included in the folder for a particular lab setup itself). TATA! You are ready to practice the commands according to the CCNA Guide. Just follow the commands and you will be able to see how things work. All commands in the CCNA Guide have been fully tested and working fine. ☺

Basically we can setup Cisco labs and practice Cisco IOS commands in 2 minutes time. ☺ Before this, we would need to look for real routers, power cords, UTP network cables, power them on, took 5 minutes, clear the configuration, etc. From the time we are motivated to practice until the lab is up and ready for practice (maybe take able 30 minutes), we may already feel tired and say: "OK, let me watch a movie and come back to this later...". ☺ Hope you get the idea of using this wonderful tool.

Finally, the **Proof of Concepts** folder contains many packet captures and command output captured for the various topics throughout the CCNA Guide. Download and install **Wireshark** *http://www.wireshark.org/* to view the packet capture files. Packet captures shows the bits and bytes of network packets. Basically I spend many days and nights capturing them to prove how networking works, and documented them down in the CCNA Guide. Basically most of the concepts have been proven using Cisco IOS commands and real network packets. Hope you get the idea. ☺

The files in the **Proof of Concept** folder are basically used to enhance you learning experience. Those info are saved separately there because it will overwhelm the most of the readers and make the CCNA Guide too lengthy if everything is included in the CCNA Guide itself. ☺

OK, I have briefed the overall usages of the Companion CD. Have fun and keep in touch! ☺

Regards,
YapCH

Chapter 1
Introduction to Computer Networking

- Welcome to the wonderful and exciting world of computer networking and Cisco certification!

- There are 3 levels of Cisco certification:

Associate level	
CCNA	Cisco Certified Network Associate
CCDA	Cisco Certified Design Associate
Professional level	
CCNP	Cisco Certified Network Professional
CCDP	Cisco Certified Design Professional
CCSP	Cisco Certified Security Professional
CCIP	Cisco Certified Internetwork Professional
CCVP	Cisco Certified Voice Professional
Expert level	
CCIE	Cisco Certified Internetwork Expert
- Routing and Switching	
- Security	
- Service Provider	
- Voice	
- Storage Networking	
- Wireless	

- Below are the available paths to become a CCNA:

1	One exam: **CCNA** (640-802), 50-60 questions, 90 minutes, USD$250.
2	Two exams: **ICND1** (640-822), 50-60 questions, 90 minutes, USD$125. **ICND2** (640-816), 45-55 questions, 75 minute, USD$125.

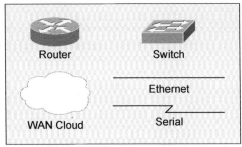

Figure 1-1: Icons and Symbols

- The 2 most common **Internetworking Models** are **OSI Reference Model** and **TCP/IP Model**. **Note:** OSI – Open Systems Interconnection.

- Below are the benefits of layered architecture:
    - i) **Reduces complexity** and **accelerates evolution**. A vendor may concentrate its research and development works on a single layer without worrying the details of other layers, because changes made in one layer will not affect other layers.
    - ii) Ensures **interoperability** among multiple vendors' products, as vendors develop and manufacture their products based on open standards.

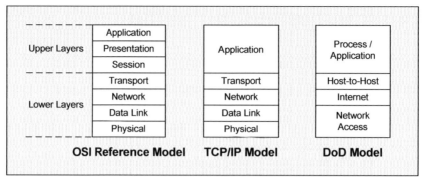

Figure 1-2: OSI Reference Model, TCP/IP Model, and DoD (Department of Defense) Model

- The **upper 3 layers** define the communication between applications running at different end systems and the communication between an application and its users.
  The **lower 4 layers** define how data is transmitted between end systems.

- Below describes the roles and functions of every layer in the OSI reference model:

Application	Acts as the **interface** between applications and the presentation layer. Applications such as web browsers are not reside in this layer. In fact they use this interface for communication with remote applications at the other end. Ex. Protocols: **HTTP, FTP, SMTP, Telnet, SNMP**.
Presentation	Defines **data formats**, presents data, and handles **compression** and **encryption**. As an example, the FTP ASCII and binary transfer modes define how FTP transfer data between 2 end systems. The receiving end will reassemble data according to the format used and pass them back to the application layer. Ex. Formats: **ASCII, EBCDIC, JPEG, GIF, TIFF, MPEG, WAV, MIDI**.
Session	Defines how to **setup / establish**, **control / manage**, and **end / terminate** the presentation layer sessions between 2 end systems. Uses port numbers to keep different application data separated from each other. Ex: **SQL, NFS, RPC, X Window, NetBIOS, Winsock, BSD socket**.
Transport	Provides **reliable** (TCP) and **unreliable** (UDP) application data delivery services, as well as **segmentation** and **reassembly** of applications data. Important concepts are **connection-oriented**, **connectionless**, **error recovery**, **acknowledgment**, **flow control**, and **windowing**. Ex. Protocols: **TCP, UDP, SPX** (Sequenced Packet Exchange).
Network	Defines **end-to-end packet delivery** and **tracking of end system locations** with **logical addressing** – IP addresses. Determines the best path to transfer data within an internetwork through the routes learning via routing protocols. Allows communication *between end systems from different networks*. There are 2 types of packets – **data packets** and **routing update packets**. Ex. Protocols: **IP, IPX, AppleTalk**.
Data Link	Defines how to transmit data over a network media (how to place network layer packets onto the network media – cable or wireless) with **physical addressing**. Allows communication *between end systems within the same network*. Ex. Protocols: LAN – **Ethernet**, WAN – **HDLC, PPP, Frame Relay, ATM**.
Physical	Defines specifications for communication between end systems and the physical media (how to place data link layer frames onto the media). Defines connector shapes, number of pins, pin usages or assignments, electrical current levels, and signal encoding schemes. Ex: **Ethernet, RS-232, V.35**.

- Below lists some comparison points between common network devices:

Routers	They are **Network** layer (L3) devices. Their main concern is **locating specific networks** – Where is it? Which is the shortest path or best way to reach there? They **create separate broadcast domains**.
Switches and **Bridges**	They are **Data Link** layer (L2) devices. Their main role is **locating specific hosts** within the same network. Devices connected to a switch do not receive data that is meant only for devices connected to other ports. They **create separate collision domains** for devices connected to them (segmentation) but the devices are still reside in the **same broadcast domain**. **Note:** VLAN technology found in enterprise-class switches are able to create separate broadcast domains (multiple networks).
Hubs	They are **Physical** layer (L1) devices. Hubs are not smart devices. They send all the bits received from one port to all other ports; hence all devices connected via a hub **receive everything** the other devices send. This is like being in a room with many people – everyone hear if someone speaks. If more than one person speaks at a time, there is only noise. Repeaters also fall under the category of L1 devices. All devices connected to a hub reside in the **same collision and broadcast domains**.

Note: A collision domain is an area of an Ethernet network where collisions can occur. If an end system can prevent another from using the network when it is using the network, these systems are considered reside in the same collision domain.

- **Data encapsulation** is the process of wrapping data from upper layer with a particular layer's header (and trailer), which creates PDU for that particular layer (for adjacent-layer interaction).

- A **Protocol Data Unit** (PDU) consists of the layer *n* control information and layer *n+1* encapsulated data for each layer (for same-layer interaction). Ex: L7PDU, L6PDU, ... L2PDU.

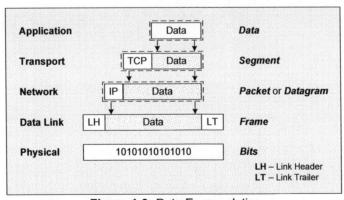

Figure 1-3: Data Encapsulation

- Below list the 2 types of interactions between layers:

Same-layer interaction	Each layer uses its own header (and trailer) to communicate between the **same layer** on **different computers**.
Adjacent-layer interaction	A particular layer provides services to its upper layer while requests its next lower layer to perform other functions. Take place on the **same computer**.

Cisco Hierarchical Model

- Defined by Cisco to simplify the design, implementation, and maintenance of responsive, scalable, reliable, and cost-effective networks.

- The 3 layers are **logical and not physical** – there may be many devices in a single layer, or a single device may perform the functions of 2 layers, eg: core and distribution.

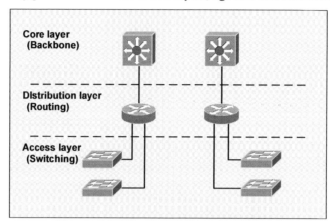

Figure 1-4: The Cisco Hierarchical Model

- Below are the 3 layers in the Cisco Hierarchical Model:

Core layer	Also referred to as the **backbone layer**. It is responsible for transferring large amounts of traffic reliably and quickly – switches traffic as fast as possible. A failure in the core can affect many users; hence fault tolerance is the main concern in this layer. The core layer should be designed for **high reliability**, **high availability**, **high redundancy**, **high speed**, and **low convergence**. Do not support workgroup access, implement access lists, VLAN routing, and packet filtering which can introduce latency to this layer.
Distribution layer	Also referred to as the **workgroup layer**. Its primary functions are routing, Inter-VLAN routing, defining or segmenting broadcast and multicast domains, network security and filtering with firewalls and access lists, WAN access, and determining (or filtering) how packets access across the core layer.
Access layer	Also referred to as the **desktop layer**. Here is where end systems gain access to the network. The access layer (switches) handles traffic for local services (within a network) whereas the distribution layer (routers) handles traffic for remote services. It mainly creates separate collision domains. It also defines the access control policies for accessing the access and distribution layers.

- In a hierarchical network, traffic on a lower layer is only allowed to be forwarded to the upper layer after it meets some clearly defined criteria. Filtering rules and operations restrict unnecessary traffic from traversing the entire network, which results in a more responsive (lower network congestion), scalable (easy to grow), and reliable (higher availability) network.

- A clear understanding of the traffic flow patterns of an organization helps to ensure the placement of network devices and end systems within the organization.

Application Layer

- **Telnet** is a TCP-based text-based terminal emulation application that allows a user to remote access a machine through a Telnet session using a Telnet client which login into a Telnet server. A user may execute applications and issue commands on the server via Telnet.

- **HyperText Transfer Protocol** (HTTP) is a TCP-based application protocol that is widely used on the World Wide Web to publish and retrieve HTML (HyperText Markup Language) pages.

- **File Transfer Protocol** (FTP) is a TCP-based application protocol that allows users to perform listing of files and directories, as well as transferring files between hosts. It cannot be used to execute remote applications as with Telnet. FTP server authentication is normally implemented by system administrators to restrict user access. Anonymous FTP is a common facility offered by many FTP servers, where users do not require an account on the server.

- **Trivial File Transfer Protocol** (TFTP) is the stripped-down version of FTP (UDP-based). It does not support directory browsing, and mainly used to send and receive files. It sends much smaller block of data compared to FTP, and does not support authentication as in FTP (insecure).

- **Network File System** (NFS) is a UDP-based network file sharing protocol. It allows interoperability between 2 different types of file systems or platforms, eg: UNIX and Windows.

- **Simple Mail Transfer Protocol** (SMTP) is a TCP-based protocol that provides email delivery services. SMTP is used to send mails between SMTP mail servers; while **Post Office Protocol 3 (POP3)** is used to retrieve mails in the SMTP mail servers.

- **X Window** is a popular UNIX display protocol which has been designed for client-server operations. It allows an X-based GUI application called an **X client** which running on one computer to display its graphical screen output on an **X server** running on another computer.

- **Simple Network Management Protocol** (SNMP) is the de facto protocol used for **network management** – fault, performance, security, configuration, and account management. It gathers data by polling SNMP devices from a management station at defined intervals. SNMP agents can also be configured to send SNMP Traps to the management station upon errors.

- **Domain Name System** (DNS) makes our life easier by providing name resolution services – **resolving hostnames into IP addresses**. It is used to resolve **Fully Qualified Domain Names** (FQDNs) into IP addresses. In DNS zone files, a FQDN is specified with a trailing dot, eg: server.test.com., specifies an absolute domain name ends with an empty top level domain label.

- What is a **Protocol**? The dictionary defines it as a standard procedure for regulating data transmission between networking devices.

This page is intentionally left blank

Chapter 2
Transport and Network Layers

Transport Layer

- Transport layer protocols provide **reliable** and **unreliable** application data delivery services. The **Transmission Control Protocol** (TCP) and **User Datagram Protocol** (UDP) are the most common transport layer protocols. There are many differences between them.

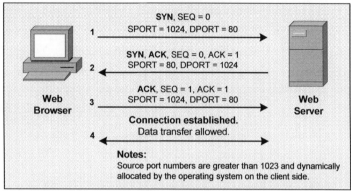

Figure 2-1: Connection-Oriented Session Establishment

- **Connection-oriented communication** is used in **reliable** transport service – TCP. Figure 2-1 shows the TCP connection establishment sequence (also known as **three-way handshake**) which allows the systems to exchange information such as initial sequence number, window size, and other parameters for reliable data transfer between a web browser (client) and a web server. These steps must be completed prior to data transmission in connection-oriented communication.

- The **SYN** and **ACK** flags are very important for the connection-oriented session establishment. When SYN bit is set, it means **synchronize the sequence numbers** (during connection setup), while ACK bit is used to indicate that **the value in the acknowledgment field is valid**. In step 2, the ACK replied by the web server acknowledges the receipt of the web browser's SYN message.

- Figure 2-2 shows the TCP connection termination sequence to gracefully shutdown a connection. An additional flag – **FIN** flag, is being used in the four-way connection termination sequence. Firstly, the web server sends a segment with the FIN bit set to 1 when the server application decided to gracefully close the connection after finished sending data (Step 1). The client would then reply with an ACK reply, which means it notices the connection termination request (Step 2). After that, the server will still wait for FIN segment from the client (Step 3). Finally, the server acknowledges the client's FIN segment (Step 4).

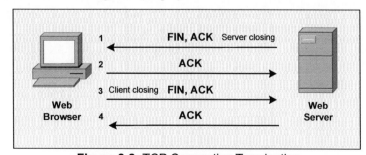

Figure 2-2: TCP Connection Termination

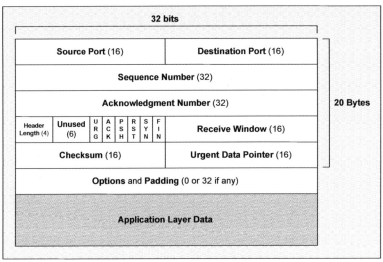

Figure 2-3: TCP Segment Structure

- **Sequence Number** is used by TCP to segment large application layer data into smaller pieces. Every TCP segment sent over a TCP connection has a sequence number, which represents the **byte-stream number relative to the 1st byte** of the application layer data.
  Acknowledgment Number is the sequence number of the **next expected bytes**. It is used by the receiver to tell the sender the next byte to send (or resend). The acknowledgment mechanism is **accumulative** – a packet with the ACK bit set and an acknowledgment number of x indicates that all bytes up to $x - 1$ have been received.

- **Error Recovery** is another important feature provided by TCP for reliable data transfer. SYN and ACK bits are also being used for this purpose. Figure 2-4 shows 2 TCP error recovery scenarios – **TCP Acknowledgment without Error** and **TCP Acknowledgment with Error**.

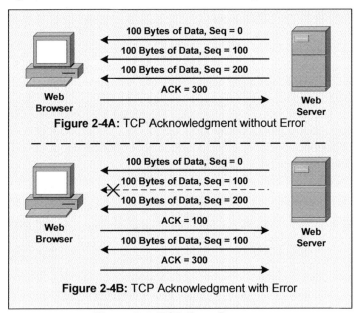

Figure 2-4A: TCP Acknowledgment without Error

Figure 2-4B: TCP Acknowledgment with Error

Figure 2-4: TCP Error Recovery

- In Figure 2-4B, the 2nd segment is lost. In order to recover the lost segment, the web client replies a segment with acknowledge number equals to 100, which means it expecting byte number 100 from the web server. The server then resends the data to the client (**retransmission**). Since the client has already received bytes 200-299 without error, it is not necessary to request again. Data is then reassembled back in order at the client end and passed to the application layer. Finally, the client continues to request data from the web server by sending an ACK = 300.

- **Positive Acknowledgment and Retransmission** (PAR) uses a timer that is set to the **retransmission timeout interval** and is being activated every time a sender sends a segment and waiting for the ACK reply. The sender will **resend all segments once the timer expired**. This provides a reliability mechanism that intends to overcome the following 2 problem scenarios:
  i)   The transmitted segment is lost or dropped.
  ii)   The ACK segment is failed to arrive at the sender.

- TCP segments **may arrive out of order** because routers can send data across different links to a destination host. Hence the TCP stack running at the receiving end **must reorder** the out of order segments before passing the data to the application layer.

- TCP **Flow Control** or **Congestion Control** provides a mechanism for the receiver to **control the sending rate** of the sender with a **windowing** mechanism. It is achieved via SEQ, ACK and Window fields in the TCP header. The receiver defines the Window size to tell the sender how many bytes are allowed to send without waiting for an acknowledgement. It represents the receiver's **available buffer**. Buffer is used to temporarily store the received bytes before the receiving application is free to process the received bytes. The sender will not send when the receiver's window is full. Increased Window size may result in increased throughput.

- The window size normally starts with small value and keeps on increment until an error occurs. The window size is negotiated dynamically throughout a TCP session and it may slide up and down, hence it is often being referred to as **sliding window**.

- **Multiplexing** allows multiple connections to be established between processes in 2 end systems. Multiplexing is a feature that allows the transport layer at the receiving end to differentiate between the various connections and **decide the appropriate application layer applications** to hand over the received and reassembled data (similar to the concept of forming virtual circuits). The **source and destination port number fields** in the TCP and UDP headers and a concept called **socket** are being used for this purpose.

- Below lists some popular applications and their associated well-known port numbers:

Application	Protocol	Port Number
HTTP	TCP	80
FTP	TCP	20 (data) and 21 (control)
Telnet	TCP	23
TFTP	UDP	69
DNS	TCP, UDP	53
DHCP	UDP	67, 68
SMTP	TCP	25
POP3	TCP	110
SNMP	UDP	161

- Port numbers 0 – 1023 are **well-known ports**, port numbers 1024 – 49151 are **registered ports**, and port numbers 49152 – 65535 are **private vendor assigned and dynamic ports**.

- **Socket** is a communication channel between 2 TCP processes. A client socket is created by specifying the IP address and the destination port to connect to the server; whereas a server socket binds to a specified port number and listens for incoming connections upon started a server application.

- **User Datagram Protocol** (UDP) is a **connectionless** (does not contact the destination before data transmission) and **unreliable** data delivery service, which also known as best effort service. No sequencing. No reordering. No acknowledgment. No error recovery. No congestion control.

- Applications uses UDP are either **tolerant to data lost**, or **perform error recovery themselves** (perform error recovery in application layer instead of transport layer).
  i)   Tolerant to data lost: **video streaming**.
  ii)   Handles its own reliability issues: **NFS** and **TFTP** (hence the use of TCP is unnecessary).

- Figure 2-5 shows the UDP segment structure. It does not contain SEQ, ACK and other fields as in TCP header. Even there are many disadvantages as mentioned above, UDP advantages over TCP are it is **faster** (no ACK process) and uses **less network bandwidth and processing resources**.

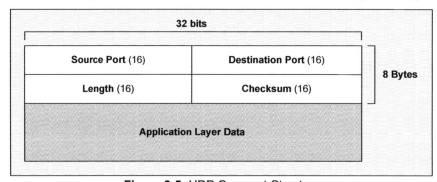

Figure 2-5: UDP Segment Structure

- In network programming, a socket would fail to bind to specified port if the port is already in use by another socket. However, a host is allowed to bind a TCP socket and a UDP socket to the **same port number** at the same time, and waiting for incoming connections, as they are treated as 2 different type of service – a host can provide TCP and UDP Echo services at the same time.

- Do not make false assumption that **connection-oriented = reliable!**
  A connection-oriented protocol does not mean it also performs error recovery, and vice-versa.

Connection Type	Reliable	Example Protocol
Connection-oriented	Yes	TCP
Connection-oriented	No	TP0 and TP2
Connectionless	Yes	TFTP and NFS
Connectionless	No	UDP

Note: TPx isTransport Protocol Class x in **ISO-TP** (OSI Transport Layer Protocols).

- Below shows the TCP and UDP comparison chart:

Feature	TCP	UDP
Connection-oriented	Yes	No
Reliable data transfer	Yes	No
Ordered data transfer	Yes	No
Flow control	Yes	No
Multiplexing	Yes	Yes

Network Layer

- The main functions performed by network layer (L3) protocols are **routing** and **addressing**.

- All devices connected to a common L2 network usually share the same network address space. A flat network is a network which all network devices reside in a same broadcast domain.

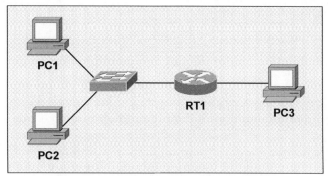

Figure 2-6: Network Setup for IP Routing

- When an end system would like to send an IP packet to another end system, it first compares the destination IP address with its own IP address. If the destination IP address is within the **same subnet** (PC1 to PC2), the originating end system will send an ARP request to resolve the MAC address of the destination end system; the resolved MAC address is then used to encapsulate the L3 packets into L2 frames for transmission across the data link to the destination end system.

- If an end system determines that the destination end system is on a **different subnet**, it encapsulates the packets into frames and sends using the **MAC address of its default gateway** and the **IP address of the destination end system**. The default gateway router will then receive the frames, performs routing table lookup, reconstructs the frames with the source MAC address of the outgoing interface, and forwards the frames out the corresponding outgoing interface.

- Routing algorithms can be classified into the following types:

Static vs. **Dynamic**	Static routes are manually configured and modified. Dynamic routes dynamically maintain routing tables upon network changes.
Single-path vs. **Multipath**	Some routing protocols support multiple paths (redundant links) to the same destination network.
Flat vs. **Hierarchical**	In a flat routing system, the routers are peers of all other routers. In a hierarchical routing system, some routers form a routing area.
Host-intelligent vs. **Router-intelligent**	Some routing algorithms allow the source end system determines the entire route to a destination (**source routing**). Most routing algorithms assume that hosts know nothing about network, and the path determination process is done by the routing algorithms.
Intradomain vs. **Interdomain**	Some routing protocols work only within a single domain (autonomous system) while others work within and between domains.

- The length of an IP address is 32-bit or 4 bytes, and usually written in **dotted-decimal notation**, where each byte (8 bits) of the 32-bit IP address is converted to its decimal equivalent. Each of the decimals numbers in an IP address is called an **octet**.
  Ex: IP address = 192.168.0.1. 1st octet = 192, 2nd octet = 168, 3rd octet = 0, and 4th octet = 1.

- Each network interface in an end system will be assigned a unique IP address.

- Network layer addresses were designed to allow **logical grouping of addresses**.

TCP/IP	network or subnet
IPX	network
AppleTalk	cable range

- IP addressing and grouping of IP addresses **ease the routing process** by assisting routers in building their routing tables. The general ideas of IP addresses grouping are:
  - All IP addresses in the same group must not be separated by a router.
  - IP addresses separated by a router must be in different groups.

- **IP subnetting** allows the creation of larger numbers of smaller groups of IP addresses, instead of simply using the class A, B, and C conventional rules. Subnetting treats a subdivision of a single class A, B, or C network as a network itself – a single class A, B, or C network can be subdivided into many **smaller groups** and non-overlapping subnets.

- When performing subnetting, the subnet portion or mask (the part between the network and host portions of an address) is created by **borrowing** bits from the host portion of the address. The size of the network portion never shrinks while the size of the host portion **shrinks** to make room for the subnet portion of the address. Figure 2-7 shows the address format when subnetting.

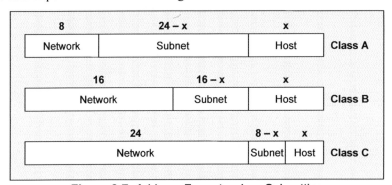

Figure 2-7: Address Formats when Subnetting

- **Subnet masks** are used in conjunction with IP addressing to define **which subnet** an IP address (in fact, an end system) resides in by identifying the network and host bits for the IP address. Routers only examine the network bits in an IP address as indicated by the subnet mask – the network address, when performing its function – examine network address, lookup network address in the routing table, and forward the packet out the corresponding outgoing interface.

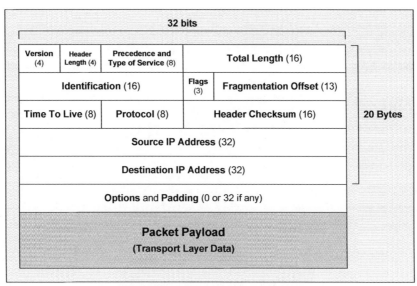

Figure 2-8: IPv4 Datagram Format

- The Identification, Flags, Fragmentation Offset fields are used for **IP fragmentation** – the process of breaking a large packet that exceed the MTU of the intermediate network medium into smaller packets called **fragments**. Network layer fragments are reassembled before they are being passed to the transport layer at the receiver. IPv6 does not support fragmentation at routers. Fragmentation can result in degradation of router performance due to the additional workloads.

- The Protocol field identifies the transport layer protocol (eg: TCP, UDP) or network layer protocol (eg: ICMP, ARP) the packet payload (the data portion of datagram) should be passed to.

- **Checksum** is a test for ensuring the integrity of data. It is a number calculated from a sequence of mathematical functions. It is typically placed at the end of the data from which it is calculated, and then recalculated at the receiving end for verification (error detection).

- IP does not run complete checksum upon the whole packet as what Ethernet does upon a frame. The Header Checksum field in the IPv4 header is a checksum that is calculated based on all the fields in the IPv4 header **only**; hence only the IPv4 header is being checked for errors. The Header Checksum field is filled with 0s when computing the checksum.

- Below are some popular protocols that can be specified in the Protocol field:

Protocol	Protocol Number
ICMP (Internet Control Message Protocol)	1 (0x01)
TCP (Transmission Control Protocol)	6 (0x06)
IGRP (Interior Gateway Routing Protocol)	9 (0x09)
UDP (User Datagram Protocol)	17 (0x11)
EIGRP (Enhanced IGRP)	88 (0x58)
OSPF (Open Shortest Path First)	89 (0x59)
IPv6 (IP Version 6)	41 (0x29)
GRE (Generic Routing Encapsulation)	47 (0x2F)
ESP (Encapsulating Security Payload)	50 (0x32)
AH (Authentication Header)	51 (0x33)
VRRP (Virtual Router Redundancy Protocol)	112
PIM (Protocol Independent Multicast)	103 (0x67)

- The following section discusses several TCP/IP network layer utility protocols.

- **Address Resolution Protocol** (ARP) → When IP (L3) has a packet to send, it must supply the destination host's hardware address to a network access protocol, eg: Ethernet or Token Ring. IP will first try to find the information from the ARP cache. If IP is unable to find it from the ARP cache, it uses ARP to **dynamically discover or learn the MAC address** for a particular IP network layer address. A sender must know the physical or MAC address of the destination host before sending out the data. Basically ARP resolves an IP address (software logical address) to a MAC address (hardware physical address).

- **ARP Requests** are **L2 broadcasts**. Since Ethernet is a broadcast media, hence all devices on a segment will receive an ARP Request. However, only the device with the requested L3 address will answer the ARP Request by sending a *unicast* **ARP Reply** back to the device that sent the ARP Request. The sender will then have the IP and MAC addresses for data transmission.
  Note: The sender might need to send out DNS request to resolve the hostname of the destination host into IP address prior to the ARP Request-Reply process.

- Hubs and repeaters are typically signal amplifiers, while switches do forward broadcasts out all ports except the incoming port. In fact they have no impact on ARP traffic.

- The **show arp** EXEC command displays the entries in the ARP cache.

- **Proxy ARP** happens when a network device replies to an ARP Request on behave of another device with the MAC address of the interface that received the ARP Request. The ARP caches of end systems might need to be flushed (with the **arp −d** command) whenever a Proxy ARP device is being introduced into a network.

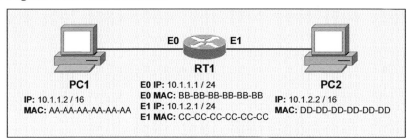

Figure 2-9: Network Setup for Proxy ARP

- Routers do not forward L2 and L3 broadcasts. Figure 2-9 shows a typical Proxy ARP scenario. Since PC1 and PC2 IP addresses are reside in the same subnet (10.1.0.0/16), PC1 will assume it is in the same segment with PC2. Problems arise as there is a router separates the 2 devices into different broadcast domains, which the ARP broadcast traffic will not be forwarded.

- RT1, the Cisco router will answer the ARP Request sent by PC1 on behave of PC2 with the MAC address of the interface that received the ARP Request − BB-BB-BB-BB-BB-BB. When PC1 receives the ARP Reply from RT1, it assumes the MAC address of PC2 is BB-BB-BB-BB-BB-BB. Finally, further traffic destined to PC2 will have 10.1.2.2 as the destination IP address and encapsulated with the MAC address BB-BB-BB-BB-BB-BB instead of DD-DD-DD-DD-DD-DD.

- Proxy ARP is enabled by default on Cisco routers. It can be enabled or disabled with the [**no**] **ip proxy-arp** interface subcommand respectively. Proxy ARP is not really a protocol; it is a service offered by routers.

- **Reverse ARP** (RARP), **Boot Protocol** (BOOTP) and **Dynamic Host Configuration Protocol** (DHCP) allow a host computer to **discover** the IP address it should use.

- **RARP** and **BOOTP** requests which are sent out as broadcasts would include a host MAC address to request for an IP address assigned to that MAC address. RARP is only able to ask for an IP address, it can't even ask for the subnet mask; whereas BOOTP which was defined later, allows many more information to be announced to a BOOTP client, eg: IP address, subnet mask, default gateway, other servers IP addresses, and the name of the file the client computer should download (a more sophisticated OS) into the client computer's RAM. Both protocols were created to allow **diskless workstations** to initialize, boot up, and start operating once turned on.

- However, both protocols are not in use today as an RARP or BOOTP server is **required to know all computers MAC addresses** – a MAC-to-IP-address mapping table, and the corresponding configuration parameters for each computer, which is a nightmare of network administration.

- **Dynamic Host Configuration Protocol** (DHCP), which is widely used in today's networks, solves the scaling and configuration issues in RARP and BOOTP. DHCP uses the same concept of BOOTP – a client makes a request, the server supplies the IP address, subnet mask, default gateway, DNS server IP address, and other information. The biggest advantage of DHCP is a DHCP server does not need to be configured with the MAC-to-IP-address mapping table.

- ARP and RARP are network and data link layer protocols whereas DHCP and BOOTP are application layer protocols.

- **Inverse ARP** (InARP) doesn't deal with IP and MAC addresses. It is used to dynamically create the mapping between local DLCIs and remote IP addresses in **Frame Relay** networks. However, many organizations prefer to statically create those mappings. This default behavior can be disabled with the **no frame-relay inverse-arp** interface subcommand.

- **Internet Control Message Protocol** (ICMP) is a management and control protocol for IP. It is often used by hosts and routers to exchange network layer info and problem notification. ICMP messages are encapsulated within IP packets and sent using the basic IP header only.

- **Hops** or **TTL** (Time-to-Live) → Each IP packet needs to pass through a certain number of routers (hops) before arrive to the destination. When a packet reaches its limit of existence in the network (TTL expired) before arrives to its destination, the last router that receives the packet will discard it, and sends an ICMP message to the sender to inform the dropping of its packet. This mechanism is used to prevent IP packets from being forwarded forever upon routing loops.

- **ping** (Packet INternet Groper) is a basic network utility that uses ICMP to test for physical and logical **network connectivity** by sending out an ICMP Echo Request message to an IP address, and expects the end system with that IP address will reply with an ICMP Echo Reply message. The ICMP identifier, sequence number, and data received in an Echo Request message must be returned **unaltered** in the Echo Reply message to the sender.

- **Traceroute** is another network utility that is being used to **discover the path** to a remote host by utilizing ICMP Time Exceeded messages.

This page is intentionally left blank

Chapter 3
Data Link and Physical Layers featuring The Ethernet

Data Link Layer

-   The data link layer defines the standards and protocols used to control the transmission of data across a physical network. The data link and physical layers work together to provide the physical delivery of data across various media types. L1 is about **encoding and sending bits**; whereas L2 is about **knowing when to send the bits, noticing when errors occurred when sending bits, and identifying the computer that needs to get the bits**.

-   Routers, which work at the network layer, don't care about where a particular host is located; they only concern about where the networks are located, and the best way to reach them. Data link layer is the one that responsible to **identify** all devices resides on a local network, ensures messages are **delivered to the appropriate device** on a LAN using hardware addresses, and translates messages from the network layer into bits for the physical layer to transmit.

-   The data link layer encapsulates network layer packets into **frames** with a **header** that contains the source and destination hardware addresses, as well as a **trailer** that contains the FCS field. Packets are never altered. In fact they are framed and encapsulated / decapsulated continuously with the corresponding type of data link layer control information that is required to pass it onto different physical media types.

-   Switches **operate faster** than routers because they perform lesser job – they don't need to process L3 headers to lookup for destination addresses as with routers. Adding routers (or hops) **increases the latency** – the amount of time a packet takes to get to its destination.

-   Most data link protocols perform the following functions:

Arbitration	Determines the appropriate timing to use the physical media to **avoid collisions**. If all devices in a LAN are allowed to send at any time as they wanted, the data frames can collide, and data in the frames are messed up. **Carrier sense multiple access with collision detection** (CSMA/CD) algorithm is used by Ethernet for arbitration.
Addressing	Ensures that the correct device **listens, receives**, and processes the frame. Ethernet uses a 6-byte **Media Access Control** (MAC) address while Frame Relay uses a 10-bit **Data Link Connection Identifier** (DLCI) address for L2 addressing.
Error Detection	Discovers whether bit errors occurred during the transmission of a frame. Most data link layer protocols include a **Frame Check Sequence** (FCS) or **Cyclical Redundancy Check** (CRC) field in the data link trailer, which allowed the receiver to notice if there is any error. This value is calculated with a mathematical formula applied to the data in the frame. **Error detection does not include recovery** – a frame is discarded if the calculated value and the FCS value are mismatched. Error recovery is the responsibility of other protocols, eg: TCP.
Identifying Encapsulated Data	Determines the data or protocol that resides in the Data field of a frame. The Protocol Type field in IEEE Ethernet 802.2 **Logical Link Control** (LLC) header is being used for this purpose.

- Below lists the 2 sublayers in the IEEE Ethernet data link layer:

Logical Link Control (LLC) (IEEE 802.2)	Provides an interface for upper layers to work with any type of MAC sublayer, eg: 802.3 Ethernet CSMA/CD, 802.5 Token Ring Token Passing, to achieve **physical media independence**. Responsible for logical **identification** and **encapsulation** of the network layer protocols. The Type field – the DSAP and SNAP fields are used to identify the network layer protocol the frame should be destined for after a frame is received. The LLC can also provide **error recovery**, and **flow control** (windowing). **Note:** LLC is the same for various physical media.
Media Access Control (MAC) (IEEE 802.3)	Defines how to **place and transmit data over the physical media** (**framing**), provides **physical addressing**, **error detection** (but no correction), and **flow control** (optional).

- Below lists the early Ethernet standards:

10Base5 and 10Base2	The early DIX Ethernet specifications. All devices were connected by **coaxial cables**, and there is no hub, switch, and patch panel. When a device sends some bits (electrical signals) to another device on the same bus, the electricity propagates to all devices on the LAN. The CSMA/CD algorithm is developed to **prevent collisions** and **recover when collisions occur**. **DIX** = **DEC** (Digital Equipment Corporation), **Intel**, and **Xerox**.
10Base-T	Solved the high cabling costs and availability problems in 10Base5 and 10Base2 Ethernet networks with the introduction of hubs. Electrical signals that come in one port were regenerated by hubs and sends out to all other ports. 10Base-T networks were **physical star**, **logical bus** topology. In 10base5 and 10Base2 networks, a single cable problem could take down the whole network; whereas in 10Base-T networks it affects only a single device.

- **Straight-through cables** are used to connect PCs and routers to hubs or switches. When a PC sends data on pins 1 and 2, the hub receives the electrical signal on pins 1 and 2. Hubs and switches must **think oppositely** compared to PCs and routers in order to correctly receive data.

- **Crossover cables** are used to connect devices that use the same pair of pins for transmitting data, eg: hub to hub, switch to switch, hub to switch, PC to PC, and PC to router.

- **Carrier Sense Multiple Access with Collision Detection** (CSMA/CD) logic or algorithm:
    i)   Senses or listens for electrical signal before transmitting a frame (**carrier sensing**).
    ii)   If the network media is idle, begins frame transmission; else, activates a random timer. Once the random timer expires, try to transmit again by first sensing the network media. If no signal is sensed, it presumes that the previous device has finished its frame transmission and now is its turn for frame transmission.
    iii)   Once begin transmitting frame, listens (via the NIC loopback circuit) to detect collision that may occur if another device also begin frame transmission at the same time.
    iv)   If a collision is detected, sends a **jamming signal** to ensure that all devices on the segment notice the collision and stop frame transmission.
    v)   All devices start a **timer** and **stop transmitting** for that period (**back-off mechanism**).
    vi)   Once the back-off timer expires, try to transmit again by first sensing the network media.
    Note: CSMA/CD is defined in IEEE 802.3 MAC sublayer specification.

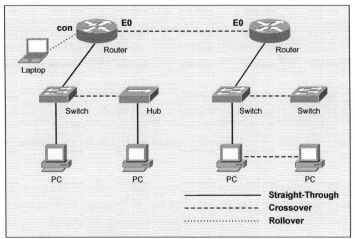

Figure 3-1: Ethernet Cabling

- Below shows the operations of a hub when an NIC transmits a frame without collision:
  i)   An NIC transmits a frame.
  ii)   The NIC loops the sent frame onto its internal receive pair through its loopback circuit.
  iii) The hub receives the frame.
  iv)   The hub internal wiring circuit propagates the frame to all other ports, except the port that the frame was received upon.

- A device is able to sense a collision with its loopback circuit on the NIC. An NIC (NIC1) loops back the frame it sent to its own receive pair. If another NIC (NIC2) also sends a frame at the same time, the signal will be received upon the receive pair of NIC1, and NIC1 would eventually notice there is a collision.

- A hub which propagates the electrical signals from 2 devices that transmit frames at the same time would send the **overlapping signals** to all NICs and will eventually detected by the NIC loopback circuits. CSMA/CD mechanism will make them stop transmission and try again later.

- **Back-off** is the **retransmission delay** when a collision is occurred and detected. Once the timer expires, all end systems have equal priority to transmit data. The more collisions in a network, the slower it will be, as the devices must resend the frames that were collided.

- The drawback of hub-based networks is that the network performance degrades or the network is virtually unusable as the number of end systems increases, as the chances that devices transmit at the same time (collisions) also increase. Hub-based networks can **never reach 100% utilization**.

- Switches remove the possibility of collisions, and hence **CSMA/CD is no longer required**. With **microsegmentation**, each individual physical port is treated as a separate bus – **each port has its own collision domain, and hence each end system has its own dedicated segment**, instead of a single shared bus (a large collision domain) as with hubs, and full-duplex operation can be achieved. **Memory buffers** are used to temporary hold incoming frames – when 2 devices send a frame at the same time, the switch can forward one frame while holding another frame in the memory buffer, and forward the second frame after the first frame has been forwarded.

- Switches interpret electrical signals or bits (L1) and reassemble them into Ethernet frames (L2), as well as process the frames to make a forwarding decision; whereas hubs simply repeat the electrical signals and it does not attempt to interpret the electrical signals as LAN frames.

- Each switch port **does not share the bandwidth**, it has it own separate bandwidth, which means a switch has 100Mbps of bandwidth **per port**. The bandwidth will be either **dedicated** to a single device (direct connection, full-duplex, 200Mbps – 100Mbps TX + 100Mbps RX) or **shared** by devices in the same collision domain (connected via a hub, half-duplex, 100Mbps).

- Switches (and bridges) learn and build their **bridging tables** by **listening to incoming frames** and **examining the source MAC addresses** of the incoming frames. An entry for a new MAC address along with the **interface that received the frame** will be created in the bridging table. This information is needed for the **forwarding** (or switching) and **filtering** operations.

- Below describe the forwarding (or switching) and filtering operations of switches (and bridges):
    - i)   A frame is received. If the MAC address of the frame is not yet in the bridging table, the switch adds the address and interface into its bridging table (it learned the MAC address).
    - ii)   If the destination is a broadcast or multicast, forward the frame out all interfaces (flooding) except the interface that received the frame (incoming interface).
    - iii)   If the destination is a unicast address that is not yet in the bridging table (unknown unicast frame), forward (flood) the frame out all interfaces except the incoming interface. The switch expects to learn the MAC address of the destination device as another frame will eventually passes through the switch when the destination replies the source.
    - iv)   If the destination is a unicast address in the bridging table, and the associated interface is not same with the incoming interface, forward the frame out the destination interface. This means the switch will not forward the frame to a segment in which the destination is on the same segment as the source. It forwards traffic from one segment to another only when necessary to preserve bandwidth on other segments (**segment = collision domain**).
    - v)   Otherwise, filter (do not forward) the frame.

- Both transparent bridges and switches use **Spanning Tree Protocol** to perform **loop avoidance**.

- **Internet Group Management Protocol** (IGMP) snooping is a multicast feature in switches which can be used to **limit the flooding of multicasts** and **optimize multicast forwarding**.

- The early Ethernet specifications use shared bus architecture, where a particular device cannot send and receive frames at the same time, as this would lead to an occurrence of collision. Devices operating in **half-duplex** mode **cannot send a frame while receiving another frame**.

- Ethernet switches allow multiple frames to be transmitted across different ports at the same time. Full-duplex operation uses 2 pairs of wires instead of 1 pair of wires as in half-duplex operation. **No collisions will occur** because different pairs of wires are used for sending and receiving data. If only one device is connected to a switch port, no collision can occur as there is only one device connected in the segment, and this allows the operation of **full-duplex** – the operation mode that enables **concurrent sending and receiving frames** between an Ethernet NIC and a switch port. An NIC must **disable its loopback circuit** if intends to operate in full-duplex mode.

- If a hub with multiple devices is connected to a switch port, collisions can still occur and thus half-duplex operation must be used. A collision domain defines a group of devices that connected to the **same physical media** (shared media) where collisions can occur when 2 devices transmit frames at the same time.

- Full-duplex operation requires a **point-to-point connection**:
    - i)   A connection between a switch and a host.
    - ii)   A connection between a switch and another switch.
    - iii)   A connection between a host and another host (with a crossover cable).

- Bridges were introduced to connect **different type of networks,** eg: Ethernet and Token Ring. Switches and bridges can communicate with each other with a **bridging protocol.** Cisco routers (acting as bridges) and switches support the following types of bridging protocols:

Transparent Bridging	Found primarily in Ethernet networks. This switching method used by device that forwards frames between LAN segments based on the bridging table. **Transparent** refers to the presence of bridge is transparent to end systems – they never notice the existence of a bridge. End systems behave the same in networks with or without transparent bridges.
Source-Route Bridging (SRB)	Found exclusively in Token Ring networks.
Translational Bridging	Facilitates communications between Ethernet transparent bridging and Token Ring source-route bridging networks. There is no open implementation standard. It was replaced by source-route transparent (SRT) bridging.
Encapsulating Bridging	Allows packets to cross a bridged backbone network.
Source-Route Transparent Bridging (SRT)	Allows a bridge to function as both a source-route and transparent bridge to enable communications in mixed Ethernet and Token Ring environments, hence fulfilling the needs of all end systems in a single device. SRT only allows transparent and source-route hosts to communicate with other hosts of the **same type**; hence it is not the perfect solution to the incompatibility problem of mixed-media bridging.
Source-Route Translational Bridging (SR/TLB)	Allows a bridge to function as both a source-route and transparent bridge. SR/TLB translates between Ethernet and Token Ring protocols to allow communication between hosts from source-route and transparent bridging networks.

- Switches behave identically to bridges in terms of the learning and forwarding operations. Generally, switches are bridges with more ports and faster processing capability. Although they have many similar attributes, there are still some differences between the their technologies.

Switches	Bridges
Faster processing (also known as **wire-speed**) because switch in hardware (ASICs – **Application-Specific Integrated Circuits**).	Slower processing because switch in software – bridges are implemented using software.
Able to interconnect LANs of unlike bandwidth. (Connecting a 10Mbps LAN and a 100Mbps LAN)	Unable to interconnect LANs of unlike bandwidth.
Support higher port density than bridges.	Normally available in 4 – 16 ports.
Support both **cut-through switching** and **store-and-forward switching**.	Only support **store-and-forward switching**.
Support VLANs.	Do not support VLANs.
Support full-duplex operation.	Do not support full-duplex operation.
Support multiple spanning tree instances.	Only support one spanning tree instance.

- Fast-forward switching and fragment-free switching are the 2 forms of **cut-through switching**. Cut-through switching operates at **wire-speed** and has **constant latency** regardless of frame size. Fragment-free is also referred to as **modified cut-through**.

- Below lists the switch internal processing and operating modes that handle frame switching:

Store-and-Forward	Offers maximum error checking at the expense of forwarding speed. A switch fully receives all bits in the frame (**store**) before forwards the frame (**forward**). It is able to filter (detect and discard) error frames by verifying the FCS of the frames. Latency is varies upon the frame size.
Fast-Forward (Cut-Through)	Offers the fastest possible forwarding at the expense of error checking. A switch can start forwarding a frame before the whole frame has been received. It performs bridging table lookup **as soon as the destination MAC address is received** (the first 14 bytes of a frame [1]). Switches are unable to filter and will propagate error frames. This switching mode reduces latency and delays as with Store-and-Forward switching.
Fragment-Free (Modified Cut-Through)	Offers a tradeoff between the switching methods above. Similar to Fast-Forward switching, but only start forwarding frames **after the first 64 bytes of frames have been received and verified**. According to the Ethernet specification, **collisions should be detected within the first 64 bytes of a frame**; such error frames due to collisions will be filtered. However, this method is unable to filter error frames due to late collisions.

Store-and-Forward is most preferred method nowadays as the latency issues become less relevant with the higher network speeds and faster switch processors.
[1] – 8 bytes Preamble + 6 bytes Destination MAC Address

- **Ethernet addressing** uses MAC addresses to identify individual (**unicast**), all (**broadcast**), or group of network entities (**multicast**). MAC addresses are unique for each NIC on a device. MAC addresses **48 bits** in length and are expressed as **12 hexadecimal digits** – with dots placed after every 4 hex digits, eg: 0000.0012.3456. A host will only process frames destined to it.
  - i) The **first 6 hex digits** indicates the **Organizationally Unique Identifier** (OUI), which are assigned and administered by the **Institute of Electrical and Electronics Engineers** (IEEE) to identify the manufacturer or vendor for an NIC.
  - ii) The **last 6 hex digits** indicate the unique serial number of an NIC and are administered by the manufacturer or vendor of the NIC.
  - iii) MAC addresses are sometimes called **burned-in addresses** (BIAs), as they are burned into ROM chips. The MAC address is copied from ROM to RAM upon the initialization.

- **Destination MAC addresses** can be either a **unicast**, **broadcast**, or **multicast** address. **Source MAC addresses** are always **unicast** addresses.
  Below describes the 3 categories of Ethernet MAC addresses:

Unicast	A MAC address that identifies a single LAN interface card.
Broadcast	An address implies that all devices on a LAN (same broadcast domain) should process the frame. It has a value of **FFFF.FFFF.FFFF**. Ethernet frames (L2) that encapsulate IP broadcast packets (L3) are usually sent to this address as well.
Multicast	Allows point-to-multipoint communication among a subset of devices on a LAN. It enables multiple recipients to receive messages without flooding the messages to all hosts on the same broadcast domain. The format of IP multicast MAC addresses is **0100.5E**xx.xxxx.

- **Framing** defines how to **interpret a sequence of bits**. Physical layer only transfer the bits across a media, and data link layer performs framing to **interpret the contents of the received bits**. **Preamble** is an alternating pattern of 1s and 0s that is used for clocking and synchronization to notify the receiving end that a frame is coming. 10Mbps and slower versions are asynchronous; while faster Ethernet versions are synchronous hence this timing information is not necessary.

- The **Preamble** is 10101010; while the **Start Frame Delimiter** (SFD) is 10101011.

- The Data field in frames is used to hold L3 packets and its size can vary from **28 to 1500 bytes**. The IEEE 802.3 specification defines 1500 bytes as the **Maximum Transmission Unit** (MTU), which means that **1500 bytes is the largest IP packet allowed to be sent across Ethernet**.

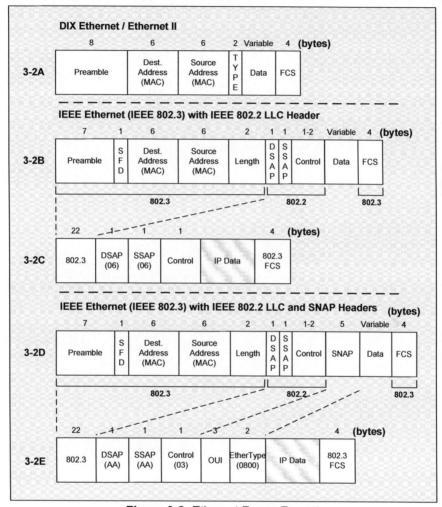

Figure 3-2: Ethernet Frame Formats

- Data link layer headers use a Protocol Type field as defined in IEEE 802.2 LLC specification – **Destination Service Access Point** (DSAP) to identify the type of network (and data link) layer data encapsulated in an Ethernet frame (Figure 3-2B). SAPs are important in situations where users are running **multiple protocol stacks**. However, IEEE did not plan this well for a large number of protocols thus the 1-byte DSAP field is insufficient to identify all possible protocols.

- As a workaround, IEEE allows the use of an extra 2-byte header – **Subnetwork Access Protocol** (SNAP) to provide the same purpose as the DSAP field for **identifying all possible protocols** (Figure 3-2D). When using SNAP, both DSAP and SSAP fields contain the value 0xAA (170) and 0x03 in the Control field, which means that there is a SNAP header after the 802.2 header. A value of 0x0800 (2048) in the SNAP EtherType field identifies an IP header as the next header. SNAP is being used in Ethernet, Token Ring, and FDDI.
Note: A value of 0x86DD SNAP EtherType field identifies an IPv6 header as the next header.

Physical Layer

- The physical layer defines the standards used to **send and receive bits** between 2 devices across physical network media, eg: maximum length of each type of cable, the number of wires inside the cable, the shape of the connector on the end of the cable, and the purpose of each pin or wire.

- The **Electronic Industries Association** and the newer **Telecommunications Industry Alliance** (EIA/TIA) are the standard organizations that define the Ethernet physical layer specifications.

- Figure 3-3 shows the wiring of the **Category 5** (CAT5) **Unshielded Twisted-Pair** (UTP) **straight-through** and **crossover** cables.

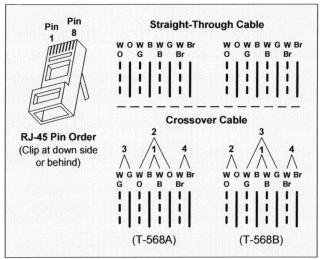

Figure 3-3: CAT5 UTP Cables and RJ-45 Connector

- Pins 1 and 2 are used for **transmitting** data; while pins 3 and 6 are used for **receiving** data.

- Sometime multiple specifications are used to define the details of the physical layer.
  Ex: **RJ-45** (connector shape, number of pins) + **Ethernet** (pins usage – pins 1, 2, 3, and 6).

- **Straight-through cable** → Pin 1 connects to pin 1 of the other end, pin 2 connects to pin 2, etc. A straight-through cable has 2 identical ends.

- **Crossover cable** → Pin 1 connects to pin 3, pin 2 connects to pin 6, and vice versa for both ends. With such pin arrangement, it connects the transmit circuit of an NIC to the receive circuit of another NIC, and vice versa, which allows both NICs to transmit and receive at the same time. It allows the creation of mini-LAN with 2 PCs without a switch or hub (point-to-point topology).

- **Rollover cable** → Pin 1 connects to pin 8 of the other end, pin 2 to pin 7, pin 3 to pin 6, etc. Mainly used to connect to the RJ-45 **console ports** which are available on most Cisco devices. Also known as **console cable**.

- Most LAN cabling uses **twisted-pairs** (a pair of wires that were twisted together) cables, as they can greatly **reduce electromagnetic interference** caused by electrical current.

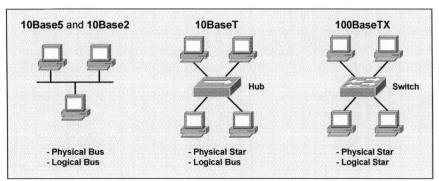

Figure 3-4: Common Network Topologies

- **Physical topology** defines how devices are physically connected; while **logical topology** defines how devices communicate (the data path) across the physical topology. The physical and logical topologies could be same or different depends on the Ethernet specifications.

- A **bus topology** uses a single cable to connect all devices (linear topology). Both ends of the cable must be terminated with a terminator to absorb signals that reach the end of the cable in order to prevent them from bouncing back at the end of the wire and causing collisions or errors. If the terminators were removed, an entire network would stop working.

- In a **star topology**, a central device has many point-to-point connections to other devices. In a 10BaseT or 100BaseTX network, multiple PCs connect to a hub or switch (the center of the star). Star topologies are also known as **hub-and-spoke** topologies.

- All type of networks has the limitations on the total length of a cable. **Repeaters** were developed to **exceed the distance limitation** of the Ethernet standard. They were deployed inline to overcome the **attenuation** problem. Any signal (including collisions) received from a port is **reamplified** or **regenerated** and **forwarded out all ports** without any interpretation of the meaning of bits. However, repeaters **do not simply amplify** the signal, as this might amplify noise as well. They act as signal conditioners that clean up signals prior to transmission.

- Hubs are multiple ports repeaters. All devices connected into a hub reside in the **same collision and broadcast domains**. Note that while a hub is a repeater, a repeater is not necessary a hub. A repeater may have only 2 connectors, while a hub can have many more.

- **Attenuation** is the **loss of signal strength** as electrical signal travels across a cable. It is measured in decibels (dB). A higher quality cable will have a **higher rated category** and **lower attenuation** – CAT5 cables are better than CAT3 cables, as they have **more wire twists per inch** and **less crosstalk** (unwanted signal interference from adjacent pairs); and therefore can run at **higher speeds** and **longer distances**.

- When an electrical signal is transmitted across a cable, it will introduce **magnetic field and radio frequency interference**s, which emit radiation that can interfere with other signals in other wires. **Crosstalk** is referred to as the situation where a wire affects another wire(s) by changing of the electrical signal which would cause **bit errors**.

- **Twisted-pair cables** (a pair of wires which are twisted together) are used to **reduce emissions**. By using an opposite current on each wire, each wire produces an identical magnetic field in opposite direction, which can **cancel** each other out (**cancellation**).

- Another way to reduce emissions is by **shielding the wires** – the use of some materials placed around them to block the electromagnetic interference. Unfortunately, this makes the cables **more expensive** (materials and manufacturing costs), and **less flexible** (cannot be bended easily, which makes it more difficult to install).

- STP max length and speed for a network segment is **100m** (328 feet) and **100Mbps** respectively.

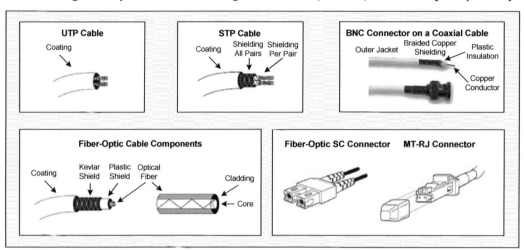

Figure 3-5: Common Network Cables and Connectors

- The TIA has defined several standards for UTP cabling and different categories of UTP (Unshielded Twisted Pair) cables. Below lists the all the UTP categories and their characteristics:

UTP Category	Max Speed Rating	Usual Applications
CAT1	< 1Mbps	Analog voice (telephones). ISDN BRI. **Not for data**.
CAT2	4Mbps	Mainly used in IBM Token Ring networks.
CAT3	10Mbps	Analog voice (telephones) and 10BaseT Ethernet (data)
CAT4	16Mbps	Mainly used in IBM Fast Token Ring networks.
CAT5	100Mbps	Mainly used in 100BaseTX Fast Ethernet networks.
CAT5e	1Gbps	Similar to CAT5 cable, but contains a physical separator between the 4 pairs to further reduce electromagnetic interference (more expensive than CAT5). Lower emissions and better for Gigabit Ethernet cabling.
CAT6	1Gbps+	Intended as a replacement for CAT5e. Capable of supporting multigigabit speeds.

- **Coaxial cabling** was used for 10Base5 and 10Base2 Ethernet networks. 10Base5 was referred to as **thicknet** while 10Base2 was referred to as **thinnet**, as 10Base5 used **thicker** coaxial cables.

- Coaxial cables are **shielded**. They have a single copper wire in the center, with plastic insulation and copper shielding.

- Connecting a host to a 10Base5 segment requires a **vampire tap** and the cabling is inflexible. No cable stripping and connectors were used. Vampire taps pierce through insulating layer and makes **direct contact** with the core of a cable. **Attachment Unit Interface** (AUI) cables (15-pin shielded and twisted-pair) were also used to connect between vampire taps (MAUs) and NICs.

- The 10Base2 Ethernet, which was developed after 10Base5 uses **thinner** and **more flexible** coaxial cabling. The cables are terminated with **BNC** (British Naval Connector, Bayonet Neill Concelman, or Bayonet Nut Connector) connectors, which was a lot easier to use than the vampire taps. A BNC T-connector was being used to connect a host into a 10Base2 segment.

- In those networks, a single cable problem could **take down** the entire Ethernet segment.

- **Transceiver** is Transmitter + Receiver. Original Ethernet was designed to use an external device called **transceiver** instead of the NIC itself for encoding and decoding of signals and bits.

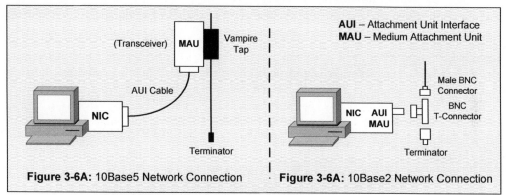

Figure 3-6: 10Base5 and 10Base2 Network Connections

- Below are the main differences between optical cabling (fiber cabling) and electrical cabling:
  i)   Supports longer distances.
  ii) Higher cost.
  iii) Does not emit electromagnetic radiation. Immune to electromagnetic interferences (EMI) and electronic eavesdropping; hence provides better security.
  iv) Supports 10Gbps Ethernet.

- Optical cabling uses a **pair of strands** (or threads) for data transmission in both directions.

- The cladding has a different **Index of Refraction** (IOR) than the core (the fiber). When the light hits the outer wall of the core, which is the inner wall of the cladding, the light will be reflected back into the core, and the light eventually travels from one end to another end of the fiber cable.

- Below lists the 2 general categories of optical cabling:

Single-mode Fiber (SMF)	Uses **very small diameter** optical fiber core. Uses **lasers** to generate light. Lasers generate a single specific wavelength, thus named as SM. SMF can generate only one signal per fiber. SMF cables and cards are **more expensive** because SMF requires more precision in the manufacturing process for the light generation hardware. SMF provides **longer distances**, **higher data rates**, and **less dispersion** than MMF.
Multimode Fiber (MMF)	Uses **larger diameter** optical fiber core. Uses **light-emitting diodes** (LEDs) to generate light. LEDs generate multiple modes or wavelengths of light where each takes slightly different path, thus named as MM. MMF is mostly deployed in **short transmission distance** environments.

Note: Modes are the number of paths that a light ray can follow when propagating down a fiber. Dispersion is the spreading of light pulses as they propagate down a fiber.

- Optical cabling can transmit up to **10Gbps** (MMF) and **100Gbps** (SMF).

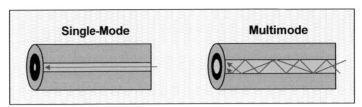

Figure 3-7: Single-Mode and Multimode Fiber Optics

- Below lists some types of fiber-optic connectors:

ST connector	Each strand is terminated with a barrel connector (like a BNC connector). **Twisted** when connected into an interface card to **secure** the connection.
SC connector	2 strands are attached together as a single connector.
MT-RJ connector	Newer type of connector (**Small Form Factor Pluggable**, SFP). Similar to RJ-45 connector that ease the connectors to switch ports installation.

- Below lists the original and expanded IEEE Ethernet 802.3 standards:

Original IEEE 802.3 Standards:	
10Base-5	Up to 500 meters long. **Physical and logical bus.** Uses **vampire taps** and **AUI cables.** Up to **2500 meters** with repeaters and 1024 users for all segments. **Terminators** were used.
10Base-2	Developed after 10Base5. Up to **185 meters** (since it is ~200 meters, thus 2 in the name). Supports up to 30 workstations on a single segment. **Physical and logical bus.** Uses **BNCs** and **T-connectors. Terminators** were used.
10Base-T	Up to **100 meters.** Uses Category 3 UTP 2-pair wiring. Each device must connect into a hub or switch, and only 1 host per segment or wire. **Physical star topology and logical bus** with RJ-45 connectors and hubs.
Expanded IEEE 802.3 Standards:	
100Base-T	Up to **100 meters.** Uses UTP.
100Base-T4	Up to **100 meters.** Uses 4 pairs of Category 3, 4, 5 UTP.
100Base-TX	Up to **100 meters.** Uses 2 pairs of Cat 5, 6, 7 UTP or STP. 1 user per segment. **Physical and logical star topology** with RJ-45 connectors and switches.
100Base-FX	Up to **400 meters.** Uses 2 strands of 62.5 or 125 microns MMF optical cable. Point-to-point topology. Uses ST or SC connector.
1000Base-CX	Copper twisted pair called **twinax** that can only run up to **25 meters.**
1000Base-T	Up to **100 meters.** Uses Category 5, 5e, 6 UTP **4-pair** wiring.
1000Base-SX	**Short-wavelength laser.** MMF using 50 or 62.5 microns core and 850 nanometer laser. Up to **275 meters** (62.5-micron) and **550 meters** (50-micron).
1000Base-LX	**Long-wavelength laser.** SMF or MMF that uses a 9-micron core and 1310 nanometer laser. Up to **550 meters** (MMF) and **10KM** (SMF). Lasers used in SMF provide higher output than LEDs used in MMF.
1000Base-XD	Extended distance up to **50KM.**
1000Base-ZX	Extended distance up to **70KM** with a 9-micro core SMF.

- The "**Base**" in IEEE 802.3 standards is referred to as **baseband signaling**, a technology where only one carrier frequency or digital signal is being used at a time on the wire – when a device transmits, it uses the entire bandwidth on the wire and does not share with other. As compared to **broadband technology**, where multiple signals are multiplexed and share a single wire.

- **Attachment Unit Interface** (AUI) is defined in all original 802.3 standards as the standard Ethernet interface that allows the data link layer to remain unchanged while supporting any existing and new physical layer technologies (eg: BNC, UTP). **Medium Attachment Unit** (MAU) transceivers (also known as **media converters**) were used to provide conversion between 15-pin AUI signals and twisted-pair Ethernet cables (eg: 10Base2, 10BaseT). Networks connected via external transceivers (eg: AUI, MAU) can operate only in 10Mbps half-duplex.

- **Media Independent Interface** (MII) is used in Fast Ethernet and Gigabit Ethernet to provide faster bit transfer rate of 4 or 8 bits at a time. As compared to AUI, which is only 1 bit at a time.

- Below lists the IEEE 802.3 Ethernet standards:

IEEE 802.3	Legacy Ethernet (10Mbps).
IEEE 802.3u	Fast Ethernet over twisted-pair copper cable (100Base-TX).
IEEE 802.3z	Gigabit Ethernet over fiber-optic (1000Base-SX and 1000Base-LX).
IEEE 802.3ab	Gigabit Ethernet over twisted-pair copper cable – CAT5 or CAT5e (1000Base-T).
IEEE 802.3ae	10-Gigabit Ethernet (fiber and copper).

Note: UTP Gigabit Ethernet may operate in half-duplex mode with the 10/100Mbps Ethernet CSMA/CD mechanism. Fiber optic Gigabit Ethernet can only operate in full-duplex mode.

- Below are some features of IEEE 802.3ae 10-Gigabit Ethernet:
  i)   Allows only **point-to-point** topology. It is targeted for connections between high speed switching devices.
  ii) Allows only **full-duplex** communication.
  iii) Supports only **optical fiber cabling**. Supports copper cabling in the future.

- **Auto-negotiation** is a feature of Fast Ethernet that allows NICs and switch ports to negotiate to discover which mode they should operate at (10Mbps or 100Mbps, half duplex or full duplex). There are doubts of the reliability of auto-negotiation, hence the speed and duplex settings for the switch ports and devices that seldom move (eg: servers, routers) should be configured **statically**. The use of auto-negotiation should be limited to access layer switches ports.

- Wireless communication uses some form of **electromagnetic energy** that propagates through the air at varying wavelengths. Electromagnetic energy can pass through matters, but the matters often reflect the energy to certain degree and absorb part of the energy. Some wavelengths require line-of-sight for communication as they are unable to pass through matters well.

- The IEEE 802.11 Wi-Fi (Wireless Fidelity) is the most common and widely deployed WLAN. A WLAN is a **shared LAN** as only one station can transmit at a time. A typical WLAN consists of PCs with wireless adapters, and a wireless access point (AP). Access points bridge traffic between the wired and wireless LANs.

- The IEEE 802.11 standards still uses IEEE 802.2 LLC, but with a different MAC header other than 802.3. An access point swaps an 802.3 header with an 802.11 header when bridging traffic.

- Below lists some IEEE 802.11 standards:

Standard	Transmits Using	Maximum Speed
802.11a	5GHz frequency band	54Mbps
802.11b	2.4GHz frequency band	11Mbps
802.11g	2.4GHz frequency band	54Mbps

Note: 802.11g is backward-compatible with 802.11b.

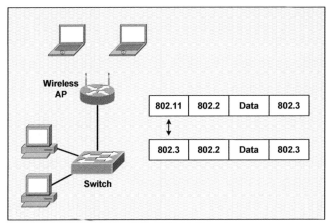

Figure 3-8: 802.11 Framing

- 802.11b transmits at 11Mbps but has a maximum throughput of 7Mbps due to the **shared bus** architecture – WLANs are half-duplex communication, all devices share the same bandwidth and only one device can transmit at a time.

- Half-duplex Ethernet uses CSMA/CD in its operation while IEEE 802.11 WLAN uses CSMA/CA (**Carrier Sense Multiple Access with Collisions Avoidance**) in its operation. Congestion avoidance monitors network traffic load to predict and avoid congestion via packet dropping. A common congestion avoidance mechanism is **Random Early Detection** (RED).

Chapter 4
Introduction to Cisco IOS

-   Almost all current Cisco routers and switches run Cisco IOS (**Internetwork Operating System**), the routing and switching software in Cisco devices.

-   Cisco IOS **command-line interface** (CLI) is the **text-based user interface** to a Cisco device for configuring, administering, and managing the Cisco device.

-   CLI can be accessed through:
    i)   Console with a **rollover cable** and **terminal emulator** application. [**line console 0**]
    ii)   AUX through a dialup device such as modem for out-of-band management. The modem is connected with a straight-through cable to the auxiliary port. [**line aux 0**]
    iii) In-band management through the network via Telnet or SSH. [**line vty 0 4**]

-   Below lists the main Cisco IOS modes:

User EXEC mode	Least privileges and limited access. Only provides a set of non-destructive **show** commands that allow examination of configuration.
Privileged mode	More **show** commands, and limited configuration commands.
Configuration mode	Configuration commands are being entered in this mode. Unable to check status with the series of **show** commands. Sub-divided into some child modes, eg: interface configuration mode, line configuration mode, router configuration mode, etc. Commands entered in this mode update the active or running configuration **immediately** after the Enter button is pressed. Configuration commands can be divided into **global configuration commands** and **subcommands**, eg: interface subcommand, subinterface subcommand, controller subcommand, line subcommand, router subcommand, etc.

-   Below describes some basic Cisco IOS commands:

enable	Switches from EXEC mode to privileged mode.
disable	Switches from privileged mode back to EXEC mode.
show version	Views the basic configuration of the system hardware, software version, the name and source of the system boot image, etc.
configure terminal	Switches from privileged mode to global configuration mode.
hostname	Changes the hostname of a Cisco device.
^Z / end / exit	Exits from the global configuration mode back to privileged mode.
exit / quit	Exits from the EXEC mode.

-   Some special IOS CLI features are **Context-Sensitive Help** with [?] and **Auto-Completion** with [TAB] can be used to display or auto-complete the **available** commands or parameters.

-   The context-sensitive help is divided into **word help** and **command syntax help**.

word help	Ex: **cl?** – Displays any command or syntax that starts with **cl**.
command syntax help	Ex: **clock ?** – Displays the available parameters after the **clock** command.

Note: The escape sequence for entering the **?** character is Ctrl+V.

- Below lists the common IOS CLI error messages:

`% Invalid input detected at '^'`	User issued an incorrect or invalid command.
`% Ambiguous command`	User used an abbreviation that did not specify enough characters for the IOS to determine or recognize the specific command that the user has intended to issue.
`% Incomplete command`	User did not specify enough parameters.
`& Unrecognized command`	User issued an unavailable command.

- Below shows a configuration example of some basic Cisco IOS commands:

```
Router>enable
Router#configure terminal
Enter configuration commands, one per line.  End with CNTL/Z.
Router(config)#hostname RT1
RT1(config)#end
RT1#
00:00:30: %SYS-5-CONFIG_I: Configured from console by console
RT1#disable
RT1>quit


RT1 con0 is now available

Press RETURN to get started.
```

- The **clock set** privileged command sets the **time** and **date** settings on Cisco devices.

```
RT1#clock set 20:20:20 20 Jan 2008
00:10:10: %SYS-6-CLOCKUPDATE: System clock has been updated from 00:10:10
UTC Mon Mar 1 1993 to 20:20:20 UTC Sun Jan 20 2008, configured from console
by console.
RT1#show clock
20:20:21.520 UTC Sun Jan 20 2008
RT1#
```

- 2 supportive line subcommands for console and telnet sessions:

logging synchronous	Stops the annoying console messages from interrupting user input and readability.
exec-timeout {*minutes*} {*seconds*}	Configures the **inactivity timeout** – automatic session logout if there is no keyboard activity. 0 min 0 sec means never expires. The default is 10 minites and 0 seconds (**exec-timeout 10 0**).

```
RT1(config)#line con 0
RT1(config-line)#logging synchronous
RT1(config-line)#exec-timeout 0 0
RT1(config-line)#^Z
00:15:00: %SYS-5-CONFIG_I: Configured from console by console
RT1#
```

Note: no exec-timeout is equivalent to **exec-timeout 0 0**.

- The **banner motd** global configuration command configures the **Message of the Day** banner. The character followed by the command – **delimiter**, is used to **define the end of the message**. Banners are commonly used as **security notices** for remote access users.

```
RT1(config)#banner motd #This is banner line 1
Enter TEXT message.  End with the character '#'.
This is line 2
#
RT1(config)#^Z
RT1#quit

RT1 con0 is now available

Press RETURN to get started.

This is banner line 1
This is line 2

RT1>
```

- The **description** {*text*} interface subcommand adds a description for a particular interface.

```
RT1(config)#interface FastEthernet 0/1
RT1(config-if)#description *** Core Switch Gi0/1 ***
RT1(config-if)#^Z
RT1#show running-config interface FastEthernet 0/1
Building configuration...

Current configuration : 95 bytes
!
interface FastEthernet0/1
 description *** Core Switch Gi0/1 ***
 no ip address
end

RT1#
```

- The **default interface** {intf-*type* intf-*num*} global configuration command **resets the configuration** for a particular interface.

```
RT1#show running-config interface FastEthernet 0/1
Building configuration...

Current configuration : 61 bytes
!
interface FastEthernet0/1
 description *** Core Switch Gi0/1 ***
 ip address 192.168.0.1 255.255.255.0
end

RT1#configure terminal
Enter configuration commands, one per line.  End with CNTL/Z.
RT1(config)#default interface FastEthernet 0/1
Interface FastEthernet0/1 set to default configuration
RT1(config)#^Z
RT1#
```

```
RT1#show running-config interface FastEthernet 0/1
Building configuration...

Current configuration : 38 bytes
!
interface FastEthernet0/1
 no ip address
 shutdown
end

RT1#
```

- The privileged mode access passwords can be defined with either **enable password** {*passwd*} or **enable secret** {*passwd*} global configuration command. Both passwords are **case-sensitive**.

enable password	Used in older version of IOS (pre-10.3). Password is saved as **clear text**.
enable secret	Mostly used in current version of IOS. Based on MD5 hash function. Instead of simple encryption, **one-way hash** algorithm is used to calculate the hash value of the password, where decryption is impossible.

- Cisco recommends the **enable secret** to be different from the **enable password** for better security. If both of them are configured, the **enable secret** password will be in effect.

```
RT1(config)#enable password cisco123
RT1(config)#enable secret cisco123
The enable secret you have chosen is the same as your enable password.
This is not recommended.  Re-enter the enable secret.

RT1(config)#enable secret cisco456
RT1(config)#^Z
RT1#show running-config | in enable
enable secret 5 $1$.1p/$BXYbAw21QzsOEfHOjUPAP.
enable password cisco123
RT1#
```

- The **terminal history size** {*num-of-lines*} EXEC command can be used to set the size of command history buffer for the **current session**; whereas the **history size** {*num-of-lines*} line subcommand will **permanently** set the size of command history buffer for a particular line. The default command history size is 10, which means the latest 10 issued commands are saved.

- **Virtual TeleTypes / Terminals** (VTY) are used for remote administration. Users connecting to a router through Telnet or SSH are unable to choose which VTY line to connect to.
  Note: The minimum number of VTY lines on a Cisco router is 5; and they cannot be deleted.

- The **password** {*passwd*} and **login** line subcommands are used in conjunction to configure the password for console and remote access login. The **password** {*passwd*} command specifies the login password; while the **login** command tells the router to display a password login prompt.

```
RT1(config)#line con 0
RT1(config-line)#password cisco123
RT1(config-line)#login
RT1(config-line)#line vty 0 4
RT1(config-line)#password cisco123
RT1(config-line)#login
RT1(config-line)#^Z
RT1#exit

RT1 con0 is now available

Press RETURN to get started.



User Access Verification

Password:
```

- The **service password-encryption** global configuration command encrypts the system passwords, eg: console and Telnet passwords.

```
RT1#show running-config | begin line con 0
line con 0
 password cisco123
 login
line vty 0 4
 password cisco123
 login
line vty 5 15
 no login
!
!
end

RT1#configure terminal
RT1(config)#service password-encryption
RT1(config)#^Z
RT1#
RT1#show running-config | begin line con 0
line con 0
 password 7 060506324F41584B56
 login
line vty 0 4
 password 7 060506324F41584B56
 login
!
end

RT1#
```

- Cisco IOS treats a mistyped command as a **hostname** and will try to resolve it using DNS. DNS resolution is a time consuming process and is enabled by default, but DNS server is rarely deployed in lab environments. The **no ip domain-lookup** global configuration command disables this default feature.

- The **erase startup-config** and **erase nvram:** privileged commands can be used to erase the startup-config in the NVRAM, which cause a Cisco router or switch to perform factory reset and enter into the initial configuration dialog upon next reboot.

- The **reload** [**at** *hh:mm day month* | **in** reload-*delay*] [*reason*] privileged command warm boot a Cisco device. The **reload cancel** privileged command cancels a scheduled reboot.

- Below lists the types of memory that can be found in Cisco devices:

RAM	Used as **working storage** for packet buffers, ARP cache, routing tables, etc. The running-config is being stored here.
ROM	Normally stores a limited-function bootable IOS image – **bootstrap code**, which is not intended for normal operation and is loaded after the POST to locate and load the full IOS image or **ROMmon** (the bootstrap code itself) by examining the configuration register.
Flash memory	Either an Intel EEPROM or a PCMCIA card. It is an **erasable**, **rewriteable** and **permanent** storage. It stores **fully functional** IOS images and is the default location where a device obtains its IOS at boot time. It can be used to store any other files as well (some routers can store configuration files here). The **show flash:** privileged command can be used to view the contents of the Flash memory.
NVRAM	**Nonvolatile RAM** that stores the startup-config.

EEPROM – Electronically Erasable Programmable Read-Only Memory.

- The **copy** {*source-file*} {*destination-file*} privileged command is used to copy files. It is mainly used to duplicate configuration files as well as backup and upgrade of IOS images.

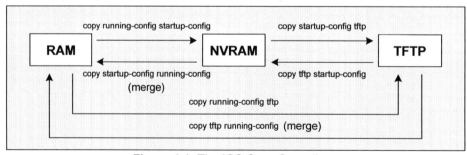

Figure 4-1: The IOS Copy Operations

- During the IOS upgrade process, the device will try to obtain the following information:
  i) The IP address of the TFTP server.
  ii) The name of the IOS image file.
  iii) Does the Flash memory have available space for the file?
  iv) Does the TFTP server actually have the specified file?
  v) Does it need to erase or delete the old IOS image?

- The TFTP server can either resides on the **same subnet** with an interface; or a **remote subnet** (requires the default route configuration).

- Below lists some image name decodes for Cisco IOS:

Code	Features and Descriptions
j	Enterprise feature set, which contains most features.
z	The IOS file is compressed. Decompression is needed when it is being loaded.
m	The IOS runs in the RAM.
k3	56-bit SSH encryption.

- Below shows the Cisco IOS software boot sequence when a device is powered on or reloaded:
  i)   Performs a **power-on self-test** (POST) to discover and verify the present and operability of the hardware, eg: memory, interfaces.
  ii)   Loads and runs the **bootstrap** or **bootloader** (which performs task iii) from ROM.
  iii)   Finds the software (normally IOS) in the order of Flash, TFTP, and ROM (for the limited-function IOS – RXBOOT) and loads it.
  iv)   Finds the startup-config configuration file and loads it into running-config. If the router is unable to find the startup-config file, it enters into the initial configuration dialog.
  Note: **bootstrap** and **bootloader** are different!

- Below list the categories of Cisco IOS operating systems:

Operating System	Purposes
Full-featured IOS	Resides in Flash memory. Loaded most of the time for operations.
Limited-function IOS (RXBoot)	Also known as the **bootloader**. Basic IP capabilities. No IP routing capability. Normally loaded during **IOS upgrade** or when replacing a faulty Flash memory. Enter with configuration register 0x2101. Resides in either ROM or Flash memory.
ROMmon (ROM Monitor)	Loaded by the **bootstrap code** when there is an error in the POST. Normally used for **manufacturing**, **low-level debugging** by the Cisco TAC engineers, and **password recovery**. Enter by sending a **break sequence** upon system boot up. Resides in ROM.

- Below are the methods that are used to define which OS to load upon system boot up:

Configuration Register	A 16-bit software register that used to control how the router boots up by telling which OS to use. Its value can be viewed from the last line of the output of the **show version** command, and is set with the **config-register** global configuration command. Its typical value on most Cisco routers is 0x2102, which tells the router to load the IOS from Flash memory and configuration from NVRAM. Configuration register is written and stored into the NVRAM. A reboot is required for the new settings to take effective, as the register value is examined only during the boot up process.
boot system command	Whenever the configuration register is set to load a full-featured IOS, the **boot system** command at the startup-config will be parsed to locate and load the IOS image file. The first IOS file in the Flash memory will be loaded if there is no **boot system** command.

- Below are some reasons for changing the configuration register:
  i)   To force the system to **boot into the ROM monitor mode** upon next reboot for debugging or password recovery purpose.
  ii)   To enable or disable the **Break function**.
  iii)   To set the console terminal **baud rate**.

This page is intentionally left blank

Chapter 5
Spanning Tree Protocol

- Most network engineers design LANs with redundant links between switches in order to provide **higher availability** as switch hardware and cable problems might occur.

- Broadcast frames could loop forever in networks with redundant links – **broadcast storm**. Switching or bridging loops might caused by broadcast of ARP requests for locating an unknown or shutdown device, as switches were designed to forward unknown unicast frames.

- Another problem is **multiple frame copies**, which could occur when a frame arrives from different segments at the same time, which could also lead to **MAC address table thrashing**.

- **Spanning Tree Protocol** (STP) was introduced to solve these problems by placing switch ports in either **forwarding** or **blocking** state in forming a single active path called the **spanning tree**. The purpose of STP is to maintain a **loop-free network topology** in networks with redundant links. STP is **enabled by default** in Cisco Catalyst switches.

- Switch ports in **forwarding** state can receive and forward frames.
  Switch ports in **blocking** state cannot receive and forward frames (but can still receive BPDUs).
  Note: If a blocking state port can receive frames, it will process and forward broadcast frames!

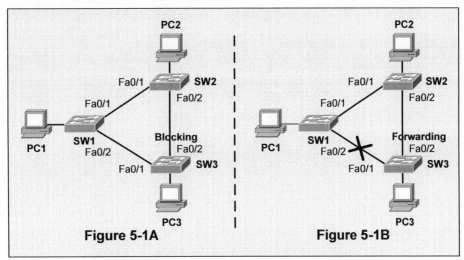

Figure 5-1: Network Setup for Spanning Tree Protocol

- Figure 5-1A shows a network after the STP convergence – SW3's Fa0/2 port is in blocking state. When PC1 sends a broadcast frame, SW1 will forward the broadcast frame to both SW2 and SW3. SW2 can forward the frame to SW3 as its Fa0/2 port is in **forwarding** state; whereas SW3 cannot forward the frame to SW2 as its Fa0/2 port is in **blocking** state.

- When the link between SW1 and SW3 fails (Figure 5-1B), SW3 will react as it no longer receiving any BPDU via its root port (Fa0/1). After the STP convergence, SW3 Fa0/2 will be changed to **forwarding** state, which allows SW3 to exchange frames with other switches.

- The drawback of STP is it would cause some frames to traverse a **longer** and **less-efficient path**. Ex: If PC3 wants to send a frame to PC2, the frame will be traversed from SW3 → SW1 → SW2.

- Below describes the STP convergence process:
  i) **Elect the root bridge.** There is **only one root bridge** per network. All root bridge's ports (which are also designated ports) are placed in **forwarding** state.
  ii) **Selects the root port on all non-root bridges.** Root port is the port that is **closest** to the root bridge, which means it is the port that receiving the lowest-cost BPDU from the root. Every non-root bridge must have a root port. All root ports are placed in **forwarding** state. **Note:** It is not always the shortest path but the fastest path to reach the root bridge.
  iii) **Selects the designated port** from the designated bridge for each LAN segment. Designated bridge is the lowest-cost bridge on each segment that **forwards the lowest-cost BPDUs** into the segment. If the costs are the same, the port of the **lower BID bridge** will be selected as the designated port. If there is a tie in the BID, the port with the **lowest port ID** will be used as the final tiebreaker (this happens when a switch connects back to itself with a cross cable). All designated ports are placed in **forwarding** state.
  iv) All other ports – **non-designated ports**, are placed in **blocking** state.

- STP root bridge election process started with each bridge claiming itself as the root bridge by sending out multicast frames called **Bridge Protocol Data Units** (BPDUs), which are used to exchange STP information between bridges. A BPDU contains the following important values:

The Bridge IDs of the Root Bridge and the Transmitting Bridge	BID is an 8-byte field that is composed of the **bridge priority** value (0-65,535, 2 bytes) and the bridge **MAC address** (6 bytes). The root bridge is the bridge with the **lowest bridge ID**. A bridge can become the root bridge by **lowering the priority value** (eventually the BID), which is normally being practiced in large switched networks.
The cost to reach the root from this bridge (Root Path Cost)	This value is set to 0 at the beginning of STP root bridge election process since all bridges claim to be the root. The lower the cost, the better chance to become a designated port. The range is 0-65,535.
Port ID	The port ID of the originating switch port of the BPDU frame.

- The bridge with the **lowest priority** becomes the root. **32,768** is the default bridge priority value. If there is a tie occurred on priority, the bridge with the **lowest MAC address** becomes the root.

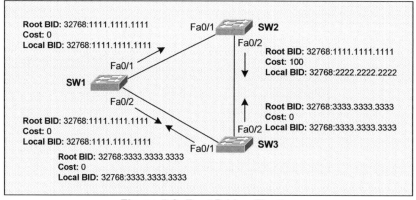

Figure 5-2: Root Bridge Election

- Figure 5-2 shows the STP root bridge election process. Each switch sends out BPDUs to claim itself as the root. Assume that SW2 receives the BPDU from SW1 faster than SW3, SW2 agrees that SW1 is the root and start forwards out SW1 BPDUs to SW3 with the **accumulated cost**. After a while, SW3 will also agree that SW1 is the root bridge after received BPDU from SW1.

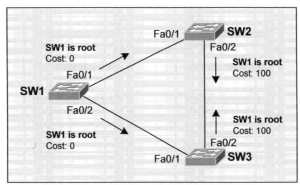

Figure 5-3: Electing the Designated Port

- SW2's Fa0/2 port will be selected as the **designated port** for the segment between SW2 and SW3 even both switches forward the same cost BPDUs into the segment, because SW2 has the **lower BID** (same priority but lower MAC address) than SW3. Below lists the state of all switch ports after the STP convergence:

Port	State	Why is it in Forwarding state
SW1, Fa0/1	Forwarding	Root bridge's interface.
SW1, Fa0/2	Forwarding	Root bridge's interface.
SW2, Fa0/1	Forwarding	Root port.
SW2, Fa0/2	Forwarding	Designated port for the segment between SW2 and SW3.
SW3, Fa0/1	Forwarding	Root port.
SW3, Fa0/2	Blocking	–

- Below list the default IEEE STP port costs:

Speed	Port Cost
10Gbps	2
1Gbps	4
100Mbps	19
10Mbps	100

- In a stable topology, the root bridge will be continuously generating BPDUs every 2 seconds. Other bridges will change the Root Path Cost in the received BPDUs to the **accumulated cost** of the particular bridge to the root and propagate the BPDUs out their designated ports. Ex: A root bridge will send out BPDUs with Root Path Cost of 0. A non-root bridge that connects to the root bridge via Fast Ethernet will send out BPDUs with Root Path Cost of 19.

- A bridge assumes the path to the root is active by constantly receiving BPDUs from the root. A non-root bridge will declare itself as the root bridge if it does not receive the BPDUs from the root for the MaxAge period, which could be caused by the **spanning-tree bpdufilter enable** interface subcommand that configures an interface to not send and receive (ignore) BPDUs.

- A BPDU also defines the following timers:

Hello Time	The time a root bridge should wait before sending out periodical BPDUs. The default interval is **2 seconds.**
MaxAge	The time a bridge should wait before trying to change the STP topology after it fails to receive the BPDUs from the root. The default interval is **20 seconds.**
Forward Delay	The time a bridge should spend for the **listening** and **learning** states when an interface needs to be changed from blocking to forwarding state. The default interval of the forward delay for both states is **15 seconds.**

- Refer back to Figure 5-1B, assume the Metro Ethernet WAN link between SW1 and SW3 experiencing problems and frames (including BPDUs) are unable to traverse across the link even the interface and line protocol are active, SW3 will react after it fails to receive the BPDUs from SW1 for the MaxAge period. SW2 does not react since it still can receive the BPDUs from SW1.

- SW3 will declare itself as the root bridge and start generating BPDUs after its MaxAge expires. However, it will receive a better BPDU (SW1 root bridge BPDUs) from SW2. SW3's Fa0/2 will become the root port and transitioned from blocking to forwarding state (after the listening and learning states). SW3 will send out a TCN BPDU out Fa0/2 when Fa0/2 is transitioned to forwarding state in order to inform the root bridge regarding the spanning tree topology change.

- A switch port **cannot be immediately transitioned** from blocking state to forwarding state, as **broadcast storms** (due to switching loop) could occur if other switches were also converging. STP uses the following 2 intermediate (or transition) states to prevent switching loop problems:

Listening	Listens for BPDUs to make sure that no loops will occur once the port is transitioned to forwarding state. Build another active topology and change the root port if necessary if found a better path to the root bridge. A port in listening state **only listens for BPDUs** and is not used to populate the MAC address table.
Learning	Learns the new location of MAC addresses and builds the bridging table. Does not forward frames yet.

Note: Blocking and Forwarding are known as stable states.

- By using default timers, a port takes up to **50 seconds** to transition from blocking to forwarding state [20 seconds MaxAge + 15 seconds Listening + 15 seconds Learning forward delays]. It is **not recommended** to modify the default STP timer intervals.

- Below summarizes the STP port states:

State	Forwards Data Frames?	Leans MACs from Received Frames?	Transitory / Stable
Blocking	No	No	Stable
Listening	No	No	Transitory
Learning	No	Yes	Transitory
Forwarding	Yes	Yes	Stable

- **EtherChannel** provides a way to **prevent the need of STP convergence** when a cable failure (fault-tolerant). STP can combine 2 to 8 parallel Ethernet links (same speed) between 2 switches into an EtherChannel which is treated as a **single logical link**. EtherChannel allows a switch to forward traffic over all the trunk links (load balancing) which provides **more bandwidth**. No STP convergence will occur as long as **at least one** of the links in the EtherChannel group is still up. In normal operation, STP blocks all links except one when there are multiple parallel links between 2 switches; whereas with EtherChannel, STP allows **all the parallel links up** and **working at the same time**, all trunks will be either in forwarding or blocking state.

- **PortFast** causes a switch port to enter the forwarding state immediately as soon as the port is physically up, without the waiting of 50 seconds (MaxAge + 2 x forward delays). PortFast should only be enabled on **access ports** that do not expect to receive STP BPDUs.

- Enabling PortFast on a port connected to another switch can create spanning tree loops. The **Cisco BPDU Guard** feature (enable with the **spanning-tree portfast bpduguard default** global configuration command) allows a port to be automatically disabled if a BPDU is received from a PortFast port, which can prevent accidental or malicious intended STP convergence.

Rapid Spanning Tree Protocol

-   **Rapid Spanning Tree Protocol** (RSTP) is introduced to **reduce the convergence time** upon network topology changes. RSTP uses the same process as STP in selecting the root bridge, root ports, and designated ports, as well as the same rules applied when determining the blocking and forwarding states of switch ports. RSTP **only works in switches that support it** and is **backward-compatible** with switches that only support traditional STP, just that the RSTP fast convergence ability is sacrificed or lost when it interoperates with STP.

-   **Link ports** are connections between 2 switches.
    Edge ports are connections to end systems, eg: PC, printer. No bridging loop can ever occur.

Switch ←→Switch (full-duplex)	Link-type Point-to-point (**P2p Peer**)
Switch ←→ Hub (half-duplex)	Link-type Shared (**Shr Peer**))
Switch ←→ PC (full-duplex)	Edge-type Point-to-point (**Edge P2p**)
Switch ←→ PC (half-duplex)	Edge-type Shared (**Edge Shr**)

-   RSTP works same as STP, but **does not work** in hub-based networks – **link-type shared**; it only works in switched networks – **link-type point-to-point** and **edge-type point-to-point**.

-   STP and RSTP port states:

Operational State	STP State (802.1D)	RSTP State (802.1w)
Disabled	Disabled	Disabled
Enabled	Blocking	Discarding
Enabled	Listening	Discarding
Enabled	Learning	Learning
Enabled	Forwarding	Forwarding

-   RSTP added 2 more port roles. Both types of port do not forward traffic (discarding state).

Alternate Port	Alternate path to the root bridge (backup of the root port). The port that received the **second best BPDU from another switch**. Can be immediately placed in forwarding state and act as the root port if the current root port fails.
Backup Port	**Backup of the designated port for a segment**. Exists only when a switch has 2 or more connections to a shared LAN segment (connect using a hub). The port that received the **same BPDU from the same switch**. Only either one of the links will be placed in forwarding state. Can be immediately placed in forwarding state if the other link fails.

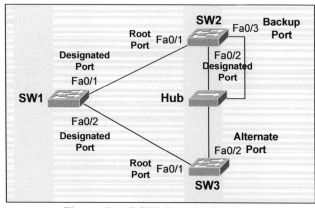

Figure 5-4: RSTP Port Designations

- A switch running RSTP only need 6 seconds (misses 3 consecutive BPDUs) to realize a lost connectivity to its direct neighbor and start to converge. In RSTP, BPDUs are also being used as keepalive mechanism between switches.

- STP and RSTP generate BPDUs differently. In 802.1D STP, a non-root bridge only generates or propagates BPDUs when it receives a BPDU (originated from the root bridge) on the root port. In 802.1w RSTP, a non-root bridge generates BPDUs with its current information every 2 seconds by default (Hello Time), even if it does not receive any BPDU from the root bridge.

- During spanning tree topology convergence, STP **passively** waits for new BPDUs; while RSTP can **proactively** negotiate with neighboring switches. When a suitable port is discovered, RSTP can immediately place it in forwarding state. Normally this can be done within 2 seconds for the whole RSTP domain.

Chapter 6
Spanning Tree Protocol Lab

Basic Catalyst Switch Configuration

- All current Cisco routers and Catalyst switches run Cisco IOS software (legacy Catalyst switches run CatOS with a series of **set**-based and **show** commands), hence Catalyst switches share a lot of command syntaxes and similarity with the configuration and administration of Cisco routers.

- Below list some basic Catalyst switch **show** commands:

show interfaces status	Displays a summary view of all interfaces status.
show mac-address-table dynamic	Displays the dynamically learned MAC addresses in the bridging table.

```
Switch#show interfaces status

Port      Name              Status         Vlan     Duplex   Speed   Type
Fa0/1                       connected      1        a-full   a-100   10/100BaseTX
Fa0/2                       connected      1        a-full   a-100   10/100BaseTX
Fa0/3                       notconnect     1        auto     auto    10/100BaseTX
Fa0/4                       notconnect     1        auto     auto    10/100BaseTX
Fa0/5                       notconnect     1        auto     auto    10/100BaseTX
Fa0/6                       notconnect     1        auto     auto    10/100BaseTX
Fa0/7                       notconnect     1        auto     auto    10/100BaseTX
Fa0/8                       notconnect     1        auto     auto    10/100BaseTX

Switch#
Switch#show mac-address-table dynamic
          Mac Address Table
-------------------------------------------

Vlan    Mac Address       Type        Ports
----    -----------       --------    -----
   1    aaaa.aaaa.aaaa    DYNAMIC     Fa0/1
   1    bbbb.bbbb.bbbb    DYNAMIC     Fa0/2
Total Mac Addresses for this criterion: 2
Switch#
```

- A switch is normally configured with a **management IP address** for remote access management. The IP address is configured on the Vlan1 interface. A switch also needs a **default gateway**, which can be configured with the **ip default-gateway** {*gw-ip-addr*} global configuration command. The **show running-config** privileged command can be used to view these settings.

```
Switch#conf t
Enter configuration commands, one per line.  End with CNTL/Z.
Switch(config)#int vlan 1
Switch(config-if)#ip add 192.168.0.11 255.255.255.0
Switch(config-if)#no shut
Switch(config-if)#exit
00:03:01: %LINK-3-UPDOWN: Interface Vlan1, changed state to up
00:03:02: %LINEPROTO-5-UPDOWN: Line protocol on Interface Vlan1, changed
state to up
Switch(config)#ip default-gateway 192.168.0.1
Switch(config)#^Z
Switch#
```

Port Security Configuration

- Port security can be used to restrict access to a switch port by **limiting** or **identifying** the MAC addresses of the expected devices. Whenever a **wrong** or **unauthorized device** connects to the secure port, the switch can issue information messages, discard frames from that device, and even shutdown the interface.

- Enabling port security on a particular switch interface:
    i)   Issue the **switchport mode access** interface subcommand as port security is only allowed on **non-trunking** (or **access**) ports.
    ii)   Enable port security with the **switchport port-security** interface subcommand.
    iii) Statically configure the MAC addresses with the **switchport port-security mac-address** {*H.H.H*} interface subcommand.

- In the following scenario, the only device authorized for network access via Fa0/1 is aaaa.aaaa.aaaa, but another device – bbbb.bbbb.bbbb has attempted an illegal network access.

```
Switch#conf t
Enter configuration commands, one per line.  End with CNTL/Z.
Switch(config)#int fa0/1
Switch(config-if)#switchport mode access
Switch(config-if)#spanning-tree portfast
Switch(config-if)#switchport port-security
Switch(config-if)#switchport port-security mac-address aaaa.aaaa.aaaa
Switch(config-if)#^Z
Switch#
Switch#show port-security int fa0/1
Port Security              : Enabled
Port Status                : Secure-down
Violation Mode             : Shutdown
Aging Time                 : 0 mins
Aging Type                 : Absolute
SecureStatic Address Aging : Disabled
Maximum MAC Addresses      : 1
Total MAC Addresses        : 1
Configured MAC Addresses   : 1
Sticky MAC Addresses       : 0
Last Source Address        : 0000.0000.0000
Security Violation Count   : 0

Switch#show port-security int fa0/1 address
          Secure Mac Address Table
-------------------------------------------------------------------
Vlan    Mac Address      Type            Ports    Remaining Age
                                                     (mins)
----    -----------      ----            -----    -------------
  1     aaaa.aaaa.aaaa   SecureConfigured  Fa0/1        -
-------------------------------------------------------------------
Total Addresses: 1

Switch#
00:10:01: %PM-4-ERR_DISABLE: psecure-violation error detected on Fa0/1,
putting Fa0/1 in err-disable state
Switch#
00:10:01: %PORT_SECURITY-2-PSECURE_VIOLATION: Security violation occurred,
caused by MAC address bbbb.bbbb.bbbb on port FastEthernet0/1.
Switch#
```

- When a secure port is in the error-disabled (shutdown) state caused by a security violation, it can be re-enabled with the series of **shutdown** and **no shutdown** interface subcommands.

- The **switchport port-security mac-address sticky** interface subcommand enables **sticky learning** – dynamically learn the MAC address from the first frame sent into a secure port, and add the MAC address as a secure MAC address to the running configuration.

- The **switchport port-security violation {protect | restrict | shutdown}** interface subcommand configures the violation mode for a secure port. The default action is shutdown. In restrict and protect modes, frames with unauthorized MAC addresses are discarded instead of shutting down the secure port, and a log entry will (**restrict**) or will not (**protect**) be made.

- The **switchport port-security maximum** [*num*] interface subcommand changes the **maximum secure MAC addresses** that will be allowed for a secure port. The default value is 1.

Spanning Tree Protocol Configuration

- STP is **enabled by default** in Catalyst switches, and hence no configuration is needed when connecting new switches that are out of the boxes, as STP will ensure that no loop can exist.

- In the following example, SW1 and SW2 were connected together at Fa0/1 and Fa0/2, and SW1 as the initial root bridge. Let's begin by listing the spanning tree information, followed by configuring SW2's Fa0/2 as the root port by changing the **STP port cost**. Finally, SW2 has been configured as the root bridge by changing the **bridge priority** with the **spanning-tree vlan** {*vlan-id*} **root primary** global configuration command.

```
SW2#sh spanning-tree

VLAN0001
  Spanning tree enabled protocol ieee
  Root ID    Priority    32768
             Address     aaaa.aaaa.aaaa
             Cost        19
             Port        1 (FastEthernet0/1)
             Hello Time   2 sec  Max Age 20 sec  Forward Delay 15 sec

  Bridge ID  Priority    32769  (priority 32768 sys-id-ext 1)
             Address     bbbb.bbbb.bbbb
             Hello Time   2 sec  Max Age 20 sec  Forward Delay 15 sec
             Aging Time 300

Interface        Role Sts Cost      Prio.Nbr Type
---------------- ---- --- --------- -------- --------------------------------
Fa0/1            Root FWD 19        128.1    P2p
Fa0/2            Altn BLK 19        128.2    P2p

SW2#debug spanning-tree events
Spanning Tree event debugging is on
SW2#
SW2#conf t
Enter configuration commands, one per line.  End with CNTL/Z.
SW2(config)#int fa0/2
SW2(config-if)#spanning-tree cost 10
SW2(config-if)#^Z
SW2#
```

```
SW2#
00:25:00: STP: VLAN0001 new root port Fa0/2, cost 10
00:25:00: STP: VLAN0001 sent Topology Change Notice on Fa0/2
00:25:00: STP: VLAN0001 Fa0/1 -> blocking
00:25:00: STP: VLAN0001 Fa0/2 -> listening
00:25:15: STP: VLAN0001 Fa0/2 -> learning
00:25:30: STP: VLAN0001 Fa0/2 -> forwarding
SW2#
SW2#sh spanning-tree

VLAN0001
  Spanning tree enabled protocol ieee
  Root ID    Priority    32768
             Address     aaaa.aaaa.aaaa
             Cost        10
             Port        2 (FastEthernet0/2)
             Hello Time   2 sec  Max Age 20 sec  Forward Delay 15 sec

  Bridge ID  Priority    32769  (priority 32768 sys-id-ext 1)
             Address     bbbb.bbbb.bbbb
             Hello Time   2 sec  Max Age 20 sec  Forward Delay 15 sec
             Aging Time 300

Interface        Role Sts Cost      Prio.Nbr Type
---------------- ---- --- --------- -------- --------------------------------
Fa0/1            Altn BLK 19        128.1    P2p
Fa0/2            Root FWD 10        128.2    P2p

SW2#conf t
Enter configuration commands, one per line.  End with CNTL/Z.
SW2(config)#spanning-tree vlan 1 root primary
SW2(config)#
00:30:00: setting bridge id (which=1) prio 24577 prio cfg 24576 sysid 1 (on)
id 6001.bbbb.bbbb.bbbb
00:30:00: STP: VLAN0001 we are the spanning tree root
00:30:00: STP: VLAN0001 Fa0/1 -> listening
00:30:00: STP: VLAN0001 Topology Change rcvd on Fa0/1
00:30:15: STP: VLAN0001 Fa0/1 -> learning
00:30:30: STP: VLAN0001 Fa0/1 -> forwarding
SW2(config)#^Z
SW2#sh spanning-tree

VLAN0001
  Spanning tree enabled protocol ieee
  Root ID    Priority    24577
             Address     bbbb.bbbb.bbbb
             This bridge is the root
             Hello Time   2 sec  Max Age 20 sec  Forward Delay 15 sec

  Bridge ID  Priority    24577  (priority 24576 sys-id-ext 1)
             Address     bbbb.bbbb.bbbb
             Hello Time   2 sec  Max Age 20 sec  Forward Delay 15 sec
             Aging Time 15

Interface        Role Sts Cost      Prio.Nbr Type
---------------- ---- --- --------- -------- --------------------------------
Fa0/1            Desg FWD 19        128.1    P2p
Fa0/2            Desg FWD 10        128.2    P2p

SW2#
```

EtherChannel Configuration

- In this section, both the trunks between SW1 and SW2 are configured as an EtherChannel.

- The **channel-group** [*channel-group-number*] **mode on** interface subcommand configures an interface as an EtherChannel interface and assigns it to an EtherChannel channel group.

- Below shows the other 2 EtherChannel modes that allow a switch to **automatically negotiate** with its neighboring switch in establishing an EtherChannel.

auto	If configured on both switch ports, an EtherChannel will **never** be established.
desirable	As long as one of the switch ports is configured with this mode, an EtherChannel will be established.

- EtherChannel configuration on SW2:

```
SW2#conf t
Enter configuration commands, one per line.  End with CNTL/Z.
SW2(config)#int fa0/1
SW2(config-if)#channel-group 1 mode on
SW2(config-if)#
00:40:00: %LINK-3-UPDOWN: Interface Port-channel1, changed state to up
00:40:01: %LINEPROTO-5-UPDOWN: Line protocol on Interface Port-channel1,
changed state to up
SW2(config-if)#int fa0/2
SW2(config-if)#channel-group 1 mode on
SW2(config-if)#^Z
SW2#sh spanning-tree

VLAN0001
  Spanning tree enabled protocol ieee
  Root ID    Priority    24577
             Address     bbbb.bbbb.bbbb
             This bridge is the root
             Hello Time   2 sec  Max Age 20 sec  Forward Delay 15 sec

  Bridge ID  Priority    24577   (priority 24576 sys-id-ext 1)
             Address     bbbb.bbbb.bbbb
             Hello Time   2 sec  Max Age 20 sec  Forward Delay 15 sec
             Aging Time 15

Interface        Role Sts Cost      Prio.Nbr Type
---------------- ---- --- --------- -------- --------------------------------
Po1              Desg FWD 12        128.65   P2p

SW2#sh etherchannel 1 summary
Flags:  D - down        P - in port-channel
        I - stand-alone s - suspended
        R - Layer3      S - Layer2
        u - unsuitable for bundling
        U - port-channel in use
        d - default port

Group  Port-channel  Protocol    Ports
------+-------------+-----------+-----------------------------------------------
1      Po1(SU)          -        Fa0/1(P)     Fa0/2(P)

SW2#
```

This page is intentionally left blank

Chapter 7
Virtual LAN and VLAN Trunking Protocol

- All devices reside in the same LAN are in the same broadcast domain. All devices connected to a switch are normally reside in the same broadcast domain. However, a technology called VLAN allows a switch to **create multiple broadcast domains**.

- A **Virtual LAN** (VLAN) is a broadcast domain created by **one or more switches**. A switch creates VLANs by assigning its interfaces to different VLANs.

- Below are some benefits of implementing VLANs:
  i) Allows **logical grouping** of users or devices based on their functions or departments instead of their physical locations.
  ii) Reduces network overhead by **limiting the size** of each broadcast domain.
  iii) Offers **enhanced network security** by keeping sensitive devices on a separate VLAN.

- VLAN trunking is used when a VLAN **span across multiple switches**. When a switch receives a frame from another switch, it uses the **frame tag** created by other switch to identify the VLAN membership of the frame and forwards it out to ports associated for the corresponding VLAN.

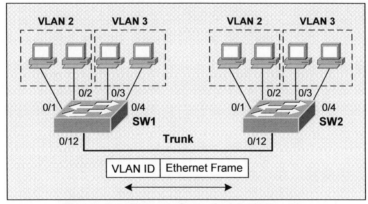

Figure 7-1: Network Setup for VLAN Trunking

- When SW1 receives a broadcast from a device in VLAN 2, it will add a header to the frame and forward to SW2. SW2 will know which interfaces it should forward to all other members of VLAN 2. The **VLAN identifier** will be removed when the frame is forwarded out an access link.

- **Where is VLAN 1?** VLAN 1 is the **administrative VLAN** which is recommended for management purposes only; even though it still can be used for workgroup access purpose.

- Catalyst switches support 2 VLAN encapsulation methods for inter-switch VLAN communication:

ISL – Inter-Switch Link	IEEE 802.1Q
Cisco-proprietary.	Industry standard. Standardized by IEEE.
Encapsulates the entire original frame with a new header and trailer (CRC), increasing the network overhead.	Does not encapsulate the original frame. Adds a 4-byte tag to the original Ethernet header and a recalculated FCS to the trailer.
Supports multiple spanning trees (one STP instance per VLAN) with **PVST+**.	Supports multiple spanning trees (one STP instance per VLAN) with **PVST+** and 802.1S **Multiple Spanning Tree Protocol** (MSTP).
Does not have the concept of native VLAN.	Uses a native VLAN.

- Both protocols utilize a 12-bit **VLAN ID** field, and hence support the same number of VLANs.

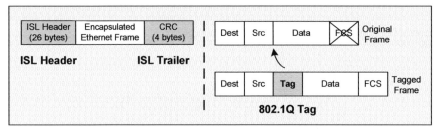

Figure 7-2: VLAN Identification and Encapsulation Formats

- Below shows the trunking actions for different types of switch port modes:

Switch Port Mode	Trunking Action
access	Never try to trunk.
trunk	Permanent trunking mode – always becomes a trunk link even if the interface at the other end is not configured as a trunk port.
dynamic desirable	Trunks to **trunk**, **dynamic desirable**, and **dynamic auto** interfaces.
dynamic auto	Trunks to **trunk** and **dynamic desirable** interfaces.

Note: A trunk link will **never be established** if the interfaces at both ends of a trunk link were configured as the **dynamic auto** mode!

- The **switchport nonegotiate** interface subcommand prevents an interface from generating **Dynamic Trunking Protocol** (DTP) frames, which are used for trunking negotiation.

- **Per-VLAN Spanning Tree Plus** (PVST+) allows each VLAN to have its own instance of spanning tree. Figure 7-3 shows 6 interfaces on 3 switches with 2 VLANs. STP parameters in each VLAN are configured to **block different interfaces in different spanning trees** for VLAN 2 and VLAN 3 on SW3. SW3 would use the link to SW1 for traffic in VLAN 3 and link to SW2 for traffic in VLAN 2. STP will converge to find a new path for a VLAN if one of the links fails.

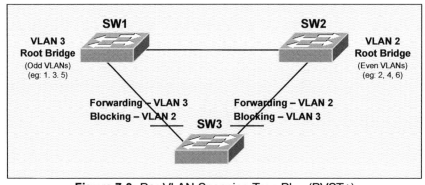

Figure 7-3: Per-VLAN Spanning Tree Plus (PVST+)

- 802.1Q defines a VLAN on a trunk as the **native VLAN**, where frames associated with the native VLAN are **not tagged**. A switch recognizes a native VLAN frame when a frame **without 802.1Q tag** is received from an 802.1Q trunk. ISL does not have this concept – every frame will be encapsulated and has an ISL header.

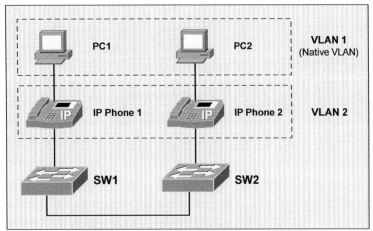

Figure 7-4: Network Setup for Native VLAN

- Figure 7-4 shows the usage of **native VLAN**. 2 PCs are connected to 2 separate switches. The organization would like to install an IP phone near each PC. Normal PCs do not understand 802.1Q but the built-in switches in the IP phones do. The IP phones are reside between the PCs and switches, and the PCs and IP phones are assigned to different VLANs. All the switch ports are configured for 802.1Q while the PCs are placed in the native VLAN. IP phones and switches can understand 802.1Q traffic between them. The IP phones can simply forward the native VLAN traffic (frames without 802.1Q tags) between the PCs and the switches.

- Switches use the same switching logic when implemented VLANs, but in per-VLAN basis – there is a MAC address table for each VLAN and the tables are separated for different VLANs. Hence, unicasts and broadcasts for a VLAN **cannot be forwarded out** to ports in other VLANs.

- L2 switches are unable to forward traffic between VLANs. L3 to L7 switches are able to perform **multilayer switching**. Below are the available methods for passing traffic between VLANs:

L3 Forwarding using a Router	In the 1st option (Figure 7-5A), each router interface is connected to an access link to a VLAN of the switch. Each router interface's IP address would be the default gateway address for each host in each VLAN. In the 2nd option (Figure 7-5B), instead of using a router interface for each VLAN, just a single Fast Ethernet interface that supports ISL or 802.1Q trunking is used, which allows all VLANs to communicate through one interface. This setup is also known as **router-on-a-stick**.
L3 Forwarding using a L3 switch	L3 switches are switches that have L2 switching and L3 routing capabilities. Performing routing with an external router and with the internal processing of an L3 switch provide the same result. L3 switches are able to run routing protocols to build their routing table, and make forwarding decisions based on destination IP addresses.

Layer 4 Switching (Content Switching)	L4 switches consider the information in the L4 headers when forwarding packets. The forwarding decision can either be based upon information in the **L4 headers** (typically the port numbers), the **IP addresses** (L3 forwarding), and even the **MAC addresses**. L4 switches support accounting by keeping track of the numbers of packets and bytes sent per TCP port number. Ex: A server farm consists of 2 replicated web servers and a FTP server. Clients' requests are directed to a single IP address which has been associated to all 3 servers. Packets destined to port 80 will be switched to either of the web servers and packets destined to port 21 will be switched to the only single FTP server. The first request of a client will be directed to either web servers and subsequent connections for that client will be switched to the same server. L4 switching requires more processing capacity that L3 switching. **NetFlow switching** can be enabled on Cisco Catalyst switches to perform L4 (and network traffic) accounting.
Layer 5 – Layer 7 Switching (Content Switching)	Refers to the type of switching that able to look into the application layer headers to make switching decisions. Also known as L7 switching, application layer switching, and content switching. It falls into a category of products called **Content Delivery Networks** (CDN).

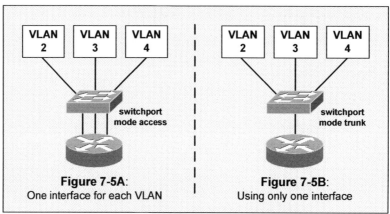

Figure 7-5A:
One interface for each VLAN

Figure 7-5B:
Using only one interface

Figure 7-5: L3 Forwarding using a Router

VLAN Trunking Protocol

- **VLAN Trunking Protocol** (VTP) is the Cisco-proprietary L2 protocol used to **exchange and maintain a consistent VLAN database** across Catalyst switches in an administrative domain. VTP **minimizes misconfiguration** and eases the configuration task by **reducing manual configuration** needs. VTP facilitates centralized VLAN management – VLAN configuration (eg: addition, deletion, and renaming of VLANs) only needs to be made on a single switch and the configuration will be propagated to all other switches in the same VTP domain.
  Ex: The changing of the name for a particular VLAN on a switch will be distributed to other switches. Hence no configuration is needed on those switches.

- Below lists the operation of VTP:
  i)   Modification of VLAN information (eg: VLAN name) in a VTP server.
  ii)   Increments the VLAN configuration revision number (+1).
  iii) The VTP server sends out a VTP advertisement with a higher revision number.
  iv)   VTP clients notice the configuration when the revision number larger than its current one.
  v)   VTP clients synchronize their VLAN configurations with the new VLAN information.

- By default, VTP servers flood VTP advertisements throughout a VTP domain every 10 minutes, or whenever there is a VLAN configuration change. VTP advertisements are sent as **multicasts**. A **VTP domain** is also known as a **VLAN management domain**.

- A higher configuration revision number indicates that the received VLAN information is more current than the current information. A switch would ignore a VTP advertisement with a revision number that is the same or lower with its current revision number.

- **Caution:** Inserting a VTP client or server with a **higher configuration revision number** into a VTP domain can **overwrite** the VLAN information on existing VTP servers and clients.

- The methods that can be used to reset the VTP configuration revision number of a switch are:
  i)   Change the VTP domain name, and change back to the original VTP domain name.
  ii)   Change to VTP Transparent mode, and change back to VTP Server mode.

- Below list the VTP operation modes:

Server (default)	There must be at least one VTP server in a VTP domain. Only VTP server switches are allowed to **create, add, modify,** and **delete** VLANs. Changes made on a VTP server switch will be advertised throughout the entire VTP domain. **Can save** VLAN config in NVRAM.
Client	Can receive and forward VTP advertisements, but **cannot** create, add, modify, nor delete VLANs. They process received advertisements and synchronize their VLAN configuration. **Cannot save** VLAN configuration in NVRAM. They synchronize the VLAN configuration with other switches upon reboot.
Transparent	Do not participate in the VTP domain (ignore VTP advertisements), but still forward VTP advertisements. Switches operate in this mode can **create, add, modify,** and **delete** their own VLANs but do not advertise the configuration to other switches (locally significant only). **Can save** VLAN config in NVRAM.

- **Note:** VTP advertisements are only propagated across (or sent over) **trunk links**. VTP advertisements can be sent over **all types of trunk links**, eg: ISL, 802.1Q, and ATM LANE. Additionally, all switches in the VTP domain must be configured to use the **same VTP version**.

- **VTP Pruning** provides a way to preserve bandwidth by configuring switches to only send broadcasts and unknown unicasts to the trunks to other switches that need the information (contain ports in a particular VLAN). VTP pruning is **disabled by default**, which means broadcasts and unknown unicasts in every VLAN is forwarded to all switches in the network.
Ex: SW1 does not have any ports configured for VLAN 2, thus broadcasts sent to VLAN 2 should not be forwarded to the trunk to SW1 (pruning flooded traffic to conserve bandwidth).
Note: VLAN 1 can never be pruned because it is an administrative VLAN.

- The [**no**] **vtp pruning** privileged or global configuration command is used to enable or disable VTP pruning respectively. VTP pruning only need to be enabled on a single VTP server mode switch throughout a VTP domain, as the setting will be propagated to other switches and cause them to enable VTP pruning as well. VTP pruning utilizes VTP advertisements for its operation.

- When PVST is in use, STP optimization for each VLAN and VTP pruning are important to ensure STP changes that occur in a particular VLAN will not affect other STP instances for other VLANs, which results in a more stable network.

Chapter 8
Virtual LAN and VLAN Trunking Protocol Lab

VLAN Configuration

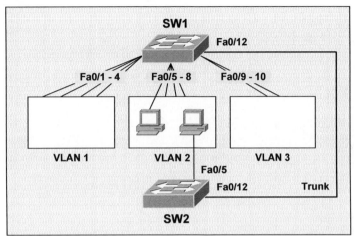

Figure 8-1: Network Setup for VLAN and VLAN Trunking Protocol

```
SW1#conf t
Enter configuration commands, one per line.  End with CNTL/Z.
SW1(config)#vlan 1
SW1(config-vlan)#name IT
Default VLAN 1 may not have its name changed.
SW1(config-vlan)#vlan 2
SW1(config-vlan)#name Sales
SW1(config-vlan)#vlan 3
SW1(config-vlan)#name Marketing
SW1(config-vlan)#exit
SW1(config)#
SW1(config)#int range fa0/5 – 8
SW1(config-if-range)#switchport mode access
SW1(config-if-range)#switchport access vlan 2
SW1(config-if-range)#spanning-tree portfast
SW1(config-if-range)#int range fa0/9 – 10
SW1(config-if-range)#switchport mode access
SW1(config-if-range)#switchport access vlan 3
SW1(config-if-range)#spanning-tree portfast
SW1(config-if-range)#^Z
SW1#sh vlan

VLAN Name                             Status    Ports
---- -------------------------------- --------- -------------------------------
1    default                          active    Fa0/1, Fa0/2, Fa0/3, Fa0/4
                                                Fa0/11, Fa0/12
2    Sales                            active    Fa0/5, Fa0/6, Fa0/7, Fa0/8
3    Marketing                        active    Fa0/9, Fa0/10
1002 fddi-default                     act/unsup
1003 token-ring-default               act/unsup
1004 fddinet-default                  act/unsup
1005 trnet-default                    act/unsup
SW1#
```

VLAN Trunking Protocol Configuration

- VTP configuration on SW1:

```
SW1#conf t
Enter configuration commands, one per line.  End with CNTL/Z.
SW1(config)#int fa0/12
SW1(config-if)#switchport trunk encapsulation dot1q
SW1(config-if)#switchport mode trunk
SW1(config-if)#no shut
SW1(config-if)#^Z
SW1#
SW1#sh int fa0/12 switchport
Name: Fa0/12
Switchport: Enabled
Administrative Mode: trunk
Operational Mode: trunk
Administrative Trunking Encapsulation: dot1q
Operational Trunking Encapsulation: dot1q
Negotiation of Trunking: On
Access Mode VLAN: 1 (default)
Trunking Native Mode VLAN: 1 (default)
Administrative Native VLAN tagging: enabled
--- output omitted ---

SW1#sh int fa0/12 trunk

Port            Mode             Encapsulation  Status        Native vlan
Fa0/12          on               802.1q         trunking      1

Port            Vlans allowed on trunk
Fa0/12          1-4094

Port            Vlans allowed and active in management domain
Fa0/12          1-3

Port            Vlans in spanning tree forwarding state and not pruned
Fa0/12          1-3
SW1#conf t
Enter configuration commands, one per line.  End with CNTL/Z.
SW1(config)#vtp domain building01
Changing VTP domain name from NULL to building01
SW1(config)#vtp password pass123
Setting device VLAN database password to pass123
SW1(config)#^Z
SW1#sh vtp status
VTP Version                     : 2
Configuration Revision          : 2
Maximum VLANs supported locally : 1005
Number of existing VLANs        : 7
VTP Operating Mode              : Server
VTP Domain Name                 : building01
VTP Pruning Mode                : Disabled
VTP V2 Mode                     : Disabled
VTP Traps Generation            : Disabled
MD5 digest                      : 0x82 0x47 0xB0 0x3D 0x78 0xFE 0xCF 0x47
Configuration last modified by 0.0.0.0 at 3-1-93 00:06:10
Local updater ID is 0.0.0.0 (no valid interface found)
SW1#
```

- VTP configuration on SW2:

```
SW2#conf t
Enter configuration commands, one per line.  End with CNTL/Z.
SW2(config)#int fa0/12
SW2(config-if)#switchport trunk encapsulation dot1q
SW2(config-if)#switchport mode trunk
SW2(config-if)#no shut
SW2(config-if)#exit
SW2(config)#vtp mode client
Setting device to VTP CLIENT mode.
SW2(config)#vtp domain building01
Changing VTP domain name from NULL to building01
SW2(config)#vtp password pass123
Setting device VLAN database password to pass123
SW2(config)#vlan 4
VTP VLAN configuration not allowed when device is in CLIENT mode.
SW2(config)#no vlan 3
VTP VLAN configuration not allowed when device is in CLIENT mode.
SW2(config)#int fa0/5
SW2(config-if)#spanning-tree portfast
SW2(config-if)#switchport mode access
SW2(config-if)#switchport access vlan 2
SW2(config-if)#^Z
SW2#
```

- Verify the VTP configuration on SW2 with the **sh vlan** and **sh int fa0/12 switchport** commands. Verify PC1 and PC2 (in the same VLAN) communication with the **ping** command.

- Below lists the 2 types of VLAN membership:

Static VLANs	Dynamic VLANs
- The most usual and secure way of creating VLANs by manual configuration of VLAN assignment. - A switch port always maintains its VLAN association. - Works well in networks with minimal user movement.	- Automatically determines the VLAN assignment for an end system based on the MAC address. - Easier management and configuration – switches will correctly assign the appropriate VLAN for moved end systems. - **VLAN Management Policy Server** (VMPS) is being used for setting up a MAC-address-to-VLAN mapping database.

Note: Catalyst 4500 and 6500 switches can be configured as a VMPS.

- Below lists the 2 types of links in switched networks:

Access links	Belongs to only one VLAN at a time and only allow a single VLAN to be used across the link (directly connected hosts are communicating in one VLAN only). VLAN information associated to a frame is removed before the frame is being forwarded out an access link. Hence hosts are unaware of the usage of VLAN and are just assume in a broadcast domain. Connecting hosts and hubs.
Trunk links	Can be part of multiple VLANs at a time and able to carry traffic for multiple VLANs when VLANs span across multiple switches. They are point-to-point links between 2 switches, switch-router, or switch-host. They are **not shown** in the output of **show vlan** EXEC command. The term **trunk** was inspired by the telephone system trunks which carry multiple conversations at a time.

- VLAN information will not be propagated over a network until a **domain name** is specified. A switch in a domain will ignore VTP advertisements from switches in other domains. A **password** must also be configured on all switches when VTP is operating in **secure mode**. **Note:** VTP domain names and passwords are **case-sensitive**.

Inter-VLAN Routing Configuration

- By implementing VLAN, hosts are only able to communicate with other members from the same VLAN. Inter-VLAN communication can be achieved with an external router or a L3 switch.

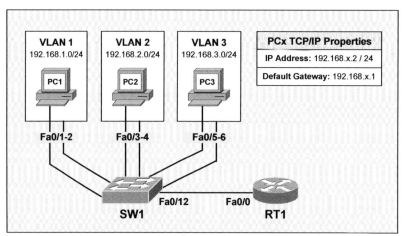

Figure 8-2: Inter-VLAN Routing with Router-on-a-Stick

- Fast Ethernet router interfaces are recommended for the router-on-a-stick setup. Note that the physical router interface is being divided into logical interfaces called **subinterfaces**.

- Inter-VLAN Routing configuration on SW1:

```
SW1(config)#int fa0/12
SW1(config-if)#switchport trunk encapsulation dot1q
SW1(config-if)#switchport mode trunk
```

- Inter-VLAN Routing configuration on RT1:

```
RT1(config)#int fa0/0
RT1(config-if)#no ip address
RT1(config-if)#no shut
RT1(config-if)#int fa0/0.1
RT1(config-subif)#encapsulation dot1q 1 native
RT1(config-subif)#ip add 192.168.1.1 255.255.255.0
RT1(config-subif)#exit
RT1(config)#int fa0/0.2
RT1(config-subif)#encapsulation dot1q 2
RT1(config-subif)#ip add 192.168.2.1 255.255.255.0
RT1(config-subif)#exit
RT1(config)#int fa0/0.3
RT1(config-subif)#encapsulation dot1q 3
RT1(config-subif)#ip add 192.168.3.1 255.255.255.0
```

Chapter 9

IP Addressing and Subnetting

- 4 bits – **nibble**. 8 bits – **byte / octet**. The values in a byte are 128 64 32 16 8 4 2 1.

- Binary to Decimal memorization chart:

Binary Value	Decimal Value
10000000	128
11000000	192
11100000	224
11110000	240
11111000	248
11111100	252
11111110	254
11111111	255

Decimal to Binary to Hex chart:

Decimal	Binary	Hexadecimal
1	0001	1
2	0010	2
3	0011	3
4	0100	4
5	0101	5
6	0110	6
7	0111	7
8	1000	8
9	1001	9
10	1010	A
11	1011	B
12	1100	C
13	1101	D
14	1110	E
15	1111	F

- IP addresses are normally written in **dotted-decimal** format, eg: 192.168.0.100, 172.16.10.10.

- An IP address can be divided into 2 portions:
  Network address that is used to identify the network.
  Host address or **node address** that is used to identify the end system on the network.

- 5 different classes of IP address were designed for **efficient routing** by defining different **leading-bits sections** for the address of different class. A router is able to identify an IP address quickly by only reading the first few bits of the address, eg: if the address starts with 0, it is a Class A address, etc. Classful routing protocols also use the **first octet rule** to determine the class of an address when assigning subnet masks for their routing operation.

Class	First Octet Range	Valid Network Numbers	Default Subnet Mask	Max number of networks	Max number of hosts
A	**00000000** – 0 **0**1111111 – 127	1.0.0.0 – 126.0.0.0	8 bits, 255.0.0.0	$2^7 - 2$, 126	$2^{24} - 2$, 16777214
B	**10000000** – 128 **10**111111 – 191	128.0.0.0 – 191.255.0.0	16 bits, 255.255.0.0	2^{14} [1], 16384	$2^{16} - 2$, 65534
C	**110000000** – 192 **110**11111 – 223	192.0.0.0 – 223.255.255.0	24 bits, 255.255.255.0	2^{21} [2], 2097152	$2^8 - 2$, 254
D [3]	**1110000** – 224 **1110**1111 – 239	224.0.0.0 – 239.255.255.255	–	–	–
E [4]	**11110000** – 240 **11111**111 – 255	240.0.0.0 – 255.255.255.255	–	–	–

[1] **14** = 6 bits in 1st octet + 8 bits in 2nd octet.
[2] **21** = 5 bits in 1st octet + 8 bits in 2nd octet + 8 bits in 3rd octet.
[3] Class D addresses are used for **multicasting**.
[4] Class E addresses are reserved for **experimental and testing** purposes.

- Private IP addresses are **non-routable** addresses that can only be used for private networking; they cannot be routed through the public Internet. They were introduced for address allocation for the communication between systems within an organization that has no intention to connect to the Internet, as well as to extend the life of the IPv4 address space.

- Below lists the reserved private IP addresses. Note that the masks or these private address ranges are not the default subnet masks for the IP address classes – /8, /16, /24.

Address Class	Reserved Address Space	Number of Networks
Class A	10.0.0.0 – 10.255.255.255 (10.0.0.0/8)	1 Class A network
Class B	172.16.0.0 – 172.31.255.255 (172.16.0.0/12)	16 Class B networks
Class C	192.168.0.0 – 192.168.255.255 (192.168.0.0/16)	256 Class C networks

Reference: RFC 1918 – Address Allocation for Private Internets.

- Some other special-purpose reserved IP addresses are 127.0.0.1, the **loopback testing address** that allows a host to test whether its TCP/IP stack is operational; and 0.0.0.0 that is used by Cisco routers to indicate the **default route**. Network 128.0.0.0, 191.255.0.0, 192.0.0.0, and 223.255.255.0 are also reserved.
Note: In fact, any IP address starts with 127 (127.0.0.0/8) is reserved for loopback testing.
Note: Ping from Cisco devices to 127.0.0.1 would fail, as the route is not in their routing tables.

IP Subnetting

- **Classful addressing** uses the subnet masks of standard classes to determine the network and host portions of an address. IPv4 networks can be divided into smaller networks called **subnets**. Subnetting allows the breaking of a large network into a number of smaller networks (subnets) using subnet masks other than the convention or standard Class A, B, and C subnet masks (/8, /16, and /24).

- Some benefits of subnetting are:
  i) Reduced network traffic and bandwidth utilization, as well as optimized network performance (as a result of reduced broadcast traffic).
  ii) More efficient use and allocation of network addresses.
  iii) Simplified administration and management.

- A **subnet address** is created by borrowing bits from the host portion of an IP address – **host bits**. A **subnet mask** is a 32-bit number that is associated with an IP address. 1 indicates **subnet bit** and 0 indicates **host bit**. The subnet mask indicates the number of bits that have been borrowed from the host portion for the subnet portion. Subnet mask is also known as **prefix length** in classless addressing rule.

- Subnet masks are assigned on end systems for them to know which subnet they resides in by knowing the network and host portions of an IP address.

- **Prefix notation** or **slash notation** indicates the number of binary 1s in a mask with a slash (**/**).
Ex: 192.168.0.100/24 → IP address = 192.168.0.100, subnet mask = 255.255.255.0.

- The largest subnet mask can only be **/30** because at least 2 bits are required for host bits.

- The Boolean AND operation:

1st Bit	2nd Bit	Operation	Result
0	0	**AND**	0
0	1	**AND**	0
1	0	**AND**	0
1	1	**AND**	1

- The **bitwise Boolean AND** operation between an IP address and its subnet mask is used to discover the **subnet number** for the IP address.

- **First address** → Add 1 to the 4th octet of the subnet number.
  Broadcast address → Change the values of all host bits in the subnet number to binary 1s.
  Last address (or **largest valid IP address**) → Broadcast address – 1.

- **Example 1:** 10.0.0.1/16

IP Address	10.0.0.1	00001010 00000000	00000000 00000001
Subnet Mask	255.255.0.0	11111111 11111111	00000000 00000000
Subnet Number	10.0.0.0	00001010 00000000	00000000 00000000
First Address	10.0.0.1	00001010 00000000	00000000 00000001
Broadcast Address	10.0.255.255	00001010 00000000	11111111 11111111
Last Address	10.0.255.254	00001010 00000000	11111111 11111110

- **Example 2:** 172.16.0.1/24

IP Address	172.16.0.1	10101100 00010000 00000000	00000001
Subnet Mask	255.255.255.0	11111111 11111111 11111111	00000000
Subnet Number	172.16.0.0	10101100 00010000 00000000	00000000
First Address	172.16.0.1	10101100 00010000 00000000	00000001
Broadcast Address	172.16.0.255	10101100 00010000 00000000	11111111
Last Address	172.16.0.254	10101100 00010000 00000000	11111110

- **Example 3:** 192.168.100.100/28

IP Address	192.168.100.100	11000000 10101000 01100100 0110	0100
Subnet Mask	255.255.255.240	11111111 11111111 11111111 1111	0000
Subnet Number	192.168.100.96	11000000 10101000 01100100 0110	0000
First Address	192.168.100.97	11000000 10101000 01100100 0110	0001
Broadcast Address	192.168.100.111	11000000 10101000 01100100 0110	1111
Last Address	192.168.100.110	11000000 10101000 01100100 0110	1110

- Total number of subnets → $2^n - 2$, where n is the number of subnet bits. [1]
  Total number of hosts → $2^n - 2$, where n is the number of host bits. [2]
  [1] minus the subnet zero and the broadcast subnet.
  [2] minus the network address (all-0s bit pattern) and the broadcast address (all-1s bit pattern).

Subnet zero	It has all binary 0s in the subnet portion. Also known as all-0s subnet.
Broadcast subnet	It has all binary 1s in the subnet portion. Also known as all-1s subnet.

- Ex: In 172.16.0.0, 255.255.255.0, 8 bits are borrowed from the 16 host bits for subnet bits. With these 8 subnet bits, there are $2^8 - 2 = 254$ subnets, and each subnet has 8 host bit, which are $2^8 - 2 = 254$ hosts are available on each subnet.

- Some materials calculate the number of subnets with the 2^n formula, which includes the subnet zero and the broadcast subnet. All-0s subnet (subnet zero) must be allowed with the **ip subnet-zero** global configuration command, which is enabled by default in IOS Release 12.0 and later. All-0s subnet and all-1s subnet (broadcast subnet) are legal subnets according to RFC 1812. **Tips:** When answering CCNA subnetting questions, use the 2^n for **TOTAL** subnets, and $2^n - 2$ for **USABLE** or **VALID** subnets.

- Subnetting decisions should always be based on growth estimations rather than current needs.

- The 6-step approach to plan for the IP addressing needs in a network:
  i) Figure out the network and host requirements
  ii) Figure out the subnet mask
  iii) Figure out the network addresses
  iv) Figure out the broadcast addresses for the networks
  v) Figure out the host addresses for the networks

- The following formulas can be used when performing subnetting:
  1) $2^x \geq$ number of required subnets
  2) $2^y - 2 \geq$ number of required hosts
  3) $x + y \leq$ total number of host bits

- The 1st formula defines how many bits need to be borrowed from the host bits to create the number of required subnets. The 2nd formula defines how many host bits are needed to accommodate the number of required hosts. Lastly, the 3rd formula makes sure that the network and host bits do not exceed the original number of host bits.
  Ex: Given a Class C network for subnetting. 5 bits are required for network bits and 4 bits are required for host bits to fulfill the requirements. $5 + 4 = 9$ bits, but Class C networks only have 8 host bits. Hence it is impossible to meet the requirement!

- **Block size** is the number of hosts that can be used in a subnet. Block sizes are typically in increments of 2^n, eg: 2, 4, 8, 16, 32, 64, and 128.

- As a qualified CCNA, one must be able to demonstrate the ability to answer subnetting questions **confidently**, **accurately**, and **fast**!

- **Practice Makes Perfect. PRACTICE! PRACTICE!! PRACTICE!!!** ☺

IP Version 6 (IPv6)

- Private addressing and Network Address Translation (NAT) were being used in conjunction as the short-term solution for the depletion or exhaustion of IPv4 global addresses. IPv6, the new version of the IP protocol, is the long-term solution for the problem.

- IPv6 uses 128 bits for IP addressing, as compared to the 32-bit in IPv4.

- IPv6 addresses are represented in 8 16-bit hexadecimal segments and are written in hexadecimal notation, with colons between each quartet.
  Ex: 10.1.1.1 in IPv4, is 0000:0000:0000:0000:0000:FFFF:FFFF:0A01:0101 in IPv6.

- The number of possible addresses in IPv6 is 2^{128} – approximately 3.4 x 10^{38} addresses.

- Besides providing a larger address space, some other additional benefits of IPv6 are:
  i)   Simplified header
  ii)   Autoconfiguration
  iii)   Security with mandatory IPSec for all IPv6 devices
  iv)   Mobility
  v)   Enhanced multicast support
  vi)   Extension headers
  vii)   Flow labels
  viii) Improved address allocation
  ix)   Address aggregation

- Although IPv6 has many advanced features, the primary reason for the move to IPv6 is the depletion of IPv4 addresses. IPv6 provides greater flexibility in assigning addresses.

- IPv6 does not use nor send out broadcasts.

- IPv6 provides solutions to some other challenges and problems found in IPv4, eg: broadcast storm, address renumbering, network layer security (IP is vulnerable to attacks).

This page is intentionally left blank

Chapter 10
Managing a Cisco Internetwork

Resolving Hostnames

- By properly setting up **hostname resolution or translation** service, a hostname instead of an IP address can be used to communicate with a device.

- Below lists the 2 available methods used to resolve hostnames to IP addresses:
  i) Build a **host table** on each device (**static host table**).
  ii) Setup a **Domain Name System** (DNS) server (**dynamic host table**).

- Below lists some Cisco IOS IP naming services commands:

ip domain-name {*name*}	Defines the default domain name of a device. Global configuration command.
ip domain-lookup	Tells the IOS to resolve unknown hostnames and wrongly typed commands using DNS. Global configuration command.
ip name-server {*svr1*} [*svr2... svr6*]	Configures the DNS name server IP addresses (max of 6). Global configuration command.
ip host {*name*} {*ip-addr*}	Creates a static entry in the host table. Global configuration command.
no ip host {*name*}	Removes a static entry from the host table. Global configuration command.
show hosts	Lists DNS and host table information. EXEC command.

```
Switch#conf t
Switch(config)#ip host router01 192.168.0.1
Switch(config)#ip host router02 192.168.0.2
Switch(config)#ip name-server 172.16.0.1 172.16.0.2
Switch(config)#^Z
Switch#
Switch#sh hosts
Default domain is not set
Name/address lookup uses domain service
Name servers are 172.16.0.3, 172.16.1.3

Codes: u - unknown, e - expired, * - OK, ? - revalidate
       t - temporary, p - permanent

Host                    Port   Flags       Age Type   Address(es)
router01                None   (perm, OK)  0   IP     192.168.0.1
router02                None   (perm, OK)  0   IP     192.168.0.2
Switch#
```

Note: The **perm** in the Flags column represents a manually configured entry; while the **temp** represents a cached DNS-resolved entry.

- It is recommended to have **at least 2 name servers** for **redundancy** and **availability** purposes.

Cisco Discovery Protocol (CDP)

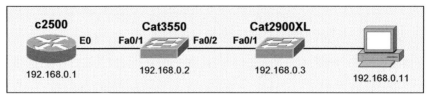

Figure 10-1: Network Setup for Cisco Discovery Protocol

- **Cisco Discovery Protocol** (CDP) is a **Cisco-proprietary** data link layer device discovery protocol designed for gathering hardware and software information of neighboring devices. Such info is useful for **troubleshooting** and **documenting** a network.

- CDP updates are sent as **multicasts**. It is a L2 protocol and runs on all physical interfaces that support SNAP (**Subnetwork Access Protocol**), eg: all LAN protocols, HDLC, Frame Relay, and ATM. The only media type CDP cannot operate over is X.25, as it does not support SNAP.

- CDP is a L2 protocol, hence it is **independent on any L3 protocol** – Cisco devices are able to discover L3 addressing details of neighboring devices even without any network layer (L3) addressing configuration.

- The **show cdp neighbors detail** EXEC displays many useful information regarding all neighboring devices.

- CDP frames do not pass through switches, they are only sent to **directly connected** devices. Ex: In Figure 10-1, c2500's CDP neighbor is only Cat3550; Cat2900XL is not its CDP neighbor.

- Below interprets the fields of the output of the **show cdp neighbors** EXEC command:

Field	Description
Device ID	The hostname of the directly connected device.
Local Interface	The interface of the local device that received the CDP packet from the directly connected device.
Holdtime	The amount of time a device will hold (keep) the received CDP information before discarding it if no more CDP packets are received.
Capability	The capabilities of the directly connected device, eg: router, switch, etc. The device capability codes are listed at the top of the command output.
Platform	The model of the directly connected device.
Port ID	The interface of the neighboring device that transmitted the CDP packet.

- Below shows some CDP command outputs on Cat3550:

```
Cat3550#sh cdp ?
  entry      Information for specific neighbor entry
  interface  CDP interface status and configuration
  neighbors  CDP neighbor entries
  traffic    CDP statistics
  |          Output modifiers
  <cr>


Cat3550#sh cdp neighbors
Capability Codes: R - Router, T - Trans Bridge, B - Source Route Bridge
                  S - Switch, H - Host, I - IGMP, r - Repeater, P - Phone

Device ID      Local Intrfce      Holdtme    Capability    Platform    Port ID
Cat2900XL      Fas 0/2            152        T S           WS-C2924-X  Fas0/1
c2500          Fas 0/1            137        R             2500        Eth0

Cat3550#sh cdp entry Cat2900XL
-----------------------
Device ID: Cat2900XL
Entry address(es):
  IP address: 192.168.0.251
Platform: cisco WS-C2924-XL,   Capabilities: Trans-Bridge Switch
Interface: FastEthernet0/2,  Port ID (outgoing port): FastEthernet0/1
Holdtime : 142 sec

Version :
Cisco Internetwork Operating System Software
IOS (tm) C2900XL Software (C2900XL-C3H2S-M), Version 12.0(5)WC10, RELEASE
SOFTWARE (fc1)
Copyright (c) 1986-2004 by cisco Systems, Inc.
Compiled Fri 28-May-04 09:52 by antonino

advertisement version: 2
Protocol Hello:  OUI=0x00000C, Protocol ID=0x0112; payload len=27,
value=0000000
0FFFFFFFF010121FF00000000000000000427C1D3C0FF0001
VTP Management Domain: ''
Native VLAN: 1
Duplex: full

Cat3550#
```

- CDP global parameters can be modified using the following global configuration commands:

cdp timer {sec}	Used to define **how often** to send the periodical CDP updates out to all CDP enabled interfaces.
cdp holdtime {sec}	Used to define **how long** a device will hold (keep) the received CDP information before discarding it if no more CDP update is received.

- CDP Version 2 (CDPv2) is the most recent release of the Cisco Discovery Protocol. It provides a reporting mechanism which can send error messages to the console or a Syslog logging server upon occurrences of unmatched 802.1Q native VLAN ID, unmatched port duplex states, etc.

- CDP is **enabled by default**.
The **no cdp run** global configuration command **completely** disables CDP on a device.
The **no cdp enable** interface subcommand disables CDP for **an interface – stop sending out and ignore** CDP packets on the interface.

```
Cat3550#sh cdp int fa0/1
FastEthernet0/1 is up, line protocol is up
  Encapsulation ARPA
  Sending CDP packets every 60 seconds
  Holdtime is 180 seconds
Cat3550#conf t
Enter configuration commands, one per line.  End with CNTL/Z.
Cat3550(config)#cdp ?
  advertise-v2  CDP sends version-2 advertisements
  holdtime      Specify the holdtime (in sec) to be sent in packets
  run           Enable CDP
  timer         Specify the rate at which CDP packets are sent      (in sec)

Cat3550(config)#int fa0/1
Cat3550(config-if)#no cdp enable
Cat3550(config-if)#^Z
Cat3550#sh cdp int fa0/1

Cat3550#
```

Telnet

- Cisco IOS allows Telnet from a Cisco device to another Cisco device. An important feature of the **telnet** EXEC command is the **suspend** feature.

- **Lab setup**: Setup the sample network as in Figure 10-1. Configure the hostname and IP address on every device, and create a host table consisting static entries for all devices on every device.

- Below lists some Cisco IOS Telnet-related commands:

telnet {*hostname* | *ip-addr*}	Used to Telnet from a device to another device.
show sessions or **where**	Used to list the suspended telnet sessions.
resume {*connection-id*}	Used to resume a suspended telnet session.
disconnect {*connection-id*}	Used to terminate a suspended telnet session.

- A Telnet session can be suspended with the following key sequence:
Ctrl + Shift + 6, release, then x.

- In the **show sessions** or **where** EXEC commands output, an **asterisk [*]** will be shown at the left of the **most recently suspended** Telnet session, which can be resumed by using the **resume** EXEC command, or by pressing Enter or Tab in EXEC or privileged mode. **Connection ID** is the identification for a Telnet session.

- Below demonstrates the usage of Telnet suspension:

```
Cat3550>telnet Cat2900XL
Trying Cat2900XL (192.168.0.3)... Open

Cat2900XL>
Cat2900XL> [Ctrl+Shift+6, x]
Cat3550>telnet c2500
Trying c2500 (192.168.0.1)... Open

c2500>
c2500> [Ctrl+Shift+6, x]
Cat3550>sh sessions
Conn Host                Address          Byte   Idle Conn Name
   1 Cat2900XL           192.168.0.3         0      0 Cat2900XL
*  2 c2500               192.168.0.1         0      0 c2500

Cat3550> [Enter]
[Resuming connection 2 to c2500 ... ]

c2500> [Ctrl+Shift+6, x]
Cat3550>resume 1
[Resuming connection 1 to Cat2900XL ... ]

Cat2900XL> [Ctrl+Shift+6, x]
Cat3550>where
Conn Host                Address          Byte   Idle Conn Name
*  1 Cat2900XL           192.168.0.3         0      0 Cat2900XL
   2 c2500               192.168.0.1         0      0 c2500

Cat3550>disconnect 1
Closing connection to Cat2900XL [confirm] [Enter]
Cat3550> [Enter]
[Resuming connection 2 to c2500 ... ]

c2500> [Ctrl+Shift+6, x]
Cat3550>where
Conn Host                Address          Byte   Idle Conn Name
*  2 c2500               192.168.0.1         0      0 c2500

Cat3550> [Enter]
[Resuming connection 2 to c2500 ... ]

c2500>
c2500>exit

[Connection to c2500 closed by foreign host]
Cat3550>
Cat3550>where
% No connections open
Cat3550>
```

Troubleshooting IP

- **Internet Control Message Protocol** (ICMP) is a TCP/IP protocol that was designed specifically to help manage and control the operation of TCP/IP networks. It provides a wide variety of information about the operational status of a network.

- ICMP is considered as a part of the network layer. ICMP messages are encapsulated within IP packets and sent using the basic IP header only, with no transport layer header at all – it is really just an extension of the network layer.

- Below lists some ICMP message types and their usages:

Message	Usage
Echo Request (Type 8) and **Echo Reply** (Type 0)	Used by the **ping** command when testing network connectivity.
Destination Unreachable (Type 3)	Used to notify the source host that there is a problem when delivering a packet.
Redirect (Type 5)	Sent by a router to notify the sender to use a better route for subsequent connection attempts.
Time Exceeded (Type 11)	Used to notify a host when a packet sent by it has been discarded due the time for a packet to exist in a network (Time-to-Live, TTL) when being delivered to the destination has expired.

- **ICMP Destination Unreachable** messages are sent to notify the sender when a message cannot be delivered to the destination host. Packet delivery can fail with many reasons. Below lists the 5 common ICMP Unreachable codes that can be sent in ICMP Destination Unreachable messages:

Unreachable Code	When it is being sent?	Typically sent by
Network Unreachable (Code 0)	Unable to match a packet's destination network in the routing table and therefore unable to forward the packet.	Routers
Host Unreachable (Code 1)	A packet has reached the router attached to the destination network, but the destination host is not responding to ARP Request sent by the router. **Note:** Cisco routers do not generate Host Unreachable ICMP messages.	Routers
Can't Fragment (Code 4)	A packet has the Don't Fragment (DF) bit set, but the router must fragment the packet in order to forward it.	Routers
Protocol Unreachable (Code 2)	A packet is delivered to the destination host, but the transport layer protocol is not available or running on that host. This is very unlikely to happen as most operating systems that support TCP/IP should have provided IP, TCP and UDP services.	Endpoint hosts
Port Unreachable (Code 3)	A packet is delivered to the destination host, but there is no application listening to the destination port number.	Endpoint hosts

- Below lists the Cisco IOS **ping** response codes:

Response Code	Description
!	ICMP Echo Reply message received.
.	The **ping** command timed out while waiting for a reply.
N	ICMP Network Unreachable message received.
U	ICMP Destination Unreachable – Host Unreachable (ICMP Type 3 Code 1) message received.
M	ICMP Can't Fragment message received.
Q	ICMP Source Quench message received, which normally indicates the destination host does not have sufficient processing buffer.
P	ICMP Destination Unreachable – Port Unreachable (ICMP Type 3 Code 3) message received.
A	Packet denied by access list.
&	TTL of packet (packet lifetime) was exceeded.
?	Unknown packet received.

- **Troubleshooting scenario:**
  Q: A host is able to ping to other hosts in the same subnet, but is unable to ping to a server in another subnet. What are the potential causes of this problem?
  A: Most likely due to subnet mask or default gateway misconfiguration on the host.

- ICMP **Source Quench** messages are used for **congestion control**. They are sent by a congested router to notify the sending host to reduce its transmission rate as packets were discarded due to insufficient packet queue buffer. It is seldom being used as congestion control is often being performed by TCP at the transport layer.

- ICMP **Time Exceeded** messages utilize the **Time-to-Live** (TTL) field in the IP header that indicates the period a packet can exist on a network when being delivered to the destination. Routers decrement the TTL by 1 whenever they forward a packet. Packets with TTL = 0 will be discarded, which can prevent IP packets from being circulated forever when routing loops occur. Upon decrementing the TTL value, a router must recalculate the Header Checksum of a packet.

- Figure 10-2 shows how the Traceroute program on PC1, a Windows workstation, utilizes the IP TTL field (in ICMP Echo Requests) and ICMP TTL Exceeded messages to find the path to PC2.

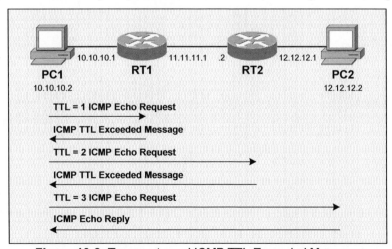

Figure 10-2: Traceroute and ICMP TTL Exceeded Messages

- Firstly, PC1 purposely sends out an ICMP Echo Request packet with TTL = 1. RT1 which receives the packet will discard it and send out a ICMP TTL Exceeded message to PC1 as the TTL of the packet is decremented to 0. PC1 continues to send out another ICMP packet with TTL = 2, which causes RT2 to discard the packet and send out another ICMP TTL Exceeded message.

- Standard Traceroute program sends sets of 3 ICMP Echo Requests for each increased TTL value. Hence the output provides 3 results for each TTL. Below shows the output of the **tracert** command on PC1:

```
C:\>tracert -d 12.12.12.2

Tracing route to 12.12.12.2 over a maximum of 30 hops

  1    <1 ms    <1 ms    <1 ms   10.10.10.1
  2     1 ms    <1 ms    <1 ms   11.11.11.2
  3     2 ms    <1 ms    <1 ms   12.12.12.2

Trace complete.

C:\>
```

- **Note:** Cisco Standard and Extended Traceroute send out **UDP packets** instead of ICMP Echo Request messages to detect intermediate hops and destination host via ICMP TTL Exceeded messages and ICMP Destination Unreachable – Port Unreachable messages respectively.

- ICMP **Redirect** messages are used when a router (RT1) processes a packet sent by an endpoint host (PC1) and notices that there is another router (RT2) with better metric to the network of the destination host (PC3), it will send out an ICMP Redirect message to the sending host (PC1) to notify it to forward future packets destined to the destination host to the better router (RT2). However, the host (PC1) can decide whether to accept or ignore the ICMP Redirect message. **Note:** PC1, RT1, and RT2 reside on the same network. The default gateway of PC1 is RT1. PC1 is sending packets to PC3 (via RT1).

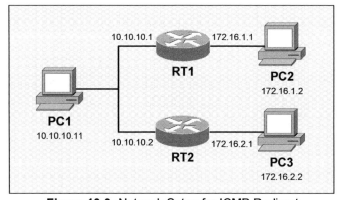

Figure 10-3: Network Setup for ICMP Redirect

Chapter 11
Distance-Vector Routing Protocols – RIP and IGRP

- IP routing is the process of transmitting packets from a network to another network. The main concern of routers is networks instead of hosts. A router can only forward packets to routes (or subnets) in its routing table. Routers are also known as **gateways**. A host would send packets destined to another network to its **default gateway** of the local network.

- **Routing protocols** are used by routers to figure out the network topology, find paths to all the networks in an internetwork, determine the best path to a network, and fill the routing tables with the routing information. Ex: RIP, IGRP, OSPF, and EIGRP.
  Routed protocols are used to define and assign logical addressing on physical interfaces, encapsulate data into packets, and liaise with the data link layer to deliver packets through an internetwork. These protocols allow packets to be forwarded by routing protocols. Ex: IP, IPX, and AppleTalk. **Note:** IBM SNA, NetBIOS, and NetBEUI are non-routable protocols.

- A router always has the routes to **directly connected** networks. For non-directly connected networks, the router must **learn and know** how to get to there. The information can be manually configured (static routing), or learn from other routers using routing protocols (dynamic routing).

- Below list the 2 types of routing protocols:

Interior Gateway Protocols	Used for exchanging routing information between routers **within** an autonomous system (Intra-AS or intradomain). Ex: RIP, IGRP, OSPF, and EIGRP.
Exterior Gateway Protocols	Used for communication **between** autonomous systems (Inter-AS or interdomain). Out of the scope of CCNA. Ex: BGP.

Note: In the past, the term **gateway** was used to define a router.

- **Autonomous system** (AS) is a collection of networks that is within the administration control of a company or organization that shares a common routing strategy.

- **Static routing** is the most basic way to tell a router **where** to forward packets to non-directly connected networks. Static routes are **manually** added to and removed from a router's routing table; hence it is very tedious and impractical to implement static routing in large networks.

- Below list the 3 classes of dynamic routing protocols:

Distance-Vector	Simple routing algorithm. Less effective and efficient compared to other classes of routing protocols. Targeted for small networks. Ex: RIP, IGRP.
Link-State	Complex routing algorithm. Frequently used in large and complex networks. Ex: OSPF.
Balanced Hybrid	Consists of both DV and LS concepts and features. Ex: EIGRP.

- Every routing protocol has its **pros** and **cons**. Good understanding of them is required to choose and implement the best solution for specific situation and requirement.

- With **Distance-Vector routing protocols**, every router in a network **advertises all its known routes** (complete routing table) to its **neighboring** routers. Finally, each router would have a complete routing table to all the subnets in the network by **combining** the received routing updates with its own routing table entries. A router running a Distance-Vector routing protocol does not know the topology of the entire network.

- Below describes the operation of Distance-Vector or Bellman-Ford algorithm:
  i)   RT1 advertises all its directly connected networks out all its interfaces.
  ii)   RT2 which received RT1 routing updates would advertise all its directly connected networks and the routes learned from RT1 out all its interfaces (RT1 would receive it too).
  iii) Routers **send** and **receive** periodic routing updates to and from their neighboring routers.
  iv)   When a router fails to receive the routing updates from a neighbor, all the routes learned from the neighbor will be removed from its routing table.

- Below shows the operation of Distance-Vector routing protocols. The routing table of each router includes the **network number**, **outgoing interface**, and **metric** (hop count) to all networks.

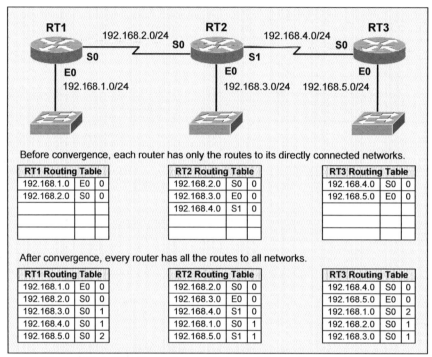

Figure 11-1: The Operation of Distance-Vector Routing Protocols

- Below are the main disadvantages of Distance-Vector routing protocols:
  i)   **High network load,** as complete routing tables (routing updates) are sent as **broadcasts**.
  ii)   **Inconsistent routing tables** and tends to have **routing loops** due to **slow convergence**.
  Note: Convergence is referred to as the process of finding the new path upon a network failure.

- Distance-Vector routing protocols are also said to be "**routing by rumor**" or "**gossip protocols**", as each router depends on its neighbors for routing information.

- **Routing loops** can occur when all routers are not updated at the same time. Figure 11-2 shows a routing loop scenario. Below describes how a routing loop could occur (refer to Figure 11-2):
  • All routers have route to Network 4. At one time, link to Network 4 fails. RT4 would inform RT3 about the bad news and RT3 would stop routing to Network 4 through RT4.
  • RT2 would notice this a while later when RT3 send out its latest routing update.
  • RT1 which was not received the routing update would send out its regular routing update. RT2 received that and was told that Network 4 can be reach through RT1!
  • Routing loop occurred at this point where packets destined to Network 4 would send to RT1, then to RT2, and back to RT1…

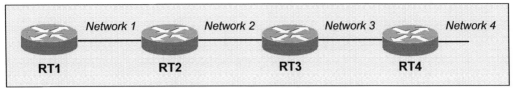

Figure 11-2: Sample Routing Loop Network

- It is **very high probability** that routers send routing updates to each other at about the same time. Figure 11-3 shows another routing loop scenario – **counting to infinity**. Imagine that RT2 sends out an update to RT1 when the link to 172.16.3.0 is failed (metric 16 represents an unreachable network in RIP). Unfortunately RT1 send out an update to RT2 at about the same time and hence RT2 learns that 172.16.3.0 can be reach through RT1. As a result, 2 versions of updates (infinite metric (16) and metric *x*) are sent out continuously until both numbers reach infinity (16). Although eventually the routing loop is being resolved, it still slow down the convergence time.

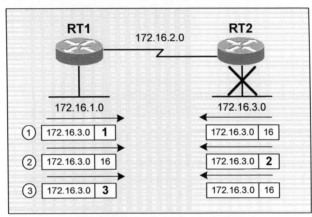

Figure 11-3: Counting to Infinity

- Below lists the solutions for preventing routing loops (Distance-Vector loop-avoidance features):

Split Horizon	Prevent a router from re-advertising the routing update information back to the same interface which the route(s) was learned, which also prohibits a router from advertising a route through an interface that the router itself is using to reach the destination. It is able to **prevent** counting to infinity problem over a **single link**.
Route Poisoning	A router will advertise a route to an unreachable network with an infinite metric to ensure all routers do not believe any rumor about the availability of the unreachable network. Poisoned routes are placed into holddown instead of waiting for the invalid timer to expire. It is used to **prevent** routing loops due to inconsistent routing updates through alternative or redundant paths.
Poison Reverse	When the network is stable, routers use split horizon. When a link has failed and a router received an infinite metric route, the route will be advertised out to **all** interfaces (route poisoning), including those prevented by split horizon. This ensures that all routers on the segment receive the poisoned route and will not use the invalid route. It is able to **prevent** counting to infinity problem. It is also known as **split horizon with poison reverse**.

Maximum Hop Count	Hop count metric increases each time a route passes through a router. It is able to **solve** counting to infinity problem by defining a **maximum hop count**. This is not a good solution since packets will still loop in the network until all routers removed or flushed the bad route from their routing tables.
Holddown	When a router (RT1) did not receive the periodic routing update for a particular subnet from another router (RT2) after the invalid timer is expired (due to the passive interface configuration or RT2 is down), the route will be placed into holddown state (`x is possibly down`). During this period, the router will **ignore** or **suppress** any incoming updates about alternative routes to that subnet (from routers other than RT2) until either a route with **better metric is received** (from RT2) or the **holddown timer expires**. It is able to **prevent** counting to infinity problem that split horizon does not solve, eg: networks with redundant links (Figure 11-4).
Triggered Updates	Without waiting for the regular scheduled routing update timer to expire, a router will **immediately** send out an update as soon as a directly connected subnet has changed state (up or down), which intends to speed up convergence time. Also known as **flash updates**.

- **Note:** Some loop-avoidance features, eg: holddown, slow down convergence. Loop-avoidance features on distance-vector routing protocols are **enabled and activated by default**.

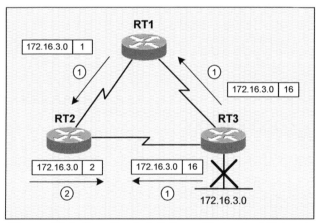

Figure 11-4: Counting to Infinity on Redundant Network

- Figure 11-4 shows another routing loop scenario – **counting to infinity on redundant network** (network with redundant links).

- Imagine that RT3 send out an update to RT1 and RT2 right after the link to 172.16.3.0 has failed. However, RT1's update timer expires at the same time and it sends out an update contains route to 172.16.3.0 to RT2 (RT1 does not send the update to RT3 due to split horizon). RT2 chooses the metric 2 route through RT1 between the RT3 **infinite metric route** and RT1 **metric 1 route**. **Note:** Routers normally (and should) advertise the metric to a destination network based on the metric in the routing table. However, RIP advertises **metric + 1** in the routing updates.

- On RT2's next update, it does not advertise the infinite metric route to 172.16.3.0 to RT3 (due to split horizon), but it does advertise the route with metric 2 to RT3. After a while, RT3 also advertise the route with metric 3 to RT1 after its update timer expires. Counting to infinity occurs in this scenario even with split horizon enabled. **Holddown** is used to prevent this problem.

RIP and IGRP

-   **Routing Information Protocol** (RIP) and **Interior Gateway Routing Protocol** (IGRP) are DV routing protocols. Both are designed for small networks and have many similarities. The main advantage of IGRP over RIP is it **provides a better measurement** when determining the best route, and **better scalability** (overcomes the limitation of RIP maximum hop count – 15).

-   **Metric** is the distance to a remote or destination network.

-   RIP uses only **hop count** to determine the best route to a subnet. If there are multiple routes to a same network with the same hop counts, RIP can perform **load balancing** over those **equal-cost** links. The total number of equal-cost routes that can be included in the routing table can be changed with the **maximum-paths** {*num*} router subcommand (max of 6, default is 4).

-   **Pinhole congestion** is a problem scenario where RIP treats links with different bandwidth or speeds (T1 vs. 56K dial up) as equal cost due to same hop count – the main disadvantage of RIP.

-   IGRP is a **Cisco-proprietary** DV routing protocol, which means all routers must be Cisco routers in order to use IGRP as the routing protocol throughout the network.

-   IGRP uses multiple factors in determining the best path to a remote network. By default, IGRP **composite metrics** are calculated via a function based on the **bandwidth** and **delay** of the link. The **reliability** and **load utilization** can also be used; whereas the MTU size is never been used.

-   The unit of bandwidth is **kbps**.
    Ex: **bandwidth** is defaults to 1544 on serial interfaces. (1544kbps = 1.544Mbps = T1 speed)

-   RIP is only able to load balance over paths with the same hop count (equal cost paths) whereas IGRP is able to load balance over unequal cost paths (unequal metric load balancing). The **variance** router subcommand configures IGRP load balancing over unequal cost paths.

-   Cisco routers perform 2 types of load balancing over parallel paths in a round robin basis. Each type has its own pros and cons.

Round robin on the per-packet basis (Process Switching)	The router simply takes turn when selecting the path for sending packets. This option provides the most even distribution across parallel paths but **does not preserve packet order**.
Round robin on the per-destination or per-session basis (Fast Switching)	The router distributes packets based on the destination address (all packets for Host1 go over first path, all packets for Host2 go over second path, etc). This option **preserves packet order**.

-   Below compares RIP and IGRP features with their default values:

Feature	RIP	IGRP
Metric	Hop count	Bandwidth, delay, reliability, and load utilization.
Update Timer	30 seconds	90 seconds
Invalid Timer	180 seconds	270 seconds (3 x update timers)
Holddown Timer	180 seconds	280 seconds (3 x update timers + 10 seconds)
Flush Timer	240 seconds	630 (7 x update timers)
Triggered Updates	Yes	Yes
Infinite Metric	16	4,294,967,295

- **Invalid Timer** specifies how long a router should wait before determine a route is invalid when it does not receive any update about that particular route. An invalid route will enter into a holddown state and is advertised as unreachable by the router to all its neighbors. Invalid or holddown state routes still used to forward packets until the holddown timer expires.

- **Flush Timer** specifies how long a router should wait before removing an invalid route from its routing table. Flush timer interval value should always **greater** than the value of invalid timer. When the flush timer has expired for a route, it is removed from the routing table. The invalid and flush timers **start at the same time** and run concurrently. For RIP, the flush timer expires before the holddown timer; hence it never has the chance to complete its holddown cycle.

- IGRP has a maximum hop count of 255 while RIP can only have a maximum hop count of 15. Hence IGRP should be selected over RIP when implementing routing on large networks.

- Both RIP and IGRP are **classful routing protocols**, which means subnet mask information are not sent along with the routing updates and do not support **Variable-Length Subnet Masks** (VLSMs). A router running a classful routing protocol assume that all remote networks have the same subnet mask as the exiting interface, and all subnetworks of the same major network use the same subnet mask.

Administrative Distance

- Metrics cannot be used to select the best path from the routes learned from different routing protocols because different routing protocols calculate their metrics differently. Ex: The metric for a route learned by RIP could be 1 while the metric for another route learned by IGRP could be 8539. Administrative distance is used to select the best path to use for this kind of situation.

- The **administrative distance** (AD) is used by routers to **rate the trustworthiness of routing information sources**. When a router learned multiple routes from different routing protocols to a same network, the **AD will be first considered** to select the best route to be stored into its routing table (the lower the better). If the multiple routes to the same network have the same AD (learnt from the same routing protocol), then only the **metric** will be used to select the best route. If multiple routes have the same AD and metric, which are normally equal-cost links, they will be used for load balancing when sending packets to the same destination network.

- Default administrative distance values:

Route Type	Default AD
Directly connected	0
Static	1
EIGRP (internal)	90
IGRP	100
OSPF	110
RIP	120
External EIGRP	170

- As seen in the table above, IGRP is more believable than OSPF. Take caution of this because when both IGRP and OSPF routing protocols are being used to learn routes to the same subnet, only the routes learned by IGRP will be added into the routing table.

- The decimal values of AD (8-bit variable) is **0 – 255**. Routes with an AD of 255 will never be used. The AD values can be manipulated on a router and **will not be exchanged** with other routers.

Chapter 12
Static Routing, Default Routing, RIP, and IGRP Lab

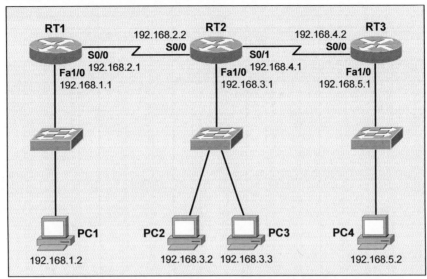

Figure 12-1: Network Setup for IP Routing Configuration

- Figure 12-1 shows the network setup for static routing, default routing, RIP, and IGRP configurations. **Note:** Both RT2 serial interfaces are DCEs.

- Initial configuration on RT1:

```
Router>en
Router#conf t
Enter configuration commands, one per line.  End with CNTL/Z.
Router(config)#hostname RT1
RT1(config)#int fa1/0
RT1(config-if)#ip add 192.168.1.1 255.255.255.0
RT1(config-if)#no shut
RT1(config-if)#int s0/0
RT1(config-if)#ip add 192.168.2.1 255.255.255.0
RT1(config-if)#no shut
RT1(config-if)#^Z
RT1#
RT1#sh ip route
Codes: C - connected, S - static, I - IGRP, R - RIP, M - mobile, B - BGP
       D - EIGRP, EX - EIGRP external, O - OSPF, IA - OSPF inter area
       E1 - OSPF external type 1, E2 - OSPF external type 2, E - EGP

Gateway of last resort is not set

C    192.168.1.0/24 is directly connected, FastEthernet1/0
RT1#
```

- Route to 192.168.2.0/24 is not shown in the routing table as the line protocol of S0/0 is down. This happens because the DCE end (RT2) does not provide the clocking yet. The **clock rate** interface subcommand defines the timing of data transmission over a synchronous serial link when back-to-back DTE/DCE serial cables instead of CSU/DSU are being used.

- Initial configuration on RT2:

```
Router>en
Router#conf t
Enter configuration commands, one per line.  End with CNTL/Z.
Router(config)#hostname RT2
RT2(config)#int s0/0
RT2(config-if)#ip add 192.168.2.2 255.255.255.0
RT2(config-if)#clock rate 56000
RT2(config-if)#no shut
RT2(config-if)#int fa1/0
RT2(config-if)#ip add 192.168.3.1 255.255.255.0
RT2(config-if)#no shut
RT2(config-if)#int s0/1
RT2(config-if)#ip add 192.168.4.1 255.255.255.0
RT2(config-if)#clock rate 56000
RT2(config-if)#no shut
RT2(config-if)#^Z
RT2#
RT2#sh ip route
Codes: C - connected, S - static, I - IGRP, R - RIP, M - mobile, B - BGP
       D - EIGRP, EX - EIGRP external, O - OSPF, IA - OSPF inter area
       E1 - OSPF external type 1, E2 - OSPF external type 2, E - EGP

Gateway of last resort is not set

C    192.168.2.0/24 is directly connected, Serial0/0
C    192.168.3.0/24 is directly connected, FastEthernet1/0
RT2#
```

- Initial configuration on RT3:

```
Router>en
Router#conf t
Enter configuration commands, one per line.  End with CNTL/Z.
Router(config)#hostname RT3
RT3(config)#int s0/0
RT3(config-if)#ip add 192.168.4.2 255.255.255.0
RT3(config-if)#no shut
RT3(config-if)#int fa1/0
RT3(config-if)#ip add 192.168.5.1 255.255.255.0
RT3(config-if)#no shut
RT3(config-if)#^Z
RT3#
RT3#sh ip route
Codes: C - connected, S - static, I - IGRP, R - RIP, M - mobile, B - BGP
       D - EIGRP, EX - EIGRP external, O - OSPF, IA - OSPF inter area
       E1 - OSPF external type 1, E2 - OSPF external type 2, E - EGP

Gateway of last resort is not set
C    192.168.4.0/24 is directly connected, Serial0/0
C    192.168.5.0/24 is directly connected, FastEthernet1/0
RT3#
```

- Test the network connectivity on all devices with the **ping** command.

- **Tips:** The **show controllers** {*intf-type intf-num*} EXEC command can be used to find out which end (DTE or DCE) is plugged into a serial interface:

```
Router#show controllers serial 0
HD unit 0, idb = 0xC2518, driver structure at 0xC79B0
buffer size 1524  HD unit 0, V.35 DCE cable
cpb = 0xE1, eda = 0x4940, cda = 0x4800
RX ring with 16 entries at 0xE14800
```

- The **terminal ip netmask-format** {**bit-count | decimal**} EXEC command can be used to change the network mask format (**prefix notation** – /xx or **dotted decimal** – x.x.x.x) in the output of the series of **show** command, eg: **show ip route**.

- Troubleshooting network problems with **ping**:

Error Message	Possible Cause
Destination host unreachable	Packet dropped **on the way to the destination**. Normally returned by an intermediate router when it is not able to find a route to the destination network.
Request timed out	Packet dropped **on the way to the destination**. Another possible cause is an intermediate router does not have a route to the network of the source host when the packet is **on the way back from** the destination network.

Static Routing Configuration

- Currently, a Request timed out error message would be received when trying to ping 192.168.2.2 from PC1. This is due to RT2 does not have a route to 192.168.1.0/24 network! This section shows the static routing configuration on all routers for them to reach all networks.

- The **ip route** {*destination-network*} {*subnet-mask*} {*next-hop-addr | outgoing-intf*} [*administrative-distance*] [**permanent**] global configuration command defines static routes.
  Note: Static routes that use the outgoing interface option instead of the next-hop address option are considered as **directly connected** static routes.
  Note: Only configure static routes pointing to an outgoing interface on point-to-point links, as the router won't be able to resolve a next-hop address in point-to-multipoint topologies.

- Static Routing configuration on RT1:

```
RT1(config)#ip route 192.168.3.0 255.255.255.0 192.168.2.2
RT1(config)#ip route 192.168.4.0 255.255.255.0 192.168.2.2
RT1(config)#ip route 192.168.5.0 255.255.255.0 192.168.2.2
RT1(config)#^Z
RT1#
RT1#sh ip route
Gateway of last resort is not set

C    192.168.1.0/24 is directly connected, FastEthernet1/0
C    192.168.2.0/24 is directly connected, Serial0/0
S    192.168.3.0/24 [1/0] via 192.168.2.2
S    192.168.4.0/24 [1/0] via 192.168.2.2
S    192.168.5.0/24 [1/0] via 192.168.2.2
```

- Static Routing configuration on RT2:

```
RT2(config)#ip route 192.168.1.0 255.255.255.0 192.168.2.1
RT2(config)#ip route 192.168.5.0 255.255.255.0 192.168.4.2
RT2(config)#^Z
RT2#
```

- Static Routing configuration on RT3:

```
RT3(config)#ip route 192.168.1.0 255.255.255.0 192.168.4.1
RT3(config)#ip route 192.168.2.0 255.255.255.0 192.168.4.1
RT3(config)#ip route 192.168.3.0 255.255.255.0 192.168.4.1
RT3(config)#^Z
RT3#
```

- The values in the bracket `[x/y]` of the routes shown in the **show ip route** EXEC command represent the **administrative distance** and **metric** respectively.

Default Routing Configuration

- Default routing is very useful in situations where learning all the more specific networks is **not desirable** or **not feasible** due to limited system resources, eg: memory, processing power. Packets destined to networks that are not in the routing table – **unknown destination networks** will be directed to the default route. A default route is also known as the **gateway of last resort**.

- Default routing can only be used on **stub networks** – networks with **only one entry and exit point** to all outside networks. RT1 and RT3 are considered in stub networks.

- Default routes can be configured by substituting the destination network and subnet mask with wildcards (0.0.0.0) in the **ip route** static routing configuration command.

- Default Routing configuration on RT1:

```
RT1(config)#no ip route 192.168.3.0 255.255.255.0
RT1(config)#no ip route 192.168.4.0 255.255.255.0
RT1(config)#no ip route 192.168.5.0 255.255.255.0
RT1(config)#ip route 0.0.0.0 0.0.0.0 192.168.2.2
RT1(config)#^Z
RT1#
RT1#sh ip route
Codes: C - connected, S - static, I - IGRP, R - RIP, M - mobile, B - BGP
       D - EIGRP, EX - EIGRP external, O - OSPF, IA - OSPF inter area
       E1 - OSPF external type 1, E2 - OSPF external type 2, E - EGP

Gateway of last resort is 192.168.2.2 to network 0.0.0.0

C    192.168.1.0/24 is directly connected, FastEthernet1/0
C    192.168.2.0/24 is directly connected, Serial0/0
S*   0.0.0.0/0 [1/0] via 192.168.2.2
RT1#
```

- Notice the Gateway of last resort in the routing table. An asterisk (*) indicates a default route.

- The **ip classless** global configuration command is important when using default routing. It is enabled by default in Cisco IOS release 12.0 and later. Default routing and classless routing are discussed further in Chapter 16 – Classful and Classless Routing and MISC TCP/IP Topics.

- Multiple routes can be configured and flagged as candidate default routes. The candidate default route with the lowest metric will be selected as the default route.

RIP Configuration

- The main command when configuring RIP and IGRP is the **network** {*classful-network-addr*} router subcommand. It **matches** one or more interfaces on a router and causes the router to perform 3 tasks on the matched directly-connected interfaces:
  - i) **Broadcast** routing updates out the matched interfaces.
  - ii) **Listen and process** incoming routing updates from the matched interfaces.
  - iii) **Include the subnet** of the matched interfaces in the routing updates to other routers.

- RIP configuration on RT1:

```
RT1(config)#no ip route 0.0.0.0 0.0.0.0 192.168.2.2
RT1(config)#router rip
RT1(config-router)#network 192.168.1.0
RT1(config-router)#network 192.168.2.0
RT1(config-router)#^Z
RT1#
```

- RIP configuration on RT2:

```
RT2(config)#no ip route 192.168.1.0 255.255.255.0 192.168.2.1
RT2(config)#no ip route 192.168.5.0 255.255.255.0 192.168.4.2
RT2(config)#router rip
RT2(config-router)#network 192.168.2.0
RT2(config-router)#network 192.168.3.0
RT2(config-router)#network 192.168.4.0
RT2(config-router)#^Z
RT2#
```

- RIP configuration on RT3:

```
RT3(config)#no ip route 192.168.1.0 255.255.255.0 192.168.4.1
RT3(config)#no ip route 192.168.2.0 255.255.255.0 192.168.4.1
RT3(config)#no ip route 192.168.3.0 255.255.255.0 192.168.4.1
RT3(config)#router rip
RT3(config-router)#network 192.168.4.0
RT3(config-router)#network 192.168.5.0
RT3(config-router)#^Z
RT3#
```

- **Note:** Remember that the administrative distances of static routes and RIP routers are 1 and 120 respectively, hence static routes must to be removed in order to use the routes learnt via RIP.

- RIPv1 and IGRP are **classful routing protocols** and therefore use **classful network addresses** in their configuration, which means that they must consider which class an interface resides in (Class A, B, or C network) when performing tasks. Classful routing protocols **do not send subnet mask information along routing updates** as they assume that all hosts and router interfaces connected to all segments throughout the network belongs to the **same classful network** and use the **same subnet mask**! RIPv1 and IGRP, which are distance-vector classful routing protocols, do not support VLSM and route summarization. **Note:** RIPv2 supports VLSM.

- The **network** {*classful-network-addr*} router subcommand is able to **figure out the IP address class** of the network address that is entered along with the command (similar to the IP address configuration dialog in Microsoft Windows). The command will change the network number entered along with the command to its **classful entry** or the **major network number**. Ex: 10.1.1.0 → 10.0.0.0; 172.16.1.0 → 172.16.0.0.

- Verify the RIP configuration on RT1, RT2 and RT3 with the **show ip route** EXEC command:

```
RT1#show ip route
Gateway of last resort is not set

C    192.168.1.0/24 is directly connected, FastEthernet1/0
C    192.168.2.0/24 is directly connected, Serial0/0
R    192.168.3.0/24 [120/1] via 192.168.2.2, 00:00:10, Serial0/0
R    192.168.4.0/24 [120/1] via 192.168.2.2, 00:00:10, Serial0/0
R    192.168.5.0/24 [120/2] via 192.168.2.2, 00:00:10, Serial0/0
RT1#
```

- The **show ip protocols** EXEC command provides an overview of **all running routing protocols** when multiple routing protocols are running on a single router. It also displays other routers that sending routing updates to the router, and all the **timer values** used for the operation of the routing protocols.

```
RT2#sh ip protocols
Routing Protocol is "rip"
  Sending updates every 30 seconds, next due in 18 seconds
  Invalid after 180 seconds, hold down 180, flushed after 240
  Outgoing update filter list for all interfaces is not set
  Incoming update filter list for all interfaces is not set
  Redistributing: rip
  Default version control: send version 1, receive any version
    Interface          Send  Recv  Triggered RIP  Key-chain
    FastEthernet1/0    1     1 2
    Serial0/0          1     1 2
    Serial0/1          1     1 2
  Automatic network summarization is in effect
  Maximum path: 4
  Routing for Networks:
    192.168.2.0
    192.168.3.0
    192.168.4.0
  Routing Information Sources:
    Gateway         Distance      Last Update
    192.168.2.1          120      00:00:10
    192.168.4.2          120      00:00:05
  Distance: (default is 120)

RT2#
```

- An RIP routing update packet can only carry network information up to **25** networks or subnets. Updates are sent out as broadcasts (with an IP address of 255.255.255.255) every 30 seconds. **Note:** IGRP can fit 104 networks in a single routing update packet.

- The **debug ip rip** privileged command is the most useful and important command for troubleshooting RIP. Issue the **terminal monitor** privileged command in order to view the debug output from a Telnet session. Notice that split horizon is enabled.

```
RT2#debug ip rip
RIP protocol debugging is on
RT2#
00:10:54: RIP: received v1 update from 192.168.2.1 on Serial0/0
00:10:54:      192.168.1.0 in 1 hops
00:11:01: RIP: received v1 update from 192.168.4.2 on Serial0/1
00:11:01:      192.168.5.0 in 1 hops
00:11:07: RIP: sending v1 update to 255.255.255.255 via FastEthernet1/0
(192.168.3.1)
00:11:07: RIP: build update entries
00:11:07:    network 192.168.1.0 metric 2
00:11:07:    network 192.168.2.0 metric 1
00:11:07:    network 192.168.4.0 metric 1
00:11:07:    network 192.168.5.0 metric 2
00:11:07: RIP: sending v1 update to 255.255.255.255 via Serial0/0
(192.168.2.2)
00:11:07: RIP: build update entries
00:11:07:    network 192.168.3.0 metric 1
00:11:07:    network 192.168.4.0 metric 1
00:11:07:    network 192.168.5.0 metric 2
00:11:07: RIP: sending v1 update to 255.255.255.255 via Serial0/1
(192.168.4.1)
00:11:07: RIP: build update entries
00:11:07:    network 192.168.1.0 metric 2
00:11:07:    network 192.168.2.0 metric 1
00:11:07:    network 192.168.3.0 metric 1
RT2#
```

- The **terminal monitor** privileged command allows console messages to be viewed in a VTY (Telnet or SSH) session.

IGRP Configuration

- IGRP configuration is very similar to RIP configuration except that IGRP needs an extra parameter – the **autonomous system** (AS) **number**. IGRP routers only exchange routing updates with routers within the same autonomous system.

- IGRP configuration on RT1:

```
RT1(config)#router igrp ?
  <1-65535>  Autonomous system number
RT1(config)#router igrp 1
RT1(config-router)#network 192.168.1.0
RT1(config-router)#network 192.168.2.0
RT1(config-router)#^Z
RT1#
```

- IGRP configuration on RT2:

```
RT2(config)#router igrp 1
RT2(config-router)#network 192.168.2.0
RT2(config-router)#network 192.168.3.0
RT2(config-router)#network 192.168.4.0
RT2(config-router)#^Z
RT2#
```

- IGRP configuration on RT3:

```
RT3(config)#router igrp 1
RT3(config-router)#network 192.168.4.0
RT3(config-router)#network 192.168.5.0
RT3(config-router)#^Z
RT3#
```

- Verify the IGRP configuration on RT1, RT2 and RT3.

```
RT1#show ip route
Gateway of last resort is not set

C    192.168.1.0 is directly connected, FastEthernet1/0
C    192.168.2.0 is directly connected, Serial0/0
I    192.168.3.0 [100/8486] via 192.168.2.2, 00:00:09, Serial0/0
I    192.168.4.0 [100/10476] via 192.168.2.2, 00:00:09, Serial0/0
I    192.168.5.0 [100/10486] via 192.168.2.2, 00:00:09, Serial0/0
RT1#
```

- **Q:** If RIP and IGRP are running at the same time, routes from which protocol will be selected?
  A: IGRP has a lower administrative distance value than RIP; hence IGRP routes will be selected. Anyway, take note that if RIP is still running in the background, it can consume unnecessary router CPU resources and network bandwidth.

- The information after the next hop IP address for a route indicates the **invalid timer** for a route in hh:mm:ss format. The timer is reset to all 0s upon an update for a particular route is received. When the invalid timer for a route is expired, the route will be marked as **possibly down** and the router will start the holddown cycle for the particular route.

- A router will still use routes in holddown state when forward packets destined to the network. This is a standard behavior of many IP routing protocols, which is based on the assumption that **temporary packet loss due to using routes to networks that might not be viable is better than immediately accepting a less desirable route to the destination network**.

- DV routing protocols **do not support discontiguous networks**. When a router running RIP or IGRP receives a route, it checks if the routing update information contains the same major network number that is configured on the receiving interface. If it does, it applies the subnet mask that is configured on the receiving interface to the newly received route; else if it doesn't (the routing update information contains a different major network number than the receiving interface), it applies the **default classful subnet mask** accordingly.
  Ex: A router receives a route to 172.16.2.0 from an interface 172.16.1.1/24, it applies the /24 mask to the route and becomes 172.16.2.0/24. Else, it applies the default /16 mask to the route and becomes 172.16.0.0/16.

- Below shows the output of the **show ip protocols** EXEC command on RT2:

```
RT2#sh ip protocols
Routing Protocol is "igrp 1"
  Sending updates every 90 seconds, next due in 56 seconds
  Invalid after 270 seconds, hold down 280, flushed after 630
  Outgoing update filter list for all interfaces is not set
  Incoming update filter list for all interfaces is not set
  Default networks flagged in outgoing updates
  Default networks accepted from incoming updates
  IGRP metric weight K1=1, K2=0, K3=1, K4=0, K5=0
  IGRP maximum hopcount 100
  IGRP maximum metric variance 1
  Redistributing: igrp 1
 Maximum path: 4
  Routing for Networks:
    192.168.2.0
    192.168.3.0
    192.168.4.0
  Routing Information Sources:
    Gateway         Distance      Last Update
    192.168.2.1         100       00:00:48
    192.168.4.2         100       00:01:03
  Distance: (default is 100)

RT2#
```

- The **debug ip igrp events** privileged command provides a summary view of the IGRP events.

```
RT2#debug ip igrp events
IGRP event debugging is on
RT2#
00:15:30: IGRP: received update from 192.168.2.1 on Serial0/0
00:15:30: IGRP: Update contains 0 interior, 1 system, and 0 exterior routes.
00:15:30: IGRP: Total routes in update: 1
00:15:42: IGRP: sending update to 255.255.255.255 via Serial0/0 (192.168.2.2)
00:15:42: IGRP: Update contains 0 interior, 3 system, and 0 exterior routes.
00:15:42: IGRP: Total routes in update: 3
RT2#
```

- The **debug ip igrp transactions** privileged command provides detailed IGRP debugging messages.

```
RT2#debug ip igrp transactions
IGRP protocol debugging is on
RT2#
00:17:32: IGRP: received update from 192.168.2.1 on Serial0/0
00:17:32:         network 192.168.1.0, metric 8486 (neighbor 110)
00:17:32: IGRP: sending update to 255.255.255.255 via Serial0/1 (192.168.4.1)
00:17:32:         subnet 192.168.1.0, metric=8486
00:17:32:         subnet 192.168.2.0, metric=8476
00:17:32:         subnet 192.168.3.0, metric=110
RT2#
```

- RT2 does not advertise the 192.168.5.0 network back to RT3 due to **split horizon**.

- The **no metric holddown** router subcommand disables holddown, in which an IGRP router may accept a route from another IGRP router as soon as the current route has became invalid.

MISC IP Routing Commands

- The **passive-interface** {*intf-type intf-num*} router subcommand is the simplest solution to prevent a routing protocol from sending its routing updates out to an interface; but the interface **can still receive** (and process) routing updates for a particular routing protocol. There is no point sending routing updates out an interface where there is no router to receive the routing updates. **Note:** Network information for passive interfaces will still be included in routing updates.

- The **maximum-paths** {*max-paths-num*} router subcommand defines the number of same metric parallel paths to a same subnet that can be added to the routing table (and perform load balancing over the links in a round-robin basis). Its value is ranging from 1 to 6, with the default of 4. Setting *max-paths-num* to 1 to disable load balancing. Only values other than 4 will be shown in the output of the show running-config command.

```
RT1(config)#router rip
RT1(config-router)#network 192.168.1.0
RT1(config-router)#passive-interface fa1/0
RT1(config-router)#maximum-paths 6
RT1(config-router)#^Z
RT1#
```

- Since the metrics calculated and used by IGRP (and EIGRP) are very unlikely to be equal, the **variance** router subcommand can be used to achieve unequal cost path load balancing.

- The **variance** {*multiplier*} router subcommand defines a **multiplier**. All routes with metric value less than or equal to **lowest metric** x **variance multiplier** are considered equal. Ex: With a lowest metric of 100 and variance of 2, all routes with a metric ≤ 200 are considered equal. **Note:** multiplier value = 1 – 128. The default is 1, which means equal cost path load balancing.

- IGRP (and EIGRP) routers perform load balancing across multiple routes with different metrics to a same subnet by distributing traffic proportionally to the ratios of the metrics of the unequal cost paths. The **traffic-share min** across-interfaces router subcommand tells a router to use **only the lowest metric route** even if the routing table has multiple unequal cost routes to a same subnet due to the **variance** command.

- With the **variance** and **traffic-share min across-interfaces** router subcommands, IGRP is able to perform **instantaneous convergence**! Because by having multiple routes to a same subnet in the routing table, whenever the best route fails, the router can simply select and use the second best route among the remaining routes.

- The **show protocols** EXEC command displays all the **routed protocols** and the interfaces and addresses that are configured for each protocol.

```
RT2#sh protocols
Global values:
  Internet Protocol routing is enabled
Serial0/0 is up, line protocol is up
  Internet address is 192.168.2.2/24
Serial0/1 is up, line protocol is up
  Internet address is 192.168.4.1/24
FastEthernet1/0 is up, line protocol is up
  Internet address is 192.168.3.1/24
RT2#
```

Chapter 13
OSPF and EIGRP

- Distance-Vector routing protocols were designed to use little memory and processing power, as routers had slow processors, less memory and processing power, and were connected with slow links. They **advertise just the basic routing information** in order to **conserve bandwidth**.

- Link-State and Balanced Hybrid routing protocols were designed under the assumptions of **faster links and more processing power in the routers**. By sending more information and more processing cycles on the routers, **faster convergence** can be achieved.

- **DV protocols** say nothing about the routers beyond the neighboring router in a routing update. **LS protocols** advertise a **large amount** of the network topology information which describes the **whole network topology** in the routing updates. The routers will also perform some **CPU-intensive computations** upon the topology information.

Open Shortest Path First (OSPF)

- **Dijkstra Shortest Path First** (SPF) algorithm is used by LS protocols to determine the best path to a network. An OSPF router contains the **map** of an area (the topology of the network or area) in its topology database. It then runs SPF algorithm to process all the topology information to come up with the best route to each network, based on the metrics or costs of all potential paths to a network in the **same area**. SPF calculations are not performed for routes from other areas.

- LS protocols **must calculate the metric** instead of simply using what have been received in routing updates as with DV protocols. The metric of a route to a network is calculated by **totaling the costs** associated with all links to the network as saved in the **topology database**.

- Cisco OSPF cost calculation is 10^8 / **bandwidth** (in bps). 100Mbps FE → 1, 10Mbps → 10. Ex: An interface with bandwidth of 64000 → 1563.

- LS protocols need to use a process to **dynamically discover neighbors** instead of just start broadcasting topology information out every interface upon initialization.

- **Neighbors** are routers running the same LS protocol and have an interface on a common subnet. As soon as routers know that they are neighbors, they can exchange their own copies of topology information as saved in the **topology database**, and then run SPF to calculate new routes.

- The process of identifying neighbors can be **complicated**, and it must happen before exchanging any topology information. CCNP syllabus covers more details about neighbor relationships.

- **Adjacency** is a relationship between 2 OSPF routers that allows the exchange of routing updates. OSPF routers only exchange routes with neighbors that have **established adjacencies**. Adjacency depends upon both the **network type** and **router configuration**. Unlike EIGRP which directly exchanges routes with all neighbors, OSPF is very choosy in forming adjacencies. Ex: Hello and dead timer values must be the **same** in order for routers to form adjacency.

- **Link-State Updates** (LSUs) are the routing updates sent by OSPF to routers that have established adjacencies. **Link-State Advertisements** (LSAs) are the items sent in an LSU. An individual LSA describes the **subnet number** and **mask**, the **cost** (metric), and **link type** about a particular subnet. OSPF sends out self-originated LSAs every 30 mins (LS refresh time).

- OSPF uses a **reliable protocol** to exchange routing information, which ensures that lost LSU packets are retransmitted; hence OSPF routers can certainly assure whether a neighbor has received all the LSAs when exchanging routing information with the replied **acknowledgment**.

- Below lists the process or sequence of learning OSPF routes for the first time:
  - i) Each router discovers its neighbors and forms neighbor relationship on each interface (with Hello packets). The list of neighbors is kept in the **neighbor table** (or **adjacency database**), which maintains a variety of details, eg: Router IDs and OSPF neighbor state.
  - ii) Each router exchanges topology information (LSAs) with its neighbors reliably.
  - iii) Each router places the learned topology information in its topology database.
  - iv) Each router runs the SPF algorithm upon all information its topology database to calculate the shortest path (best route) to each subnet in the database.
  - v) Each router places the best route to each subnet in its routing table.

- LS protocols require more memory and processing cycles than DV protocols due to the SPF calculations. Additionally, their routing updates use more bytes compared to DV routing updates. However, the overall number of bytes **can be smaller** as OSPF **does not advertise all routes** in every update interval as in DV protocols. Some good design practices must be followed to reduce the memory and processing requirements.

- **Router ID** (RID) is an IP address that is used to identify a router in the OSPF neighbor and topology databases. The highest IP address of any configured loopback interface will be selected. If no loopback interface is configured with an address, the highest IP address of all physical interfaces will be selected. **Note:** Logical interfaces have higher priority than physical interfaces.

- **Designated Router** (DR) is elected whenever OSPF routers are connected to the same multi-access or broadcast network in order to minimize the number of adjacencies formed and the overhead when exchanging routing updates. The DR is elected to receive and disseminate routing information with the other routers on the broadcast network, link, or segment, which can **ensure the synchronization** of their topology databases. All routers in the shared network only required to establish adjacencies and exchange routing updates with the DR and BDR. The **highest priority** interface will become the DR for a segment, and the Router ID is used as the tiebreaker if the priority values are the same. The priority value range is 0 – 255, with a default value of 1. A priority value of 0 indicates an interface that is not intended to be elected as a DR or BDR – a DROTHER on the segment. **Note:** Do not confuse multi-access with multipoint!

- **Backup Designated Router** (BDR) is the **standby** for the DR on multi-access networks. A BDR also forms adjacency with all OSPF routers on the same network and becomes the DR when the current DR fails. A BDR receives routing updates from adjacent routers, but doesn't flood LSUs.

- For each multi-access network segment, there is a DR and a BDR as well as other routers. Ex: 10 VLANs in a switching domain will have 10 DRs and 10 BDRs; one pair per VLAN.

- DR and BDR are elected on **both** broadcast and non-broadcast multi-access (NBMA) networks. **Broadcast multi-access** networks allow multiple devices to connect and access to the same network, and provide broadcast ability (a single packet can be delivered to all nodes on the network), eg: Ethernet. **Non-broadcast multi-access** (NBMA) networks allow multi-access, but do not have the broadcast ability like Ethernet, eg: X.25, Frame Relay, and ATM. They **require special configuration** to function properly and **neighbors are manually defined**. When an OSPF router initializes, it will **form adjacencies** only with the DR and the BDR on the multi-access segment that it is connected to. It does not simply form adjacency with a router.

- **Point-to-point** is a type of network topology which consists a direct connection between 2 routers that provides a single communication path either physically (a direct serial connection) or logically (a point-to-point Frame Relay virtual circuit). This type of topology **does not elect a DR or BDR**.

- **Point-to-multipoint** is a special type of NBMA network topology which consists of a series of connections between an interface on one router and multiple interfaces on other routers, and all the interfaces belong to a same network. This type of topology **does not elect a DR or BDR**.

- Routers running LS routing protocols **establish** and **maintain** (during steady state) neighbor relationships by exchanging periodical small messages called **Hello packets**. Hello packets are sent by DR and BDR to all routers with the IP multicast address 224.0.0.5 (AllSPFRouters). The Hello interval varies upon media types – 30 seconds for NBMA and 10 seconds for others (faster links receive more-frequent Hellos). As long as a router continues to receive Hello packets from its neighbors, the link and the neighboring router are considered up and running. Hello packets serve the same purpose as periodical full routing updates in DV routing protocols which notify neighbor routers that a router is up and running and the routes through it are valid.

- When a router fails to receive Hellos from a neighbor for the **dead interval**, the router believes the silent router has failed. The router will mark the silent router as 'down' in its topology database and then converge by running SPF algorithm to calculate the new routes. Dead timer interval is 4 x Hello interval, which is 120 seconds for NBMA and 40 seconds for others.

- LS routing protocols **do not need** loop avoidance features as in DV routing protocols, eg: split horizon, poison reverse, and holddown. SPF algorithm prevents loops as natural due to the processing of the topology database and maintaining the knowledge of the network topology.

- OSPF sends LSUs only when a topology change is detected (event-triggered updates). When a link or router fails, a router that noticed the failure will immediately flood the new status to its neighbors, and from those routers to their neighbors. Eventually all routers will receive the new status information. This is similar to triggered updates in DV routing protocols, but this behavior is just a feature of LS routing protocols and does not have a specific term.

- In DV routing protocols, most of the convergence time is taken by the loop-avoidance features; whereas in LS routing protocols, there is no such time-consuming loop-avoidance features, which means LS protocols can converge very quickly.

- With proper design, OSPF can convergence as fast as 5 seconds after a router notices a failure. Good design is also very important for OSPF scalability in large networks.

- The 3 **scalability issues** in large OSPF networks are:
  i) Large topology database requires more memory on each router.
  ii) Calculation and processing grow exponentially with the size of the topology database.
  iii) A single interface or link status change (up – down) forces every router to run SPF!

- Unlike RIP, OSPF can operate in a hierarchy basis. Areas are used to establish a hierarchical network and the largest entity within the hierarchy is an area. Although it is capable of receiving routes from and sending routes to other areas, OSPF is still an interior gateway routing protocol. An AS can be divided into a number of areas, which are groups of networks and routers.

- Hierarchical OSPF implementations reduce routing overhead, speed up convergence, confine network instability to a single area, and scalable to very large networks.

- OSPF areas break up a network so that routers in one area know less topology information about the subnets in other area and do not need to know about the routers in other area. With smaller topology databases, routers consume less memory and processing power for SPF calculations. Areas are considered as logical subdivisions of an autonomous system.

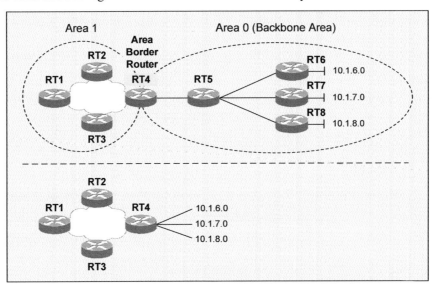

Figure 13-1: OSPF Scalability with Hierarchical Design

- By dividing the network into multiple areas, the routers reside in Area 1 are shielded from the details of Area 0. RT4 is known as an **OSPF Area Border Router** (ABR), as it resides on the border of 2 different areas and belongs to both areas. RT4 only advertises **summary information** about the subnets in Area 0 instead of full topology information of Area 0. In such a way, RT1, RT2, and RT3 would think the network topology as the lower part of Figure 13-1 (fewer routers). Eventually, SPF calculations would take less time and memory due to smaller topology databases.
  Note: Routers in Area 0 are also shielded from the details of Area 1.
  Note: Router that connects autonomous systems together is known as **Autonomous System Boundary Router** (ASBR).

- There **must be** an **area 0** (backbone area) in OSPF, which is typically configured on the routers that resides in the backbone of the network. All other OSPF areas must connect to area 0.

- Using areas improves all 3 of the scaling problems discussed earlier.
  i) Smaller topology databases require less memory and processing time and hence faster convergence.
  ii) Confine network instability to single areas of the network – when a link in an area changes state, the routers in other areas do not need to perform SPF calculation.

- Do not confuse this concept with **route summarization**, which reduces the number of subnets advertised to other routers, as OSPF ABRs **do not reduce the number of subnets** when advertising routing updates to another area. Both concepts are **different**!

- The ABR has the topology database for both areas and runs SPF when a link changes its state in either area. Using areas does not actually reduce memory requirements and the number of SPF calculations for ABRs. ABRs often have more memory and much powerful processors.

- **Stub area** is an OSPF feature for further reduce the size of the topology database for routers in a stub area. Variants of areas are Totally Stubby Area, Not-So-Stubby Area (NSSA), and Totally Not-So-Stubby Area. CCNP syllabus covers more details on this topic.

- The main disadvantages of LS protocols are the extra planning and design effort, and the consumption of CPU and memory resources which might affect the overall router performance.

Enhanced Interior Gateway Routing Protocol (EIGRP)

- EIGRP has many similar attributes to OSPF:
  i)   Dynamically discovers each other as neighbors using Hello packets.
  ii)   Synchronizes routing tables between neighbors after established neighbor relationships.
  iii) Uses EIGRP Hello packets (keepalives) to maintain neighbor relationships.

- EIGRP reliably exchanges or advertises its **entire / full routing table** when it discovers a new EIGRP neighbor. Besides that, it sends traditional distance-vector updates instead of link-state updates as with OSPF. Those updates contain information about destination networks and the cost of reaching them in the perspective of the advertising router.

- A proprietary reliable multicast protocol, **Reliable Transport Protocol** (RTP) is being used by EIGRP to exchange routing update messages between EIGRP routers.

- EIGRP does not send out periodic routing updates as with DV routing protocols and OSPF. Routing updates are sent only when link or topology changes occur – triggered updates.

- EIGRP sends multicasts to the 224.0.0.10 Class D multicast IP address. Each EIGRP router is aware of who are its neighbors, and maintains a list of neighbors that have replied for each multicast it sends out. EIGRP will resend the same data by unicasts if it doesn't get any reply from a neighbor. A neighbor is declared dead after it didn't get a reply after **16** unicast attempts. EIGRP also assigns **sequence number** to each packet in order for it to detect old, redundant, or out-of-sequence information. These features are very important for EIGRP, as any loss of update packet or out-of-order update packet processing can cause routing database corruption.

- EIGRP routers must become neighbors before exchanging routing information between them. The following conditions must be met for establishing neighbor relationship successfully:
  i)   Hello or ACK received.
  ii)   Same AS number (only routers reside in the same AS would share route information).
  iii) Same EIGRP K values.

- Every EIGRP router would maintain a **neighbor table**, which contains the information about EIGRP adjacencies and neighbors.

- EIGRP (and IGRP) is able to add multiple unequal-metric routes in its routing table and perform **unequal cost path load balancing** with the **variance** {*multiplier*} router subcommand.
  Note: A path must also a feasible successor (backup route) for it to be used for load balancing.

- **EIGRP Loop Avoidance** → DV avoids loops by having a variety of features. LS avoids loops by having all routers to aware of the full network topology. EIGRP avoids loops by building a topology table that includes the **best backup routes** for used when the current best route fails. EIGRP runs **Diffusing Update Algorithm** (DUAL) to identify which backup or alternative route to use immediately when the best route fails, without the worry of causing a loop.

- EIGRP uses the same formula as used by IGRP, which is based on **bandwidth** and **delay** to calculate the metric associated with a route. **EIGRP metric = IGRP metric multiplied by 256**.

- EIGRP (and IGRP) uses 4 elements or factors in calculating the best route: **bandwidth**, **delay**, **reliability**, and **load utilization**. The bandwidth and delay factors are being used by default. The 5th element – **Maximum Transmission Unit** (MTU), which is never been used in EIGRP metric calculation, is important when performing route redistribution upon EIGRP routes.

- **Successor** or **Feasible Distance** is the **lowest metric best path** as populated in the topology and routing tables. **Feasible Successor** is the **best alternative loop-free backup path** that can be used without causing a loop. EIGRP is able to maintain unlimited number of feasible successors per destination in the **topology table** (only in the topology table, not the routing table). The topology table is populated by the PDMs to store the routing information from the neighbors – destination networks, advertised routers, and advertised distance. EIGRP selects the best route to be inserted into the routing table based on the routing information stored in the topology table.

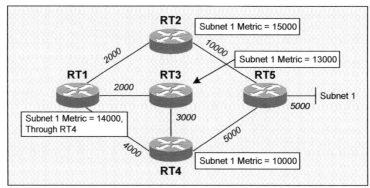

Figure 13-2: EIGRP Successor and Feasible Successors

- A feasible successor route for a particular destination network is selected when the computed metric of a particular neighbor to the destination network – **advertised distance**, is less than the local computed metric to the destination network – **feasible distance**. In Figure 13-2, RT1 computes the best route to Subnet 1 with a metric of 14000, through RT4. Route through RT3 is considered as a feasible successor as RT3's computed metric to Subnet 1 is 13000, and EIGRP believes that using the route will not cause a loop and will be added into RT1's topology table as a feasible successor route. Finally, RT2's computed metric is 15000, which is larger than 14000, and thus RT1 does not consider the route through RT2 as a feasible successor.

- When a successor route fails and the router has a feasible successor route, convergence can occur **instantly** without the worry of causing a loop. What if there is no feasible successor route? EIGRP uses a distributed proprietary algorithm called **Diffusing Update Algorithm** (DUAL) to **send queries to neighbors** asking for a loop-free route to the subnet when there is no backup route (feasible successor) exists. The newly learned route will be added to the routing table.

- EIGRP **converges quickly while avoiding loops**. It converges much more quickly than DV protocols, as it does not implement the loop-avoidance features which slow down convergence. EIGRP does not face the scaling issues in LS protocols, and hence **extra design effort is not required**; additionally it also uses less memory and processing resources than LS protocols. EIGRP sends only **partial routing updates** instead of full routing table updates as with DV protocols or periodic updates as with LS protocols, which reduces the network overhead. Finally, EIGRP also supports VLSM and multiple network layer routed protocols, eg: IP, IPX, and AppleTalk with **Protocol Dependent Modules** (PDMs).

- The only limitation of EIGRP is that it is Cisco-proprietary, which means it cannot be implemented in environments with routers from various vendors. Anyway, a possible solution is **route redistribution**, where a router exchanges routes between 2 routing protocols.

- EIGRP is suitable for very large networks. These networks are normally divided into multiple EIGRP autonomous systems (ASs). Route information can be shared among different ASs via redistribution. **Internal EIGRP routes** (AD = 90), are routes that originated by EIGRP routers within an AS. Another type of routes – **external EIGRP routes** (AD = 170), are routes that originated from another EIGRP AS, or redistributed from another routing protocol, eg: OSPF. **Note:** The maximum hop count for EIGRP (and IGRP) is 255, with the default value 100. The **metric maximum-hops** {*hop-count*} router subcommand changes this value.

- IGRP, OSPF, and EIGRP features comparison chart:

Feature	IGRP	OSPF	EIGRP
Discover neighbors before exchanging routing information	No	Yes	Yes
Build some form of topology table besides the routing table	No	Yes	Yes
Converge quickly	No	Yes	Yes
Calculate metric based on bandwidth and delay (by default)	Yes	No. Cost	Yes
Send full routing information on every routing update cycle	Yes	No	No
Implement distance-vector loop-avoidance features	Yes	No	No
Public standard	No	Yes	No

- RIPv2, OSPF, and EIGRP support **variable length subnet mask** and **discontiguous networks**. When selecting the suitable routing protocol to be implemented on a network environment, the **simplest** routing protocol that meets the requirements should be selected.

Type of Network	Suitable Routing Protocol
- No redundant links or parallel paths. - Not requires VLSM or discontiguous subnets.	RIPv1
- Has redundant links or parallel paths. - Not requires VLSM or discontiguous subnets.	IGRP
- No redundant links or parallel paths. - Requires VLSM and/or support of discontiguous subnets.	RIPv2
- Has redundant links or parallel paths. - Requires VLSM and/or support of discontiguous subnets.	OSPF or EIGRP

- **Discontiguous networks** are networks that have subnets of a major network separated by a different major network. Figure 13-3A shows a typical discontiguous network where subnets 172.16.10.0 and 172.16.20.0 are connected together with (or separated by) a 10.1.1.0 network. Discontiguous networks won't ever work with RIPv1 and IGRP; and they don't work **by default** with RIPv2 and EIGRP as well, as they perform autosummarization by default.

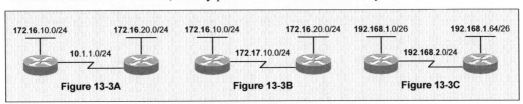

Figure 13-3: Sample Discontiguous Networks

- **Autosummarization** → EIGRP supports route summarization, which is commonly used to reduce the size of routing tables. However, EIGRP performs **autosummarization** by default, which means routes belong to the classful networks different than the classful network of the interface that sends out the routing updates (routing updates cross 2 major networks) will be **summarized** as a single summary route up to the **classful network boundary** of the addresses. Figure 13-4 shows a discontiguous network with autosummarization, which would never work! RIP, RIPv2, and IGRP also perform autosummarization by default, except OSPF. The autosummarization feature can be disabled. The best practice is disable autosummarization with the **no auto-summary** router subcommand and performs manual route summarization with the **ip summary-address** interface subcommand when necessary.
  Classful network boundary: 172.16.10.0/24 → 172.16.0.0/16. 10.1.1.0/24 → 10.0.0.0/8.

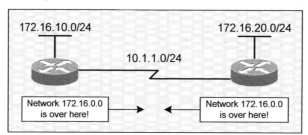

172.16.10.0/24

172.16.20.0/24

10.1.1.0/24

Network 172.16.0.0 is over here!

Network 172.16.0.0 is over here!

Figure 13-4: EIGRP Autosummarization

- Figure 13-4 shows 2 EIGRP routers advertise the same network – 172.16.0.0/16, which in fact they should advertise 2 different networks – 172.16.10.0/24 and 172.16.20.0/24.

- RIPv2 and EIGRP do not support discontiguous networks by default due to autosummarization; OSPF supports discontiguous networks by default as it does not perform autosummarization.

- The EIGRP **automatic redistribution** feature eases IGRP to EIGRP routing protocol migration. Introduce a router to reside between the IGRP and EIGRP domains which runs IGRP and EIGRP concurrently, and configure all EIGRP routers with the same AS number of IGRP domain. EIGRP will automatically redistribute IGRP routes into EIGRP (as external routes, AD 170), and the EIGRP routes are being redistributed into IGRP as well.
  Note: It may take a while (around 90 seconds) for the IGRP-EIGRP redistributing border router to generate the IGRP routing updates for the EIGRP routes into the IGRP routing domain.

- Comparison between Distance-Vector, Link-State, and Balanced Hybrid routing protocols:

Distance-Vector	Uses Bellman-Ford algorithm for route computation. Each router sends all its routing table entries (large updates) **only to neighboring routers**. [1]
Link-State	Uses Shortest Path First algorithm for route computations. Each router sends only a portion of its routing table (small partial updates) that describes its link status (up/down, cost) to all routers within an area. [1] LS protocols **flood** routing updates to **all routers within an area**. [2]
Balanced Hybrid	Have attributes associated with both DV and LS protocols – uses the routing-by-rumor mechanism (DV feature) and uses the Hello packets in neighbor discovery and maintenance (LS feature). Balanced Hybrid protocols send **small updates only to neighboring routers**. [2]

[1] and [2] are comparison points between DV and LS protocols, as well as between LS and BH protocols respectively.

For environments with routers from various vendors, use OSPF. For environments with only Cisco routers, use EIGRP.

Chapter 14
OSPF and EIGRP Lab

OSPF Single-Area Configuration

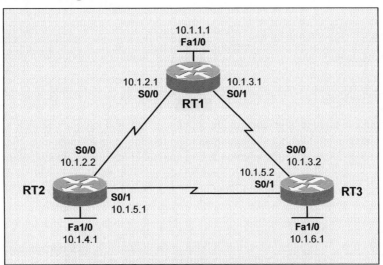

Figure 14-1: Network Setup for OSPF Single-Area

- The **router ospf** {*process-id*} global configuration command enables an OSPF process and enters into the OSPF configuration mode. It requires a parameter called the **OSPF Process ID**. When a router runs multiple OSPF processes, the Process IDs are used to distinguish the processes and databases. Unlink the autonomous system number in EIGRP router configuration, the OSPF Process ID is **locally significant** and does not need to match the Process IDs on other routers in order for the OSPF routers to establish adjacency and exchange routing information.

- Running multiple OSPF processes on a router is not recommended, as it creates multiple independent database instances that add extra overhead to the router.
  Note: Running multiple OSPF processes on a router is not the same as running multi-area OSPF.

- OSPF Single-Area configuration on RT1:

```
RT1(config)#router ospf ?
  <1-65535>  Process ID
RT1(config)#router ospf 1
RT1(config-router)#network 10.0.0.0 0.255.255.255 area ?
  <0-4294967295>  OSPF area ID as a decimal value
  A.B.C.D         OSPF area ID in IP address format

RT1(config-router)#network 10.0.0.0 0.255.255.255 area 0
RT1(config-router)#^Z
RT1#
```

- OSPF Single-Area configuration on RT2:

```
RT2(config)#router ospf 1
RT2(config-router)#network 10.1.0.0 0.0.255.255 area 0
RT2(config-router)#^Z
RT2#
```

- OSPF Single-Area configuration on RT3:

```
RT3(config)#router ospf 1
RT3(config-router)#network 10.1.3.2 0.0.0.0 area 0
RT3(config-router)#network 10.1.5.2 0.0.0.0 area 0
RT3(config-router)#network 10.1.6.1 0.0.0.0 area 0
RT3(config-router)#^Z
RT3#
```

- The **network** {*ip-addr*} {*wildcard-mask*} **area** {*area-id*} router subcommand identifies the interfaces that belong to an OSPF process, the interfaces to transmit and receive routing updates, the OSPF area that the interfaces reside on, and the networks to be included in the routing updates.

- OSPF **network** router subcommand differs from RIP and IGRP **network** router subcommands in its way of matching interfaces. It includes a parameter called the **wildcard mask**. Binary 1s in the wildcard mask are considered wildcard bits or **don't care bits**, means that the router does not need to care what binary value is in the corresponding bits. Wildcard masks are also used in access control list configuration.

- Binary 0s in the wildcard mask indicates that the corresponding bits of an interface IP address **must be matched exactly**. Ex: 1.1.1.1 and 0.0.0.0 would match 1.1.1.1 only. 1.1.0.0 and 0.0.255.255 would match anything in the range 1.1.0.0 – 1.1.255.255. It is often **simpler** and **safer** to use the 0.0.0.0 wildcard mask to identify each OSPF interface individually.

- Verify the OSPF Single-Area configuration on RT1:

```
RT1#sh ip route
Gateway of last resort is not set

     10.0.0.0/24 is subnetted, 6 subnets
C       10.1.1.0 is directly connected, FastEthernet1/0
C       10.1.2.0 is directly connected, Serial0/0
C       10.1.3.0 is directly connected, Serial0/1
O       10.1.4.0 [110/65] via 10.1.2.2, 00:00:32, Serial0/0
O       10.1.5.0 [110/128] via 10.1.2.2, 00:00:32, Serial0/0
                 [110/128] via 10.1.3.2, 00:00:32, Serial0/1
O       10.1.6.0 [110/65] via 10.1.3.2, 00:00:32, Seria0/1
RT1#
```

- Verify the OSPF Single-Area configuration on RT2:

```
RT2#sh ip route
Gateway of last resort is not set

     10.0.0.0/24 is subnetted, 6 subnets
O       10.1.1.0 [110/65] via 10.1.2.1, 00:00:48, Serial0/0
C       10.1.2.0 is directly connected, Serial0/0
O       10.1.3.0 [110/128] via 10.1.2.1, 00:00:48, Serial0/0
                 [110/128] via 10.1.5.2, 00:00:48, Serial0/1
C       10.1.4.0 is directly connected, FastEthernet1/0
C       10.1.5.0 is directly connected, Serial0/1
O       10.1.6.0 [110/65] via 10.1.5.2, 00:00:48, Serial0/1
RT2#
```

- Verify the OSPF Single-Area configuration on RT3:

```
RT3#sh ip route
Gateway of last resort is not set

     10.0.0.0/24 is subnetted, 6 subnets
O       10.1.1.0 [110/65] via 10.1.3.1, 00:01:09, Serial0/0
O       10.1.2.0 [110/128] via 10.1.3.1, 00:01:09, Serial0/0
                 [110/128] via 10.1.5.1, 00:01:09, Serial0/1
C       10.1.3.0 is directly connected, Serial0/0
O       10.1.4.0 [110/65] via 10.1.5.1, 00:01:09, Serial0/1
C       10.1.5.0 is directly connected, Serial0/1
C       10.1.6.0 is directly connected, FastEthernet1/0
RT3#
```

MISC OSPF Commands

- The **show ip route ospf** EXEC command displays only OSPF routes in the routing table.

```
RT1#sh ip route ospf
     10.0.0.0/24 is subnetted, 3 subnets
O       10.1.4.0 [110/65] via 10.1.2.2, 00:02:01, Serial0/0
O       10.1.5.0 [110/128] via 10.1.2.2, 00:02:01, Serial0/0
                 [110/128] via 10.1.3.2, 00:02:01, Serial0/1
O       10.1.6.0 [110/65] via 10.1.3.2, 00:02:01, Serial0/1
RT1#
```

- The **show ip ospf** EXEC command displays OSPF information for all OSPF processes running on a router, eg: Router ID, area information, SPF statistics, LSA timer information, etc. Notice that the RID on RT1 is 10.1.3.1, which is the **highest IP address** (physical) of the router.

```
RT1#sh ip ospf
 Routing Process "ospf 1" with ID 10.1.3.1
 Supports only single TOS(TOS0) routes
 Supports opaque LSA
 SPF schedule delay 5 secs, Hold time between two SPFs 10 secs
 Minimum LSA interval 5 secs. Minimum LSA arrival 1 secs
 Number of external LSA 0. Checksum Sum 0x0
 Number of opaque AS LSA 0. Checksum Sum 0x0
 Number of DCbitless external and opaque AS LSA 0
 Number of DoNotAge external and opaque AS LSA 0
 Number of areas in this router is 1. 1 normal 0 stub 0 nssa
 External flood list length 0
    Area BACKBONE(0)
        Number of interfaces in this area is 3
        Area has no authentication
        SPF algorithm last executed 00:03:10 ago
        SPF algorithm executed 3 times
        Area ranges are
        Number of LSA 3. Checksum Sum 0x015FCD
        Number of opaque link LSA 0. Checksum Sum 0x0
        Number of DCbitless LSA 0
        Number of indication LSA 0
        Number of DoNotAge LSA 0
        Flood list length 0

RT1#
```

- The **show ip ospf database** EXEC command displays the OSPF **topology database**, which contains the number of routers in the autonomous system and the RID of the neighboring router. It shows the Router ID (Link ID), the RID of the advertising router (ADV Router), the version of the OSPF database which used to detect old or duplicate LSUs (Seq#), and the number of links (including point-to-point links, transit links, stub networks, and virtual links) detected for a particular router (Link count). The output is **broken down by the OSPF processes and areas**.

```
RT1#sh ip ospf database

        OSPF Router with ID (10.1.3.1) (Process ID 1)


               Router Link States (Area 0)

Link ID         ADV Router       Age       Seq#        Checksum Link count
10.1.3.1        10.1.3.1         170       0x80000003 0x00234A 5
10.1.5.1        10.1.5.1         172       0x80000003 0x0066FC 5
10.1.6.1        10.1.6.1         169       0x80000003 0x00D587 5
RT1#
```

- The **show ip ospf interface** [*intf-type intf-num*] EXEC command displays all interface-related OSPF information for all interfaces or a particular interface. It shows the interface state, interface IP address, area assignment, Process ID, Router ID, network type, cost, priority, DR/BDR election information (if applicable), timer intervals, adjacent neighbor information, and authentication configuration information (if applicable).

```
RT1#sh ip ospf interface
FastEthernet1/0 is up, line protocol is up
  Internet Address 10.1.1.1/24, Area 0
  Process ID 1, Router ID 10.1.3.1, Network Type BROADCAST, Cost: 1
  Transmit Delay is 1 sec, State DR, Priority 1
  Designated Router (ID) 10.1.3.1, Interface address 10.1.1.1
  No backup designated router on this network
  Timer intervals configured, Hello 10, Dead 40, Wait 40, Retransmit 5
    Hello due in 00:00:00
  Index 1/1, flood queue length 0
  Next 0x0(0)/0x0(0)
  Last flood scan length is 0, maximum is 0
  Last flood scan time is 0 msec, maximum is 0 msec
  Neighbor Count is 0, Adjacent neighbor count is 0
  Suppress hello for 0 neighbor(s)
--- output omitted ---
```

- The **show ip ospf neighbor** [*intf-type intf-num*] [*neighbor-id*] [**detail**] EXEC command is a very useful command because it summarizes the important OSPF information regarding neighbors and the adjacency state, as well as the DR/BDR information (only if applicable, as DR and BDR are not used on point-to-point and point-to-multipoint interfaces) for all interfaces or a particular interface. The neighbors are identified with their Router IDs (highest IP address).

```
RT1#sh ip ospf neighbor

Neighbor ID      Pri   State        Dead Time   Address      Interface
10.1.5.1          1    FULL/  -     00:00:29    10.1.2.2     Serial0/0
10.1.6.1          1    FULL/  -     00:00:35    10.1.3.2     Serial0/1
RT1#
```

- The **show ip protocols** EXEC command provides an overview of **all running routing protocols** when multiple routing protocols are running on a single router. The following command output shows the Process ID, Router ID, the number of OSPF areas and their types, networks and areas configured for OSPF, and OSPF Router IDs of the neighbors.

```
RT1#sh ip protocols
Routing Protocol is "ospf 1"
  Outgoing update filter list for all interfaces is not set
  Incoming update filter list for all interfaces is not set
  Router ID 10.1.3.1
  Number of areas in this router is 1. 1 normal 0 stub 0 nssa
  Maximum path: 4
  Routing for Networks:
    10.0.0.0 0.255.255.255 area 0
  Routing Information Sources:
    Gateway          Distance      Last Update
    10.1.3.1              110      00:02:21
    10.1.6.1              110      00:02:21
    10.1.5.1              110      00:02:21
  Distance: (default is 110)

RT1#
```

- The **debug ip ospf adj** privileged command displays the OSPF adjacency events, eg: DR/BDR election.

- The **debug ip ospf events** privileged command displays information on OSPF-related events, eg: adjacency formation, flooding information, DR/BDR election, and SPF calculation.

- The **debug ip ospf packet** privileged command displays the contents of all sent and received OSPF packets.

- Cisco OSPF link cost is calculated based on **bandwidth**, whereas other vendors may use other methods for link cost / metric calculation. Hence when connecting routers from different vendors, the OSPF cost might need to be adjusted to match other vendor's router. Both routers must have the **same cost** for a particular link for the OSPF to operate properly.

- Since OSPF cost is based on bandwidth, the OSPF cost of an interface can also be changed with the **bandwidth** {*bw*} interface subcommand. If an interface's cost is not set, the formula 10^8 / bandwidth is used by default. Changing an interface's bandwidth changes its OSPF cost as well. Cisco OSPF cost calculation → 10^8 / **bandwidth** (in bps). 100Mbps FE → 1, 10Mbps → 10. A higher bandwidth indicates a lower cost, making higher speed links more preferable.

- Gigabit Ethernet = 0.1, but since only integer value can be used, so OSPF uses a cost of 1 for both FE and GE links. The **reference bandwidth**, which is the value of the numerator in the cost calculation formula, can be changed with the **auto-cost reference-bandwidth 1000** router subcommand. This command changes the numerator to 1000Mbps (10^9), and hence the formula becomes 10^9 / **bandwidth**. Finally, the cost calculation will be 1 for GE and 10 for FE.
  * 10^8 = 100,000,000 = 100Mbps
  * 10^9 = 1,000,000,000 = 1000Mbps = 1Gbps
  Note: OSPF always rounds down when the calculation results in a fraction.

- The **ip ospf cost** {*cost*} interface subcommand manipulates the OSPF cost associated with a particular interface. This command **overrides** the default formulated cost. The OSPF cost value ranges from 1 – 65,535. The OSPF cost has no unit of measurement, it is just a number.

OSPF Multiarea Configuration

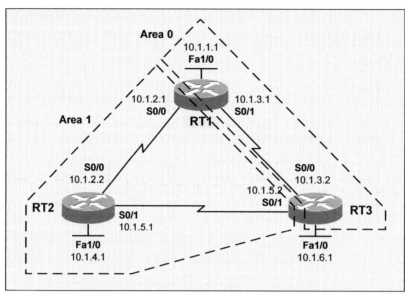

Figure 14-2: Network Setup for OSPF Multiarea

- OSPF hierarchical and multiarea design adds complexity to the router configuration. However, OSPF multiarea configuration is simple once understood OSPF single-area configuration. The difficult part would be network design – deciding which subnets should be placed in which areas. After the area design is complete, the configuration would be straightforward and easy.

- OSPF Multiarea configuration on RT1:

```
RT1#router ospf 1
RT1(config-router)#network 10.1.1.1 0.0.0.0 area 0
RT1(config-router)#network 10.1.2.1 0.0.0.0 area 1
RT1(config-router)#network 10.1.3.1 0.0.0.0 area 0
RT1(config-router)#^Z
RT1#
```

- OSPF Multiarea configuration on RT2:

```
RT2#router ospf 1
RT2(config-router)#network 10.0.0.0 0.255.255.255 area 1
RT2(config-router)#^Z
RT2#
```

- OSPF Multiarea configuration on RT3:

```
RT3#router ospf 1
RT3(config-router)#network 10.1.3.2 0.0.0.0 area 0
RT3(config-router)#network 10.1.5.2 0.0.0.0 area 1
RT3(config-router)#network 10.1.6.1 0.0.0.0 area 0
RT3(config-router)#^Z
RT3#
```

- RT1 and RT3 cannot match all their 3 interfaces with a single **network** router subcommand, as both routers have an interface that resides in a **different area** than the other 2 interfaces. However, this is possible for RT2 since all its interfaces are in the same area.

- Verify the OSPF Multiarea configuration on RT1:

```
RT1#sh ip route
Gateway of last resort is not set

      10.0.0.0/24 is subnetted, 6 subnets
C        10.1.1.0 is directly connected, FastEthernet10
C        10.1.2.0 is directly connected, Serial0/0
C        10.1.3.0 is directly connected, Serial0/1
O        10.1.4.0 [110/65] via 10.1.2.2, 00:02:04, Serial0/0
O        10.1.5.0 [110/128] via 10.1.2.2, 00:02:04, Serial0/0
O        10.1.6.0 [110/65] via 10.1.3.2, 00:07:41, Serial0/1
RT1#
```

- Verify the OSPF Multiarea configuration on RT2:

```
RT2#sh ip route
Gateway of last resort is not set

      10.0.0.0/24 is subnetted, 6 subnets
O IA    10.1.1.0 [110/65] via 10.1.2.1, 00:03:05, Serial0/0
C        10.1.2.0 is directly connected, Serial0/0
O IA    10.1.3.0 [110/128] via 10.1.2.1, 00:03:05, Serial0/0
                  [110/128] via 10.1.5.2, 00:03:05, Serial0/1
C        10.1.4.0 is directly connected, FastEthernet1/0
C        10.1.5.0 is directly connected, Serial0/1
O IA    10.1.6.0 [110/65] via 10.1.5.2, 00:03:05, Serial/01
RT2#
```

- Verify the OSPF Multiarea configuration on RT3:

```
RT3#sh ip route
Gateway of last resort is not set

      10.0.0.0/24 is subnetted, 6 subnets
O        10.1.1.0 [110/74] via 10.1.3.1, 00:09:48, Serial0/0
O        10.1.2.0 [110/128] via 10.1.5.1, 00:04:11, Serial0/1
C        10.1.3.0 is directly connected, Serial0/0
O        10.1.4.0 [110/74] via 10.1.5.1, 00:04:11, Serial0/1
C        10.1.5.0 is directly connected, Serial/01
C        10.1.6.0 is directly connected, FastEthernet1/0
RT3#
```

- **Note:** The routes learned by RT2 from the other 2 routers are shown as **OSPF interarea** (IA) **routes,** as those subnets are reside in Area 0, while RT2 resides in Area 1.

- Below lists the different terminology used for the OSPF tables:

OSPF neighbor table	OSPF adjacency database
OSPF topology table	OSPF topology database or link-state database
OSPF routing table	OSPF forwarding database

- A router requires an operational interface (line up, protocol up) with an IP address when initializing the OSPF process; or else the `can't allocate router-id` error message will be generated and the OSPF process will not be started.

- **Loopback** interfaces are logical interfaces (not real router interfaces). They are important in OSPF configuration. Without using loopback interfaces, the **highest physical IP address** on a router will become the RID, which is used for DR election and link-state database exchange. When using loopback interfaces in OSPF configuration, the RID of a router will never change as they never go down (always active) and hence can produce a stable network. Cisco suggests to use logical interfaces (eventually become the RIDs) as the best practice for OSPF configuration.

- MISC OSPF Router ID notes:
  i)   Use a private IP addressing scheme for loopback interface IP address configuration.
  ii) A newly configured and enabled loopback interface with an IP address higher than the current RID will only take effect as the new RID when after a router reboot or set the loopback interface address as the RID with the **router-id** router subcommand followed by issuing the **clear ip ospf process** privileged command. This prevents a newly enabled loopback interface with an IP address higher than the current RID from restarting the OSPF process which will trigger SPF calculation and network service interruption.
       Note: The **clear ip ospf process** privileged command is unable to make the IP address of a loopback interface to take effect as the new RID.
  iii) RID is selected at the moment when the OSPF process starts. It will remain even if the interface with the IP address that is selected as the RID is disabled and even removed. A router reboot or the **router-id** router subcommand is required to change the RID.
  iv) Loopback interface address overrides any physical interface address even if there is a physical interface address that is numerically higher than the loopback interface address. Additionally, the highest IP address of any logical interface will be selected as the RID.
  v)   RID can also be set **persistently** with the **router-id** {*rid-ip-addr*} router subcommand. The RID set with this command **overrides** loopback interface address, which means a physical interface address can be set as the RID even it is numerically lower than the current RID selected from a loopback interface address. The RID set with the **router-id** OSPF router subcommand requires a router reboot or issue the **clear ip ospf process** privileged command for it to take effect as the new RID.
  Note: The **router-id** OSPF router subcommand behaves differently on stand-alone routers and routers with established OSPF neighbors. It takes effect immediately on stand-alone routers – the RID is changed immediately upon issuing the command; while the **clear ip ospf process** privileged command must be issued on latter situation for a newly configured RID to take effect.

- The formula for calculating the number of adjacencies will to be formed between DROTHER routers with the DR and BDR routers on a multi-access network is $2(n - 1)$, where n is the number of routers on the network.

- OSPF does not support unequal-cost load balancing. If OSPF has 2 unequal cost links to a destination network, only the lowest-cost link will be used, and the other link will remain idle. One may manually change the cost of the interfaces with the **ip ospf cost** {*cost*} interface subcommand in order to utilize both links for load balancing purpose.

EIGRP Configuration

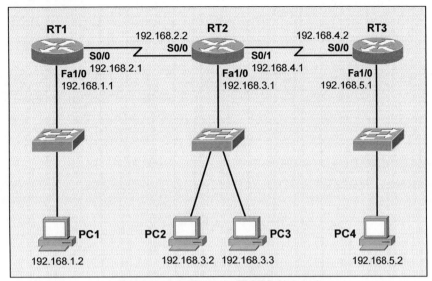

Figure 14-3: Sample EIGRP Network

- All routers in an EIGRP domain must be configured in the **same AS number**.

- EIGRP configuration on RT1:

```
RT1(config)#router eigrp ?
  <1-65535>  Autonomous system number

RT1(config)#router eigrp 10
RT1(config-router)#network 192.168.1.0
RT1(config-router)#network 192.168.2.0
RT1(config-router)#^Z
RT1#
```

- EIGRP configuration on RT2:

```
RT2(config)#router eigrp 10
RT2(config-router)#network 192.168.2.0
RT2(config-router)#network 192.168.3.0
RT2(config-router)#network 192.168.4.0
RT2(config-router)#^Z
RT2#
```

- EIGRP configuration on RT3:

```
RT3(config)#router eigrp 10
RT3(config-router)#network 192.168.4.0
RT3(config-router)#network 192.168.5.0
RT3(config-router)#^Z
RT3#
```

- Verify the EIGRP configuration on RT1:

```
RT1#sh ip route
Gateway of last resort is not set

C    192.168.1.0/24 is directly connected, FastEthernet1/0
C    192.168.2.0/24 is directly connected, Serial0/0
D    192.168.3.0/24 [90/2172416] via 192.168.2.2, 00:04:41, Serial0/0
D    192.168.4.0/24 [90/2681856] via 192.168.2.2, 00:04:41, Serial0/0
D    192.168.5.0/24 [90/2684416] via 192.168.2.2, 00:04:41, Serial0/0
RT1#
```

- Verify the EIGRP configuration on RT2:

```
RT2#sh ip route
Gateway of last resort is not set

D    192.168.1.0/24 [90/2172416] via 192.168.2.1, 00:05:25, Serial0/0
C    192.168.2.0/24 is directly connected, Serial0/0
C    192.168.3.0/24 is directly connected, FastEthernet1/0
C    192.168.4.0/24 is directly connected, Serial0/1
D    192.168.5.0/24 [90/2172416] via 192.168.4.2, 00:05:25, Serial0/1
RT2#
```

- Verify the EIGRP configuration on RT3:

```
RT3#sh ip route
Gateway of last resort is not set

D    192.168.1.0/24 [90/2684416] via 192.168.4.1, 00:05:57, Serial0/0
D    192.168.2.0/24 [90/2681856] via 192.168.4.1, 00:05:58, Serial0/0
D    192.168.3.0/24 [90/2172416] via 192.168.4.1, 00:05:58, Serial0/0
C    192.168.4.0/24 is directly connected, Serial0/0
C    192.168.5.0/24 is directly connected, FastEthernet1/0
RT3#
```

- The **show ip eigrp interfaces** EXEC command displays the information about EIGRP-enabled interfaces.

```
RT2#sh ip eigrp interfaces
IP-EIGRP interfaces for process 10

                 Xmit Queue    Mean   Pacing Time   Multicast    Pending
Interface  Peers Un/Reliable   SRTT   Un/Reliable   Flow Timer   Routes
Se0/0      1     0/0           207    5/190         250          0
Se0/1      1     0/0           217    5/190         250          0
Fa1/0      1     0/0           1      0/10          50           0
RT2#
```

- The **show ip eigrp neighbors** EXEC command displays the information about EIGRP adjacencies and discovered neighbors.

```
RT2#sh ip eigrp neighbors
H   Address            Interface       Hold Uptime    SRTT    RTO   Q   Seq
                                       (sec)          (ms)          Cnt Num
1   192.168.2.1        Se0/0            10 00:16:07   207    1242   0   7
0   192.168.4.2        Se0/1            13 00:16:03   217    1302   0   5
```

Below explains the fields in the output of the command:

H (handle)	Indicates the order by time a particular neighbor was discovered.
Hold (in second)	Hold time. Indicates how long this router will wait for a Hello packet from a particular neighbor before declaring the neighbor is down.
Uptime	Indicates how long the neighbor relationship has been established.
SRTT (in ms)	**Smooth Round-Trip Time.** Indicates how long it takes for an EIGRP packet to be sent from this router to a neighbor, and receiving an acknowledgment for the multicast packet sent to the neighbor. If an ACK packet isn't received within this interval, EIGRP will switch to unicasts to attempt to complete the communication. The interval between the multicast-to-unicast attempt is specified by the RTO.
RTO (in ms)	**Retransmission Time Out.** Indicates how long EIGRP should wait for an ACK packet before retransmitting a packet in the retransmission queue to a neighbor.
Queue Count	Indicates the numbers of outstanding Update, Query, or Reply packets waiting for retransmission. Consistently large values often indicate a problem.
Seq Num	Indicates the sequence number of the last update from a neighbor. Used to maintain synchronization, avoid duplicate and out-of-sequence messages.

- The **show ip eigrp topology** EXEC command displays all EIGRP successor and feasible successor routes in the EIGRP topology table. Routes preceded by a P are **passive state** routes.
  Note: Successor routes are stored in both routing and topology tables, while feasible successor routes are stored only in the topology table.

```
RT2#sh ip eigrp topology
IP-EIGRP Topology Table for AS(10)/ID(192.168.4.1)

Codes: P - Passive, A - Active, U - Update, Q - Query, R - Reply,
       r - reply Status, s - sia Status

P 192.168.1.0/24, 1 successors, FD is 2172416
        via 192.168.2.1 (2172416/28160), Serial0/0
P 192.168.2.0/24, 1 successors, FD is 2169856
        via Connected, Serial0/0
P 192.168.3.0/24, 1 successors, FD is 28160
        via Connected, FastEthernet1/0
P 192.168.4.0/24, 1 successors, FD is 2169856
        via Connected, Serial0/1
P 192.168.5.0/24, 1 successors, FD is 2172416
        via 192.168.4.2 (2172416/28160), Serial0/1
```

Passive	The router has path to this network and is not performing route computation for it.
Active	The router has lost the path to this network and is performing route computation to search for a replacement route. An active route exists when the router has no feasible successor to a destination network. A route never needs to enter into active state when the router always has feasible successors for the particular destination network.

- When a link to a neighbor fails, all successor and feasible successor routes through that neighbor enter into active state and the router is required to perform route computation.

- The xxx and yyy in the via A.B.C.D (xxx/yyy), *interface* entry in the **show ip eigrp topology** EXEC command represent **feasible distance** and **advertised distance** respectively.

- EIGRP uses the following 5 types of packets:

Hellos	Used for neighbor discovery. Do not require acknowledgement.
Updates	Used to tell a newly discovered neighbor the reachability of destination networks. Requires acknowledgment.
Queries	Used to ask for a replacement route when there is no feasible successor to a network. Requires acknowledgment.
Replies	Used to response to query packets to tell the originator not to recompute the route as there is feasible successor. Requires acknowledgment.
ACKs	Used to acknowledge updates, queries, and replies.

- The EIGRP **passive-interface** {*intf-type intf-num*} router subcommand prevents an interface from sending and receiving Hello packets, which eventually stop it from forming adjacencies and exchanging routing updates with other routers which reside on the passive interface subnet.

- RIP passive interfaces prevent the sending but allow the receiving of routing updates. Hence the router can still learn about the networks advertised by other routers.
  EIGRP passive interfaces neither send nor receive routing updates. Additionally no neighbor relationship will be formed, as EIGRP passive interfaces suppress the exchange of Hello packets.

- EIGRP performs autosummarization in discontiguous networks by default, and some networks might not work due to this feature. The best practice is disable autosummarization and performs manual summarization with **ip summary-address** interface subcommand when necessary. EIGRP autosummarization can be disabled with the **no auto-summary** router subcommand.

```
Router(config)#router eigrp 10
Router(config-router)#network 10.0.0.0
Router(config-router)#network 172.16.0.0
Router(config-router)#no auto-summary
```

Note: classful network addresses are used in EIGRP (and IGRP) configuration.

- The **maximum-paths** {*num*} router subcommand defines the total number of links allowed for **equal-cost path load balancing**. Its value is ranging from 1 to 6, with the default of 4. The **variance** router subcommand can be used to achieve unequal cost path load balancing.

- EIGRP (and IGRP) has a default maximum hop count of 100, but it can be changed to 255. Normally it is unnecessary to change the value, as hop count isn't used in the path metric calculation. It is only being used to **limit the scope** of an autonomous system.

```
Router(config)#router eigrp 10
Router(config-router)#metric maximum-hops ?
  <1-255>  Hop count
```

Chapter 15
Variable-Length Subnet Masks and Route Summarization

Variable-Length Subnet Masks

- VLSM allows more than one subnet mask to be used within a single Class A, B, or C network. VLSM allows the creation of efficient network addressing plan by using different subnet masks for different networks – some subnets to be larger and some to be smaller, which is able to **reduce the wasted IP addresses** in each subnet, and hence allows the creation of more subnets.

- A routing protocol that supports VLSM (eg: RIPv2, EIGRP, and OSPF) must be used for routers to learn VLSM routes in a network. A routing protocol that supports VLSM advertises not only the subnet number, but also the subnet mask along with its routing updates.

- The most efficient subnet mask for point-to-point links is 255.255.255.252 (/30). It provides 1 network address, 2 host addresses, and 1 broadcast address, which is sufficient for 2 end systems on a point-to-point link.

- The following table shows the network addresses for the common subnet masks:

Mask	Subnet Bits	Host Bits	Block Size	Network Addresses
/24	0	8	256 addresses	.0
/25	1	7	128 addresses	.0, or .128
/26	2	6	64 addresses	.0, .64, .128, or .192
/27	3	5	32 addresses	.0, .32, .64, .96, .128, .160, .192, or .224
/28	4	4	16 addresses	.0, .16, .32, … (multiplier of 16)
/29	5	3	8 addresses	.0, .8, .16, … (multiplier of 8)
/30	6	2	4 addresses	.0, .4, .8, … (multiplier of 4)

- **Caution:** Watch out for the **subnets overlap** issue when implementing VLSM networks.

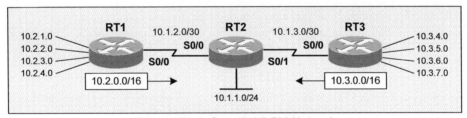

Figure 15-1: Sample VLSM Network

- Below shows the routing table on RT2 in the sample VLSM network with 2 separate masks (/24 and /30) configured on interfaces, along with autosummarized EIGRP routes from other routers:

```
RT2#sh ip route
Gateway of last resort is not set

     10.0.0.0/8 is variably subnetted, 5 subnets, 3 masks
D       10.2.0.0/16 [90/2195456] via 10.1.2.1, 00:00:07, Serial0/0
D       10.3.0.0/16 [90/2195456] via 10.1.3.2, 00:06:27, Serial0/1
C       10.1.1.0/24 is directly connected, Ethernet1/0
C       10.1.2.0/30 is directly connected, Serial0/0
C       10.1.3.0/30 is directly connected, Serial0/1
RT2#
```

Note: EIGRP autosummarization is enabled in this scenario.

- Below shows the beauty of VLSM. By having just a single Class C network – 192.168.0.0/24, an amount of 12 networks can be created with VLSM!

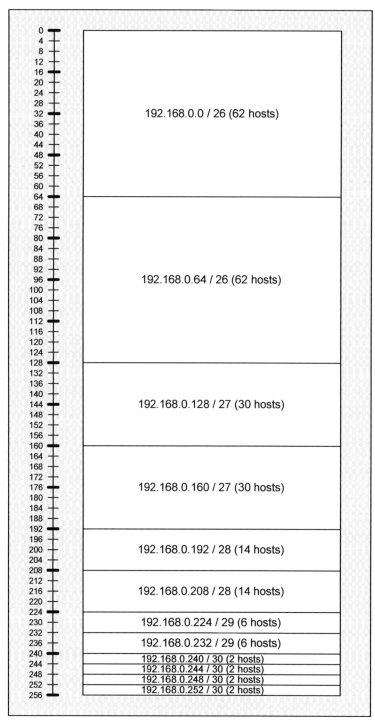

Figure 15-2: Sample VLSM Table

Route Summarization

- The larger the network, more routes to advertise, larger routing update packets, more bandwidth the updates take, and hence reducing the bandwidth available for data transmission. Besides that, large IP networks also produce large routing tables, which consume **more router memory**, and take **more time and CPU cycles** to perform routing table lookup when routing a packet.

- **Route summarization** reduces the size of routing updates and tables while still maintain routing information to all destination networks. It is also known as **route aggregation** or **supernetting**.

- Route summarization also able to **reduce convergences**. Upstream routers that received the summary route do not have to reconverge whenever there is a status change in the component subnets, which can effectively insulate upstream routers from problems such as **route flapping**. Route flapping is when a network goes up and down on a router, causing it to constantly advertise the status about the network.

- A requirement for route summarization is a classless routing protocol (eg: RIPv2, EIGRP, OSPF, IS-IS, and BGP) must be running, as they support **variable-length subnet masks** (VLSMs) and carry subnet mask information along with the routing updates.

- A **summary route** substitutes multiple original component routes. Once configured, the routing protocol advertises only the single summary route instead of multiple specific component routes.

- Route summarization works great in **contiguous networks** that were designed and planned for it.

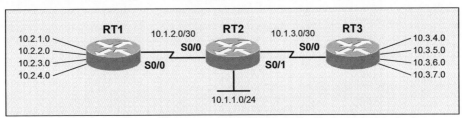

Figure 15-3: A Network Designed and Planned for Route Summarization

- Below shows the routing table on RT2 before route summarization, with EIGRP as the routing protocol. It shows 4 routes to 10.2.x.x subnets out its Serial0/0 interface to RT1, and 4 routes to 10.3.x.x subnets out its Serial0/1 interface to RT3:

```
RT2#sh ip route
Gateway of last resort is not set

     10.0.0.0/8 is variably subnetted, 11 subnets, 2 masks
C       10.1.1.0/24 is directly connected, Ethernet1/0
C       10.1.2.0/30 is directly connected, Serial0/0
C       10.1.3.0/30 is directly connected, Serial0/1
D       10.2.1.0/24 [90/2195456] via 10.1.2.1, 00:02:13, Serial0/0
D       10.2.2.0/24 [90/2195456] via 10.1.2.1, 00:02:13, Serial0/0
D       10.2.3.0/24 [90/2195456] via 10.1.2.1, 00:02:13, Serial0/0
D       10.2.4.0/24 [90/2195456] via 10.1.2.1, 00:02:13, Serial0/0
D       10.3.4.0/24 [90/2195456] via 10.1.3.2, 00:00:18, Serial0/1
D       10.3.5.0/24 [90/2195456] via 10.1.3.2, 00:00:18, Serial0/1
D       10.3.6.0/24 [90/2195456] via 10.1.3.2, 00:00:19, Serial0/1
D       10.3.7.0/24 [90/2195456] via 10.1.3.2, 00:00:19, Serial0/1
RT2#
```

- RT1 and RT3 are **summarizing routers**, which advertise summary routes to other routers.

- Route summarization configuration differs with different routing protocols. The **ip summary-address eigrp** {*as-num*} {*address*} {*mask*} interface subcommand is used to create a summary route that is to be advertised out an interface for an EIGRP autonomous system. **Note:** EIGRP route summarization takes effect immediately upon the issuance of the manual summarization command and would tear down EIGRP neighbor relationship; this ensure neighbors remove previous topology information, and accept to the new topology information upon the neighborship is recovered.

- Route Summarization configuration on RT1 and RT3:

```
RT1#conf t
Enter configuration commands, one per line.  End with CNTL/Z.
RT1(config)#int s0/0
RT1(config-if)#ip summary-address eigrp 100 10.2.0.0 255.255.0.0
RT1(config-if)#
------------------------------------------------------------------
RT3#conf t
Enter configuration commands, one per line.  End with CNTL/Z.
RT3(config)#int s0/0
RT3(config-if)#ip summary-address eigrp 100 10.3.0.0 255.255.0.0
RT3(config-if)
```

- Below shows the routing tables on RT1 and RT3 after route summarization:

```
RT1#sh ip route

Gateway of last resort is not set

     10.0.0.0/8 is variably subnetted, 9 subnets, 2 masks
D       10.1.1.0/24 [90/2195456] via 10.1.2.2, 00:04:36, Serial0/0
C       10.1.2.0/30 is directly connected, Serial0/0
D       10.1.3.0/30 [90/2681856] via 10.1.2.2, 00:04:36, Serial0/0
D       10.2.0.0/16 is a summary, 00:04:41, Null0
C       10.2.1.0/24 is directly connected, Ethernet1/0
C       10.2.2.0/24 is directly connected, Ethernet1/1
C       10.2.3.0/24 is directly connected, Ethernet1/2
C       10.2.4.0/24 is directly connected, Ethernet1/3
D       10.3.0.0/16 [90/2707456] via 10.1.2.2, 00:03:05, Serial0/0
RT1#
------------------------------------------------------------------
RT3#sh ip route

Gateway of last resort is not set

     10.0.0.0/8 is variably subnetted, 9 subnets, 2 masks
D       10.1.1.0/24 [90/2195456] via 10.1.3.1, 00:05:32, Serial0/0
D       10.1.2.0/30 [90/2681856] via 10.1.3.1, 00:05:34, Serial0/0
C       10.1.3.0/30 is directly connected, Serial0/0
D       10.2.0.0/16 [90/2707456] via 10.1.3.1, 00:05:32, Serial0/0
D       10.3.0.0/16 is a summary, 00:05:37, Null0
C       10.3.4.0/24 is directly connected, Ethernet1/0
C       10.3.5.0/24 is directly connected, Ethernet1/1
C       10.3.6.0/24 is directly connected, Ethernet1/2
C       10.3.7.0/24 is directly connected, Ethernet1/3
RT3#
```

- Static routes can be said to support VLSM, as they can be used to define summary routes for routing protocols that do not support VLSM, eg: RIP and IGRP.

- Below shows the routing table on RT2 after route summarization:

```
RT2#sh ip route
Gateway of last resort is not set

     10.0.0.0/8 is variably subnetted, 5 subnets, 2 masks
D       10.2.0.0/16 [90/2195456] via 10.1.2.1, 00:03:34, Serial0/0
D       10.3.0.0/16 [90/2195456] via 10.1.3.2, 00:02:06, Serial0/1
C       10.1.1.0/24 is directly connected, Ethernet1/0
C       10.1.2.0/30 is directly connected, Serial0/0
C       10.1.3.0/30 is directly connected, Serial0/1
RT2#
```

- RT1 no longer seeing the 4 10.3.x.x routes, and RT3 no longer seeing the 4 10.2.x.x routes. With route summarization, both routers advertise only the **summary routes**. Route summarization conserve great amount of bandwidth (smaller routing update packets) and minimizes processing for routing updates.

- EIGRP route summarization configuration introduces a route destined to the Null0 interface, where packets matching the route will be discarded. Whenever the summarizing router receives a packet destined for the summary route but the specific route does not exist in the routing table, the packet will be matched to the null route and being discarded. This prevents the summarizing router from forwarding the packet to its default route which would possibly create a routing loop. The null route will only be seen on the summarizing router.

- To find the **best summary route**, locate the bits of the subnet numbers that have the common bit pattern, from left to right (highest-order bits) – this is the subnet mask for the summary route.

- Best summary route for RT1:
  00001010 00000010 00000001 00000000 – 10.2.1.0
  00001010 00000010 00000010 00000000 – 10.2.2.0
  00001010 00000010 00000011 00000000 – 10.2.3.0
  00001010 00000010 00000100 00000000 – 10.2.4.0
  The best summary route for RT1 is 10.2.0.0, subnet mask 255.255.248.0.

- Best summary route for RT3:
  00001010 00000011 00000100 00000000 – 10.3.4.0
  00001010 00000011 00000101 00000000 – 10.3.5.0
  00001010 00000011 00000110 00000000 – 10.3.6.0
  00001010 00000011 00000111 00000000 – 10.3.7.0
  The best summary route for RT3 is 10.3.4.0, subnet mask 255.255.252.0.

This page is intentionally left blank

Chapter 16
Classful and Classless Routing, and MISC TCP/IP Topics

Classful and Classless Routing

- Routing protocols can be classified into different categories. eg: distance-vector, link-state, and balanced-hybrid. Routing protocols can also be classified as either classful or classless.

- Classful routing protocols **must consider** class rules when making a routing decision. They were designed to use little memory and processing power; hence they advertise just the basic routing information and **do not send subnet mask information** along with the subnet number in the routing updates in order to conserve bandwidth. A router running a classful routing protocol assume that all remote networks have the same subnet mask as the exiting interface, and all subnetworks of the same major network use the same subnet mask.

- Classless routing (prefix routing) protocols **ignores** class rules when making a routing decision. They transmit the subnet mask information along with the subnet number in the routing updates, which is also known as **prefix routing**.

- The class rules imply that a routing protocol must consider the Class A, B, or C network number that a subnet resides when performing its tasks.

- Interior IP routing protocols comparison chart:

Routing Protocol	Classful / Classless	Sends Subnet Mask along with Routing Updates	Supports VLSM	Supports Route Summarization
RIPv1	Classful	No	No	No
IGRP	Classful	No	No	No
RIPv2	Classless	Yes	Yes	Yes
EIGRP	Classless	Yes	Yes	Yes
OSPF	Classless	Yes	Yes	Yes

- As classful routing protocols do not advertise subnet mask information along the routing updates, a router will guess the subnet mask when it received a classful routing protocol routing updates. Classful routing protocols expect a **Fixed-Length Subnet Mask** (FLSM) throughout a network, and this does not cause any problem as long as all subnets are in the same class.

- Classless routing protocols have more advantages over classful routing protocols as they support some advanced and important features, eg: VLSM and route summarization. Besides that, classless routing protocols also overcome some network design issues that exist only in classful routing protocols, eg: autosummarization.

- **Autosummarization** happens when a router has interfaces in more than one Class A, B, or C networks. When advertising routes with classful addresses different than the classful address of the interface that sends out the routing updates, the routes will be **summarized** as a single summary route up to the **classful network boundary** of the addresses.
  Ex: 172.16.1.0/24 and 172.16.2.0/24 (Class C) are summarized as 172.16.0.0/16 (Class B).

- Autosummarization works fine in contiguous networks, but this behavior can causes problems in **discontiguous networks** – networks that have 2 subnets of a classful network separated by another different classful network. Classful routing protocols do not support discontiguous networks; while classless routing protocols do support discontiguous networks.

- RIPv1 and IGRP perform autosummarization **by default**, and **cannot be disabled** – it is a feature of classful routing protocols. For RIPv2 and EIGRP, the autosummarization feature which enabled by default can be disabled with the **no auto-summary** router subcommand. Autosummarization allows RIPv2 and EIGRP to be backward-compatible with their predecessors – RIPv1 and IGRP.

- OSPF and IS-IS do no perform autosummarization and do not even have this feature.

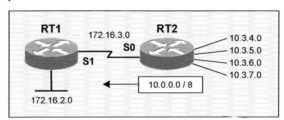

Figure 16-1: Autosummarization

- Below shows the routing table on RT1 with just a single route to network 10.0.0.0/8 due to the autosummarization feature of RT2 (RIPv1).

```
RT1#sh ip route
Gateway of last resort is not set

     172.16.0.0/24 is subnetted, 2 subnets
C       172.16.2.0 is directly connected, Ethernet0
C       172.16.3.0 is directly connected, Serial1
R    10.0.0.0/8 [120/1] via 172.16.3.2, 00:00:15, Serial1
RT1#
RT1#debug ip rip
RIP protocol debugging is on
RT1#
00:08:54: RIP: received v1 update from 172.16.3.2 on Serial1
00:08:54:      10.0.0.0 in 1 hops
RT1#
```

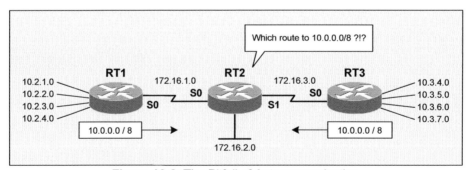

Figure 16-2: The Pitfall of Autosummarization

- Below shows the routing table of RT2, with RIPv1 as the routing protocol. RT2 has 2 routes to 10.0.0.0/8 network due to autosummarization. RT2 will perform load balancing across the paths since they are equal-cost paths to the same destination, which will definitely cause malfunctioning on applications!

```
RT2#sh ip route
Gateway of last resort is not set

     172.16.0.0/24 is subnetted, 3 subnets
C       172.16.1.0 is directly connected, Serial0
C       172.16.2.0 is directly connected, Ethernet0
C       172.16.3.0 is directly connected, Serial1
R    10.0.0.0/8 [120/1] via 172.16.1.1, 00:00:20, Serial0
                [120/1] via 172.16.3.2, 00:00:15, Serial1
RT2#
```

- This problem can be solved by migrating to a classless routing protocol with autosummarization disabled, eg: RIPv2, EIGRP. Remember to disable autosummarization as it is enabled by default.

- As mentioned before, routing protocols are considered either classful or classless. Nevertheless, IP routing can also be considered either classful or classless as well.

- The concepts of classful and classless routing are **independent** of any routing protocol, as the concepts still applicable to IP routing even if only static routes are being used.
  Note: Classlessness can be a characteristic of a routing protocol or a router.

- Classful or classless routing affects how a router uses its default route. A very good topic for the discussion of classful and classless routing is **default routing**, where packets destined to networks with no specific routes in the routing table will be directed to the default route.

- The [**no**] **ip classless** global configuration command enables and disables classless routing respectively. Disabling classless routing is equivalent to enabling classful routing.

- **Note:** The classless IP behavior is enabled by default in Cisco IOS Release 12.0 and later.
  Note: The classless IP behavior has no effect on some later Cisco IOS 12.3 releases.

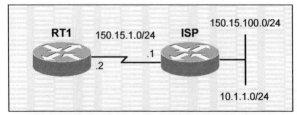

Figure 16-3: Sample Default Routing Network

```
RT1#conf t
Enter configuration commands, one per line.  End with CNTL/Z.
RT1(config)#no ip classless
RT1(config)#ip route 0.0.0.0 0.0.0.0 150.15.1.1
RT1(config)#^Z
RT1#
```

```
RT1#sh ip route
Gateway of last resort is 150.15.1.1 to network 0.0.0.0

     150.15.0.0/24 is subnetted, 1 subnets
C       150.15.1.0 is directly connected, Serial0/0
S*   0.0.0.0/0 [1/0] via 150.15.1.1
RT1#
RT1#ping 10.1.1.1

Type escape sequence to abort.
Sending 5, 100-byte ICMP Echos to 10.1.1.1, timeout is 2 seconds:
!!!!!
Success rate is 100 percent (5/5), round-trip min/avg/max = 36/36/40 ms
RT1#ping 150.15.100.1

Type escape sequence to abort.
Sending 5, 100-byte ICMP Echos to 150.15.100.1, timeout is 2 seconds:
.....
Success rate is 0 percent (0/5)
RT1#conf t
Enter configuration commands, one per line.  End with CNTL/Z.
RT1(config)#ip classless
RT1(config)#^Z
RT1#ping 150.15.100.1

Type escape sequence to abort.
Sending 5, 100-byte ICMP Echos to 150.15.100.1, timeout is 2 seconds:
!!!!!
Success rate is 100 percent (5/5), round-trip min/avg/max = 36/38/40 ms
RT1#
```

- As seen from the output above, **ping** to 150.15.100.1 with classful routing failed, but **ping** has succeeded with classless routing. This shows even if there is a default route in the routing table, it might not be used!

- Cisco IOS uses either classful or classless routing logic when matching a destination IP address with the routes in the routing table and decide when to use the default route.

- **The classful logic – no ip classless**:
  i)   RT1 needs to send a packet to 150.15.100.1.
  ii)   RT1 matches Class B network – 150.15.0.0, a directly connected network.
         Due to it is running classful routing, the default route cannot be used!
  iii)   RT1 does not have a more specific route to 150.15.100.0 from its routing table.
  iv)   RT1 discards the packet as the default route cannot be used.

- **The classless logic – ip classless**:
  i)   RT1 needs to sends a packet to 150.15.100.1.
  ii)   RT1 does not have a more specific route to 150.15.100.0.
  iii)   The default route is being used as there is no specific route matched.

- With classful routing, the default route is only being used when a packet's destination Class A, B, or C major network number is not in the routing table.
  Ex: A packet destined to 10.2.1.1 is discarded by a classful router with a routing table that consisting routes to 10.0.0.0/8, 10.1.1.0/24, 10.1.2.0/24, as the major network of 10.2.1.1 – 10.0.0.0/8, is in the routing table.

- With classless routing, the default route is used whenever a packet does not match a more specific route in the routing table (unknown subnets of known a classful network).

- If the supernet or default route is learned via a classless routing protocol (eg: OSPF, IS-IS), the classful nature (the **no ip classless** global configuration command is configured) of a router is ignored – a classful router may use a default route to reach networks that are not listed in the routing table regardless of the **ip classless** command.

Secondary IP Addressing

- Secondary addressing provides a solution to the problem of running out of addresses in a subnet (due to poor network design) by allowing multiple networks (or subnets) to reside on the same data link media. An interface may have an **unlimited** number of secondary addresses.

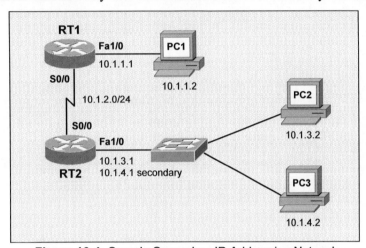

Figure 16-4: Sample Secondary IP Addressing Network

- Secondary IP Addressing configuration on RT2:

```
RT2(config)#int fa1/0
RT2(config-if)#ip add 10.1.3.1 255.255.255.0
RT2(config-if)#ip add 10.1.4.1 255.255.255.0 secondary
RT2(config-if)#no shut
RT2(config-if)#^Z
RT2#
RT2#sh ip route
Gateway of last resort is not set

     10.0.0.0/24 is subnetted, 4 subnets
R       10.1.1.0 [120/1] via 10.1.2.1, 00:00:10, Serial0/0
C       10.1.2.0 is directly connected, Serial0/0
C       10.1.3.0 is directly connected, FastEthernet1/0
C       10.1.4.0 is directly connected, FastEthernet1/0
RT2#
```

- By implementing secondary IP addressing on RT2, all PCs are able to ping each other.

- **Note:** RT2 would use its primary IP address (10.1.3.1) as the source IP address when it communicates with hosts in the secondary network (10.1.4.0/24).

- **Note:** A router uses the primary IP address when communicating with other hosts reside on both the same and remote networks, even when there are other secondary IP addresses configured.

MTU and Fragmentation

- **Maximum Transmission Unit** (MTU) defines the maximum amount of network layer data that a data link layer frame can carry; or the largest packet size that an interface can handle. This ensures that an IP packet that encapsulates a TCP segment will fit into a single frame. The default MTU value on Ethernet interfaces is **1500 bytes**.

- The following information can be gathered with a packet sniffer, eg: Ethereal, Wireshark:

Max application data size	1460 bytes
Max TCP segments size	1480 bytes
Max IP packets size	1500 bytes
Max Ethernet frames size	1514 bytes [1]

TCP and IP headers are 20 bytes in length.
[1] 14 bytes = 6 bytes Source MAC address + 6 bytes Destination MAC address + 2 bytes Type.
The actual Ethernet frame size should be 1518 bytes (1514 bytes + 4 bytes FCS).

Preamble	Start Frame Delimiter	Destination MAC Address	Source MAC Address	802.1Q Tag (optional)	EtherType / Length	Payload	FCS (CRC)	Inter Frame Gap (IFG)
7 octets of 10101010	1 octet of 10101011	6 octets	6 octets	(4 octets)	2 octets	46 – 1500 octets	4 octets	12 octets

64 – 1522 octets

Figure 16-5: IEEE 802.3 Ethernet Frame Structure

- An Ethernet frame begins with Preamble and Start Frame Delimiter.
Preamble and Start Frame Delimiter are not displayed by packet sniffing software as they are stripped away at OSI Layer 1 by the Ethernet adapter before being passed on to the OSI Layer 2, which is where packet sniffers collect their data from. There are OSI Physical Layer sniffers which can capture and display the Preamble and Start Frame Delimiter, but they are expensive and are mainly used to detect problems related to the physical layer.

- Routers are unable to forward a packet out an interface if the packet is larger than the MTU. **Fragmentation** is the process of breaking an IP packet into smaller pieces (≤ MTU). Fragmented packets are reassembled before being passed to the transport layer protocol.

- Fragmentation is performed at network layer (L3) using the 16-bit Identification, 3-bit Flags, and 13-bit Fragmentation Offset bits in the IP header. The 3-bit Flags field contains the Don't fragment bit, More fragments bit, and a reserved bit.

Chapter 17
Scaling the Internet with CIDR and NAT

- In the early era of Internet, an organization would ask for and get assigned one or more registered (public) IP addresses. However, the very fast growing of Internet has resulted the depletion or exhaustion of registered IP addresses.

- One of the solutions is increase the number of IP addresses, which IPv6 was introduced for this purpose. IPv6 has been developed but will take times to be implemented, as it requires modifications of the Internet infrastructure. IPv5 is an experimental protocol and never deployed.

- **Private addressing** and **NAT** work in conjunction to provide the short-term solution to IPv4 address depletion or exhaustion. The long-term solution is still IPv6.

- **Classless Interdomain Routing** (CIDR) was introduced to address the problem of large routing tables in the Internet backbone routers.

Classless Interdomain Routing (CIDR)

- An Internet router with routes to every Class A, B, and C networks on Earth is **impossible**! CIDR is basically subnetting and summarization performed at the Internet Service Provider level.

- CIDR allows routers to **summarize** or **aggregate** a group of IP addresses to appear as a unified and larger entity to other routers – **supernetting**. IP addresses and subnet masks are written in the slash notation (/) format in CIDR. **Border Gateway Protocol Version 4** (BGP4) is the most commonly used interdomain or exterior routing protocol in the Internet that supports CIDR to reduce the detailed routing information to other organization networks in order to reduce the routes in the Internet router routing tables (smaller routing tables).

- **Subnetting** creates networks with masks that are **longer** than the classful network masks. Normally VLSM is being used.
  Supernetting creates networks with masks that are **shorter** than the classful network masks. Normally CIDR is being used.
  Note: Classful network masks are /8, /16, and /24.

- CIDR values:

Subnet Mask	CIDR Value	Subnet Mask	CIDR Value
255.0.0.0	/8	225.255.240.0	/20
255.128.0.0	/9	255.255.248.0	/21
255.192.0.0	/10	255.255.252.0	/22
255.224.0.0	/11	255.255.254.0	/23
255.240.0.0	/12	255.255.255.0	/24
255.248.0.0	/13	255.255.255.128	/25
255.252.0.0	/14	255.255.255.192	/26
255.254.0.0	/15	255.255.255.224	/27
255.255.0.0	/16	255.255.255.240	/28
255.255.128.0	/17	255.255.255.248	/29
255.255.192.0	/18	255.255.255.252	/30
255.255.224.0	/19		

- Figure 17-1 shows the usage of CIDR – multiple routes to multiple Class C networks are grouped into a single route, which can reduces the size of ISP 2, ISP 3, and ISP 4 routing tables.

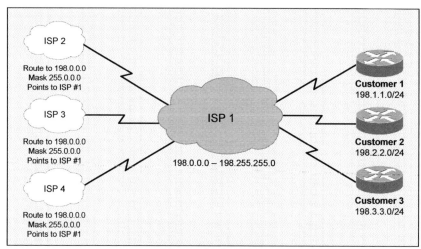

Figure 17-1: CIDR

- Without using CIDR, all ISPs routing tables would have a separate route to each of 2^{16} Class C networks that begin with 198. By implementing CIDR, a single route to 198.0.0.0/8 is sufficient to route all networks whose IP addresses begin with 198 to ISP 1. CIDR helps Internet routers to reduce the size of their routing tables by reducing the number of entries in the routing tables.

- CIDR is an extension to VLSM and route summarization. It is also referred to as **prefix routing**.

- The difference between route summarization and CIDR is as below:
  i)   Route summarization is generally done up to the classful network number boundary. (Fixed masks – /8, /16, /24).
  ii) CIDR is commonly used to combine and summarize several classful networks and goes beyond the classful network number boundary. (Flexible masks).

Private Addressing

Address Class	Reserved Address Space		Number of Networks
Class A	10.0.0.0 – 10.255.255.255	(10.0.0.0/8)	1 Class A network
Class B	172.16.0.0 – 172.31.255.255	(172.16.0.0/12)	16 Class B network
Class C	192.168.0.0 – 192.168.255.255	(192.168.0.0/16)	256 Class C network

Reference: RFC 1918 – Address Allocation for Private Internets.

- Public IP addresses cannot be duplicated in the Internet. However, organizations may use the mentioned private IP addresses when assigning IP addresses for hosts within the organizations. NAT is commonly being used to provide Internet access for organizations that using private addressing by performing translation between private and public addresses.

- Private addressing and NAT work in conjunction to provide the short-term solution to IPv4 address depletion or exhaustion.

Network Address Translation (NAT)

- NAT allows a host with **non-registered** IP address (private network) to connect to the Internet. NAT provides a small level of network security by hiding the internal network addressing schemes from external networks (advertise only a single address for the entire private network). NAT is often used on firewall systems.

- NAT performs translation between private IP addresses (inside local) and publicly registered IP addresses (inside global) on all IP packets that pass through a router that performing NAT. Figure 17-2 shows a typical NAT scenario.

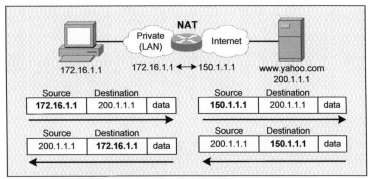

Figure 17-2: Network Address Translation

- The NAT router would change the source IP address of all packets that leaving the organization to its address (150.1.1.1). The Yahoo web server which receives the packets would reply with packets destined back to 150.1.1.1. The router changes back the destination IP address of all packets replied by Yahoo to the private host IP address (172.16.1.1) and forward to the host.

- Cisco IOS supports the following common NAT features:
  i)   Static NAT
  ii)   Dynamic NAT
  iii) Port Address Translation, PAT (also known as Dynamic NAT with Overloading)
  iv)   Overlapping Address Translation (commonly use when organizations merge)

- Below describes the different types of IP addresses that are being used in the operation of NAT:

Inside local address (Inside private)	The IP address that is assigned to a host in the inside network (private network) before any translation.
Inside global address (Inside public)	A routable IP address that is normally assigned by an ISP to represent one or more inside local hosts to the outside network. This is the translated IP address that is seen by the outside network.
Outside local address (Outside private)	The IP address that appears to the inside network to represent an outside host. It is used by all inside hosts to communicate with the outside host. Mostly used when **translating overlapping addresses**. It is usually a private IP address.
Outside global address (Outside public)	The routable IP address that is assigned to a host in the outside network.

- NAT is being performed when a packet is being routed or switched…
  i)   From an IP NAT inside interface to an IP NAT outside interface.
  ii)   From an IP NAT outside interface to an IP NAT inside interface.

- **Static NAT** performs **one-to-one mapping** between inside local and inside global addresses. Figure 17-3 shows a typical static NAT scenario. An organization that has 254 private hosts would need a single registered Class C IP subnet (/24 – 254 usable IP addresses) to provide Internet access to all its hosts, which is definitely a waste of public IP addresses!

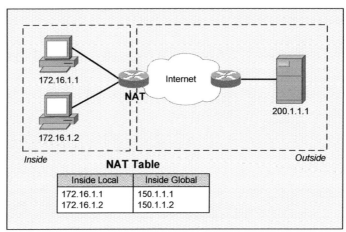

NAT Table

Inside Local	Inside Global
172.16.1.1	150.1.1.1
172.16.1.2	150.1.1.2

Figure 17-3: Static NAT

- **Dynamic NAT** performs **dynamic mapping** between an inside local and inside global addresses from a pool of public IP addresses. An available registered IP address from the NAT pool will be allocated to a private host when it communicates with a host on the Internet. The major limitation of dynamic NAT is it can only provide Internet access to a very limited number of private hosts (the number of registered IP addresses of the NAT pool).

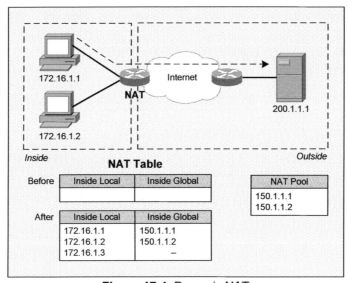

NAT Table

	Inside Local	Inside Global
Before		

NAT Pool
150.1.1.1
150.1.1.2

	Inside Local	Inside Global
After	172.16.1.1	150.1.1.1
	172.16.1.2	150.1.1.2
	172.16.1.3	–

Figure 17-4: Dynamic NAT

- **Port Address Translation** (PAT) was introduced to overcome the limitations of static and dynamic NAT methods. It performs **many-to-one mapping** between multiple unregistered private IP addresses and a single registered public IP address by using transport layer ports. PAT is also known as **Overload NAT** or **Dynamic NAT with Overloading**.

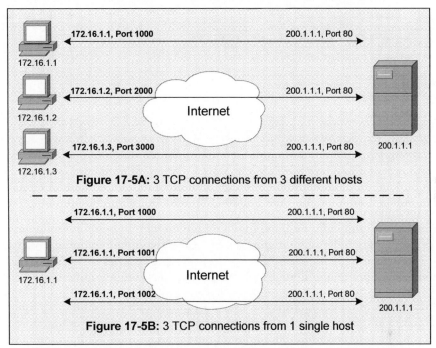

Figure 17-5A: 3 TCP connections from 3 different hosts

Figure 17-5B: 3 TCP connections from 1 single host

Figure 17-5: TCP Connections from Multiple Hosts and a Single Host

- Figure 17-5 shows that a server doesn't care how many clients are connected to it at a time. The server is able to differentiate connections to it by the combination of client IP addresses (network layer) and port numbers (transport layer).

- PAT utilizes the advantage of the TCP/IP **multiplexing** feature, where connections are unique with the combination of IP addresses and port numbers. A NAT router would have a NAT table entry for storing every unique combination of IP addresses and port numbers when hosts in private network traverse through it to the Internet. The port numbers assigned are random and will not be from the well-known port number range – 1 to 1023. These entries are used for **reverse-translation** upon reply packets from the Internet back to the hosts in private network.

- PAT does not only translate IP addresses, it also translates port numbers. Theoretically, 65536 connections to the hosts on the Internet can be made with a single registered public IP address.

- Cisco routers don't assign the source port on the inside global address randomly; the router assigns ports from a series of pools. The ranges are:
1 – 511, 512 – 1023, 1024 – 4999, and **5000 – 65535**.
For instance, if the inside host used port 500 as its source port, the router will choose a port between 1 and 511 for the source port when it translates the address. *TBC*

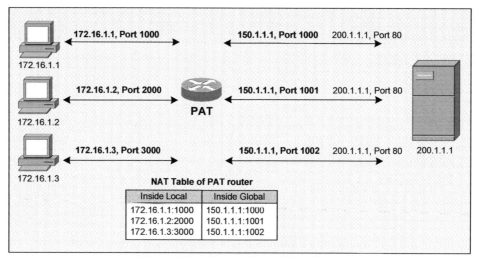

Figure 17-6: Port Address Translation

- **Overlapping Address Translation** is a special NAT operation that is being used when addresses in the inside network overlap with addresses in the outside network, which can exist when an organization does not use private addressing (illustrated in Figure 17-7), or when 2 companies that have similar IP addressing scheme merge due to business requirements.

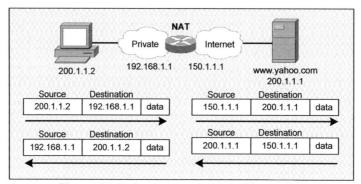

Figure 17-7: Overlapping Address Translation

- Figure 17-7 shows a network with overlapping addresses. Whenever the client sends a packet destined to *www.yahoo.com* (200.1.1.1), the packet would never arrive at the server, because the client might assume 200.1.1.1 is on the same LAN with it, hence it would not even try to forward packets destined to 200.1.1.1 to its default gateway!

- NAT is able to solve this problem by **translating both the source and destination addresses** of the packet passes through the NAT router, by having a NAT static mapping configuration for translation between the **outside global** address – 200.1.1.1, and the **outside local** address – 192.168.1.1, which represents the real outside host to the inside network.

- The client first sends out a DNS request to *www.yahoo.com*. When the DNS reply comes back from the outside network, the NAT router would intercept and change the DNS reply so that the client in the private network would think that 192.168.1.1 is the IP address of *www.yahoo.com*.

- Finally, the NAT router would change both the source and destination addresses for all packets send to (SRC: inside local → inside global; DST: outside local → outside global) and reply from (SRC: outside global → outside local; DST: inside global → inside local) *www.yahoo.com*.

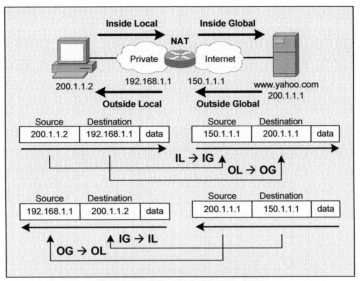

Figure 17-8: NAT Terminology

NAT Terminology	IP address in Figure 17-8
Inside local	200.1.1.2
Inside global	150.1.1.1
Outside local	192.168.1.1
Outside global	200.1.1.1

- The main disadvantage of implementing NAT is the loss of end-to-end IP traceability and hence some new applications or technologies such as mobile IP and end-to-end security cannot be implemented in NAT environments.

This page is intentionally left blank

Chapter 18
Network Address Translation Lab

Static NAT Configuration

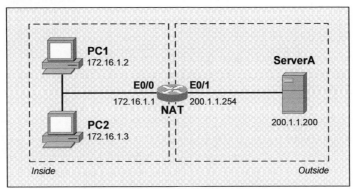

Figure 18-1: Network Setup for NAT

- Static NAT requires the fewest configuration steps as compared to other NAT implementations. Each interface needs to be identified as either an inside or outside interface with the **ip nat {inside | outside}** interface subcommand, as well as the configuration for static mapping between each pair of inside local and inside global addresses. Only packets arriving on an inside or outside NAT interface are subject for translation.

- Static NAT configuration on NAT:

```
NAT#conf t
Enter configuration commands, one per line.  End with CNTL/Z.
NAT(config)#int e0/0
NAT(config-if)#ip nat inside
NAT(config-if)#int e0/1
NAT(config-if)#ip nat outside
NAT(config-if)#exit
NAT(config)#ip nat inside source static 172.16.1.2 200.1.1.2
NAT(config)#ip nat inside source static 172.16.1.3 200.1.1.3
NAT(config)#^Z
NAT#
NAT#sh ip nat translations
Pro Inside global      Inside local       Outside local      Outside global
--- 200.1.1.2          172.16.1.2         ---                ---
--- 200.1.1.3          172.16.1.3         ---                ---
NAT#
NAT#sh ip nat statistics
Total active translations: 2 (2 static, 0 dynamic; 0 extended)
Outside interfaces:
  Ethernet0/1
Inside interfaces:
  Ethernet0/0
Hits: 0  Misses: 0
Expired translations: 0
Dynamic mappings:
NAT#
```

- Below shows the IP NAT debugging messages when PC1 (172.16.1.2) telnet into ServerA (200.1.1.200). The **debug ip nat** privileged command displays every packet that is being translated by the NAT operation.
  The * indicates that a packet was translated and fast switched to the destination.

```
NAT#debug ip nat
IP NAT debugging is on
NAT#
00:10:10: NAT: s=172.16.1.2->200.1.1.2, d=200.1.1.200 [0]
00:10:10: NAT: s=200.1.1.200, d=200.1.1.2->172.16.1.2 [0]
00:10:10: NAT*: s=172.16.1.2->200.1.1.2, d=200.1.1.200 [1]
00:10:10: NAT*: s=172.16.1.2->200.1.1.2, d=200.1.1.200 [2]
00:10:10: NAT*: s=172.16.1.2->200.1.1.2, d=200.1.1.200 [3]
00:10:10: NAT*: s=200.1.1.200, d=200.1.1.2->172.16.1.2 [1]
00:10:10: NAT*: s=200.1.1.200, d=200.1.1.2->172.16.1.2 [2]
00:10:10: NAT*: s=200.1.1.200, d=200.1.1.2->172.16.1.2 [3]
NAT#
```

- Below shows the output of **netstat** command at ServerA.

```
C:\>netstat -a

Active Connections

  Proto   Local Address          Foreign Address        State
  TCP     ServerA:telnet         200.1.1.2:1050         ESTABLISHED
```

- The static mappings are created with the **ip nat inside source static** {inside-local-addr} {inside-global-addr} global configuration command. The **inside** keyword tells NAT to translate the IP addresses in packets sourced from the **inside network** destined to the outside network. The **source** keyword tells NAT to translate the **source IP address** of the packets. The **static** keyword indicates a static entry, which **will not be removed from the NAT table** due to timeout or the **clear ip nat translation *** privileged command.

- The **show ip nat translations** EXEC command displays the active NAT mappings.
  The **show ip nat statistics** EXEC command displays the counters for translated packets and NAT table entries, as well as some basic configuration information.

- The **ip nat inside source static** {**tcp** | **udp**} {inside-local-addr} {local-port-num} {inside-global-addr | **interface** {inside-global-intf intf-type intf-num}} {global-port-num} global configuration command can be used when outside users would like to access an inside resource, eg: an FTP Server. This command seems to be difficult to understand at the first glance. However, it would work, as **inside source** would translate the destination IP addresses in packets that travel from outside to inside network. This is also known as **port forwarding**.

- **inside source** translates the source IP addresses in packets traverse from inside to outside, and translates the destination IP addresses in packets traverse from outside to inside.

- **inside destination** translates the destination IP addresses in packets traverse from inside to outside, and translates the source IP addresses in packets traverse from outside to inside.

- **outside source** translates the source IP addresses in packets traverse from outside to inside, and translates the destination IP addresses in packets traverse from inside to outside. Mostly used when translating overlapping addresses.

Dynamic NAT Configuration

-   An access list is created to include all the hosts on the inside network that are allowed to use NAT to communicate with outside network. The **ip nat pool** {*pool-name*} {*start-ip*} {*end-ip*} {**netmask** *netmask* | **prefix-length** *prefix-length*} global configuration command defines the pool of inside global addresses that can be dynamically allocated for dynamic NAT operation.

-   Dynamic NAT configuration on NAT:

```
NAT#conf t
Enter configuration commands, one per line.  End with CNTL/Z.
NAT(config)#no ip nat inside source static 172.16.1.2 200.1.1.2
NAT(config)#no ip nat inside source static 172.16.1.3 200.1.1.3
NAT(config)#
NAT(config)#access-list 1 permit 172.16.1.2
NAT(config)#access-list 1 permit 172.16.1.3
NAT(config)#ip nat pool pool01 200.1.1.1 200.1.1.2 netmask 255.255.255.252
NAT(config)#ip nat inside source list 1 pool pool01
NAT(config)#^Z
NAT#
NAT#sh ip nat translations
NAT#sh ip nat statistics
Total active translations: 0 (0 static, 0 dynamic; 0 extended)
Outside interfaces:
  Ethernet0/1
Inside interfaces:
  Ethernet0/0
Hits: 250  Misses: 0
Expired translations: 0
Dynamic mappings:
-- Inside Source
access-list 1 pool pool01 refcount 0
 pool pool01: netmask 255.255.255.252
        start 200.1.1.1 end 200.1.1.2
        type generic, total addresses 2, allocated 0 (0%), misses 0
NAT# [PC1 Telnet into ServerA]
00:15:33: NAT: s=172.16.1.2->200.1.1.1, d=200.1.1.200 [0]
00:15:33: NAT: s=200.1.1.200, d=200.1.1.1->172.16.1.2 [0]
00:15:33: NAT*: s=172.16.1.2->200.1.1.1, d=200.1.1.200 [1]
00:15:33: NAT*: s=172.16.1.2->200.1.1.1, d=200.1.1.200 [2]
NAT#
NAT#sh ip nat translations
Pro Inside global      Inside local       Outside local       Outside global
--- 200.1.1.1          172.16.1.2         ---                 ---
NAT#sh ip nat statistics
Total active translations: 1 (0 static, 1 dynamic; 0 extended)
Outside interfaces:
  Ethernet0/1
Inside interfaces:
  Ethernet0/0
Hits: 260  Misses: 1
Expired translations: 0
Dynamic mappings:
-- Inside Source
access-list 1 pool pool01 refcount 1
 pool pool01: netmask 255.255.255.252
        start 200.1.1.1 end 200.1.1.2
        type generic, total addresses 2, allocated 1 (50%), misses 0
NAT#
```

- The access list indicates whether a NAT router should translate the source IP address in a packet. Only packets with the source or destination addresses that are **permitted** (matched) in the access list will be translated. Packets with the source or destination addresses that are not matched by the access list will not be translated and the will be forwarded normally.

- With the **ip nat inside source list 1 pool pool01** command configured, packets that traverse from inside to outside with a source IP address matched by ACL 1 (172.16.1.2, 172.16.1.3) will be translated to the an inside global address in the NAT pool pool01 (200.1.1.1, 200.1.1.2).

- The entries in the NAT table will be removed after a period of inactivity (timeout). The **clear ip nat translation *** privileged command can be used to forcefully remove all dynamic NAT entries in the NAT table. The NAT table is stored in memory and is cleared upon router reboot. **Note:** Static NAT entries can only be removed with the **no** form of the static NAT commands in the global configuration mode.

PAT Configuration

- PAT configuration on NAT:

```
NAT#conf t
Enter configuration commands, one per line.  End with CNTL/Z.
NAT(config)#no ip nat pool pool01
%Pool pool01 in use, cannot destroy
NAT(config)#^Z
NAT#
NAT#clear ip nat translation *
NAT#conf t
NAT(config)#no ip nat pool pool01
NAT(config)#no ip nat inside source list 1 pool pool01
NAT(config)#
NAT(config)#ip nat inside source list 1 interface Ethernet0/1 overload
NAT(config)#^Z
NAT#
NAT# [PC1 and PC2 Telnet into ServerA]
NAT#
NAT#sh ip nat translations
Pro Inside global      Inside local       Outside local       Outside global
tcp 200.1.1.254:1055   172.16.1.2:1055    200.1.1.200:23      200.1.1.200:23
tcp 200.1.1.254:1060   172.16.1.3:1060    200.1.1.200:23      200.1.1.200:23
NAT#
NAT#sh ip nat statistics
Total active translations: 2 (0 static, 2 dynamic; 2 extended)
Outside interfaces:
  Ethernet0/1
Inside interfaces:
  Ethernet0/0
Hits: 285  Misses: 3
Expired translations: 0
Dynamic mappings:
-- Inside Source
access-list 1 interface Ethernet0/1 refcount 2
```

Alternative configuration:
NAT(config)#**ip nat pool pool02 200.1.1.254 200.1.1.254 netmask 255.255.255.252**
NAT(config)#**ip nat inside source list 1 pool pool02 overload**

Chapter 19
IP Access Control Lists

- Access control list (ACL) is an effective and important network security feature. With the ability to classify inbound and outbound packets going through the router or switch interfaces, Access lists are able to define rules that **allow** or **deny** certain type of packets flowing through a network. Ex: Employees in Department A, Building A are not allowed to access Server B in Building B; Everyone is denied the access to Server C except Department B.

- ACLs are categorized as **Standard** (simpler logic) and **Extended** (more complex logic) ACLs.

- ACLs can permit and deny packets based on L3 (IP address) and L4 (port number) information.

Standard IP Access Lists

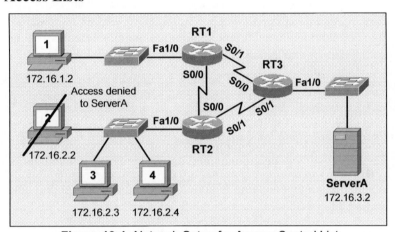

Figure 19-1: Network Setup for Access Control List

- Figure 19-1 shows a sample scenario that demonstrates the usage of ACLs – deny the access of PC2 to ServerA. It shows the packet flow for PC2 to access ServerA would typically go through a switch, RT2, RT3, another switch, and finally ServerA. In order to block the packets sent by PC2 to arrive at ServerA, the best place to apply ACL filtering logic would be on RT2 or RT3. Figure 19-2 shows the internal processing in RT3 when a packet enters it through S0/1 and exits through Fa1/0.

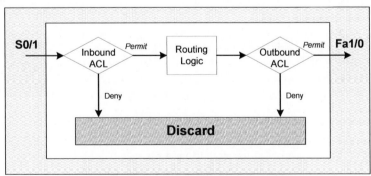

Figure 19-2: Internal Processing in RT3

- **Access Control List** (ACL) is the term used by Cisco for **packet filtering**.

- Below are some key features and terminology of Cisco IOS access lists:
  i)   Filter can be applied when packets **entering an interface** (before the routing decision).
  ii)   Filter can be applied when packets **leaving an interface** (after the routing decision).
  iii) **Permit** → Do not filter a packet (forward).
  iv)   **Deny** → Filter out a packet (discard).

- ACLs are being processed in **sequential order**. There is always an implicit **deny any** statement at the end of every access list. Packets which do not match any permit statement through out an access list will be filtered due to the implicit **deny any** rule. The implicit **deny any** rule can be overridden with an explicit **permit any** rule as the last entry in the ACL. An access list should always have at least one **permit** statement.

- There are 2 major operations upon an access list: **matching** and **action.**

Matching	Examines every packet and determines whether it matches a particular ACL statement.
Action	Performs an action (**forward** or **discard**) upon the packet when it matches a particular ACL statement.

- IP, TCP, UDP packets headers are examined in order to retrieve the IP addresses and port numbers information used in the matching operation.

- What Cisco IOS ACLs examine?

Standard ACLs	Only source IP address. Decisions are made based on source IP addresses. Do not differentiate the types of traffic, eg: WWW, Telnet.
Extended ACLs	Source and destination IP addresses, source and destination port numbers, and specific TCP/IP protocols, eg: ICMP, GRE, etc.

- Below describes the steps of how Cisco IOS processes a packet that enters or exits an interface with an inbound or outbound access list applied respectively:
  i)   The matching parameters of the first **access-list** statement are compared with the packet.
  ii)   If there is a match, the action defined in the particular **access-list** statement is performed (forward or discard). Processing ended for this packet.
  iii) If the matching parameters of a particular **access-list** statement are not matched, repeat Step 1 and Step 2 with the next statement in the access list until there is a match (top-down processing).
  iv)   If there is no match after processing all access list entries, drop the packet (due to the implicit **deny any** statement).

- Below lists the syntax of a **standard access list** statement:
  access-list {*access-list-number*} {**deny | permit**} {*source-addr*} [*source-wildcard*]

- The matching of access-list can be either an entire IP address or just part of an IP address. Refer back to Figure 19-1, ACLs can be defined to only deny the access of PC2 (match any packet with the source IP address of 172.16.2.2) or all PCs in PC2 subnet (match any packet with a source IP address that begins with 172.16.2.x).

- **Wildcard masks** are used in access lists to match a single host, a subnet, or a range of networks by specifying the portion of an IP address that should be examined by the ACL process. Its usage is identically in both standard and extended IP access lists.

- **Do not confuse wildcard masks with subnet masks!**
  0s indicate bits in the address that **must be exactly matched**.
  1s indicate bits in the address that **do not need to be matched**. Also known as **"don't care"** bits.

- Below lists 2 wildcard mask examples:
  0.0.0.0   00000000.00000000.00000000.00000000. The entire IP address must be matched.
  0.0.0.255 00000000.00000000.00000000.11111111. Just the first 24 bits must be matched.

- A wildcard mask can be calculated by **subtracting the subnet mask** from 255.255.255.255:
  i)   To match all hosts in a network with subnet mask of 255.255.240.0, the wildcard mask
         is 255.255.255.255 – 255.255.240.0 = **0.0.15.255**.
  ii)   To match all hosts in a network with subnet mask of 255.255.128.0, the wildcard mask
         is 255.255.255.255 – 255.255.128.0 = **0.0.127.255**.

Extended IP Access Lists

- Extended ACLs provide complex and powerful matching logic with the ability to examine many
  parts of a packet. A match of an extended access list entry requires that **all defined matching
  parameters are matched**. Action will be taken after the matching process.

- Below lists the syntax of an **extended access list** statement:
  access-list {*access-list-number*} {**deny** | **permit**} {*protocol*} [**host**] {*source-addr*}
  [*source-wildcard*] [*src-port*] [**host**] {*destination-addr*} [*destination-wildcard*] [*dst-port*]

- Extended ACL examples:

access-list Statement	What It Matches
access-list 101 deny ip any host 172.16.1.1	Any IP packet, any source IP address, with a destination of 172.16.1.1.
access-list 101 deny tcp any gt 1023 host 172.16.1.1 eq 23	TCP segments with any source address, source port greater than 1023, with a destination of 172.16.1.1 and destination port of 23.
access-list 101 deny tcp any host 172.16.1.1 eq 23	Same as previous example, but any source port can be matched as the source port parameter is removed.
access-list 101 deny udp 172.16.2.0 0.0.0.255 lt 1023 any	UDP segments with a source address in network 172.16.2.0, source port less than 1023, with any destination IP address.

- Below lists the Cisco IOS ACL operators used for matching TCP and UDP port numbers:

lt	Less than
gt	Greater than
eq	Equal to
neq	Not equal to
range	Range of port numbers

- Below lists some other usages of ACLs:
    i)   Permit or deny remove access (Telnet) to a device via the VTY lines. This is achieved by defining the host(s) that granted the access. Access by undefined hosts will be denied.
    ii)   Defining interesting traffic that triggers dialing to remote locations (dial-on-demand).
    iii) Categorizing or classifying packets for queuing (eg: which queue a packet should enter) or other QoS-type services.
    iv)   Route filtering when applied to routing protocols as **distribute lists**, which controls the networks that will or will not be advertised by the routing updates.

Named IP Access Lists

- Named ACLs work just like numbered standard and extended ACLs. There is no difference between items that can be matched with numbered ACLs and named ACLs. However, they made our life easier as human prefer to remember names than numbers. Besides that, lines or entries in a named IP access list **can be deleted (and added) individually**; whereas the whole list of a numbered access list will be **removed** when the **no access-list** {*acl-num*} command is issued.

- It can take large amount of time and effort in creating, troubleshooting, and updating ACLs in real environments. Below shows some guidelines and considerations when implementing ACLs:
    i)   Only one ACL per direction, per (routed) protocol, per interface; which means only one inbound ACL and one outbound ACL per routed protocol can be applied on an interface.
    ii)   A newly added entry will be placed at the bottom of the access list. A **text-editor** is highly recommended for creating and editing ACLs.
    iii) Create or modify ACLs with a text editor. **Copy and paste** the configuration to the router upon creation or modification.
    iv)   Place IP standard ACLs as close to the destination as possible. Because standard ACLs can prevent the source from accessing other allowed services in the network when they are placed close to the source.
    v)   Place IP extended ACLs as close to the source as possible to ensure that the matched packets are discarded as soon as possible in order to **filter unwanted traffic** and **preserve network bandwidth**.
    vi)   ACLs are only able to filter traffic that **passes through** a router. They cannot filter traffic that **originates from** a router – an outbound access list applied upon a router interface would not stop the communication (eg: Telnet, SSH) with the router.
    vii) Inbound access lists are more effective than outbound access lists, as they can minimize the overhead of routing table lookups.
    viii) Disable an ACL from its associated interface with the **no ip access-group** {*acl-num*} interface subcommand before making changes to it. This is to avoid packets from being filtered temporarily when adding ACL statements into an active ACL on an interface. **Note:** If an empty access list is applied to an interface, all traffic through it is permitted.
    ix)   Organize the ACLs to place the **more specific** statements / entries / tests **early** in an ACL. **Ex1:** 1st statement permits all packets from 10.1.1.1, 2nd statement denies all packets from 10.1.1.0/24 subnet. The 1st permit statement tends to be more specific than the more general deny statement and hence should be place earlier in the ACL. **Ex2:** 1st statement denies all packets from 172.16.0.0/16 subnet, 2nd statement permits all packets from 172.16.10.10. The 2nd permit statement tends to be more specific than the more general deny statement and hence should be placed earlier in the ACL.
    x)   An undefined ACL equals to **permit any**. Applying an ACL to an interface before defining the access list entries is dangerous, because the result goes from **permit any** to a **deny most** (due to the implicit **deny any**) as soon as the first ACL entry is entered! Always define the access list before applying it to an interface!

Chapter 20
IP Access Control Lists Lab

- Remember that access lists use excessive router processing resources. Hence always implement access lists as short as possible, as effective as possible, and as efficient as possible.

Standard IP Access Lists Configuration

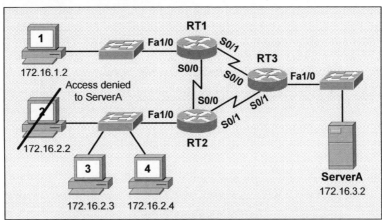

Figure 20-1: Network Setup for Access Control List

- Standard IP ACLs filter packets by examining **only the source IP address** in a packet. Standard ACLs are created with the access-list number 1-99 or 1300-1999 (expanded range), inclusively. There is no difference between a number to another.

- IP ACLs configuration commands:

Command	Description
access-list {*access-list-num*} {**deny** | **permit**} [**host**] {*source-addr*} [*source-wildcard*]	Global configuration command used to add an entry into a standard access list.
access-list {*access-list-num*} **remark** {*text*}	Global configuration command used to add a comment for an access list.
ip access-group {*access-list-num*} {**in** | **out**}	Interface subcommand used to apply an access list on an interface.
access-class {*access-list-num*} {**in** | **out**}	Line subcommand used to apply an access list on VTY remote access lines.
no access-list {*access-list-num*}	Global configuration command used to remove an access list entirely.

- **TO-DO:** Implement standard ACLs to deny the access of PC2 to ServerA.

- Standard ACLs should be placed **as near to the destination as possible**, as standard ACLs often discard packets that are allowed to forward (or pass) when they are placed close to the source. Ex: If an inbound ACL is placed on RT2's Fa1/0, PC2 will never go further than RT2! Hence the best place to deploy the ACL is on RT3's Fa1/0 with an **outbound** standard ACL.

- Another reason is security loopholes might exist when a link between routers fails – packets that pass through another new path might no longer be passing through the ACL-secured interface.

- Standard IP Access Lists configuration on RT3:

```
RT3(config)#access-list 10 remark *** Deny PC2 – ServerA ***
RT3(config)#access-list 10 deny 172.16.2.2
RT3(config)#access-list 10 permit any
RT3(config)#int fa1/0
RT3(config-if)#ip access-group 10 out
RT3(config-if)#^Z
RT3#
```

- The following 2 standard access list statements are identical:
  access-list 10 permit any
  access-list 10 permit 0.0.0.0 255.255.255.255

- The **log** parameter can be specified at the end of an access list to sends a message to the console (and logging facilities) every time the access list is matched.

- **Note:** Whenever there is a **deny** statement in an ACL, remember to create an explicit **permit** statement to allow valid traffic to pass through (all ACLs have an implicit **deny** statement).

Extended IP Access Lists Configuration

- An extended access list statement can be used to examine **multiple portions** of a packet header, and all parameters must be matched in order to match a particular packet to the ACL statement. This feature makes extended ACLs much more complex and powerful than standard ACLs.

- Extended ACLs are created with the access-list number 100-199 or 2000-2699 (expanded range), inclusively.

- **TO-DO:** Implement extended ACLs to achieve the following security policies:
  i)   Deny PC2 access to ServerA's web server.
  ii)   Deny PC1 access to hosts on RT2 Ethernet.
  iii) Allow PC3, a NMS, access to ServerA's SNMP service.
  iv)   All other combinations are allowed.

- Extended IP Access Lists configuration on RT2:

```
RT2(config)#access-list 110 deny tcp host 172.16.2.2 host 172.16.3.2 eq www
RT2(config)#access-list 110 deny ip 172.16.2.0 0.0.0.255 host 172.16.1.2
RT2(config)#access-list 110 permit udp host 172.16.2.3 host 172.16.3.2 eq snmp
RT2(config)#access-list 110 permit ip any any
RT2(config)#int fa1/0
RT2(config-if)#ip access-group 110 in
```

- Extended ACLs should be placed **as close to the source as possible** to ensure that the matched packets are discarded as soon as possible to **preserve network bandwidth**.

- The second line of configuration which denying packets flow from RT2 Ethernet subnet to PC1 effectively stops the communication between them, which is how the 2nd requirement is met. Else the extended ACL will be placed at RT1 Fa1/0 (as close to the source as possible).

- The **show ip interface** [*intf-type intf-num*] EXEC command displays the **placement** and **direction** of the ACLs applied on a router or a particular interface.

```
RT2#sh ip interface fa1/0
FastEthernet1/0 is up, line protocol is up
  Internet address is 172.16.2.1/24
  Broadcast address is 255.255.255.255
  Address determined by setup command
  MTU is 1500 bytes
  Helper address is not set
  Directed broadcast forwarding is disabled
  Outgoing access list is not set
  Inbound access list is 110
  Proxy ARP is enabled
  Local Proxy ARP is disabled
  Security level is default
  Split horizon is enabled
  ICMP redirects are always sent
  ICMP unreachables are always sent
  ICMP mask replies are never sent
  IP fast switching is enabled
  IP fast switching on the same interface is disabled
  IP Flow switching is disabled
  IP CEF switching is disabled
  IP Feature Fast switching turbo vector
  IP multicast fast switching is enabled
  IP multicast distributed fast switching is disabled
--- output omitted ---
```

- The **show access-lists** [*acl-num*] EXEC command displays all ACLs with their configured parameters. However, it does not show the association between access lists and interfaces.

Named IP Access Lists Configuration

- Benefits of using named ACLs instead of numbered ACLs:
  i)   Human have better chance to remember names than numbers.
  ii)   **Deleting individual lines** in an access list is possible with the **no** {*acl*} negate statement.

- Named ACLs use a global configuration command to enter into ACL configuration mode, which is the mode for configuring named ACLs statements.

- Named IP Access Lists configuration on RT2:

```
RT2#conf t
Enter configuration commands, one per line.  End with CNTL/Z.
RT2(config)#ip access-list extended example01
RT2(config-ext-nacl)#deny tcp host 172.16.2.2 host 172.16.3.2 eq www
RT2(config-ext-nacl)#deny ip 172.16.2.0 0.0.0.255 host 172.16.3.2
RT2(config-ext-nacl)#permit udp host 172.16.2.3 host 172.16.3.2 eq snmp
RT2(config-ext-nacl)#permit ip any any
RT2(config-ext-nacl)#int fa1/0
RT2(config-if)#ip access-group example01 in
RT2(config-if)#^Z
RT2#
```

```
RT2#sh access-lists example01
Extended IP access list example01
    10 deny tcp host 172.16.2.2 host 172.16.3.2 eq www
    20 deny ip 172.16.2.0 0.0.0.255 host 172.16.3.2
    30 permit udp host 172.16.2.3 host 172.16.3.2 eq snmp
    40 permit ip any any
RT2#
RT2#conf t
Enter configuration commands, one per line.  End with CNTL/Z.
RT2(config)#ip access-list extended example01
RT2(config-ext-nacl)#no permit udp host 172.16.2.3 host 172.16.3.2 eq snmp
RT2(config-ext-nacl)#^Z
RT2#sh access-lists example01
Extended IP access list example01
    10 deny tcp host 172.16.2.2 host 172.16.3.2 eq www
    20 deny ip 172.16.2.0 0.0.0.255 host 172.16.3.2
    40 permit ip any any
RT2#
```

Restricting VTY (Telnet) Access

-   Controlling Telnet access to a large router with hundreds of interfaces by applying inbound extended IP ACLs that limit the Telnet traffic on each interface is **inefficient** and **impractical**! This approach also affects router performance and introduces more data transmission delay as a router would examine every packet that is entering and leaving an interface with ACLs applied. The common solution is apply a standard IP access list to the VTY lines, where only Telnet packets destined to the router will be examined.

-   Steps for creating standard ACLs to restrict Telnet access:
    i)   Create a standard IP access list that permits only the host or hosts in a particular subnet that are granted for Telnet access. Due to the implicit **deny any** at the end of the list, it will deny the access for other hosts that are not specified within the permit lists.
    ii)   Apply the access list to the VTY lines with the **access-class** {*acl-num*} {**in** | **out**} line subcommand. The **in** keyword controlling incoming remote access connections; while the **out** keyword controlling outgoing remote access connections to other devices.

-   In the sample configuration below, only the host 192.168.0.2 and hosts in the 192.168.1.0/24 subnet will be granted for Telnet access to the router.

```
Router(config)#access-list 10 permit 192.168.0.2
Router(config)#access-list 10 permit 192.168.1.0 0.0.0.255
Router(config)#line vty 0 4
Router(config-line)#access-class 10 in
```

MISC Access Lists Configuration Notes

-   Cisco IOS will convert {*ip-addr*} **0.0.0.0** into **host** {*ip-addr*};
    and **0.0.0.0 255.255.255.255** into the **any** keyword.

-   The **host** keyword or the 0.0.0.0 wildcard mask is **mandatory** when defining a single host in extended ACLs; but it is **optional** when defining a single host in standard ACLs configuration.

Chapter 21
WAN Basics, Remote Access Technologies, and Serial PPP

- Organizations often extend their LANs to WANs, **Wide Area Networks** for connections to remote sites. WANs allow the information **exchange**, **communication** and **collaboration** between customers, suppliers, and among employees effectively.

- Cisco supports many types of WAN protocols. CCNA covers Serial PPP (leased lines), ISDN, and Frame Relay.

- Below lists some common WAN terminologies:
  i) **Customer Premises Equipment** (CPE) is the equipment that is owned by the service subscriber and is located at the subscriber's premise, eg: router.
  ii) **Demarcation Point** is the spot where the responsibility of the service provider ends and the CPE begins. The demarc is not a device or cable – it is a concept of where each party responsibility starts and ends. When someone reported a WAN problem to the Telco and the Telco replied that they have performed tests and are fine up to the demarc, the problem must be caused by the CPE and is not the responsibility of the Telco.
  iii) **Local Loop** is the connection from the demarc to the Telco switch in the closest service provider switching office – the local CO (central office).
  iv) **Toll network** is a collection of trunk links inside a service provider's network.

- Below lists the common WAN connection types in the order of costing (from higher to lower):

Leased Lines	Also referred to as **PPP** or **dedicated** connections. They are **pre-established** connections which allow communication at any time (hence a circuit does not need to be established before data transmission). Their **cost is very high**. HDLC and PPP encapsulation protocols are frequently used on them. They provide **high bandwidth** and **constant data rate** for data transfer.
Packet Switching	This WAN service allows the **sharing of bandwidth** with other companies to save money. It only works well for data transfer in **bursty** nature; hence leased lines would be the better choice if constant data transfer is required. Ex: X.25, Frame Relay, and ATM.
Circuit Switching	Circuit switching operates much like a **normal telephone call**. The advantage of this WAN service is **low cost**, where subscribers only pay for the duration of the usage. A **dedicated** circuit is **established**, **maintained**, and **terminated** for each communication session (hence a circuit needs to be established before data communication). In circuit-switched networks, the resources along the path are **reserved** for the duration of the communication session. It normally provides **low bandwidth** for data transfer. Ex: Modem dial-ups and ISDN.

- **Data Terminal Equipment** (DTE) and **Data Communications Equipment** (DCE): DTEs are mostly router interfaces that connect to DCEs, eg: **Channel Service Unit / Data Service Unit** (CSU/DSU), which are connects into the demarcation point (the start of the Telco responsibility). CSUs/DSUs provide **signal timing** (clocking) for communication between DTEs and DCE devices (Telco switch). CSUs/DSUs reside in the physical layer of the OSI model.

- A WAN network normally consists of 2 DTE networks connect through a DCE network. The DCE network includes the CSU/DSU at both ends, the Telco wiring, and Telco switches. DCE devices provide clocking to DTE interfaces, eg: router serial interfaces.

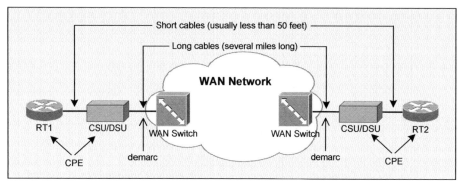

Figure 21-1: Basic WAN Components and Terminology

- The demarc points are **not always fixed**. In some cases, the CSU/DSU might owned by the Telco. In some other cases, the Telco even owns and manages the routers at customer sites.

- Cisco routers mostly manufactured with an *internal* CSU/DSU, hence eliminates the connection to an external CSU/DSU.

- **Clock rate** is important when defining the **speed** of a circuit or link. Both CSU/DSU and router need to be configured to operate and communicate at an agreed **same speed**. CSUs/DSUs provide clocking signal to routers for them to react, send and receive data at the correct rate. Hence the CSU/DSU is considered **clocking** the synchronous link.

- **DCE** – Data Communication Equipment. Device that provides clocking. Typically a CSU/DSU. **DTE** – Data Terminal Equipment. Device that receives clocking. Typically a router located at subscriber premise.

- DCE cables are very useful for **home labs**. 2 routers, a DTE cable and a DCE cable (used to form a back-to-back serial connection) is sufficient to simulate a point-to-point WAN link connection without the purchase of CSU/DSU.

- DCE cables swap the transmission and reception circuits on the DTE cables.

- A **back-to-back serial cable** incorporates both DCE and DTE ends.

- Cisco offers a variety of WAN interface cards (WICs), eg: synchronous and asynchronous serial WICs, ISDN BRI WICs, DSL WICs, and Analog Modem WICs.

- Below list the speeds or bit rates of common WAN link types:

Line Type	Name of Signaling Type	Speed / Bit Rate
64	DS0	64kbps
T1	DS1	1.544Mbps (24 DS0s + 8kbps management overhead)
T3	DS3	44.736Mbps (28 T1s + management overhead)
E1	ZM	2.048Mbps (32 DS0s)
E3	M3	34.368Mbps (16 E1s + management overhead)
J1	Y1	2.048Mbps (32 DS0s. Japan standard.)

* DSx = Digital Signal level *x*
* kbps = kilo bits per second
* T1 and T3 = US standards. E1 and E3 = Europe standards.
* T3 = 28 T1s. E3 = 16 E1s.

ATM, SONET, and SDH

- **Asynchronous Transfer Mode** (ATM) and **Synchronous Optical Network** (SONET) work in conjunction to provide high-speed voice and data services. SONET provides L1 functions – defines how to transmit high-speed data over optical links, while ATM provides L2 functions over SONET – framing, addressing, and error detection.

- **Synchronous Digital Hierarchy** (SDH) represents the same standards as SONET outside US.

- Below list the speeds and bit rates for all SONET and SDH link types:

SONET Optical Carrier Level	SONET STS Level	SDH STM Level	Speed / Bit Rate
OC-1	STS-1	STM-0	52Mbps
OC-3	STS-3	STM-1	155Mbps
OC-12	STS-12	STM-4	622Mbps
OC-24	STS-24	STM-8	1.2Gbps
OC-48	STS-48	STM-16	2.4Gbps
OC-96	STS-96	STM-32	5Gbps
OC-192	STS-192	STM-64	10Gbps
OC-768	STS-768	STM-256	40Gbps

Synchronous Transport Signal (STS) and **Synchronous Transport Module** (STM) are referred to as the frame format for SONET and SDH respectively.

- ATM does not forward frames, it forwards **cells**. IP packets and Ethernet frames can vary in size, but ATM cells are **fixed** 53-byte in length – 5 bytes header and 48 bytes payload. The ATM header contains 2 fields – **Virtual Path Identifier** (VPI) and **Virtual Channel Identifier** (VCI) that function like Frame Relay DLCI for identifying virtual circuits. ATM switches forward ATM cells based on the VPI/VCI pair.

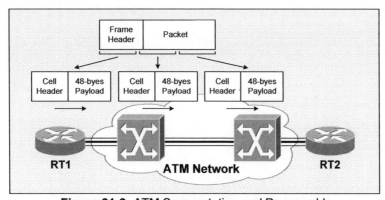

Figure 21-2: ATM Segmentation and Reassembly

- The **Segmentation and Reassembly** (SAR) of Ethernet frames and ATM cells are performed by the routers that are connected to the ATM network.

- ATM has similar functions to Frame Relay, and hence is also being considered as a type of packet-switching service. However, it is more often referred to as a **cell-switching** service.

- Frame Relay, ATM, and MPLS are **connection-oriented** packet-switched networks; while SONET/SDH is a connection-oriented circuit-switched network. They are considered connection-oriented as virtual channels or virtual circuits must be established across the network prior to data transmission. **Note:** Refer to Page 238 for explanation of connectionless networks.

Remote Access Technologies

- Remote access technologies are normally **lower cost home-based** Internet access if compared to corporate Internet access (eg: leased lines, Frame Relay, ATM). Most remote access technologies use the PSTN for basic physical access, eg: modems, ISDN, and DSL.

- **Public Switched Telephone Network** (PSTN) was built to support **telephones** voice traffic. Microphones were being used to convert sound waves into **analog electrical signals**, and being transported over the PSTN network to the speaker of the telephone at the other end. A **circuit** must be established prior to communication.

- The core of the PSTN has evolved to use **digital signals** instead of analog signals, which results in **higher bandwidth** and **lower calling cost**. Analog-to-digital (A/D) conversion is normally performed by voice switches located at the Telco's **Central Offices** (COs).

- **Codec** (Encoder + Decoder) is an A/D converter (ADC) that is being used for processing voices.

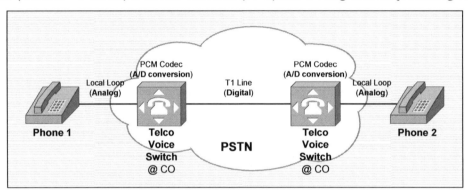

Figure 21-3: Analog Voice Calls over a Digital PSTN

- The original standard for the conversion of analog voice signals to digital signals is **Pulse-Code Modulation** (PCM), which defines that an analog voice signal should be sampled 8000 times per second by an A/D converter. **Sampling rate** is the rate at which the samples of a specific waveform amplitude are collected within a specific period of time (eg: one second).

- The PCM standard defines the use of 256 different binary values per sample (to represent different combination of **amplitude**, **frequency**, and **phase**). 256 values = 8 bits. 1 second = 8 x 8000 = 64kbps. This is the **basic transmission speed** that represents the necessary bandwidth for a single PCM-encoded voice call. Due of this specification, the first digital PSTN was built on a speed of 64kbps, and a single 64kbps channel was denoted as the **Digital Signal Level 0** (DS0).

Analog Modems

- They allow 2 computers to communicate with digital signals, but **without any physical changes** on the local loops and Telco's Cos (transmit analog signals). A modem converts or encodes the digital signals from a computer to analog signals, and sends the analog signals to the PSTN. Another modem at the other end decodes the analog signals received from the PSTN back to digital signals, and sends the digital signals to the computer at the other end.

- Modems are used in analog lines while CSUs/DSUs are used in digital lines.

- **Modem** → Modulation + Demodulation.
  Modulation is the process of encoding a set of binary digits into an analog electrical signal.
  Demodulation is the process of decoding an analog electrical signal into a set of binary digits.

- During the establishment of a modem dial-up circuit, a modem signals the tones associated with the telephone keypad. These tones, which are generated by phones as well, are interpreted as **dual-tone multi-frequency** (DTMF) tones by a CO switch. Once the circuit is established by the Telco, the modems at both ends **must agree** the modem standard to use for communication. There are many modem standards and most modems **support several standards**. Modems are able to probe, negotiate, and use the best standard that is supported by the modems at both ends.

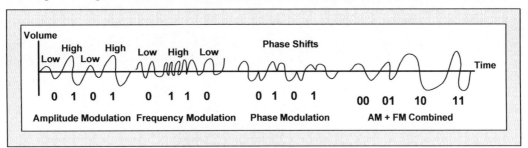

Figure 21-4: Modulation Schemes

- Modulation scheme with combination of AM and FM:

Amplitude	Frequency	Binary Code
Low	Low	00
Low	High	01
High	Low	10
High	High	11

- **Amplitude modulation** (AM) represents info by varying the **amplitude** of the carrier signal.
  Frequency modulation (FM) represents info by varying the **frequency** of the carrier signal.

- **Baud** is a measure of the number of symbol changes or signaling events per second. A **baud** is a single encoded analog energy that can represent **1 or more bits**. To archive higher bit rates, modems use certain **modulation techniques** to encode more than 1 bit in the analog signal. With the **AM + FM combined** modulation scheme in Figure 21-4, a modem which is running at 14000 baud per second can transmit data at 28000bps.

- Most computers use PPP as the data link (L2) protocol over the L1 service provided by modems. PPP is the good choice as modems traffic is transmitted **asynchronously**, while PPP support both synchronous and asynchronous communications.

- Other reasons why PPP is being used in modem communications are:
  i)   PPP provides the capability to **dynamically assign an IP address** for a device connected to the other end of a PPP link.
  ii) PPP supports **authentication** (via PAP and CHAP), which is commonly being used to authenticate dial-in users for the access to the ISP network.

- V.92 is the current modem specification defined by **International Telecommunications Union** (ITU). It transmits at 56kbps (downstream) and 33kbps (upstream), which is same as V.90 but offers a reduced handshake time (faster connection setup), increased compression throughput, and the on-hold feature.

Digital Subscriber Lines (DSL)

- DSL just defines how to transmit data between a customer site and the local CO. Data do not flow through DS0 channels inside the PSTN, but through some ISP IP networks. It does not need to be compatible with the core of PSTN and hence is able to provide higher transmission rates. The speed does not degrade when more users are added to the network.

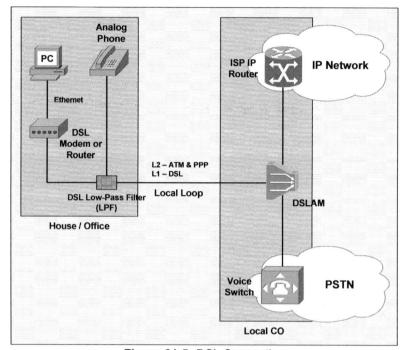

Figure 21-5: DSL Connection

- The local loop connects to the **DSL Access Multiplexer** (DSLAM) at the local CO, which is responsible for **splitting** the data and voice signals from the local loop.

- DSL allows **concurrent** data transmission and voice call, as it doesn't use the voice frequencies. Phones generate analog signals at 0–4000Hz, while DSL modems generate analog signals higher than 4000Hz – the interference is minimal. **Filters** are often being used to prevent interference.

- DSL is considered an **always-on** Internet connection service. It does not require a circuit to be setup before data transmission as with modems and ISDN.

- Its downstream speeds range from 1.5–8Mbps, while upstream speeds range from 64–800kbps.

- The ADSL maximum supported distance to home is 18000 feet (or ~5500 meters).

- Other DSL standards or variants include **HDSL** (High bit rate DSL), **IDSL** (ISDN DSL), **MSDSL** (Multi-rate Symmetric DSL), **PDSL** (Powerline DSL), **RADSL** (Rate-Adaptive DSL), **SDSL** (Symmetric DSL), **SHDSL** (Single-Pair High-Speed DSL), **UDSL** (Uni-DSL), and **VDSL** (Very High Speed DSL). **Annex A** is referred to as ADSL over PSTN (UK) while **Annex B** is referred to as ADSL over ISDN (Germany).

- DSL routers usually include the DSL modem features, and other networking features, eg: IP routing (allows Internet connection for multiple PCs), DHCP server, NAT, and port forwarding.

- DSL is a L1 service. It uses ATM as the L2 protocol for the communication between the DSL modem (or router) and the ISP router. DSL uses **PPP over ATM** (PPPoA) protocol to encapsulate PPP frames in the ATM AAL5 (ATM Adaptation Layer 5) cells. DSL transmit ATM cells over DSL, instead of SONET. ATM cells are received and processed by the ISP router. PPP and ATM are both L2 protocols, but they provide different functions in DSL connections. PPP provides features such as address assignment, authentication, encryption, and compression.

- A DSL modem (or router) uses **PPP over Ethernet** (PPPoE) when performing bridging function for a PC and a DSLAM when the PC connects to the DSL network using a PPPoE client. The WAN IP address is dynamically assigned to the PC instead of the DSL router.

Cable Modems

- This remote access technology does not use a phone line for physical connectivity. It transmits computer data in digital signals over cable TV coaxial cabling (analog). A splitter called **f-connector**, is being used to split data received from drop cable to multiple cable TVs and the cable modem in a subscriber house.

- **Cable Modem Termination System** (CMTS) is deployed at various concentration points or hubs in the cable network to provide high-speed Internet access, voice, and other networking services to home and business subscribers. The Cisco uBR (Universal Broadband Router) CMTS Series is designed for deployments at MTUs (multi-tenant units), eg: apartments and hotels.

- The speed **degrades** as more subscribers are added to the network, as the bandwidth is shared among subscribers.

- **Downstream** data referred to as the data going toward the home.
Upstream data referred to as the data going outward the home.

- Cable networks broadcast downstream traffic (logical bus networks). Security is a main concern.

- CATV (Community Antenna Television) standards use **Multimedia Cable Network System** (MCNS) as the data link protocol for arbitration, addressing, and error detection.

- As the cables could be very long, the CSMA/CD algorithm used in Ethernet is **not effective** to detect collisions in cable networks. MCNS defines some multiplexing methods – **Time-Division Multi Access** (TDMA), where home users are allocated time slots per second to send upstream data, and **Frequency-Division Multiplexing** (FDM) to receive downstream data. FDM is a form of signal multiplexing where multiple baseband signals are modulated at different frequency and bundled as a composite signal that could be transmit over a single physical circuit. FDM was normally used in traditional analog telephone networks. Modern telephone networks that employ digital transmission use **Time-Division Multiplexing** (TDM) instead of FDM.

- **Multiplexing** is the process of converting multiple logical signals into a single physical signal for transmission across a physical channel.

- MCNS defines the following encoding schemes (**QAM** = Quadrature Amplitude Modulation):
  i)   QAM-64 → 6 bits per baud.
  ii)   QAM-256 → 8 bits per baud.

- **MISC Notes:** Analog modems and DSL support both symmetric and asymmetric speeds; while ISDN, Frame Relay, and cable modems can only run across synchronous links or circuits.

Point-to-Point Serial Links (Leased Lines)

- The 2 most popular data link (L2) protocols that are being used over point-to-point serial links:

HDLC	**High-Level Data Link Control**. It was derived from Synchronous Data Link Control (SDLC) created by IBM. The HDLC specification **was not intended** to encapsulate (or support) multiple network layer protocols across the same link. It **does not** include a Protocol Type field and hence unable to identify the encapsulated network layer packets. Vendors that support HDLC **must define** their own **proprietary** HDLC headers that contain the Protocol Type field to identify the network layer protocols. Due to this reason, HDLC implementations are proprietary – Cisco routers **will not work** in connections to other vendor routers. It is the **default encapsulation type** used on Cisco synchronous serial interfaces. HDLC does not support error recovery.
PPP	**Point-to-Point Protocol**. It is an industry-standard protocol that provides an **open standard** for creating point-to-point links **between different vendor equipments**. It uses a **standardized** Protocol Type field – Network Control Protocol (NCP) field in the header to identify the encapsulated network layer packets. It supports authentication, multilink connections, and can operates over synchronous and asynchronous links. PPP uses HDLC to encapsulate and transmit packets over point-to-point links. PPP supports error recovery but is disabled by default.

Note: HDLC was developed by the International Organization for Standardization (ISO).

- HDLC does not need the arbitration feature as in Ethernet. Because on point-to-point serial links, routers can send over the 4 wires (2 twisted-pair wires) circuit at any time, and the signal (eventually data) will arrived at the other end of the link.

- Both HDLC and PPP frames include an **address field**, but it is **not being used** and **not really needed** over point-to-point links.

- Do not confuse error detection with error recovery! Almost all data link layer protocols including HDLC and PPP perform **error detection** with the FCS field in their trailers. Frames that fail the FCS check will be noticed and discarded (error detection). Error recovery is normally being performed by higher-layer protocols, eg: TCP.

Point-to-Point Protocol (PPP)

- When PPP was being developed, it includes **many additional features** that never been seen in other WAN data link protocols up to that time.

- The PPP specification includes the following 2 subprotocols or sublayers:
  - i) **Link Control Protocol** (LCP). Responsible for establishing, configuring, testing, maintaining, and terminating PPP connections. PPP was designed to work with several network layer protocols, hence each PPP link has a LCP and a NCP for the corresponding L3 protocol encapsulated and transmitted over the PPP link.
  - ii) **Network Control Protocols** (NCPs). Responsible for encapsulating network layer protocols and assigning network layer addresses to the remote end over PPP links after the link establishment and authentication phases. The negotiated network layer protocols can then be transmitted across the PPP connection.
    Ex: IP Control Protocol (IPCP) for IP, IPX Control Protocol (IPXCP) for IPX, and AppleTalk Control Protocol (ATCP) for AppleTalk. A router configured for PPP encapsulation will try to identify the network layer protocol and use the appropriate network control protocol for the corresponding L3 protocol transmitted over the PPP link.

- PPP establishes a connection in 3 phases – link establishment (LCP negotiation), authentication (optional), and network layer protocol negotiation (NCP negotiation). Both ends must agree on the same parameters to establish a link, and authenticate each other using the authentication protocol and option negotiated during the LCP negotiation. Authentication must be success prior to NCP negotiation.

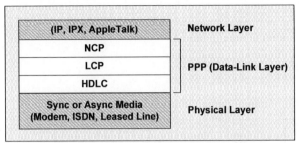

Figure 21-6: Point-to-Point Protocol Stack

- PPP also uses LCP to negotiate the following functions or features:

Function	LCP Feature	Description
Error Detection	Link Quality Monitoring (LQM)	Monitors link quality. PPP LCP at the receiving end sends messages that describe the number of correctly received packets and bytes to the other end. The sending end calculates the percent of loss. A link can be terminated after a configured error rate is exceeded.
Looped Link Detection	Magic number	Endpoints send PPP LCP messages that include a magic number, which is **different** for each endpoint. A looped link is detected when an endpoint receives an LCP message with its own magic number instead of the magic number of the other peer. PPP can be configured to terminate detected looped links.
Multilink	Multilink PPP	Allows connections of multiple parallel channels between 2 routers, and perform **load balancing** across the multiple links. Commonly used in ISDN links.
Authentication	Password Authentication Protocol (PAP) and Challenge Handshake Authen. Protocol (CHAP)	PPP initiates an authentication process to verify the identity of the device on the other end of the serial link. Normally used in dial-up links (eg: modems, ISDN, and DSL).
Callback	PPP Callback	The calling router (**client**) first contacts the remote router (**server**) and authenticates itself. After the authentication process, the remote router terminates the connection and then reinitiates a connection to the calling router. Normally used to minimize the long distance dialing cost on the client side.
Compression	Stacker and Predictor	Compresses data at source and reproduces data at destination. Predictor uses more memory than Stacker; while Stacker is more CPU intensive than Predictor.

- Comparisons between synchronous and asynchronous links:

Synchronous Links	Asynchronous Links
Have identical frequencies. Each individual character is encapsulated in control bits – the Start / Stop bits, which designate the beginning and ending of each character.	Send digital signals without timing. They agree on the same speed, but there is no checking or adjustment of the rates if they are slightly different.
Send frame continuously. Send idle frames called **Receiver Ready** when there is no data transmission over the link. The purpose is to maintain the **clock synchronization**.	No bits are sent during idle times. Only 1 byte is sent per transfer.
Allow more throughputs (due to clock synchronization).	Require less expensive hardware (because do not require clock synchronization).
Normally used for links between routers.	Normally used for dial-up links (modems).

Isochronous transmission allows asynchronous data transfer over a synchronous link. However, it requires constant bit rate for reliable transport.

- Below list some other common WAN data link protocols:

Protocol	Error Recovery?	Protocol Type Field?	Other Attributes
Synchronous Data Link Control (**SDLC**)	Yes	No	Developed by IBM. Supports multipoint links. It assumes an IBM SNA header after the SDLC header. Replaced by HDLC.
High-level Data Link Control (**HDLC**)	No	No [1]	Developed by IBM. Default on Cisco synchronous serial links.
Qualified Logical Link Control (**QLLC**)			Developed by IBM to transport SNA traffic over X.25 networks.
Link Access Procedure, Balanced (**LAPB**)	Yes	No [1]	Mainly used in X.25 networks. LAPB operates similar to HDLC, but is restricted to be used only in point-to-point links.
Link Access Procedure – D Channel (**LAPD**)	No	No	Mainly used on ISDN D channels for signaling in establishing and terminating ISDN circuits. Evolved from LAPB.
Link Access Procedure for Frame-Mode Bearer Services (**LAPF**)	No	Yes	Mainly used over Frame Relay links (between a DCE and a DTE). Similar to LAPD.
Point-to-Point Protocol (**PPP**)	Yes but disabled by default	Yes	Designed for multiprotocol interoperability.

[1] Cisco's implementation of LAPB and HDLC includes a proprietary Protocol Type field.

- PPP and ATM can operate on synchronous and asynchronous links; while HDLC and Frame Relay can only operate on synchronous links.

- PPP, HDLC, and LAPB are the data link layer protocols (or encapsulations) that can be used on ISDN B channels. PPP uses HDLC to encapsulate and transmit packets over point-to-point links.

Chapter 22
Serial PPP Connections Lab

PPP Encapsulation Configuration

- In a point-to-point link with 2 serial interfaces (eg: leased line), A DCE supplies clocking for both serial interfaces. The **clock rate** {*num*} interface subcommand sets the clock rate (in bps) on the interface that connects to a DCE cable.

- Ensure that the same WAN data link protocol (eg: HDLC or PPP) is configured on both ends of a point-to-point link. Otherwise the routers will misinterpret the incoming frames due to different frame formats of different WAN data link protocols.

- The **encapsulation** {*encap-type*} interface subcommand sets the encapsulation type on serial interfaces.

- Serial interfaces do not support Ethernet and Token Ring encapsulations.

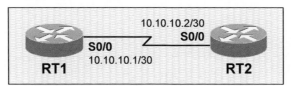

Figure 22-1: Network Setup for Serial PPP

- PPP Encapsulation configuration on RT1:

```
RT1#sh int s0/0
Serial0/0 is administratively down, line protocol is down
  Hardware is M4T
  MTU 1500 bytes, BW 1544 Kbit, DLY 20000 usec,
     reliability 255/255, txload 1/255, rxload 1/255
  Encapsulation HDLC, crc 16, loopback not set
  Keepalive set (10 sec)
--- output omitted ---
RT1#
RT1#conf t
Enter configuration commands, one per line.  End with CNTL/Z.
RT1(config)#int s0/0
RT1(config-if)#encapsulation ppp
RT1(config-if)#clock rate 56000
RT1(config-if)#ip add 10.10.10.1 255.255.255.252
RT1(config-if)#no shut
RT1(config-if)#^Z
RT1#
```

- The subnet mask 255.255.255.252 (/30) provides 4 IP addresses – 1 network address, 2 host addresses, and 1 broadcast address.

- PPP Encapsulation configuration on RT2:

```
RT2#conf t
Enter configuration commands, one per line.  End with CNTL/Z.
RT2(config)#int s0/0
RT2(config-if)#encapsulation ppp
RT2(config-if)#ip add 10.10.10.2 255.255.255.252
RT2(config-if)#no shut
RT2(config-if)#^Z
RT2#
00:10:10: %LINK-3-UPDOWN: Interface Serial0/0, changed state to up
00:10:13: %LINEPROTO-5-UPDOWN: Line protocol on Interface Serial0/0, changed
state to up
RT2#ping 10.10.10.1

Type escape sequence to abort.
Sending 5, 100-byte ICMP Echos to 10.10.10.1, timeout is 2 seconds:
!!!!!
Success rate is 100 percent (5/5), round-trip min/avg/max = 36/37/40 ms
RT2#
```

- Verify the PPP Encapsulation configuration on RT2:

```
RT2#sh int s0/0
Serial0/0 is up, line protocol is up
  Hardware is M4T
  Internet address is 10.10.10.2/30
  MTU 1500 bytes, BW 1544 Kbit, DLY 20000 usec,
     reliability 255/255, txload 1/255, rxload 1/255
  Encapsulation PPP, crc 16, loopback not set
  Keepalive set (10 sec)
  LCP Open
  Open: IPCP, CDPCP
--- output omitted ---
```

- The **debug ppp negotiation** privileged command displays PPP link establishment and negotiation information, including LCP and NCP information.

- The **debug ppp error** privileged command displays the errors related to PPP.

- **Serialx is xxxx, line protocol is xxxx**
  The 1st parameter refers to status of the physical layer (L1). It is **up** when it receives carrier detect; while it is **down** when there is a cable or interface problem (hardware failure).
  The 2nd parameter refers to status of the data link layer (L2). It is **down** when there is a **keepalive**, **clocking** (clock rate), **framing** (encapsulation type), or **authentication** (password and authentication protocol) misconfiguration. **Note:** Usernames are **not** case-sensitive.
  Note: Both interface ends must be configured with the same keepalive value or setting.

- The **clear counters** [*intf-type intf-num*] privileged command clears the statistic counters for all interfaces or a particular interface.

- The **no encapsulation ppp** command is **equivalent** to the **encapsulation hdlc** command, as it causes routers to revert back to the default encapsulation type – HDLC.

PPP Authentication Configuration

- Authentication allows a device to ensure that it is communicating with the correct device. Authentication is normally being initiated by the called party.

- The 2 authentication protocols that can be used on PPP links are **Password Authentication Protocol** (PAP) and **Challenge Handshake Authentication Protocol** (CHAP).

- PAP sends the username and password in clear text (very insecure) across a PPP link in the first message during the link establishment phase.

- During the PAP authentication phase, the calling device will sends its username (or hostname) and password to the called device. The called device compares this information with a list of locally stored usernames and passwords and will reply with an accept or reject message accordingly. PAP is a **two-way** handshake mechanism.

- CHAP does not send passwords directly; CHAP passwords are exchanged as MD5 hash values. The authentication phase takes place after the link establishment phase. CHAP begins with a **challenge** message, which states a random number. The challenged router (2nd router) replies with a calculated **Message Digest 5** (MD5) one-way hash result based on the password and the random number. The 1st router calculates the same hash result with the same set of password and random number, and compares its result with the result replied from the challenged router. CHAP is a **three-way** handshake mechanism.

- PPP authentication is defined as a **one-way authentication** method (the **ppp authentication {pap | chap}** command can be **just** issued on **either** end of a PPP link). However, **two-way authentication** can be achieved by issuing the **ppp authentication** command on both ends.

- **one-way authentication** is the minimum possible authentication. The called party verifies the identity of the calling party. Also known as **unidirectional** authentication.
  two-way authentication is where the calling party can also verify the identity of the called party. Also known as **bidirectional** authentication.

- If both PAP and CHAP are enabled with the **ppp authentication {chap pap | pap chap}** interface subcommand, the 1st method specified is used. If another peer suggests the 2nd method or refuses the 1st method, the 2nd method is used.

- For one-way PAP authentication, the **username** {*remote-hostname*} **password** {*passwd*} statement is only required on the called device to verify the username and password sent by the calling device; whereas for two-way PAP authentication, it is required on both devices.

- The **username password** statement is required on **both devices** for both unidirectional and bidirectional CHAP authentication. In unidirectional CHAP authentication (a local device authenticating a remote device), it is first used by the remote device (RT2) to response to the challenge generated by the local device (RT1), and then used by the local device (RT1) to verify the response from the remote device (RT2).

- In PPP authentication configuration, the hostname of the remote router will be configured as the **username** on the local router, and the same **shared secret** password will be configured on both routers. **Note:** Passwords are case sensitive but usernames are **not** case-sensitive.

- The function of the **username** {*remote-username*} **password** {*passwd*} statement is different for PAP and CHAP. With PAP, it is only used to verify that an incoming username and password; whereas CHAP uses it to generate the response to a challenge (on remote router) and verify a response (on local router).

- Bidirectional (two-way) CHAP Authentication configuration on RT1:

```
RT1#conf t
Enter configuration commands, one per line.  End with CNTL/Z.
RT1(config)#username RT2 password cisco123
RT1(config)#int s0/0
RT1(config-if)#ppp authentication chap
00:15:21: %LINEPROTO-5-UPDOWN: Line protocol on Interface Serial0/0, changed
state to down
RT1(config-if)#^Z
RT1#
```

- Bidirectional (two-way) CHAP Authentication configuration on RT2:

```
RT2#conf t
Enter configuration commands, one per line.  End with CNTL/Z.
RT2(config)#username RT1 password cisco123
00:16:01: %LINEPROTO-5-UPDOWN: Line protocol on Interface Serial0/0, changed
state to up
RT2(config)#int s0/0
RT2(config-if)#ppp authentication chap
RT2(config-if)#^Z
RT2#
```

- Below shows the output of the **debug ppp authentication** privileged command on RT2 when the serial link was disconnected and connected back again. It shows the inner scenes behind the PPP link establishment and authentication phases.
  Note: With bidirectional authentication, each router sends and receives CHAP challenges.

```
RT2#debug ppp authentication
PPP authentication debugging is on
RT2#
00:21:35: %LINK-3-UPDOWN: Interface Serial0/0, changed state to up
00:21:35: Se0/0 PPP: Using default call direction
00:21:35: Se0/0 PPP: Treating connection as a dedicated line
00:21:35: Se0/0 CHAP: O CHALLENGE id 40 len 24 from "RT2"
00:21:35: Se0/0 CHAP: I CHALLENGE id 9 len 24 from "RT1"
00:21:35: Se0/0 CHAP: O RESPONSE id 9 len 24 from "RT2"
00:21:35: Se0/0 CHAP: I RESPONSE id 40 len 24 from "RT1"
00:21:35: Se0/0 CHAP: O SUCCESS id 40 len 4
00:21:35: Se0/0 CHAP: I SUCCESS id 9 len 4
00:21:35: %LINEPROTO-5-UPDOWN: Line protocol on Interface Serial0/0, changed
state to up
RT2#
```

- An **O** indicates an **outgoing** message while an **I** indicates an **incoming** message.

Chapter 23
Frame Relay

- Frame Relay is one of the most common WAN protocols used today. It is a **high performance** WAN protocol that provides L2 and L1 services. It provides features such as **dynamic bandwidth allocation** and **congestion control**. It relies on upper-layer protocols (eg: TCP) for error recovery. Remember Frame Relay with the word "*frame*", the data link layer (L2) PDU.

- Frame Relay is a **packet-switched** technology, where packets are being switched to the destination end device, as the cloud normally have dozens of Frame Relay switches. End devices in a packet-switched network are able to **share** the network media and the available bandwidth. Frame Relay assumes that all customers will never constantly transfer data at the same time. LAN protocols, eg: Ethernet and Token Ring are also categorized packet-switched networks.

- Frame Relay, X.25, and ATM networks are **non-broadcast multi-access** (NBMA) networks – multi-access networks that allow **more than 2 devices to access or attach to a network**, but **do not support broadcast** as in multi-access environments (eg: Ethernet).

- Frame Relay is a successor to X.25. However, some error-correction features, eg: **windowing** (flow control) and **retransmission** of lost data offered by X.25 have been removed. This is because Frame Relay operates on links with **high reliability** compared to links in X.25 networks (noisy lines in the old X.25 networks). X.25 provides Layer 3 services while Frame Relay is strictly a Layer 2 protocol, which allows Frame Relay to provide **higher performance** than X.25 since it doesn't need to spend time in processing Layer 3 PDUs. Frame Relay can only run across synchronous links while X.25 can run across both asynchronous and synchronous links.

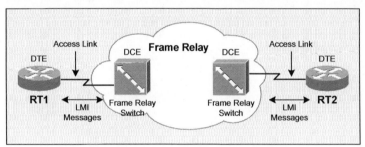

Figure 23-1: Frame Relay Components

- Figure 23-1 shows the basic components of a Frame Relay network. **Access link** is a leased line installed between a router and a nearby Frame Relay switch. The routers are considered as DTEs and the Frame Relay switches are considered as DCEs.

- Frame Relay **only defines** the communication between the routers and the Frame Relay switches. It **does not** define the data transmission within the Frame Relay network.

- **Local Management Interface** (LMI) protocol defines the signaling standard which is exchanged regularly between a router and a Frame Relay switch (between DTE and DCE), and not between routers (DTE and DTE). It supports **keepalive messages** for monitoring the status of the local link between the DTE and DCE (up or down) to verify that data is flowing, and **status messages** for **monitoring VC status** (which VC is up and which VC is down). It also provides **multicasting support** and **global DLCI addressing**.

- Keepalive messages ensure that PVCs remain up and running even without any network activity. They are **originated** from the DTE and responded by the DCE with **status reply** messages.

- 3 LMI protocol options are available in Cisco IOS – **cisco** (default)**, q933a** (ITU-T), and **ansi.** LMI is **locally significant**, hence the routers at both ends do not need to use the same LMI type. LMI must be configured to **match** the LMI configuration on the local Frame Relay switch.

- Frame Relay uses **virtual circuit** (VC) – the **logical connection** created between 2 DTE devices. Thousands of devices are connected to a Frame Relay network, and VC is used to represent a link between 2 routers. A VC can be either a PVC or SVC.

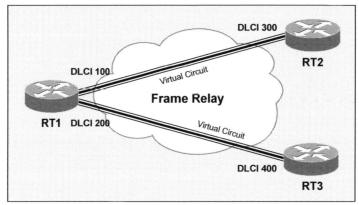

Figure 23-2: Frame Relay Virtual Circuits and DLCIs

- **Permanent Virtual Circuits** (PVCs) are **permanent** established connections that allow communication without call setup. PVCs are being setup and preconfigured by service provider (the **leased line** concept). PVCs are the most common type in use today.

- **Switched Virtual Circuits** (SVCs) are **temporary** established connections that are dynamically established when needed. A VC is established before data transmission and terminated after data transmission (the **dial-up** or **phone call** concept). SVCs are very rarely being used today.

- **Data Link Connection Identifier** (DLCI) is the **Frame Relay address** in a Frame Relay header (10-bit number) that used to identify a VC between 2 DTEs. It allows a Frame Relay interface to distinguish between different VCs as many VCs can be terminated on a same interface. Ex: 3 branch offices are connected to the HQ. Without Frame Relay, the HQ router would need 3 serial interfaces for point-to-point connections (leased lines) to all branches (a scalability issue). With Frame Relay, the HQ router just needs a **single physical access link** to a service provider's Frame Relay network and use DLCI to identify all the PVCs to branch offices. Frame Relay is less expensive than point-to-point links (leased lines) when connecting multiple sites together.

- The DLCI addresses in Frame Relay perform the same functions as MAC addresses on Ethernet. Frame Relay is a L2 protocol. Whenever a Frame Relay switch forwards an IP datagram encapsulated in a Frame Relay frame, it would read the destination DLCI address in the frame and forward to the corresponding VC accordingly.

- In Figure 23-2, RT1 has 2 VCs but only one access link (**multiple VCs can share the same access link**). A DLCI of 100 identifies the VC that connects to RT2 and a DLCI of 300 identifies the VC that connects to RT3. Whenever RT1 would like to forward a packet to RT2, it encapsulates the Layer 3 packet with a Frame Relay header with a DLCI of 100 which represents the VC to RT2, and a trailer and send out the frame (it becomes a L2 frame). The Frame Relay switches will then correctly forward the frame to RT2. On RT2, a different DLCI number can be used to identify the same VC.

- Frame Relay DLCIs are **locally significant**, which means that addresses only need to be unique on a particular local access link – there can be only one 123, Jalan ABC, 58000, Kuala Lumpur, but there can be a 123, Jalan ABC in every city.

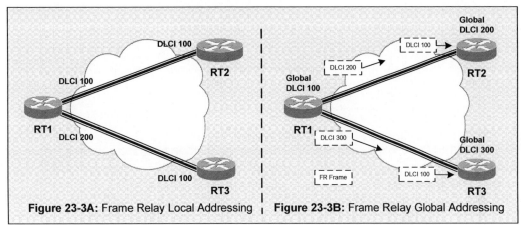

Figure 23-3A: Frame Relay Local Addressing | **Figure 23-3B:** Frame Relay Global Addressing

Figure 23-3: Frame Relay Local Addressing and Global Addressing

- **Local addressing** → DLCIs must be unique on an access link to represent different VCs, but the same DLCI number can be used on multiple access links in the Frame Relay network.

- **Global addressing** is a way of choosing DLCI numbers when planning a Frame Relay network by making DLCI addressing look like LAN addressing. But a Frame Relay header **only has a single DLCI field**, not both Source and Destination DLCI fields as expected in data link headers. Figure 23-3B shows a frame sent by RT1 to RT2 with DLCI 200 in the header, the Frame Relay switch which RT2 connected to **will change** the field to DLCI 100 before it forwards to RT2. As a result, **the sender treats the DLCI field as a destination address while the receiver treats the DLCI field as a source address**.

- **Link Access Procedure Frame Bearer Services** (LAPF) specification defines the Frame Relay frame header and trailer used to encapsulate L3 packets. Always remember that the header **only has a single DLCI field, not both Source and Destination DLCI fields** as in other L2 headers.

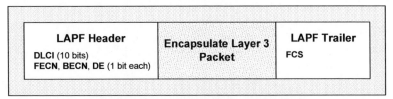

Figure 23-4: LAPF Header and Trailer

- The LAPF specification does not have a Protocol Type field which is important to identify the encapsulated Layer 3 protocols, eg: IP, IPX, AppleTalk. The 2 implementations are the default **Cisco-proprietary encapsulation** and RFC 1490 / 2427 **IETF encapsulation** (enabled with the **encapsulation frame-relay ietf** interface subcommand) when connecting to non-Cisco router.

- Frame Relay switches don't care and ignore the Frame Relay encapsulation type, but the DTEs at both ends must be configured to use the same encapsulation type. Additionally, the encapsulation type can be different for each VC.

- Comparisons between Frame Relay LMI and Encapsulation:

LMI	Encapsulation
Defines the messages used between a DTE and a DCE.	Defines the headers used between 2 DTEs.
Important for managing and monitoring the access link and VC status.	Important for DTEs to support multiprotocol traffic.
The LMI type must match between the DTE and DCE	The encapsulation type must match between the DTEs.

- **Access Rate** (AR) is the **maximum speed** or **bandwidth rate** of a circuit or access link.

- When Frame Relay was introduced, people who were using leased line services were reluctant to switch to it as the **bandwidth is shared** among customers (packet-switched networks). **Committed Information Rate** (CIR) is the **minimum guaranteed** or **agreed bandwidth** on a VC by the service provider. If the Frame Relay network has extra available bandwidth, users are allowed to temporary **exceed** their guaranteed bandwidth up to the access rate (bursting). The **Discard Eligibility** (DE) bit of the frames that are sent in excess of the CIR is marked, which means they can be discarded when congestion occurs in the Frame Relay network.

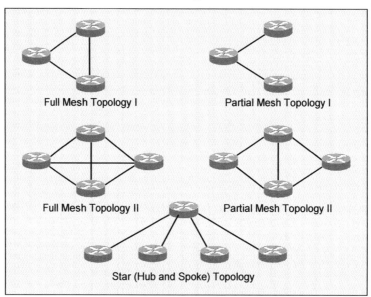

Figure 23-5: Frame Relay Topologies

- Below list the common Frame Relay topologies:

Full-Mesh (any-to-any)	Each router has direct connections to every router to provide **redundancy**. Very robust architecture as if a link fails, a router still able to reach another router via another link. Disadvantage is it is the **most expensive** to implement.
Partial-Mesh	**Less expensive** than full-mesh topology. This approach mostly used to implement redundant connections between important sites and single connections to connect less important sites into a central site.
Star (Hub and Spoke)	Consists of a central site with connections to all remote sites. The **most common** Frame Relay topology, and the **least expensive** topology as it requires the least number of VCs.

- The formula for calculating the number of links in a full-mesh network that has n nodes is $\frac{n(n-1)}{2}$.

- Below list the options for assigning IP subnets and IP addresses on Frame Relay interfaces:

One IP subnet containing all Frame Relay DTEs	Mostly used in **full-mesh** Frame Relay networks. This approach does not need subinterfaces configuration. Less usage nowadays as most organizations implement partial-mesh networks.
One IP subnet per VC	Mostly used in **partial-mesh** Frame Relay networks. Look like a set of point-to-point serial links. This approach needs point-to-point subinterfaces configuration. Most commonly implemented.
Hybrid approach	Mostly used in networks with a **mixture of full-mesh and partial-mesh** Frame Relay networks.

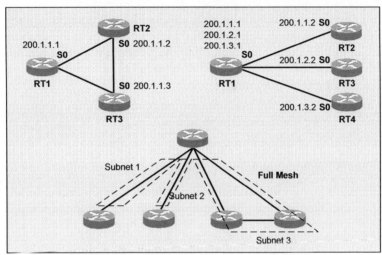

Figure 23-6: Frame Relay Layer 3 Addressing

- **Subinterface** is a Cisco IOS configuration feature that allows a physical interface to be partitioned into multiple virtual interfaces and have multiple IP addresses on multiple interfaces. Subinterfaces allow a partial-mesh network to be divided into smaller full-mesh networks.

- Cisco routers support **point-to-point** and **multipoint** subinterfaces:

Point-to-Point	Used to establish a **single** PVC to another router. A single VC is considered in the same group that consists of 2 routers (Subnet 1 and 2 in Figure 23-6). Each PPP connection has its own subnet and acts like a leased line.
Multipoint	Used to establish **multiple** PVCs to multiple routers. More than 2 routers are considered in the same group (Subnet 3 in Figure 23-6). All participating [sub]interfaces are in the same subnet and act like a multi-access network.

- Point-to-point subinterfaces can be used to handle the issues caused by **split horizon** in **partial-mesh** and **hub-and-spoke** Frame Relay networks implemented with multipoint [sub]interfaces.

- **Q:** When the term **multipoint interface** and **multiple subinterface** are used?
  A: Multipoint interface refers to FR multipoint configuration on a main interface, eg: Serial0.
      Multipoint subinterface refers to FR multipoint configuration on a subinterface, eg: Serial0.1.

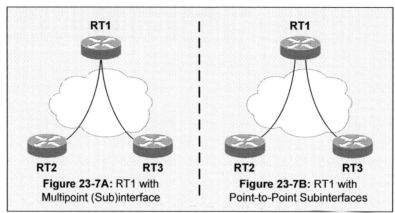

Figure 23-7A: RT1 with Multipoint (Sub)interface

Figure 23-7B: RT1 with Point-to-Point Subinterfaces

Figure 23-7: Split Horizon in Frame Relay Networks

- Split horizon defines that a routing update received from an interface cannot be readvertised back to that same interface, hence this prevents RT1 (with a multipoint [sub]interface) from forwarding the routing updates received from RT2 to RT3 and vice versa. Migration to point-to-point subinterfaces configuration is recommended to overcome this problem. By having each subinterface in a separate subnet, routing updates received from a subinterface can be propagated to other subinterfaces, even though they belong to the same physical interface.

- Another possible solution is **disable split horizon** on a particular multipoint [sub]interface. The **no ip split-horizon eigrp** {*as-num*} interface subcommand disables split horizon for EIGRP on a particular multipoint [sub]interface.
Note: Changing the split horizon configuration of an interface would reset EIGRP neighbor relationships with other routers connected to the interface.

```
00:04:45: %DUAL-5-NBRCHANGE: IP-EIGRP(0) 100: Neighbor 200.1.1.2 (Serial0/0)
is down: split horizon changed
00:05:40: %DUAL-5-NBRCHANGE: IP-EIGRP(0) 100: Neighbor 200.1.1.2 (Serial0/0)
is up: new adjacency
```

- **Note:** EIGRP is categorized as a **distance-vector** routing protocol hence it inherits the split horizon feature of DV routing protocols.

- Frame Relay does require Layer 3 broadcast support, eg: routing updates. However, Frame Relay cannot simply send a single frame to a Frame Relay network and get forwarded to multiple destinations as like LAN broadcasts; it sends copies of the broadcast to each VC. Broadcast overhead exists when sending routing updates in networks with large number of routes and VCs. The issues regarding Frame Relay broadcasts are out of the scope of CCNA.

- ATM are normally being used to build the core of the Frame Relay networks due to the advantages of ATM. **Frame Relay Network and Service Interworking** refers to the use of ATM between 2 Frame Relay switches. Both types use ATM as a transport media.

FRF.5	Defines how a Frame Relay switch can convert a Frame Relay VC to an ATM VC and back to a Frame Relay VC. The result is **transparent** to both the end devices (routers).
FRF.8	Defines how 2 end devices (routers) can communicate when a router is connected to a Frame Relay network and another one is connected to an ATM network.

- **FRF.5** → Both DTEs are connected to Frame Relay switches, and ATM is deployed between the Frame Relay switches. Frame Relay end devices communicate over an intermediate ATM network.
  FRF.8 → One DTE is connected to a Frame Relay switch while another one is connected to an ATM switch. It allows a Frame Relay end device to communicate with an ATM end device.

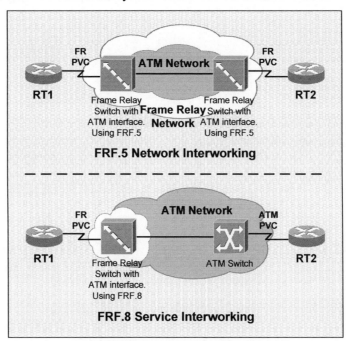

Figure 23-8: Frame Relay Interworking

- Frame Relay reduces network overhead with several congestion notification mechanisms. Frame Relay uses 3 bits in the Frame Relay LAPF header for congestion control:

DE (Discard Eligibility)	The DE bit for Frame Relay frames which transmit exceed the CIR is set to 1 (oversubscription), which means the frames can be discarded by Frame Relay switches when the network is congested (lower delivery priority or best-effort delivery).
FECN (Forward Explicit Congestion Notification)	Indicates that congestion is occurring in the **same direction** to the destination DTE – the path from the source to the destination DTE.
BECN (Backward Explicit Congestion Notification)	Indicates that congestion is occurring in the **opposite direction** to the destination DTE.

- When a frame arrives at a carrier switch that is experiencing congestion, the FECN bit of the frame is set to 1, and the frame would then be forwarded to the **receiving DTE** to inform the destination DTE that the path the frame just traversed is congested. Similarly, the BECN bit can be set in the return frame going back to the **sending DTE**. However, both bits are up to the upper-layer protocols (eg: TCP) of the receiving DTEs or routers (which receive frames with FECN or BECN set) for reaction – **ignore the notification** or **activate flow control**.

- An IOS feature called **Traffic Shaping** can be configured to send data at an average sending rate that is slower than the actual clock rate of an interface, eg: a T1 link with a 128kbps CIR.

This page is intentionally left blank

Chapter 24
Frame Relay Lab

Full-Mesh Frame Relay Network with One IP Subnet (Multipoint Interfaces)

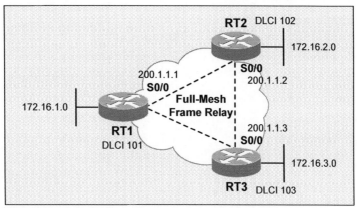

Figure 24-1: Full-Mesh Frame Relay Network with One IP Subnet

- Frame Relay configuration on RT1, RT2, and RT3:

```
RTx(config)#int s0/0
RTx(config-if)#encapsulation frame-relay
RTx(config-if)#ip add 200.1.1.{x} 255.255.255.0
RTx(config-if)#no shut
RTx(config-if)#exit
RTx(config)#router eigrp 1
RTx(config-router)#network 200.1.1.0
RTx(config-router)#network 172.16.0.0
RTx(config-router)#no auto-summary
```

- **Note:** Watch out for split horizon issues on multipoint [sub]interfaces. Refer to Page 162 for the discussion and the resolution of this issue.

- Frame Relay configuration can be relatively simple due to the following default IOS settings:
  - i) The LMI type is automatically sensed. LMI information is exchanged every 10 seconds. If a router unable to autosense the LMI type, it would use Cisco as the LMI type.
  - ii) The encapsulation type (of the LAPF headers) is Cisco, instead of IETF.
  - iii) PVC DLCIs are learned via LMI status messages.
  - iv) Inverse ARP is enabled by default. It is triggered when a router received the LMI Status Reply message that declares a VC is active. The router then uses Inverse ARP to discover and determine the network address of a remote device by advertising itself by sending an Inverse ARP to each active local DLCI. Inverse ARP messages are sent every 60 seconds.

  Note: LMI keepalive messages and LMI status messages are different! LMI keepalive messages are exchanged between DTE and DCE while LMI status messages are only sent in LMI Status Reply messages which are sent from DCE to DTE.

- Frame Relay switches do not care about the encapsulation type and IP addressing. They only care about the LMI type and the CIR.

- A router will be able to figure out the LMI type used in the Frame Relay switch without manual configuration, using the LMI autosense feature. Manual configuration disables LMI autosense.

- IETF Frame Relay encapsulation type must be used when there is a non-Cisco router (RT3). Below shows the new configuration on all routers to support the following new requirements:
    i)   RT3 uses IETF encapsulation on all VCs on the interface.
    ii)   RT1 and RT2 LMI type should be ANSI, and LMI autosense should not be used.

```
RT1 and RT2 configuration:
!
interface Serial0/0
 encapsulation frame-relay
 frame-relay lmi-type ansi
 frame-relay interface-dlci 103 ietf
 ip address 200.1.1.{x} 255.255.255.0
!

RT3 configuration:
!
interface Serial0/0
 encapsulation frame-relay ietf
 ip address 200.1.1.3 255.255.255.0
!
```

- RT3 changes its encapsulation type on both VCs on the interface with the **ietf** keyword in the **encapsulation** command. However, RT1 and RT2 cannot change their configuration in this way, as only one of their VCs needs to use IETF encapsulation, another one still use Cisco encapsulation. The encapsulation type can be changed in **per-VC basis** (use IETF encapsulation on VC to RT3) with the **frame-relay interface-dlci** {*dest-dlci*} **ietf** interface subcommand.

- Service provider's Frame Relay switches (DCE) send LMI status messages to routers (DTE) to update the virtual circuit status to one of the following 3 states:

ACTIVE	Everything is up, the connection is active, and the routers can exchange data.
INACTIVE	The router's interface is up and communicating with the local Frame Relay switch, but the remote router's connection to its Frame Relay switch is having problem.
DELETED	No LMI message is being received from the local Frame Relay switch. It could be a DLCI mapping problem, a line failure, or no service exists between the router and the Frame Relay switch – the local Frame Relay switch is not announcing and doesn't know about the DLCI.

Frame Relay Address Mapping

- It is an important Frame Relay concept for mapping a L3 address with its corresponding L2 address, which is similar to the ARP process used for L3-to-L2 address mapping to figure out the MAC address of the destination device on the same LAN before data transmission. Mapping is only needed on **multiaccess networks** (point-to-point networks do not require mapping).

- Below shows the output of some Frame Relay address mapping commands on RT1:

```
RT1#sh frame-relay pvc

PVC Statistics for interface Serial0 (Frame Relay DTE)

                Active      Inactive     Deleted        Static
    Local       2           0            0              0
    Switched    0           0            0              0
    Unused      0           0            0              0

DLCI = 102, DLCI USAGE = LOCAL, PVC STATUS = ACTIVE, INTERFACE = Serial0/0

    input pkts 55           output pkts 52          in bytes 4907
    out bytes 4845          dropped pkts 0          in FECN pkts 0
    in BECN pkts 0          out FECN pkts 0         out BECN pkts 0
    in DE pkts 0            out DE pkts 0
    out bcast pkts 8        out bcast bytes 482
    pvc create time 00:10:51, last time pvc status changed 00:09:41

DLCI = 103, DLCI USAGE = LOCAL, PVC STATUS = ACTIVE, INTERFACE = Serial0/0

    input pkts 39           output pkts 18          in bytes 2564
    out bytes 4845          dropped pkts 0          in FECN pkts 0
    in BECN pkts 0          out FECN pkts 0         out BECN pkts 0
    in DE pkts 0            out DE pkts 0
    out bcast pkts 8        out bcast bytes 482
    pvc create time 00:10:51, last time pvc status changed 00:05:30
RT1#
RT1#sh frame-relay map
Serial0/0 (up): ip 200.1.1.2 dlci 102(0x66,0x1860), dynamic,
             broadcast,, status defined, active
Serial0/0 (up): ip 200.1.1.3 dlci 103(0x67,0x1870), dynamic,
             broadcast,, status defined, active
RT1#
```

- The **show frame-relay pvc** EXEC command can also be used to display the information of Frame Relay congestion control, eg: the number of FECN and BECN packets.

- There is no DLCIs address mapping configuration on all routers. So how the routers know the appropriate DLCI numbers to use in the Frame Relay LAPF headers when forwarding the encapsulated packets to each other?

- The DLCIs address mapping can be built with either **static** configuration, or via a **dynamic** process called **Inverse ARP**. Inverse ARP resolves an IP address from a DLCI.

- The Inverse ARP process differs from the ARP process on LANs. As soon as a VC is up, the Inverse ARP process starts with the learning the DLCI via LMI messages, and the router then **sends an Inverse ARP Request message to announce its network layer address** over the VC, hence allow its neighbor router to build a mapping between its L3 and L2 addresses (DLCI).

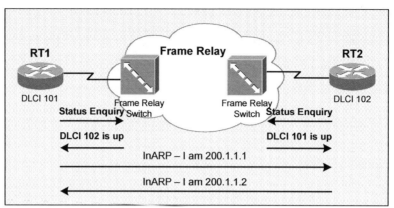
Figure 24-2: Inverse ARP

- Inverse ARP messages for Figure 24-2:

Sending Router	DLCI When the Frame is Sent	Receiving Router	DLCI When the Frame is Received	Information in the InARP Message
RT1	102	RT2	101	I am 200.1.1.1
RT1	103	RT3	101	I am 200.1.1.1
RT2	101	RT1	102	I am 200.1.1.2
RT2	103	RT3	102	I am 200.1.1.2
RT3	101	RT1	103	I am 200.1.1.3
RT3	102	RT2	103	I am 200.1.1.3

- Below shows the static mapping configuration on all routers instead of dynamic mapping with Inverse ARP. The **frame-relay map** commands are required when Inverse ARP is disabled. Frame Relay is a NBMA network, the **broadcast** keyword indicates that IP broadcasts can be forwarded to this address, which is necessary for the operations of dynamic routing protocols.

```
RT1(config)#int s0/0
RT1(config-if)#no frame-relay inverse-arp
RT1(config-if)#frame-relay map ip 200.1.1.2 102 broadcast
RT1(config-if)#frame-relay map ip 200.1.1.3 103 broadcast
------------------------------------------------
RT2(config)#int s0/0
RT2(config-if)#no frame-relay inverse-arp
RT2(config-if)#frame-relay map ip 200.1.1.1 101 broadcast
RT2(config-if)#frame-relay map ip 200.1.1.3 103 broadcast
------------------------------------------------
RT3(config)#int s0/0
RT3(config-if)#no frame-relay inverse-arp
RT3(config-if)#frame-relay map ip 200.1.1.1 101 broadcast
RT3(config-if)#frame-relay map ip 200.1.1.2 102 broadcast
```

- **Note:** Issue the **no frame-relay inverse-arp** interface subcommand before issuing the **no shutdown** interface subcommand. This ensures that the interface does not perform InARP when it is being enabled.

- The **clear frame-relay inarp** privileged command clears the dynamic Frame Relay DLCI mappings created by Inverse ARP.

Partial-Mesh Frame Relay Network with One IP Subnet Per VC (Point-to-Point Subinterfaces Configuration)

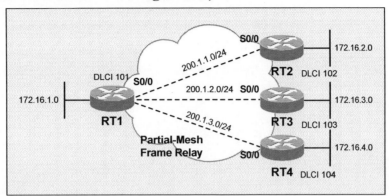

Figure 24-3: Partial-Mesh Frame Relay Network with One IP Subnet Per VC

- Figure 24-3 shows a Frame Relay network with point-to-point subinterfaces configuration. IP address is not configured on the physical interface in Frame Relay subinterfaces configuration.

- Frame Relay Point-to-Point Subinterfaces configuration on RT1:

```
RT1(config)#int s0/0
RT1(config-if)#encapsulation frame-relay
RT1(config-if)#no shut
RT1(config-if)#
RT1(config-if)#int s0/0.102 point-to-point
RT1(config-subif)#ip add 200.1.1.1 255.255.255.0
RT1(config-subif)#frame-relay interface-dlci 102
RT1(config-fr-dlci)#exit
RT1(config-subif)#int s0/0.103 point-to-point
RT1(config-subif)#ip add 200.1.2.1 255.255.255.0
RT1(config-subif)#frame-relay interface-dlci 103
RT1(config-fr-dlci)#exit
RT1(config-subif)#int s0/0.104 point-to-point
RT1(config-subif)#ip add 200.1.3.1 255.255.255.0
RT1(config-subif)#frame-relay interface-dlci 104
RT1(config-fr-dlci)#exit
RT1(config-subif)#
```

- Frame Relay Point-to-Point Subinterfaces configuration on RT2, RT3, and RT4:

```
RTx(config)#int s0/0
RTx(config-if)#encapsulation frame-relay
RTx(config-if)#no shut
RTx(config-if)#int s0/0.101 point-to-point
RTx(config-subif)#ip add 200.1.{x-1}.2 255.255.255.0
RTx(config-subif)#frame-relay interface-dlci 101
RTx(config-fr-dlci)#exit
RTx(config-subif)#
```

- Inverse ARP is not required for point-to-point subinterfaces; hence it is disabled by default.

- The **interface serial***x.y* **point-to-point** global configuration command creates a logical subinterface numbered *y* under physical interface **serial***x*, and the **frame-relay interface-dlci** {*dlci*} subinterface subcommand statically associates and maps a local DLCI with an IP address on a subinterface. This ensures a router associate the correct PVC with the corresponding subinterface when it receives LMI messages regarding a PVC (up / down).

- The subinterface and DLCI number **do not have to be matched** on both end routers of a PVC. However, it is a best practice to assign a subinterface number that matches the DLCI value assigned to the subinterface for **easier administration and troubleshooting**.

- Below shows the output of the **show frame-relay map** EXEC command on RT1:

```
RT1#sh frame-relay map
Serial0/0.102 (up): point-to-point dlci, dlci 102(0x66,0x1860), broadcast
          status defined, active
Serial0/0.103 (up): point-to-point dlci, dlci 103(0x67,0x1870), broadcast
          status defined, active
Serial0/0.104 (up): point-to-point dlci, dlci 104(0x68,0x1880), broadcast
          status defined, active
RT1#
```

- The output is different from the output of the same command in previous example of full-mesh network without subinterfaces – there is no corresponding Layer 3 address for each entry. This is because these subinterfaces are point-to-point subinterfaces. Whenever a packet is being sent out from a particular subinterface, the router would know the DLCI to use to encapsulate the packet (similar to using an outgoing interface in static routing – a router sends data without knowing the IP address of the router at the other end). Mapping with Inverse ARP or static mapping configuration is only needed **when more than one VC associated** with a particular interface or subinterface, as this is the time when a router would confuse about which DLCI to use.

- LMI messages are exchanged between a DTE (router) and DCE (Frame Relay switch) which allows the DTE to detect whether it has connectivity to its local Frame Relay switch. The **debug frame-relay lmi** privileged command displays the information about the exchange of LMI messages. LMI keepalive messages (**Status Enquiry** messages) are **originated** from the DTE, as indicated with the **out** keyword; and the DCE would response with **Status Reply** messages, as indicated with the **in** keyword. LMI status messages are originated from the DCE to inform the DTE regarding the status of virtual circuits. The **no keepalive** interface subcommand disables the use of LMI messages, which include LMI keepalive and status messages.

```
RT1#debug frame-relay lmi
Frame Relay LMI debugging is on
Displaying all Frame Relay LMI data
RT1#
00:14:30: Serial0/0(out): StEnq, myseq 44, yourseen 43, DTE up
00:14:30: datagramstart = 0xE015DC, datagramsize = 13
00:14:30: FR encap = 0xFCF10309
00:14:30: 00 75 01 01 01 03 02 2C 2B
00:14:30:
00:14:30: Serial0/0(in): Status, myseq 44, pak size 13
00:14:30: RT IE 1, length 1, type 1
00:14:30: KA IE 3, length 2, yourseq 44, myseq 44
RT1#
```

Hybrid Full and Partial-Mesh Frame Relay Network (Point-to-Point and Multipoint Subinterfaces Configuration)

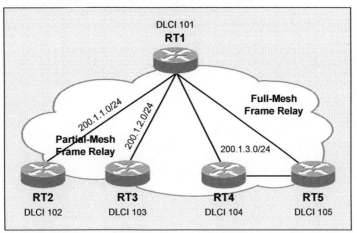

Figure 24-4: Hybrid Full-Mesh and Partial-Mesh Frame Relay Network

- Frame Relay Point-to-Point and Multipoint Subinterfaces configuration on RT1:

```
!
interface Serial0/0
 encapsulation frame-relay
!
interface Serial0/0.102 point-to-point
 ip address 200.1.1.1 255.255.255.0
 frame-relay interface-dlci 102
!
interface Serial0/0.103 point-to-point
 ip address 200.1.2.1 255.255.255.0
 frame-relay interface-dlci 103
!
interface Serial0/0.888 multipoint
 ip address 200.1.3.1 255.255.255.0
 frame-relay interface-dlci 104
 frame-relay interface-dlci 105
!
interface FastEthernet1/0
 ip address 172.16.1.1 255.255.255.0
!
```

- Frame Relay Point-to-Point Subinterface configuration on RT2 and RT3:

```
!
interface Serial0/0
 encapsulation frame-relay
!
interface Serial0/0.101 point-to-point
 ip address 200.1.{x-1}.2 255.255.255.0
 frame-relay interface-dlci 101
!
interface FastEthernet1/0
 ip address 172.16.x.1 255.255.255.0
!
```

- Frame Relay Multipoint Subinterface configuration on RT4:

```
!
interface Serial0/0
 encapsulation frame-relay
!
interface Serial0/0.888 multipoint
 ip address 200.1.3.2 255.255.255.0
 frame-relay interface-dlci 101
 frame-relay interface-dlci 105
!
interface FastEthernet1/0
 ip address 172.16.4.1 255.255.255.0
```

- Frame Relay Multipoint Subinterface configuration on RT5:

```
!
interface Serial0/0
 encapsulation frame-relay
!
interface Serial0/0.888 multipoint
 ip address 200.1.3.3 255.255.255.0
 frame-relay interface-dlci 101
 frame-relay interface-dlci 104
!
interface FastEthernet1/0
 ip address 172.16.5.1 255.255.255.0
```

- A **multipoint subinterface** is used when multiple VCs are associated with a subinterface.

- No mapping configuration is required, as Inverse ARP is enabled by default on multipoint subinterfaces; while point-to-point subinterfaces never require mapping configuration.

- The output of the **show frame-relay map** EXEC command on RT1 includes the L3 address mapping information on multipoint subinterfaces (learnt via Inverse ARP):

```
RT1#sh frame-relay map
Serial0/0.102 (up): point-to-point dlci, dlci 102(0x66,0x1860), broadcast
          status defined, active
Serial0/0.103 (up): point-to-point dlci, dlci 103(0x67,0x1870), broadcast
          status defined, active
Serial0/0.888 (up): ip 200.1.3.2 dlci 104(0x68,0x1880), dynamic,
            broadcast,, status defined, active
Serial0/0.888 (up): ip 200.1.3.3 dlci 105(0x69,0x1890), dynamic,
            broadcast,, status defined, active
```

- The disadvantage of Inverse ARP is whenever the PVC data link layer is up, a DTE router needs to learn the status and DLCIs of VCs and waits for the Inverse ARP process to occur, which can take a **considerable amount of time**! Whereas with manually resolved PVCs, data transmission is allowed as soon as the data link layer is up. Routers send InARP Request packets every 1 min. A remote router that receives the InARP Request packet would reply with an InARP Reply packet. Eventually both routers would have the L3-to-L2 address mapping to reach each other.

- The **no interface** {*subif-num*} global configuration command is **insufficient** to remove a subinterface. The subinterface will still exist in the router's memory. A router **reboot** is required. This also applied when **changing the subinterface type** (reboot is required).

Chapter 25
Wireless Networking

- Wireless LAN technologies provide mobility, flexibility, increased productivity, and cost savings compared to wired LAN deployment. WLANs allow users to access resources regardless their location, as long as within the wireless signal coverage area. However, wireless communication brings a trade-off between flexibility and mobility versus battery life and usable bandwidth. Wireless LANs are not the replacement for wired LANs, but an extension of the wired LANs.

- Wireless data transmission is similar to data transmission in a hub-based Ethernet network, which both use the same frequency to transmit and receive data – half-duplex communication. Additionally, all the users within the same access point range share the available bandwidth.

- **Radio Frequencies** (RFs) are radio waves that are radiated into the air from an antenna. They can be absorbed, refracted, or reflected by walls, water, and metal, which resulting in low signal strength. WLANs still worth the existence and deployment even though they don't offer the same robustness as wired networks due to the vulnerability to these surrounding environmental factors.

- Higher frequencies provide higher data rates, but shorter transmitting distances. Lower frequencies provide greater transmitting distances, but lower data rates. Hence a good understanding of all the various types of WLANs is vital for implementing and deploying the best WLAN solutions that meet the specific requirements of different situations.

- **Wireless Access Points** (WAPs) provide connectivity between wireless client devices and the wired network. Additionally, 2 wireless end systems can form an exclusive point-to-point independent **ad-hoc wireless network** without using an access point.

- 802.11 specifications were developed to have no licensing and operating requirement (or fees) in most countries to ensure users the freedom to install and operation WLANs.

- Below lists the various agencies that create, maintain, govern, and enforce the use of wireless standards worldwide – wireless devices, frequencies, and how the frequency spectrums operate:

Institute of Electrical and Electronics Engineers (IEEE – *www.ieee.org*)	Creates and maintains the series of 802.11 wireless standards.
Federal Communications Commission (FCC – *www.fcc.gov, wireless.fcc.gov*)	Regulates the use of wireless devices in the US by releasing public safety policies.
European Telecommunications Standards Institute (ETSI – *www.etsi.org*)	Chartered to produce communications standards in Europe. Similar to FCC in US.
Wi-Fi Alliance (*www.wi-fi.com*)	Tests and promotes WLAN interoperability. Grants certifications for interoperability among 802.11 products from various vendors.
WLAN Association (WLANA – *www.wlana.org*)	Educates and raises consumer awareness regarding WLAN technologies and security.

- As WLANs transmit over radio frequencies, the FCC regulates WLAN usages with the same types of laws used to govern AM/FM radios. The IEEE creates standards based on the frequencies released by FCC for public use. The FCC has released 3 **unlicensed** (license-free) bands for public use – 900MHz, 2.4GHz, and 5.8GHz. The 900MHz and 2.4GHz bands are referred to as the **Industrial, Scientific, and Medical** (ISM) bands, while the 5GHz band is referred to as the **Unlicensed National Information Infrastructure** (UNII) band. Deploying WLANs in a range other than the 3 public bands needs to obtain a specific license from the FCC.

- **Rate Shifting** or **Adaptive Rate Selection** (ARS) is the ability of WLAN clients to change data transfer rates while moving, without losing connectivity and does not require user intervention. An access point can support multiple clients at varying speeds depending upon the client locations. WLAN clients will always try to communicate with the highest possible data rates. A device operating at 802.11b 11Mbps can shift down to 5.5Mbps, 2Mbps, and 1Mbps farthest from the access point.

  A device operating at 802.11a or 802.11g 54Mbps can shift down to 48Mbps, 36Mbps, 24Mbps, 18Mbps, 12Mbps, 9Mbps, and 6Mbps farthest from the access point.

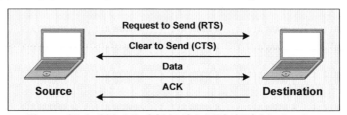

Figure 25-1: 802.11b CSMA/CA RTS/CTS Mechanism

- **Carrier Sense Multiple Access with Collision Avoidance** (CSMA/CA) is used in wireless networking, where CSMA/CD cannot be implemented – it is impossible to listen while sending. CSMA/CA is vital in wireless networking environments where the common **hidden terminal** and **exposed terminal** wireless networking problems exist.

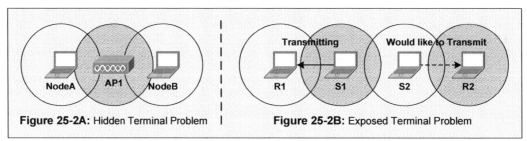

Figure 25-2: Hidden Terminal and Exposed Terminal Problems

- The **hidden terminal** problem is where nodes are out of range of other nodes – A is in range of B, but not in range of C; A cannot know that B is transmitting to C. Figure 25-2A shows a scenario where NodeA is visible from AP1, but is not visible from NodeB, which is also visible from AP1. Collisions occur when NodeA and NodeB transmit data simultaneously to AP1.

- The **exposed terminal** problem is where a node is prevented from transmitting to other nodes due to a neighboring transmitter. Figure 25-2B shows a scenario with 2 transmitters (S1 and S2) and 2 receivers (R1 and R2), where the receivers are out of range of each other, and the transmitters are in range of each other. When S1 is transmitting to R1, S2 is prevented from transmitting to R2, as S2 concludes after the carrier sense process that it will interfere S1 and R1 transmission. Actually S2 can transmit to R2 without interference, as R2 is out of range of S1.

- The **RTS/CTS mechanism** intends to reduce frame collisions caused by the hidden terminal and exposed terminal problems by alerting all nodes within the range of the sender and/or receiver to stop transmitting data for a certain period. A sender would send a RTS frame when it would like to transmit data, while the intended receiver would then reply with a CTS frame. The RTS/CTS mechanism is considered a 2-way handshake process before transmitting a data frame.

- Nodes that receive only the CTS frame are prevented from transmitting data for a certain period, which solving the hidden terminal problem. A node that receives only the RTS frame but not the corresponding CTS frame are allowed to transmit to other neighboring nodes, which solving the exposed terminal problem.

- Below lists the 3 factors that can affect radio wave propagation:

Reflection	Occurs when RF waves bounce off objects, eg: metal, glass.
Scattering	Occurs when RF waves strike uneven surfaces.
Absorption	Occurs when RF waves are absorbed by objects, eg: water.

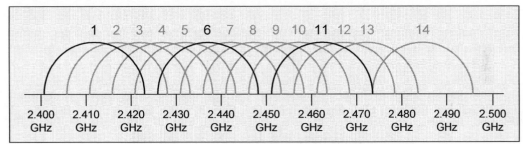

Figure 25-3: ISM 2.4GHz DSSS Frequency Channels

- Figure 25-3 shows the 14 different channels that the FCC released in the 2.4GHz range, each channel with 22MHz wide. In the US, only the first 11 channels are configurable. 802.11b and 802.11g specifications utilize these channels. 802.11g is backward compatible with 802.11b.

- Each channel delivers 11Mbps or 54Mbps of bandwidth. All clients that associate with an access point on a channel share the available bandwidth. Additional access points must be added for more bandwidth capacity.

- Channels 1 (2.412GHz), 6 (2.437GHz), and 11 (2.462GHz), with the separation of 25MHz between their center frequencies are considered non-overlapping, which allows the deployment of 3 access points in the same area (either in the same or different subnet) without experiencing interference (error-tolerant mechanism).

- Communication between a wireless network adapter and an access point occurs over the same radio frequency channel. A channel is first configured in the access point, and the wireless adapter automatically tunes its transceiver to the radio frequency channel of the access point with the strongest signal. Wireless clients perform roaming by periodically scans all access points and reassociates with the access point with the strongest signal. Access points within range of each other and having overlapping signals should be configured with non-overlapping frequency channels in order to provide seamless roaming.

- The 802.11a standard delivers a maximum data rate of 54Mbps with 12 non-overlapping frequency channels that divided into 3 5GHz UNII bands – **Lower** (for indoor), **Middle** (for indoor and outdoor), and **Upper** (for outdoor). Each UNII band is 100MHz wide. **Note:** 5.8GHz to be precise.

- By operating in the 5GHz radio band, 802.11a is also immune to interference from devices that are operating in the 2.4GHz band, eg: microwave ovens, cordless phones, and Bluetooth devices. However, 802.11a is restricted to almost line of sight, hence requiring the installation of more access points than 802.11b/g to cover an area. The strength of 2.4GHz band wireless signals is that they are not affected by water, metal, and thick walls.

- 802.11a is not backward compatible with 802.11b/g because they operate in different frequencies – 5GHz and 2.4GHz.

- The FCC added 11 new channels for the 5GHz 802.11a band in the 802.11h specification, which apparently provide the public to access to up to 23 non-overlapping channels!

- **Dynamic Frequency Selection** (DFS) is an 802.11h mechanism that continuously monitors, tests, and detects a device's operating range for the presence of radar signal that using the same 5GHz frequency band as the UNII band. If it discovers any radar signal, it will either ceases its operations at the occupied channel or chooses different channel to transmit and inform all the associated stations in order to prevent interference from occurring between the UNII band 802.11a WLANs and radar systems.

- **Transmit Power Control** (TPC) is another 802.11h mechanism that prevents too much unwanted interference between different wireless networks by automatically reduce the device transmission output power when there are other WLANs exist within the operating range. Another advantage is allowing a wireless adapter to dynamically fine-tune its transmission power to use just enough power to preserve its connection to the access point, which conserving its battery power and reducing interference with neighboring WLAN nodes. TPC is being widely used in the mobile phone industry. **Note:** Increasing the power increase the range of a WLAN.

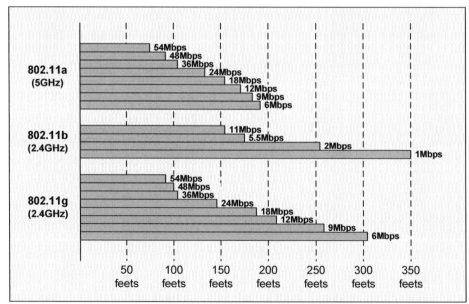

Figure 25-4: Standards Range and Speed Comparisons

- Figure 25-4 shows the range and speed comparisons between 802.11 standards using an indoor open-office environment as a factor and the default power settings. It shows that in order to obtain the full 54Mbps data rate of both 802.11a and 802.11g, a wireless client needs to be within 50 – 100 feets away from the access point.

- Upgrading from 802.11b to 802.11g requires purchasing of new wireless hardware instead of software upgrade, as 802.11g radios use different chipsets in order to deliver higher data rates.

- 802.11b uses the **Direct Sequence Spread Spectrum** (DSSS) modulation technique for data transmission which is not as robust as the **Orthogonal Frequency Division Multiplexing** (OFDM) modulation technique used in both 802.11g and 802.11a.
  Note: When 802.11g devices are operating at the 802.11b transfer rates, they are actually using the same modulation technique as 802.11b uses – DSSS. A WLAN with 4 802.11g clients and 1 802.11b client that connected to the same access point are forced to run the 802.11b CSMA/CA mechanism which really makes throughput suffer. It is recommended to enable the **802.11g-only** mode on an access point in order to optimize performance.

- 802.11n is a new WLAN standard that allows even higher speeds at greater distances. 802.11n is built upon the 802.11 standards by adding **Multiple-Input Multiple-Output** (MIMO), which employs multiple transmitter and receiver antennas to achieve higher data rates and throughput. 802.11n can have up to 8 [smart] antennas, but most of today's 802.11n access points use 4 – 2 for transmitting simultaneously while another 2 for receiving simultaneously. 802.11n uses wider channel bandwidth (40MHz) for operation compared to 22MHz as in legacy 802.11 operation.

- The 802.11n standard is not yet been ratified, which means that the "Pre-N" products on the shelf today are proprietary.

- **Bluetooth** is another wireless standard for short-range radio connections between laptops, mobiles phones, digital cameras, headsets, and other portable devices. It can be considered as a standard for **Personal Area Networks** (PANs).

- Cisco offers a complete line of indoor and outdoor wireless LAN solutions, eg: access points, WLAN controllers, WLAN client adapters, security and management servers, wireless management devices, as well as wireless integrated switches and routers.

- An Infrastructure mode WLAN is either as a **Basic Service Set** (BSS) with an access point or as an **Extended Service Set** (ESS) with multiple access points where multiple BSSs connected by a common **distribution system** with all configured with the same SSID for roaming purposes. Non-root devices (eg: bridges, repeater APs) can only connect to a root device as repeaters.

- Cisco Unified Wireless Network Solution (UWN) allows intelligent Cisco access points and Cisco WLAN Controllers (WLCs) to be managed through the controller web interface, the controller itself, or via the Cisco Wireless Control System (WCS). The Cisco WCS works in conjunction with Cisco Aironet Series Lightweight Access Points, Cisco WLAN Controllers, and Cisco Wireless Location Appliance to provide a centralized management platform for the planning, designing, configuring, controlling, managing, and monitoring of enterprise WLANs.

- The Cisco WCS can manage the WLAN controllers and eventually the entire WLAN from a single GUI interface. It can also provide a detailed insight into the network coverage, the trending of network statistics, device locations, etc.

- An access point in this type of network requires **zero configuration** after initial installation, which means that it can be connected in an indoor or outdoor environment and configured automatically based on the information provided by WLAN controller. It will even check for channel overlapping and interference and assign a non-overlapping channel. If it detects an overlapping channel within its area, it will lower its transmitting level to limit interference – the **automated RF/radio management** and **automated channel planning** features.

- Every packet from every access point must go to the WLAN controller in order to be placed either on the wired network or back to the wireless network. The WLAN controller decides the packet's destiny based on the Cisco-proprietary **Lightweight Access Point Protocol** (LWAPP) information that is encapsulated on it. The WLAN controller may analyze the data collected by the LWAPP-based lightweight access points. LWAPP can control multiple access points at once, which can reduce the effort for configuring, monitoring, and troubleshooting large WLANs.

- Deploy at least 2 redundant WLAN controllers to avoid the single point of failure. The WLAN controllers can be managed either at the WCS or the individual controller.

- Traditional WAPs which function on a stand-alone basis are also known as fat or **autonomous** APs which contain all wireless processing capabilities. The access points operate in isolation and the 802.11 traffic is visible to an individual access point only. They are difficult for management, as they must be managed individually, which can increase operation costs and staffing requirements. Fat access point deployments are fine for small deployments, but are impractical for enterprise-class WLAN deployments, which normally supporting hundreds of clients. **Note:** There is also a security risk if a fat access point is stolen or compromised.

- **Split-MAC architecture** splits the processing of the 802.11 protocol between a Cisco LWAPP-based lightweight (thin) access point that handles real-time aspects of the 802.11 specification and a centralized Cisco WLAN controller that handles functions that are not time-sensitive.

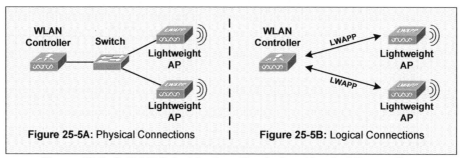

Figure 25-5: Split-MAC Architecture Physical and Logical Connections

- Figure 25-5 shows the physical and logical connections between the lightweight access points and the WLAN controller in the Split-MAC architecture. The access points are not directly connected to the controller. They are connected to 10/100/1000Mbps switch ports.
  Note: Another class of the Centralized WLAN Architecture family is **Local-MAC** architecture.

- LWAPP defines the following activities that governs the communications between access points and WLAN controllers:
  i)   **Access point device discovery and authentication**. When an access point is being connected to a WLAN, it uses LWAPP to discover an available WLAN controller in order to certify itself as a valid network device.
  ii) **Access point information exchange, as well as configuration and software control**. The access point download and upgrade its software if its code version is differs from the WLAN controller code version, and configure itself with the appropriate information, eg: SSID, channel assignment, and security parameters.
  iii) **Communication control and management between access point and wireless devices**. LWAPP handles packet encapsulation, fragmentation and reassembly, and formatting of the data that is being transferred between access points and WLAN controllers.

- Cisco lightweight access points handle the following 802.11 real-time requirements:
  i) The frame exchange handshake between a client and AP when transferring a frame.
  ii) Transmitting beacon frames.
  iii) Buffering and transmitting frames for clients in power save operations.
  iv) Responding to Probe Request frames originated from clients.
  v) Forwarding notifications for the received probe requests to the controller.
  vi) Providing real-time signal quality information of every received frame to the controller.
  vii) Monitoring each radio channel for noise, interference, and the existence of other WLANs.
  viii) Monitoring for the presence or introduction (newly installed) of other access points.
  ix) Encryption and decryption except in the case of VPN/IPSec clients.

- All other remaining functionalities that are not time-sensitive are handled by WLAN controllers. Time sensitivity is not a concern but controller-wide visibility is required. The following are some of the MAC-layer functions that are provided and handled by Cisco WLAN controllers:
  i) 802.11 authentication (security).
  ii) 802.11 association, reassociation, and disassociation (mobility).
  iii) 802.11 frame translation and bridging.

- LWAPP reduces the amount of processing of access points, and allows the resources on the access point to focus on wireless access, rather than traffic handling, authentication, encryption, filtering, and policy enforcement which are handled by WLAN controllers. This approach improves the effectiveness of **centralized WLAN management and security**.

- Below lists the operation modes of Cisco WLAN controllers:

Direct Connect Mode	The access points directly connected to the Ethernet or PoE interfaces on a WLAN controller. The WLAN controller connects back to the existing LAN infrastructure for seamless network integration.
Appliance Mode	The access points directly connected to the existing LAN switches. They communicate with the WLAN controller via LWAPP.
Hybrid Mode	The WLAN controller operates in both Direct Connect and Appliance modes.

- Below lists the ports and interfaces of Cisco WLAN controllers:

Distribution System Port (built-in)	Connects a WLAN controller to a switch port for communication between the WLAN controller and wired LAN.
Service Port (built-in)	Reserved for out-of-band management, similar to the console port of routers and switches. It is managed via the Service-Port interface and must be connected to an access mode switch port. Only Cisco 4400 series WLAN controllers have a service port.
Management Interface (mandatory)	The default interface for in-band management. It is also used for Layer 2 communications between the WLAN controller and lightweight access points in Layer 2 LWAPP communication mode (same subnet). It may reside on the same VLAN or subnet as the AP-manager interface.
AP-Manager Interface (mandatory)	A WLAN controller may have one or more AP-manager interfaces for Layer 3 communications between the WLAN controller and lightweight access points in Layer 3 LWAPP communication mode (different subnets). Configuring an AP-manager interface on the same VLAN or subnet as the management interface results in optimal access point association, but this is not a requirement.

Virtual Interface (mandatory)	It is used to support mobility management, DHCP relay, and serves as the redirect address for guest web authentication login window. All WLAN controllers within a mobility group must be configured with the same virtual interface IP address in order to support inter-controller roaming.
Service-Port Interface (optional)	It is mapped by the system to the service port. It must be configured with an IP address on a different supernet from the management, AP-manager, and any dynamic interfaces. Static routes must be configured instead of default gateway for remote network access to the service port.
Dynamic Interface (optional)	Dynamic interfaces, which are also known as VLAN interfaces, are used to define VLANs for WLAN clients. A WLAN controller can support up to 512 dynamic interfaces (VLANs).

- If a WLAN controller in appliance mode fails, its dropped access points will poll the network for another WLAN controller. Another online WLAN controller's management interface that listens to the network for AP polling messages will auto-discover, re-associate, and communicate with as many access points as it can.

- The **Cisco Wireless Mesh** networking architecture is decentralized where each node only needs to transmit as far as to the next nearest node. Wireless nodes act as repeaters to transmit data from nearly nodes to peers that are too far away or impractical for a wired deployment – network solution for networks that span a really large distance, as well as over rough or difficult terrains.

- Mesh networks are extremely reliable where nodes are connected with many redundant connections between nodes. If a node is out of service due to hardware or software failure, its neighbors can simply find another route – **self-healing**. Extra capacity and higher fault tolerance can be achieved by adding more nodes.

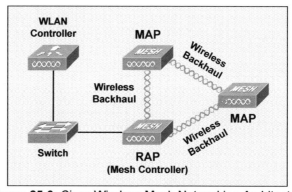

Figure 25-6: Cisco Wireless Mesh Networking Architecture

- Figure 25-6 shows a typical mesh network deployment – a RAP connected to the infrastructure, and the MAPs connect to each other as well as the WLAN controller through the RAP.

- **Backhaul interface** is the 5GHz 802.11a protocol used to route packets between access points. Ex: A MAP/PAP serves wireless clients on the 2.4GHz 802.11b wireless protocol but routes the packets to its parent (RAP) on the 5GHz 802.11a band.

- **Root Access Points** or **Roof-top Access Points** (RAPs) are connected to the wired network and serves as the root or gateway to the wired network. RAPs have a wired connection to a Cisco WLAN controller. They use backhaul wireless interface to communicate with neighboring MAPs / PAPs. RAPs are the parent node that connect a bridged or mesh network to the wired network, hence there can only be one RAP for any bridged or mesh network segment.

- **Mesh Access Points** (MAPs) or **Pole-top Access Points** (PAPs) are remote access points that do not have wired connection to a Cisco WLAN controller – they are completely wireless! If a MAP/PAP is connected to the wired network, it will try to become a RAP upon boot up. If a RAP loses its wired network connection, it will attempt to become a MAP/PAP and will search for and connect to a RAP. A MAP/PAP may also have a wired connection to another remote network segment to extend a local network by bridging the network segments.

- The Cisco Aironet series lightweight access points can operate in either RAP or MAP/PAP mode (or role).

- Cisco LWAPP-enabled mesh access points must be configured, monitored, and operated through a Cisco WLAN Controller deployed in the Cisco Mesh Networking Solution.

- Wireless mesh connections between access points are formed with radio to provide many possible paths from a single node to other nodes. The paths through a mesh network can change in response to traffic loads, radio conditions, and traffic prioritization.

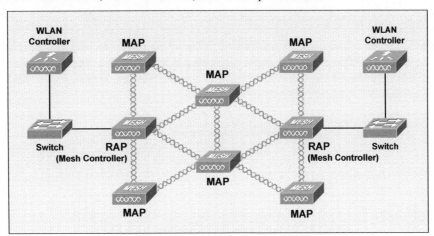

Figure 25-7: Large Meshed Outdoor Deployment

- Every Mesh AP runs the **Adaptive Wireless Path Protocol** (AWPP), a new Cisco-proprietary protocol designed specifically for wireless mesh networks. Mesh APs run AWPP continuously to identify and communicate among them to determine and establish the best and alternate paths back to the wired network via the RAP, results in self-configuring and self-healing mesh networks that provide consistent coverage upon topology changes or other conditions that weaken the signal strength. AWPP choose the paths back to the wired network by considering all the relevant wireless network elements for each path, eg: interference, signal strength, and the number of hops required to get to a WLAN controller.

Wireless Security

- Organizations that are not deploying WLANs fast enough often find their employees take the matter themselves and deploy unauthorized access points and WLANs – **rogue access points**, which would create significant security breaches in the network infrastructure.

- Wireless eavesdropping, war driving hacking, and rogue access points (unauthorized access points that allow unauthorized access to a network) are the main security concerns of WLANs.

- Below lists the 3 categories of wireless network security:

Basic Wireless Security	Achieved via SSID, WEP, and MAC address filtering.
Enhanced Wireless Security	802.1X Port-based Network Access Control Authentication and 802.11i (WPA and WPA2).
Wireless Intrusion Detection	Provides detections of rogue access point, unauthorized access, and intrusions by using access points to scan the RF airwaves and report the activity in the wireless network.

- All wireless access points are shipped with **open access** mode and broadcast their identity – **Service Set Identifier** (SSID). An SSID identifies the membership with an access point and eventually a WLAN. All wireless devices that would like to communicate are configured with the SSID of an access point to establish connectivity to the access point. SSIDs are case sensitive and should not exceed 32 characters. Joining an open access wireless network (eg: hot spots) by only knowing its SSID is referred to as **open authentication**. The reason for shipping open access products is a common marketing plan to penetrate the networking newbie markets. **Note:** Even if SSID broadcasting is turned off, it is possible to discover the SSID by monitoring the network and wait for a client communicate with the access point. SSIDs are sent in clear text as regulated in the original 802.11 specification!

- An access point periodically broadcasts its SSID and other network information every few seconds by default. This action can be stopped in order to prevent a war driving hacker from discovering the SSID and the WLAN. However, as the SSID is included in wireless **beacon** management frames, a sniffing device is able to discover the SSID and eventually the WLAN.

- **Wired Equivalent Privacy** (WEP) addresses the problem of SSID broadcasts by encrypting the traffic between wireless clients and access points. When joining a WEP-protected wireless network, an access point would send a clear-text challenge to the wireless client who must return it encrypted using the correct WEP key. Once the access point able to decipher the client's response, it proves that the client has valid keys and therefore has the rights to join the WLAN. WEP comes in 2 encryption strengths – 64-bit and 128-bit. Joining a WEP wireless network is referred to as **shared-key authentication**. WEP authentication architecture is not scalable due to the lack of centralized authentication platforms. In contrast, 802.1X-based solutions provide centralized and scalable security management platforms which can support dynamic per-user, per-session authentication (and encryption) for wireless connections.

- However, WEP is not considered secure – the challenges and the encrypted responses could be sniffed and reverse-engineered to deduce the keys used by the wireless clients and access points.

- **MAC address filtering** can be configured on an access point for the MAC addresses of the wireless clients that are granted access to a WLAN. However, this approach is also not secure as wireless data frames could be sniffed to discover and spoof the valid MAC addresses.

- Stronger security enhancement standards were created to mitigate the weaknesses of the security features provided by the original 802.11 standards. 802.1X provides enhanced authentication upon open and shared-key authentications; while 802.11i (WPA and WPA2) provides enhanced encryption upon WEP.

- 802.1X provides access control per-user, per-session via mutual strong authentication for both wired and wireless networks. It can also provide encryption depends on the authentication method used. It allows wireless clients and access points to exchange WEP encryption keys automatically based on the IEEE **Extensible Authentication Protocol** (EAP), where an access point acts as a proxy that perform the heavier encryption computational.

- **Wi-Fi Protected Access** (WPA) is introduced by the Wi-Fi Alliance as an intermediate solution to WEP while the IEEE 802.11i standard is being fully ratified. The 802.11i standard will formally replace WEP. WPA supports both authentication and encryption.

- WPA is implemented by granting access to an access point only to the wireless clients that have the correct passphrase. Although WPA is more secure than WEP, if the pre-shared key is stored on the wireless client and the client is lost or stolen, the PSK stored in the client device can be compromised (even though isn't that easy to do so) and establish access to the wireless network. **WPA Personal** performs authentication using less scalable pre-shared keys (PSK) only; while **WPA Enterprise** performs authentication using 802.1X and EAP.

- WPA uses the **Temporal Key Integrity Protocol** (TKIP) as the encryption algorithm, which dynamically change keys during its operation. The key mixing and rekeying mechanisms increase the complexities of decoding the keys and improve protection against the well-known **key recovery attack** on WEP. TKIP also incorporated with a **message integrity check** (MIC) algorithm that prevents the packet payload from being altered and retransmitted (**replay attack**). **Note:** The main flaw of CRC mechanism used in WEP is that it is possible to alter the packet payload and update the CRC without even knowing the WEP key.

- WPA implements a subset of the 802.11i specification; while WPA2 implements all the mandatory elements of the 802.11i specification, notably a new AES-based encryption algorithm – CCMP (Counter Mode with Cipher Block Chaining Message Authentication Code Protocol), which is considered fully secure. In addition to stricter encryption requirements, WPA2 also enhanced to support fast roaming by allowing a wireless client to pre-authenticate with the access point which it is moving toward to, while maintaining a connection to the access point which it is moving away from. 802.11i is often referred to as WPA2 or RSN (**Robust Security Network**).

- **Extensible Authentication Protocol** (EAP) is an authentication framework that is frequently used in WLANs and Point-to-Point connections. It supports multiple authentication methods, eg; EAP-MD5, EAP-TLS, EAP-TTLS, EAP-PSK, EAP-IKEv2, EAP-SIM, and EAP-AKA. 802.11i security standard (WPA2) has adopted 5 EAP types as its authentication mechanisms.

- **Lightweight Extensible Authentication Protocol** (LEAP) is a Cisco-proprietary EAP method developed prior to the ratification of the 802.11i security standard.

Wireless Management

- WLANs require the same level of management that wired networks do. WLANs network management tasks include site survey, interference detection, and RF/radio management services (scanning and monitoring).

- Cisco **Unified Wireless Network** (UWN) is an evolution of the Cisco **Structured Wireless-Aware Network** (SWAN). The main components of UWN are Cisco Aironet wireless access points and clients, SWAN-aware Cisco routers and Catalyst switches, as well as CiscoWorks **Wireless LAN Solution Engine** (WLSE) wireless security and management servers.

- Cisco UWN addresses all the wireless deployment, management, control, and security issues. It provides the same level of scalability, reliability, ease of deployment, security, and management for WLANs as is expected for wired LANs.

- Cisco UWN requires wireless clients to send RF/radio management (RM) data to a Cisco Aironet access point, Cisco router, or Catalyst switch running **Wireless Domain Services** (WDS), which is basically a set of Cisco IOS software features that enhance client mobility and simplify WLAN deployment and management. All access points and clients that register themselves with WDS and participate in radio management and WLAN monitoring would forward information about the radio environment (eg: interference and rogue access point detections, as well as client association and disassociation activities) to the WDS device. The WDS device aggregates all the RM data and authentication information and forwards them to a WLSE.

- Cisco UWN has the ability to generate alert when a rouge WAP or client connect to the network, as all connecting devices report to the WDS device for authentication.

- **Fast Secure Roaming** is a new feature included in WDS. It provides seamless roaming and rapid reauthentication when wireless clients switch between access points reside in the same subnet.

Wireless Network Design

- Site surveys are treated as unnecessary in this age of inexpensive wireless access points, where wireless deployment is economical. However, site surveys should still be performed to determine the optimal access point locations to minimize channel interference while maximizing the range.

- The following questions should be asked during WLAN site surveys:
  i)   Which wireless system and solution is best suited for the environments and requirements?
  ii)   Does the line-of-sight requirement exist between antennas?
  iii) Where should the access point to be placed for it to be as close as possible to clients?
  iv)   What are the potential sources of interference in the building (eg: cordless phones, microwave ovens, natural interference, other access points that using the same channel, and other WLANs that deployed by other organizations within the same building)?
  v)   Should any federal, provincial, or local regulations and legislations be considered in the deployment?

- Some access points have an autoconfiguration option which can autoconfigure themselves for the least-used wireless channel after listening on the network. However, this is not always desirable. As an example, an access point that is installed on the 6th floor might select a channel that it perceived to be available. If the channel is already used by a WAP on the 1st floor, a wireless client on the 3rd floor could have connectivity issues due to the overlapping channels at there. **Note:** The access points can belong to either same or different subnets.

- **Overlapping channels** in a wireless network operate similarly to an overcrowded wired network plagued by continuous collisions. Performance will suffer and wireless clients might not be able to establish stable connections. This can be easily solved by using non-overlapping channels.

- As WLAN deployments are relatively inexpensive compared to wired network, and throughput is proportionally to the proximity of access points, network engineers often install access points to provide overlapping signals. Using the overlapping signal design, the coverage area (radius) is narrower but the overall throughput is improved. Overlapping signals also eliminate dead spots. **Note:** Overlapping signals must be radiated in non-overlapping channels.

- **Signal strength** is the measurement of the connection between a client and an access point; while **link quality** is the measurement of bandwidth after the noise or interference is removed.

- Access points can operate in a dedicated point-to-point bridging mode when joining the LANs in 2 buildings. However, the access points no longer operate as access point for wireless clients.

- Wireless IP phones have different requirements of wireless network connectivity than common wireless clients. The main consideration for deploying wireless IP phones is **roaming**. With Layer 2 roaming, a device switches connectivity to another access point within its original subnet – the device keeps its IP addresses and hence switching between access points would not be noticed by users; while with Layer 3 roaming, a device switches connectivity from an access point in its subnet to another access point in another subnet – the device would have to change its IP address and default gateway. There will be an interruption to the connection and an IP phone call would be disconnected, which is unacceptable to users.

- When deploying wireless IP phones, the network needs to be equipped with a Cisco Catalyst 6500 Series **Wireless LAN Services Module** (WiSM) that runs WDS and aggregates access point RF/radio management information to an WLSM in order to enable seamless L2 and L3 roaming as well as client mobility management.

- Prior to WLSE, L3 roaming was an issue because an IP phone would end up in another subnet which is different from its IP address and default gateway.

Cisco Wireless LAN Configuration

- A wireless interface is just another interface on a router. However, enabling the wireless interface requires more configurations than enabling a FastEthernet interface. Unlike access points, the interface on the following router is a routed interface, which is the reason why the IP address is configured under the physical interface. Normally the IP address is configured under the management VLAN or **Bridge Virtual Interface** (BVI) on access points.

```
Router(config)#int dot11radio0/3/0
Router(config-if)#desc *** 1stFloor WLAN ***
Router(config-if)#ip add 10.10.10.1 255.255.255.0
Router(config-if)#no shut
Router(config-if)#ssid 1stFloor-WLAN
Router(config-if-ssid)#guest-mode [1]
Router(config-if-ssid)#authentication open [2]
Router(config-if-ssid)#infrastructure-ssid [3]
Router(config-if-ssid)#no shut
```

[1] – The **guest-mode** SSID subcommand configures the radio interface to broadcast the SSID.
[2] – Open authentication allows wireless clients to join the open access wireless network (eg: hot spots) by only knowing its SSID. Additionally, the **authentication shared** SSID subcommand configures an access point for shared-key authentication.
[3] – The **infrastructure-ssid** SSID subcommand designates a SSID as an infrastructure SSID, which allows an access point to communicate to other access points, or other devices on the wired network. Repeater access points and non-root bridges use the specified SSID to associate with root access points and root bridges respectively (infrastructure associations).

- In **Infrastructure mode**, all wireless clients communicate with each other through an access point instead of direct communication; whereas in **Ad hoc mode**, wireless clients communicate directly with each other without using an access point.

- Below shows the configuration on a Cisco Aironet access point. Note that the IP address is configured under the **Bridge Virtual Interface** (BVI) instead of the Dot11radio interface, as the interface is not a routed interface as in the previous example. Additionally, the IP address is used for management only and does not affect the operation of the access point nor the WLAN.

```
CiscoAP(config)#int dot11Radio0
CiscoAP(config-if)#desc *** 2ndFloor WLAN ***
CiscoAP(config-if)#no shut
CiscoAP(config-if)#ssid 2ndFloor-WLAN
CiscoAP(config-if-ssid)#guest-mode
CiscoAP(config-if-ssid)#authentication open
CiscoAP(config-if-ssid)#infrastructure-ssid
CiscoAP(config-if-ssid)#no shut
CiscoAP(config-if-ssid)#exit
CiscoAP(config)#int bvi1
CiscoAP(config-if)#ip add 11.11.11.1 255.255.255.0
CiscoAP(config-if)#no shut
```

Chapter 26
ISDN

- Most organizations have permanent and always-on WAN connections (eg: leased line, Frame Relay) to their branch offices. **Backup** WAN connections are also important, as the primary WAN connections might fail for some reasons. ISDN is a popular choice for backup connections.

- **Integrated Services Digital Network** (ISDN) is a **circuit-switched** and **dialed** digital WAN service. Dialed circuits are cheaper than leased-lines and packet-switched WAN services, and supports **concurrent** and **integrated** voice, data, and video transmission over **existing PSTNs**.

- ISDN uses **digital signals**, which allows faster transmission speed compared to analog lines. ISDN bandwidth is measured in increments of 64kbps.

- ISDN was introduced after analog modems. It has phased out as a home-based Internet access technology due to the existence of other competing remote access technologies, eg: DSL.

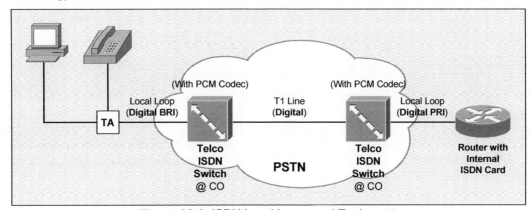

Figure 26-1: ISDN Local Loops and Equipments

- Routers often use ISDN interfaces that can directly connect to the Telco, while PCs typically require an ISDN device called an **ISDN terminal adapter** (TA). Most people misinterpret it as ISDN modem, as it was connected like an external modem. However, this is **inaccurate**, as ISDN uses digital signals and there is no modulation and demodulation processing as in analog modem communications. The functionality of TA has been incorporated into most ISDN routers.

- ISDN requires the installation of **new line** from Telco ISDN switch, as analog phone lines normally connect to a voice switch (for processing analog voice signals) whereas ISDN uses digital signals.

- ISDN has 2 types of interfaces: **Basic Rate Interface** (BRI) and **Primary Rate Interface** (PRI). Both provide multiple digital bearer channels (B channels) for data communication. Multiple B channels can be bundled together to increase the available bandwidth to a remote site.

- **B channels** are the **bearer** channels (bear or carry the data). It used for **data transmission**. A single B channel operates at the speed of 64kbps.

- **D channels** are the **signaling** channels. Phone number for dialing to the destination site is sent through D channel during the establishment phase of an ISDN connection. It is used for call control functions, which are **call setup**, **signaling**, and **call termination**.

- ISDN offers **very fast** call setup than analog modem dialup connections, which may take 30 – 60 seconds. ISDN circuits can be established in a second or two.

- Below lists the B and D channels on ISDN BRI and PRI:

Interface Type	Number of Bearer (B) Channels	Number of Signaling (D) Channels	Descriptive Term
BRI	2 (64kbps)	1 (16kbps)	2B+D
T1 PRI (1.544Mbps)	23 (64kbps)	1 (64kbps)	23B+D
E1 PRI (2.048Mbps)	30 (64kbps)	1 (64kbps)	30B+D

Note: E1 PRIs are being used in most parts of the world.

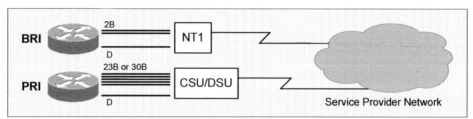

Figure 26-2: The B and D Channels on ISDN BRI and PRI

- Below lists the ITU-T ISDN standards and protocols:

Dealing With	Protocols	Key Examples
ISDN on existing telephone network	E-series	**E.163** – International telephone numbering plan **E.164** – International ISDN addressing
ISDN concepts, aspects, interfaces, and services	I-series	**I.100 series** – Concepts, structures, and terminology **I.400 series** – User-Network Interface (**UNI**)
Switching and signaling	Q-series	**Q.921** – Link Access Procedure – D Channel (**LAPD**) **Q.931** – ISDN network layer between terminal and ISDN switch (**SS7, DSS1**)

- Below lists the ISDN I-Series and Q-Series specifications:

Layer as in OSI Model	I-Series	Equivalent Q-Series Specification	Description
3	ITU-T I.450 ITU-T I.451	ITU-T Q.930 ITU-T Q.931	Defines ISDN signaling messages – call setup and termination messages. Ex: **SS7**.
2	ITU-T I.440 ITU-T I.441	ITU-T Q.920 ITU-T Q.921	Defines the **LAPD** protocol used on the D channel for **encapsulating** and **ensures the delivery** of the signaling information.
1	ITU-T I.430 ITU-T I.431	– –	Defines connectors, encoding, framing, and reference points.

Tips: From the 2nd digit of a standard, Q-series matches OSI Layers. For I-Series, minus 2.
Note: The ISDN D signaling channel comprises of the functionalities of Layer 1 to 3 of the OSI reference model.

- ISDN standards were published by International Telecommunications Union Telecommunication Standardization Sector (**ITU-T**).

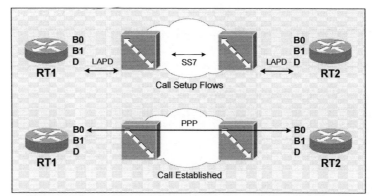

Figure 26-3: ISDN Call Setup Signaling over the D Channel

- **LAPD** is used as a data link protocol across the ISDN D channel, which is used to **encapsulate and deliver signaling messages**. LAPD does not define the signaling messages itself. **Signaling** is referred to as the requests which are being used to establish a circuit.

- During the establishment of a dialed ISDN circuit, LAPD is used for sending signals between the router and ISDN switch through ISDN D channel. **Signaling System 7** (SS7) is used for **signaling between Telco ISDN switches** for establishing ISDN connections. It is the same protocol that is used by phone companies for the establishment of phone calls.

- Sequence of events occurred during the establishment of a BRI or PRI circuit:
  i) The D channel between a router and an ISDN switch is **always up**. When a call is initiated, the called number will be sent to the ISDN switch through the D channel.
  ii) The local ISDN switch uses SS7 to setup a path and pass the called number to the remote ISDN switch at the other end.
  iii) The ISDN switch at the other end signals the destination router through the D channel.
  iv) A B channel is established. Another B channel is available for data transmission or phone call. Both B channels can be used simultaneously for higher bandwidth (2B+D).

- An ISDN switch uses **Service Profile Identifier** (SPID) to authenticate a device connecting to it.

- The D channel always remains up for new signaling messages to be sent and received – signals are sent **outside the data transmission channels**. This is referred to as **out-of-band signaling**.

- **Point-to-Point Protocol** (PPP) is commonly being used as the data link protocol on B channels. **High-Level Data Link Control** (HDLC) can be used as well.

- **Q:** ISDN supports voice and data over the same digital local loop. How does an ISDN digital circuit transport analog voice signals?
  A: An ISDN TA is able to perform PCM encoding and decoding functions and sends the analog voice signals over a B channel. When an analog phone generates DTMF tones, the TA interprets the tones and generates a signaling message over the D channel. After a circuit has been setup over one of the B channels, the TA begins to use its PCM codec to encode incoming analog signals from the phone into PCM digital signals, and sends them over the established B channel.
  Note: DTMF (**Dual-Tone Multi-Frequency**) is also known as **Touch Tone** or **Tone Dialing**. DMTF assigns specific frequencies to phone keys which used for **signaling during call setup**.

- ISDN was designed to reuse the existing customer devices as much as possible in order to **accelerate the acceptance** of the technology. As a result, ITU defined several options of the equipments required for ISDN access to provide **several migration paths** for the public. Customers have the options to purchase the required equipments according to their budgets.

- **Function** is referred to as device or hardware.
  Reference Point is referred to as **demarcation** or **interface** a function connects to.

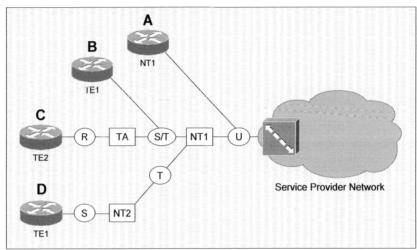

Figure 26-4: ISDN Function Groups and Reference Points

Router	Type of Interface Used
A	ISDN card, U interface (BRI interface with an integral NT1)
B	ISDN card, S/T interface (BRI interface without an integral NT1)
C	Router with a serial interface or PC with a RS–232 connection to the R ref. point
D	ISDN card, S/T interface

- Below lists the ISDN function groups:

Function Group	Description
TE1	An ISDN-compliant device (eg: router). Understands ISDN standards. Can be directly connected to the local loop. Uses an S or S/T ref. point.
TE2	Non ISDN-complaint device – a node that does not understand ISDN protocols and specifications (PC or router). Uses an R reference point.
TA	It converts TE2 non-ISDN signals to ISDN BRI signals. Uses R and S reference points. (**Note:** TAs are often misinterpreted as ISDN modems)
NT1	A device that implements the ISDN physical layer (L1) specifications. Converts between the 4-wire BRI signals of an S/T interface (from routers) and the 2-wire BRI signals of a U interface (to Telco). Uses a U reference point and directly connects to the local loop (Telco), and connects with S/T or T reference points to other CPEs.
NT2	A more complicated device (performs L2 and L3 functions) that uses a T reference point to Telco outside North America or to an NT1 inside North America. Connects with an S reference point to other CPEs.
NT1/NT2	A combined NT1 and NT2 in the same device. Can be directly connected to the local loop (Telco). Very common in North America.

- **TE** is referred to as Terminal Equipment / Endpoint.
  TA is referred to as Terminal Adapter.
  NT is referred to as Network Termination.

- Below lists the ISDN reference points (demarcations):

Reference Point	Connects Between
R	TE2 and TA (a non-ISDN device and a TA). TE2s and TAs are regular.
S	TE1 and NT1 or NT2, or TA and NT1. TE1s are special.
T	NT1 and NT2.
U	NT1 and Telco.
S/T	NT1 and TE1 or TA (when NT2 is not being used) or TE1 and a combined NT1/NT2 (when NT2 is being used).

- U = U.S. demarcation. S, T, S/T = Non-U.S. demarcation.

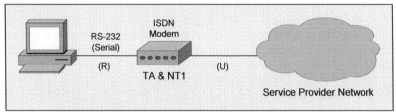

Figure 26-5: ISDN Home User and Reference Points

- By looking at the back of a Cisco router, one may evaluate its ISDN connection ability.

BRI	The router has an ISDN BRI. It is a TE1 as a native ISDN interface has already built-in.
U	The router has a built-in NT1.

  else an existing serial interface will be used to connect it to a TA to provide BRI connectivity.

- **Q:** What will happen if we connect a router with a U interface to an NT1?
  A: This will damage the router interface, as the router U interface already has a built-in NT1.

- ITU defines the mentioned ISDN access options for BRI, as it was targeted at consumer market; whereas PRI was targeted at corporate customers, due to its larger number of B channels (larger bandwidth). ITU **did not define** function groups and reference points for ISDN PRI. PRI wiring is not multipoint; there is **only a straight connection** between a CSU/DSU and a PRI interface.
  Note: BRI wiring (or configuration) supports multipoint, where there are 2 phone numbers, one for each B channel. With multipoint configuration, 2 devices may share a BRI line, and a phone number (in fact, **Service Profile Identifier**, SPID) will be assigned for each device.

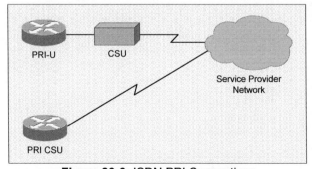

Figure 26-6: ISDN PRI Connections

- ISDN PRIs are often being used for connecting PSTN circuits to **Private Branch Exchange** (PBX) systems, which are telephone exchanges that serving small offices.

- Physical layer always includes some specifications about encoding and framing to allow network devices to send and receive bits over the media. The details normally can be ignored. However, some understanding on encoding and framing is important for ISDN PRI configuration, as when configuring PRI connections on Cisco routers, the encoding and framing information and options (as provided by the Telco) must be configured correctly for proper operation.

- **PRI Encoding** → In physical layer, encoding defines how to represent 1s and 0s with different energy levels, eg: **+5 volt** = 1 and **−5 volt** = 0.
  The available encoding schemes for T1 ISDN PRI are **Alternate Mark Inversion** (AMI) and **Binary 8 with Zero Substitution / Bipolar 8 with Zero Substitution** (B8ZS).
  The only encoding scheme for E1 ISDN PRI is **High-Density Bipolar 3** (HDB3).

- **PRI Framing** → PRI lines send and receive a serial stream of bits. In ISDN physical layer, framing defines how to interpret a serial stream of bits to identify the individual component channels of a bit stream – this bit is part of the D channel, or the 1st B channel, or …
  The available framing formats for T1 ISDN PRI are **Super Frame** (SF) and **Extended Super Frame** (ESF). SF is the older format.
  The available framing formats for E1 ISDN PRI are **CRC4** and **NO-CRC4**.

Encoding	AMI and B8ZS (T1). HDB3 (E1).
Framing	SF and ESF (T1). CRC4 and NO-CRC4 (E1).

- **Alternate Mark Inversion** (AMI) is a T1 encoding scheme that encodes 0s as 01 during each bit cell, and 1s as 11 or 00 alternately during each bit cell. The sending device must maintain ones density but not independently of the data stream. It is contrast with B8ZS.
  Binary 8 with Zero Substitution (B8ZS) is another T1 encoding scheme which is being interpreted at the remote end of a connection. It uses a special substitution code whenever 8 consecutive 0s are transmitted over a T1 circuit. It is contrast with AMI.

- **T1** = 24 different 64kbps DS0 channels + a 8kbps management channel (1.544Mbps)
  E1 = 32 different 64kbps DS0 channels (2.048Mbps)
  T1 = 23B+1D. E1 = 30B+1D + 1 used for synchronization.

- ISDN BRI uses a single encoding scheme (2B+D) and a single format for framing. Hence, it has **no encoding and framing configuration options** as in PRI.

- ISDN E channel (Echo channel) is a 64kbps control channel used for circuit switching. Information of this channel can be found in the 1984 ITU-T ISDN specification, but it was dropped since the 1988 version of the specification.

- ISDN H channel (High-speed channel) is a full-duplex ISDN primary rate channel which performs the same function as B channel, but operates at rates exceeding DS0 (64kbps). Below shows its implementations and the corresponding transmission rates:

H0	384kbps (6 B channels)
H10	1472kbps (23 B channels)
H11	1536kbps (24 B channels)
H12	1920kbps (30 B channels)

Chapter 27
ISDN and Dial-on-Demand Routing Lab

Dial-on-Demand Routing

- DDR is an important and useful IOS feature when using dialed connections, eg: ISDN. It allows routers to dynamically initiate and terminate circuit-switched connections.

- A router can be configured to consider certain traffic as **interesting traffic** while other traffic as **boring traffic**. When a router receives interesting traffic that is destined for a remote network, a circuit is established, and the traffic is transmitted normally. If the router receives boring traffic when a circuit is already established, that traffic is also being transmitted normally. The router maintains an idle timer that is reset only when it receives interesting traffic. When there is no more interesting traffic is being transmitted over the circuit for a certain period (the idle timer), the established circuit would be terminated.

- Below are some examples of interesting traffic:
  - i)   Traffic destined to a particular host.
  - ii) Traffic destined to a particular application layer protocol, eg: HTTP, FTP, SSH, etc.
  - iii) Traffic from a particular network layer protocol, eg: ICMP, OSPF, EIGRP, etc.

- DDR can be used to establish dial circuit on asynchronous and synchronous serial interfaces, as well as ISDN BRI and PRI interfaces. An established ISDN link acts like a leased line.

Legacy DDR Configuration

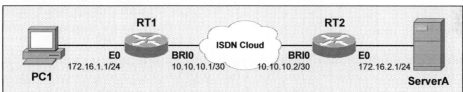

Figure 27-1: Sample ISDN Network with One Remote Site

- Figure 27-1 shows an ISDN network with 1 remote site, with RT1 as the ISDN dialing router.

- The 4 main steps in Legacy DDR configuration:
  - i)   Routing packets out the dial interface.
  - ii) Determining the subset of the routed packets (**interesting packets**) that triggers the dialing process.
  - iii) Dialing (or Signaling).
  - iv) Determining when to terminate the connection.

DDR Step 1: Routing packets out the dial interface.

- DDR does not dial until some traffic is routed out the dial interface. A packet must pass through some routing processes, and decided by the dialing router to route it through the dial interface.

- Notes on static routes configuration:
  - i)   All routers must have static routes to all known networks.
  - ii) Default routing can be used on stub networks.

- Routing protocols are unable to learn routes over inactive links. In Figure 27-1, RT1 unable to learn routes to 172.16.2.0/24 via a routing protocol, as the BRI connection is not yet established. Static routes are normally being used for this kind of scenario.

- Static Route configuration on RT1:

```
RT1#conf t
Enter configuration commands, one per line.  End with CNTL/Z.
RT1(config)#ip route 172.16.2.0 255.255.255.0 10.10.10.2
RT1(config)#
```

DDR Step 2: Determining the subset of the routed packets (**interesting packets**) that triggers the dialing process.

- Only interesting packets can cause a dial to occur. But when the dialed circuit is established, both interesting and boring traffic can be transmitted across the circuit.

- There are 2 methods of defining interesting packets to trigger a DDR call:
  i) **All packets**. Any packet from any host in RT1 Ethernet subnet destined to any host in 172.16.3.0/24 network can trigger the dialing process.
  ii) **Packets that are permitted by an access list**. Ex: Only packets from hosts in RT1 Ethernet subnet destined to ServerA, a web server, can trigger the dialing process.

- ISDN Interesting Traffic configuration on RT1:

```
RT1(config)#access-list 101 permit tcp any host 172.16.2.2 eq www
RT1(config)#dialer-list 1 protocol ip permit   (not being used in this configuration)
RT1(config)#dialer-list 2 protocol ip list 101
RT1(config)#
RT1(config)#int bri0
RT1(config-if)#ip address 10.10.10.1 255.255.255.248
RT1(config-if)#dialer-group 2
RT1(config-if)#
```

- The **dialer-group 2** interface subcommand associates RT1 BRI0 interface with dialer list 2, which refers to the IP extended ACL 101. The interesting packets are HTTP packets that destined to ServerA, a web server. The **dialer-list** global configuration command is used to specify the DDR interesting traffic.

- With **dialer-group 1** configured on the BRI0 interface, any IP traffic that tries to exit the interface is considered interesting traffic and can cause a dial to occur.

DDR Step 3: Dialing (or Signaling).

- The dialing router needs to know the phone number of the other router for the dialing process to establish a circuit.

- The **dialer string** {*string*} interface subcommand specifies the dialing string (phone number) to be used for signaling when there is only a single remote site.

- ISDN Signaling configuration on RT1 with a single remote site:

```
RT1(config-if)#dialer string 11111111
RT1(config-if)#^Z
RT1#
```

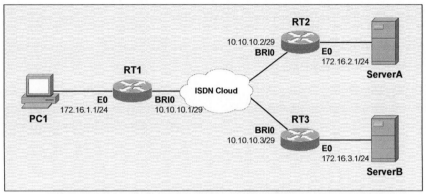

Figure 27-2: Sample ISDN Network with Multiple Remote Sites

- However, with multiple remote sites, the dialing router must know the phone number of the sites, as well as the phone number to use when calling to each site.

- The **dialer map** interface subcommand specifies the parameters to reach a destination router, eg: next-hop address, hostname, and the phone number (dial string).

- **Note:** PAP or CHAP authentication is required when dialing to more than one site with ISDN. Both authentication methods require **PPP encapsulation**. CHAP is used in this example.

- Since RT1 receives CHAP challenges from 2 different remote sites, thus it must know which router is sending the CHAP request. The **name** {*hostname*} parameter in the **dialer map** command tells the router which **username** command to use for the CHAP authentication.

- The **broadcast** keyword indicates whether broadcasts (eg: routing updates) can be sent across a PPP link. It does not really forward data link broadcasts.

- ISDN Signaling configuration on RT1 with multiple remote sites:

```
RT1#conf t
Enter configuration commands, one per line.  End with CNTL/Z.
RT1(config)#ip route 172.16.3.0 255.255.255.0 10.10.10.3
RT1(config)#access-list 101 permit tcp any host 172.16.3.2 eq ftp
RT1(config)#username RT2 password cisco123
RT1(config)#username RT3 password cisco456
RT1(config)#
RT1(config)#int bri0
RT1(config-if)#encapsulation ppp
RT1(config-if)#ppp authentication chap
RT1(config-if)#no dialer string 11111111
RT1(config-if)#dialer map ip 10.10.10.2 broadcast name RT2 11111111
RT1(config-if)#dialer map ip 10.10.10.3 broadcast name RT3 22222222
```

DDR Step 4: Determining when to terminate the connection.

- Both interesting and boring packets can be transmitted through an established circuit, but only the interesting packets are considered worthy of keeping the link up and spending more money. An idle timer is able to track the time since the last interesting packet is sent across the circuit. When there is no more interesting traffic is being transmitted over the circuit for a certain period (the idle timer), the established circuit will be terminated.

- The **idle-timeout** timer specifies the idle timer for a call. This timer terminates the call if no interesting traffic has been transmitted for the specified period. The default is 120 seconds.

- The **fast-idle** timer is another shorter idle timer that specifies a faster disconnect timer when there is another call waiting for an interface and the interface is idle. The waiting call does not have to wait for the idle timer to expire to terminate an idle circuit. The default is 20 seconds.

- ISDN Idle Timers configuration on RT1:

```
RT1(config)#int bri0
RT1(config-if)#dialer idle-timeout 300   (5 minutes)
RT1(config-if)#dialer fast-idle 10
```

ISDN BRI Configuration

- An ISDN router needs to know the type of ISDN switch it connects to. This can be done with the **isdn switch-type** {*sw-type*} global command or interface subcommand. The switch type configured in interface configuration mode *overrides* the global setting for a particular interface.

- ISDN switches use a free-form decimal value – **Service Profile Identifier** (SPID) to authenticate the device that is connecting to it. Before any Q.931 call setup messages are accepted, the dialed-in ISDN switch will ask for the configured SPIDs. The call setup flows are accepted only if the SPIDs match as what is configured in the ISDN switch. The SPIDs are given by the service provider and are configured on the ISDN BRI D channel.

- ISDN BRI configuration on RT1:

```
RT1(config)#isdn switch-type basic-ni
RT1(config)#int bri0
RT1(config-if)#isdn spid1 12345678   (setting the SPID for the 1st B channel)
RT1(config-if)#isdn spid2 87654321   (setting the SPID for the 2nd B channel)
```

- Complete ISDN BRI and DDR configuration on RT2 and RT3:

```
RTx(config)#username RT1 password cisco{xxx}   (123 for RT2, 456 for RT3)
RTx(config)#ip route 172.16.1.0 255.255.255.0 172.16.2.1
RTx(config)#int bri0
RTx(config-if)#ip add 10.10.10.{x} 255.255.255.0
RTx(config-if)#encapsulation ppp
RTx(config-if)#ppp authentication chap
RTx(config-if)#isdn switch-type basic-ni
RTx(config-if)#no shut
```

- Complete ISDN BRI and DDR configurations on RT1:

```
!
username RT2 password 0 cisco123
username RT3 password 0 cisco456
!
isdn switch-type basic-ni
!
interface BRI0
 ip address 10.10.10.1 255.255.255.248
 encapsulation ppp
 dialer idle-timeout 300
 dialer fast-idle 60
 dialer map ip 10.10.10.2 name RT2 broadcast 11111111
 dialer map ip 10.10.10.3 name RT3 broadcast 22222222
 dialer-group 2
 isdn switch-type basic-ni
 isdn spid1 12345678
 isdn spid2 87654321
 ppp authentication chap
!
ip route 172.16.2.0 255.255.255.0 10.10.10.2
ip route 172.16.3.0 255.255.255.0 10.10.10.3
!
access-list 101 permit tcp any host 172.16.2.2 eq www
access-list 101 permit tcp any host 172.16.3.2 eq ftp
dialer-list 1 protocol ip permit
dialer-list 2 protocol ip list 101
!
```

MISC ISDN BRI and DDR show and debug Commands

- The **show dialer interface** {*intf-type intf-num*} EXEC command displays useful diagnosis information, eg: timer values, call setup reason, call length, and the hostname of the remote router.

```
RT1#sh dialer int bri0

BRI0 - dialer type = ISDN

Dial String      Successes   Failures    Last DNIS   Last status
11111111                 6          3    00:00:00    successful   Default
22222222                 5          2    00:15:09        failed   Default
0 incoming call(s) have been screened.
0 incoming call(s) rejected for callback.

BRI0:1 - dialer type = ISDN
Idle timer (300 secs), Fast idle timer (60 secs)
Wait for carrier (30 secs), Re-enable (15 secs)
Dialer state is data link layer up
Dial reason: ip (s=172.16.1.2, d=172.16.2.2)
Time until disconnect 30 secs
Current call connected 00:12:30
Connected to 11111111 (RT2)

BRI0:2 - dialer type = ISDN
Idle timer (300 secs), Fast idle timer (60 secs)
Wait for carrier (30 secs), Re-enable (15 secs)
Dialer state is idle
RT1#
```

- The **show interfaces bri** {*num*:**0 | 1**} EXEC command displays the ISDN B channel status, configurations, and statistics, eg: the number of input and output packets.

```
RT1#sh int bri0:1
BRIO:1 is up, line protocol is up
  Hardware is BRI
  MTU 1500 bytes, BW 64 Kbit, DLY 20000 usec,
     reliability 255/255, txload 1/255, rxload 1/255
  Encapsulation PPP, LCP Open
  Open: CDPCP, IPCP, loopback not set
  Keepalive set (10 sec)
--More-
```

- The **show isdn active** EXEC command displays general information about active calls.

- The **show isdn status** EXEC command can be used to display information of ISDN Layer 1, 2, and 3 statuses between a router ISDN interface and the ISDN switch, which are very useful for ISDN troubleshooting.

```
RT1#sh isdn status
Global ISDN Switchtype = basic-ni
ISDN BRIO interface
    Layer 1 Status:
        ACTIVE
    Layer 2 Status:
        TEI = 64, State = MULTIPLE_FRAME_ESTABLISHED
    Layer 3 Status:
        1 Active Layer 3 Call(s)
    Active dsl 0 CCBs = 1
        CCB:callid=8003, callref-0, sapi=0, ces=1, B-chan=1
    Number of active calls = 1
    Number of available B channels = 1
    Total Allocated ISDN CCBs = 1
RT1#
```

	B Channel	D Channel
Layer 3	IP / IPX	SS7 / DSS1 (Q.931)
Layer 2	HDLC / PPP	LAPD (Q.921)
Layer 1	I.430 / I.431	

Figure 27-3: ISDN Standards on B and D Channels

- The **debug isdn q921** privileged command displays the details of the LAPD protocol on the ISDN D channel between a router ISDN interface and the ISDN switch (Layer 2 information).

- The **debug isdn q931** privileged command displays the information of ISDN call setup and termination activities (Layer 3 information).

- The **debug dialer events** and **debug dialer packets** privileged commands display the packets that were routed out the dial interface and triggered the dialing process.

ISDN PRI Configuration

- The 4 main steps in ISDN PRI configuration:
    i) Configure the **ISDN switch type** to be connected to.
    ii) Configure the T1 or E1 encoding and framing options.
    iii) Configure the T1 or E1 channel range for the DS0 channels used on this PRI.
    iv) Configure the interface settings (eg: PPP encapsulation, PPP authentication, IP address, dialer configuration) on the **subinterface that representing the D channel**.

- The controller configuration mode is being used to configure ISDN PRI physical layer parameters, eg: encoding, framing, and the number of DS0 channels used on the PRI.
  Note: controller interface – L1 configuration; serial interface – L2 and L3 configurations.

- Normally all 24 DS0 channels in the PRI will be fully utilized – 23 B channels and a D channel.

- ISDN PRI T1 controller configuration on RT1:

```
RT1#conf t
Enter configuration commands, one per line.  End with CNTL/Z.
RT1(config)#controller t1 1/0
RT1(config-controller)#linecode b8zs
RT1(config-controller)#framing esf
RT1(config-controller)#pri-group timeslots 1-24
RT1(config-controller)#no shut
RT1(config-controller)#exit
RT1(config)#
```

Note: The **pri-group timeslots 1-31** controller subcommand is used instead when configuring ISDN E1 controllers.

- ISDN PRI T1 configuration on RT1:

```
RT1(config)#int serial1/0:23
RT1(config-if)#ip add 10.10.10.1 255.255.255.248
RT1(config-if)#encapsulation ppp
RT1(config-if)#ppp authentication chap
RT1(config-if)#dialer idle-timeout 300
RT1(config-if)#dialer fast-idle 10
RT1(config-if)#dialer map ip 10.10.10.2 broadcast name RT2 11111111
RT1(config-if)#dialer map ip 10.10.10.3 broadcast name RT3 22222222
RT1(config-if)#dialer-group 2
RT1(config-if)#no shut
RT1(config-if)#^Z
RT1#
```

- DDR configuration is configured on the D channel. A T1 connection consists of 24 channels (numbered from 0 to 23); while an E1 connection consists of 31 channels (numbered from 0 to 31). The subinterfaces 23 and 15 represent the D channel of T1 and E1 respectively.
  Note: T1 = US standards.

- There is no SPID configuration required, as ISDN PRI circuits **do not** use SPID.

DDR Dialer Profiles Configuration

- Legacy DDR associates dial configuration details with physical interfaces. When there are multiple BRIs or PRIs available, legacy DDR is only able to dial to a set of sites with an interface, and another set of sites with the other interface.

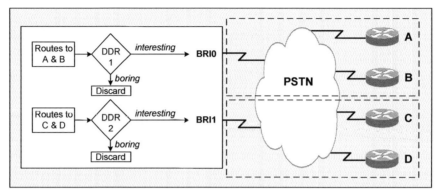

Figure 27-4: Legacy DDR with 2 BRIs and 4 Remote Sites

- The router in Figure 27-4 can be configured to route packets to site A and B through BRI0, and route packets to site C and D through BRI1, with 2 different dialer groups on the BRI interfaces.

- The limitation of legacy DDR in this scenario is it cannot be configured to dial to all remote sites with **any available B channel on either BRI**, as the configured static routes would route packets out a single BRI and hence only a single BRI can be used to reach a particular remote site.

- Dialer profiles overcome the limitation and allow **greater flexibility** by disassociating the dial configuration details from the physical interfaces, and **pool multiple interfaces** to allow a router to use an available B channel on any interface in the pool to dial and connect to a remote site.

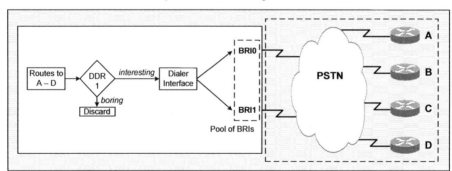

Figure 27-5: DDR Dialer Pool with 2 BRIs and 4 Remote Sites

- With DDR dialer profiles configuration, most of the DDR interface configurations are moved from physical interfaces to virtual interfaces called **dialer interfaces**.

- A BRI or PRI physical interface can be a **member** of a pool of available ISDN interfaces. Whenever an interesting packet is being routed out the dialer interface and triggered ISDN DDR, any ISDN interface with an available B channel will be selected from the pool for dialing.

- DDR Dialer Profiles configuration on RT1:

```
!
username RT2 password 0 cisco123
username RT3 password 0 cisco456
!
isdn switch-type basic-ni
!
interface BRI0
 no ip address
 encapsulation ppp
[7] dialer pool-member 1
 isdn switch-type basic-ni
 isdn spid1 12345678
 isdn spid2 87654321
 ppp authentication chap
!
interface BRI1
 no ip address
 encapsulation ppp
[7] dialer pool-member 1
 isdn switch-type basic-ni
 isdn spid1 23456789
 isdn spid2 98765432
 ppp authentication chap
!
[3] interface Dialer1
 ip address 10.10.10.1 255.255.255.252
 encapsulation ppp
[6] dialer pool 1
[4] dialer remote-name RT2
 dialer idle-timeout 300
 dialer fast-idle 60
 dialer string 11111111
 dialer-group 1
 ppp authentication chap
!
[3] interface Dialer2
 ip address 11.11.11.1 255.255.255.252
 encapsulation ppp
[6] dialer pool 1
[4] dialer remote-name RT3
 dialer idle-timeout 300
 dialer fast-idle 60
[5] dialer string 22222222 class dclass-56kpbs
 dialer-group 2
 ppp authentication chap
!
[1] ip route 172.16.2.0 255.255.255.0 10.10.10.2
 ip route 172.16.3.0 255.255.255.0 11.11.11.2
!
[5] map-class dialer dclass-56kpbs
 dialer isdn speed 56
!
[2] access-list 101 permit tcp any host 172.16.2.2 eq www
 access-list 102 permit tcp any host 172.16.3.2 eq ftp
 dialer-list 1 protocol ip list 101
 dialer-list 2 protocol ip list 102
!
```

- **Note:** IP addresses are configured on dialer interfaces instead of the physical interfaces.

- With DDR dialer profiles configuration, a dialer interface is created for each remote site. The **dialer string** command is used instead of the **dialer map** command since there is only one remote site associated with each dialer interface. All dialer interfaces reside in **different subnets**, which is like having virtual point-to-point links to each remote site.

- DDR dialer profiles configuration explanations:
  1) Each **ip route** command points to a **different next-hop address** in **different subnet**.
  2) There are 2 different ACLs as different **dialer-list** commands were created for each site.
  3) The 2 different virtual **dialer interfaces** contain the commands for dialing to each site.
  4) The name of a remote router which was configured as a parameter in the **dialer-map** command is replaced with the **dialer remote-name** {*name*} interface subcommand.
  5) The dialer interface 2 is configured to use a 56kbps B channel with a dialer class.
  6) Dialer interfaces are logical and not physical, hence are unable to dial an actual call. The dialer pool logic associated with a dialer interface will pick an available B channel from a **dialer pool** when initiating a call.
  7) The 2 BRI interfaces (total 4 B channels) are configured with their corresponding SPIDs, and are associated to a pool with the **dialer pool-member 1** interface subcommand.

Note: In dial backup scenarios, it is important to disable IP route cache on ISDN interfaces using the **no ip route-cache** interface subcommand to ensure that the router does not cache any destination as reachable through the ISDN interface and continue to send traffic for those destinations through the ISDN interface until the route cache entry times out, even the primary serial interface is restored.

Multilink PPP (MLP / MLPPP) Configuration

- It allows the creation of **multiple links** between routers, which traffic can be load balanced upon.

- Load balancing over parallel links without MLPPP is **unpredictable** and can be **underutilized**, as the Cisco routers default switching mode – **fast switching** would send all packets destined to the same IP address over the same link. Whenever some high volume data is being transmitted to a single IP address, the packets would only be transmitted over a same single link.

- A PC can dial 2 ISDN B channels instead of one for faster connection. MLPPP breaks or fragments each packet into 2 **equal-sized** packets, sends each fragment across each link, and reassembles them back at the other end of the link.

- The **dialer load-threshold** {*load*} [**inbound** | **outbound** | **either**] interface subcommand defines when to bring up the 2nd B channel. The load threshold range is 1 – 255, where 255 tells the BRI to bring up the 2nd B channel only when the 1st channel is 100% loaded. The second parameter is **inbound**, **outbound**, or **either**. It calculates the actual load on the interface either on inbound traffic, outbound traffic, or either direction. The default is **outbound**.
  Note: Multilink PPP is also referred as **Bandwidth on Demand** (BoD).

- PPP Multilink configuration:

```
Router(config)#int bri0
Router(config-if)#ppp multilink
Router(config-if)#dialer load-threshold 190 either
```

The **dialer load-threshold 190 either** interface subcommand tells the BRI interface to bring up the 2nd B channel if either the inbound or outbound traffic load excesses 75%.

Chapter 28
Route Redistribution

- Route redistribution is being used to redistribute (or transfer) routes **between routing domains**. It is beyond the scope of CCNA. However the practical knowledge is very important for becoming a better and more capable internetworking professional or network engineer.

- The main issue to address in route redistribution is **metric**.

- Each routing protocol has its own method of determining the best path to a destination network. RIP uses hop counts, IGRP and EIGRP use a composite metric (bandwidth, delay, reliability, and load), OSPF uses bandwidth, etc. Due to the differences in metric calculations, when redistributing routes from one routing protocol into another, all **metrics will be lost**. Network engineers will have to manually specify the cost metric for each routing domain.

- Another issue to address with route redistribution is that some routing protocols are **classful**, while some are **classless**, which makes redistributing VLSM and CIDR routes from a classless routing protocol into a classful routing protocol a challenging task.

- Route redistribution can get very complicated and can introduce many other problems. Sometimes the solutions to a problem are even more complicated than the problem itself.

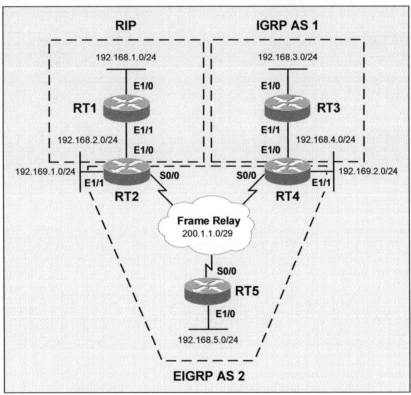

Figure 28-1: Sample Route Redistribution Network

- Below show the routing tables on all routers before route redistribution:

```
RT1#sh ip route
Gateway of last resort is not set

C    192.168.1.0/24 is directly connected, Ethernet1/0
C    192.168.2.0/24 is directly connected, Ethernet1/1

--------------------------------------------------

RT2#sh ip route
Gateway of last resort is not set

R    192.168.1.0/24 [120/1] via 192.168.2.1, 00:00:10, Ethernet1/0
C    192.168.2.0/24 is directly connected, Ethernet1/0
D    192.168.5.0/24 [90/1787392] via 200.1.1.3, 00:00:35, Serial0/0
C    192.169.1.0/24 is directly connected, Ethernet1/1
D    192.169.2.0/24 [90/1787392] via 200.1.1.2, 00:00:35, Serial0/0
C    200.1.1.0/29 is directly connected, Serial0/0

--------------------------------------------------

RT3#sh ip route
Gateway of last resort is not set

C    192.168.3.0/24 is directly connected, Ethernet1/0
C    192.168.4.0/24 is directly connected, Ethernet1/1

--------------------------------------------------

RT4#sh ip route
Gateway of last resort is not set

I    192.168.3.0/24 [100/1200] via 192.168.4.1, 00:00:25, Ethernet1/0
C    192.168.4.0/24 is directly connected, Ethernet1/0
D    192.168.5.0/24 [90/1787392] via 200.1.1.3, 00:07:30, Serial0/0
D    192.169.1.0/24 [90/1787392] via 200.1.1.1, 00:07:30, Serial0/0
C    192.169.2.0/24 is directly connected, Ethernet1/1
C    200.1.1.0/29 is directly connected, Serial0/0

--------------------------------------------------

RT5#sh ip route
Gateway of last resort is not set

C    192.168.5.0/24 is directly connected, Ethernet1/0
D    192.169.1.0/24 [90/1787392] via 200.1.1.1, 00:08:15, Serial0/0
D    192.169.2.0/24 [90/1787392] via 200.1.1.2, 00:08:15, Serial0/0
C    200.1.1.0/29 is directly connected, Serial0/0
```

Route Redistribution Configuration

- Route redistribution redistributes routes from the source protocol into the destination protocol, which is achieved by entering the router configuration mode for the destination protocol and followed by the **redistribute** router subcommand to bring in the routes of the source protocol.

- The **redistribute** {*protocol*} {*as-num* | *process-id*} {*metric*} router subcommand is used to redistributes routes from one routing protocol to another routing protocol.

- The *as-num* parameter is applicable only to routing protocols that use AS number identifiers, eg: IGRP and EIGRP; while the *process-id* parameter is applicable only to OSPF.

- RT2 is the boundary of for RIP and EIGRP, while RT4 is the boundary of IGRP and EIGRP. These are the places to redistribute routes between routing domains (or protocols).

- Route Redistribution from EIGRP into RIP configuration on RT2:

```
RT2(config)#router rip
RT2(config-router)#redistribute eigrp 2 metric 1
RT2(config-router)#
```

- The configuration above set all routes coming from EIGRP AS 2 as 1 hop count since RIP uses hop counts as the metric.

- Below shows the routing table on RT1 to verify the EIGRP is properly redistributed into RIP:

```
RT1#sh ip route
Gateway of last resort is not set

C    192.168.1.0/24 is directly connected, Ethernet1/0
C    192.168.2.0/24 is directly connected, Ethernet1/1
R    192.168.5.0/24 [120/1] via 192.168.2.2, 00:00:15, Ethernet1/1
R    192.169.1.0/24 [120/1] via 192.168.2.2, 00:00:15, Ethernet1/1
R    192.169.2.0/24 [120/1] via 192.168.2.2, 00:00:15, Ethernet1/1
R    200.1.1.0/24 [120/1] via 192.168.2.2, 00:00:15, Ethernet1/1

RT1#
```

- Route Redistribution from RIP into EIGRP configuration on RT2:

```
RT2(config)#router eigrp 2
RT2(config-router)#redistribute rip metric ?
  <1-4294967295>  Bandwidth metric in Kbits per second
RT2(config-router)#redistribute rip metric 2000 ?
  <0-4294967295>  EIGRP delay metric, in 10 microsecond units
RT2(config-router)#redistribute rip metric 2000 200 ?
  <0-255>  EIGRP reliability metric where 255 is 100% reliable
RT2(config-router)#redistribute rip metric 2000 200 255 ?
  <1-255>  EIGRP Effective bandwidth metric (Loading) where 255 is 100% loaded
RT2(config-router)#redistribute rip metric 2000 200 255 1 ?
  <1-65535>  EIGRP MTU of the path
RT2(config-router)#redistribute rip metric 2000 200 255 1 1500
RT2(config-router)#
```

- The configuration above defines 2000 bandwidth metric, 200 microseconds delay, and considers all links to be 100% reliable and have minimum traffic for all routes redistributed from RIP. EIGRP route redistribution configuration requires configuring all the composite metric values.

- **Note:** The subnet mask of the route to the Frame Relay network is /24 instead of /29. This is because EIGRP has summarized the route to its classful boundary. Additionally, classful routing protocols (eg: RIP) which do not understand VLSM and CIDR would drop the routing updates.

- Below shows the routing table on RT5 to verify the RIP is properly redistributed into EIGRP:

```
RT5#sh ip route
Gateway of last resort is not set

D EX 192.168.1.0/24 [170/2221056] via 200.1.1.1, 00:15:30, Serial0/0
D EX 192.168.2.0/24 [170/2221056] via 200.1.1.1, 00:15:30, Serial0/0
C    192.168.5.0/24 is directly connected, Ethernet1/0
D    192.169.1.0/24 [90/2195456] via 200.1.1.1, 00:08:15, Serial0/0
D    192.169.2.0/24 [90/2195456] via 200.1.1.2, 00:08:15, Serial0/0
C    200.1.1.0/29 is directly connected, Serial0/0

RT5#
```

- Route Redistribution from EIGRP into IGRP configuration on RT4:

```
RT4(config)#router igrp 1
RT4(config-router)#redistribute eigrp 2 metric 2000 200 255 1 1500
RT4(config-router)#
```

- Route Redistribution from IGRP into EIGRP configuration on RT4:

```
RT4(config)#router eigrp 2
RT4(config-router)#redistribute igrp 1 metric 2000 200 255 1 1500
RT4(config-router)#
```

- Below shows the routing table on RT3 to verify the EIGRP is properly redistributed into IGRP:

```
RT3#sh ip route
Gateway of last resort is not set

I    192.168.1.0/24 [100/8776] via 192.168.4.2, 00:00:30, Ethernet1/1
I    192.168.2.0/24 [100/8776] via 192.168.4.2, 00:00:30, Ethernet1/1
C    192.168.3.0/24 is directly connected, Ethernet1/0
C    192.168.4.0/24 is directly connected, Ethernet1/1
I    192.168.5.0/24 [100/8676] via 192.168.4.2, 00:00:30, Ethernet1/1
I    192.169.1.0/24 [100/8676] via 192.168.4.2, 00:00:30, Ethernet1/1
I    192.169.2.0/24 [100/1200] via 192.168.4.2, 00:00:30, Ethernet1/1
I    200.1.1.0/24 [100/8576] via 192.168.4.2, 00:00:30, Ethernet1/1

RT3#
```

- **Note:** All RIP routes are also shown in RT3 routing table, as the RIP routes have been redistributed into EIGRP at RT2. So when EIGRP routes are being redistributed into IGRP at RT4, all the RIP routes are being redistributed into IGRP as well.

Cisco IOS Upgrade and Password Recovery Procedures

Cisco Router IOS Upgrade Procedure

```
Router>
Router>en
Router#conf t
Enter configuration commands, one per line.  End with CNTL/Z.
Router(config)#config-register 0x2101
Router(config)#^Z
Router#
Router#sh ver
Cisco Internetwork Operating System Software
IOS (tm) 2500 Software (C2500-IS-L), Version 12.3(12), RELEASE SOFTWARE
(fc3)
Technical Support: http://www.cisco.com/techsupport
Copyright (c) 1986-2004 by cisco Systems, Inc.
Compiled Tue 30-Nov-04 02:33 by kellythw
Image text-base: 0x03094EA4, data-base: 0x00001000

ROM: System Bootstrap, Version 5.2(8a), RELEASE SOFTWARE
BOOTLDR: 3000 Bootstrap Software (IGS-RXBOOT), Version 10.2(8a), RELEASE
SOFTWARE (fc1)

Router uptime is 1 minutes
System returned to ROM by power-on
System image file is "flash:c2500-is-l.123-12.bin"

cisco 2500 (68030) processor (revision N) with 14336K/2048K bytes of memory.
Processor board ID 05534538, with hardware revision 00000000
Bridging software.
X.25 software, Version 3.0.0.
Basic Rate ISDN software, Version 1.1.
1 Ethernet/IEEE 802.3 interface(s)
2 Serial network interface(s)
1 ISDN Basic Rate interface(s)
32K bytes of non-volatile configuration memory.
16384K bytes of processor board System flash (Read ONLY)

Configuration register is 0x2102 (will be 0x2101 at next reload)

Router#reload

System configuration has been modified. Save? [yes/no]: no
Proceed with reload? [confirm]
*Mar  1 00:01:33.871: %SYS-5-RELOAD: Reload requested by console. Reload
Reason: Reload command.
System Bootstrap, Version 5.2(8a), RELEASE SOFTWARE
Copyright (c) 1986-1995 by cisco Systems
2500 processor with 14336 Kbytes of main memory

                    Restricted Rights Legend

Use, duplication, or disclosure by the Government is
subject to restrictions as set forth in subparagraph
(c) of the Commercial Computer Software - Restricted
Rights clause at FAR sec. 52.227-19 and subparagraph
(c) (1) (ii) of the Rights in Technical Data and Computer
Software clause at DFARS sec. 252.227-7013.
```

```
                   cisco Systems, Inc.
                   170 West Tasman Drive
                   San Jose, California 95134-1706


Cisco Internetwork Operating System Software
IOS (tm) 3000 Bootstrap Software (IGS-RXBOOT), Version 10.2(8a), RELEASE
SOFTWARE (fc1)
Copyright (c) 1986-1995 by cisco Systems, Inc.
Compiled Tue 24-Oct-95 15:46 by mkamson
Image text-base: 0x01020000, data-base: 0x00001000

cisco 2500 (68030) processor (revision N) with 14332K/2048K bytes of memory.
Processor board serial number 05534538 with hardware revision 00000000
X.25 software, Version 2.0, NET2, BFE and GOSIP compliant.
ISDN software, Version 1.0.
1 Ethernet/IEEE 802.3 interface.
2 Serial network interfaces.
1 ISDN Basic Rate interface.
32K bytes of non-volatile configuration memory.
16384K bytes of processor board System flash (Read/Write)




Press RETURN to get started!


Router(boot)>
Router(boot)>en
Router(boot)#conf t
Enter configuration commands, one per line.  End with CNTL/Z.
Router(boot)(config)#int e0
Router(boot)(config-if)#ip add 172.16.0.1 255.255.255.0
Router(boot)(config-if)#no shut
Router(boot)(config-if)#^Z
Router(boot)#
Router(boot)#ping 172.16.0.2
Type escape sequence to abort.
Sending 5, 100-byte ICMP Echos to 172.16.0.2, timeout is 2 seconds:
!!!!!
Success rate is 100 percent (5/5), round-trip min/avg/max = 1/203/1004 ms
Router(boot)#copy tftp flash

System flash directory:
File  Length    Name/status
  1   16522128  c2500-is-l.123-12.bin
[16522192 bytes used, 255024 available, 16777216 total]
Address or name of remote host [255.255.255.255]? 172.16.0.2
Source file name? c2500-is-l.123-18.bin
Destination file name [c2500-is-l.123-18.bin]?
Accessing file 'c2500-is-l.123-18.bin' on 172.16.0.2...
Loading c2500-is-l.123-18.bin from 172.16.0.2 (via Ethernet0): ! [OK]

Erase flash device before writing? [confirm]
Flash contains files. Are you sure you want to erase? [confirm]
```

```
Copy 'c2500-is-l.123-18.bin' from server
  as 'c2500-is-l.123-18.bin' into Flash WITH erase? [yes/no]yes
Erasing device... eeeeeeeeeeeeeeeeeeee ...erased
Loading c2500-is-l.123-18.bin from 172.16.0.2 (via Ethernet0): !!!!!!!!!!!!!!
!!!!!!!!!!!!!!!!!!!!!!!!!!!!!!!!!!!!!!!!!!!!!!!!!!!!!!!!!!!!!!!!!!!!!!!!!!!!!!
!!!!!!!!!!!!!!!!!!!!!!!!!!!!!!!!!!!!!!!!!!!!!!!!!!!!!!!!!!!!!!!!!!!!!!!!!!!!!!
!!!!!!!!!!!!!!!!!!!!!!!!!!!!!!!!!!!!!!!!!!!!!!!!!!!!!!!!!!!!!!!!!!!!!!!!!!!!!!
[OK - 16265152/16777216 bytes]

Verifying checksum...  OK (0x40BF)
Flash copy took 0:09:10 [hh:mm:ss]
Router(boot)#
Router(boot)#conf t
Enter configuration commands, one per line.  End with CNTL/Z.
Router(boot)(config)#config-register 0x2102
Router(boot)(config)#^Z
Router(boot)#sh ver
Cisco Internetwork Operating System Software
IOS (tm) 3000 Bootstrap Software (IGS-RXBOOT), Version 10.2(8a), RELEASE
SOFTWARE (fc1)
Copyright (c) 1986-1995 by cisco Systems, Inc.
Compiled Tue 24-Oct-95 15:46 by mkamson
Image text-base: 0x01020000, data-base: 0x00001000

ROM: System Bootstrap, Version 5.2(8a), RELEASE SOFTWARE

Router uptime is 11 minutes
System restarted by reload
Running default software

cisco 2500 (68030) processor (revision N) with 14332K/2048K bytes of memory.
Processor board serial number 05534538 with hardware revision 00000000
X.25 software, Version 2.0, NET2, BFE and GOSIP compliant.
ISDN software, Version 1.0.
1 Ethernet/IEEE 802.3 interface.
2 Serial network interfaces.
1 ISDN Basic Rate interface.
32K bytes of non-volatile configuration memory.
16384K bytes of processor board System flash (Read/Write)

Configuration register is 0x2101 (will be 0x2102 at next reload)

Router(boot)#reload
System configuration has been modified. Save? [yes/no]: no
Proceed with reload? [confirm]
```

- **Note:** Issue the **boot system** global configuration command if applicable.

Catalyst Switch IOS Upgrade Procedure (Cisco IOS Release 12.0)

```
Switch>
Switch>en
Switch#conf t
Enter configuration commands, one per line.  End with CNTL/Z.
Switch(config)#int vlan 1
Switch(config-if)#ip add 172.16.0.1 255.255.255.0
Switch(config-if)#no shut
Switch(config-if)#^Z
Switch#
Switch#ping 172.16.0.2

Type escape sequence to abort.
Sending 5, 100-byte ICMP Echos to 172.16.0.2, timeout is 2 seconds:
!!!!!
Success rate is 100 percent (5/5), round-trip min/avg/max = 1/202/1002 ms
Switch#
Switch#dir
Directory of flash:/

   2  -rwx      1809119   Aug 10 2004 23:04:33   c2900xl-c3h2s-mz.120-5.WC10.bin
   3  -rwx       105970   Jul 18 2000 01:26:29   c2900XL-diag-mz-120.5.2-XU
   4  drwx          704   Aug 10 2004 23:05:26   html
  18  -rwx          994   Mar 01 1993 00:00:46   config.text
  20  -rwx          329   Mar 01 1993 00:00:50   env_vars
   5  -rwx         8192   Aug 10 2004 23:04:34   e2rb.bin
  17  -rwx          109   Aug 10 2004 23:05:28   info

3612672 bytes total (571392 bytes free)
Switch#
Switch#del flash:c2900xl-c3h2s-mz.120-5.WC10.bin
Delete filename [c2900xl-c3h2s-mz.120-5.WC10.bin]?
Delete flash:c2900xl-c3h2s-mz.120-5.WC10.bin? [confirm]
Switch#del flash:html/*.*
Delete filename [html/*.*]?
Delete flash:html/homepage.htm? [confirm]
--- output omitted ---
Switch#rmdir flash:html
Rmdir filename [html]?
Delete flash:html? [confirm]
Removed dir flash:html
Switch#dir
Directory of flash:/

   3  -rwx       105970   Jul 18 2000 01:26:29   c2900XL-diag-mz-120.5.2-XU
  18  -rwx          994   Mar 01 1993 00:00:46   config.text
  20  -rwx          329   Mar 01 1993 00:00:50   env_vars
   5  -rwx         8192   Aug 10 2004 23:04:34   e2rb.bin
  17  -rwx          109   Aug 10 2004 23:05:28   info

3612672 bytes total (3495424 bytes free)
Switch#
```

```
Switch#tar /xtract tftp://172.16.0.2/c2900xl-c3h2s-tar.120-5.WC14.tar flash:
Loading c2900xl-c3h2s-tar.120-5.WC14.tar from 172.16.0.2 (via VLAN1): !!!!!!
extracting c2900xl-c3h2s-mz.120-5.WC14.bin (1811599 bytes)!!!!!!!!!!!!!!!!!!!!!
!!!!!!!!!!!!!!!!!!!!!!!!!!!!!!!!!!!!!!!!!!!!!!!!!!!!!!!!!!!!!!!!!!!!!!!!!!!!!!!!!
!!!!!!!!!!!!!!!!!!!!!!!!!!!!!!!!!!!!!!!!!!!!!!!!!!!!!!!!!!!!!!!!!!!!!!!!!!!!!!!!!
extracting e2rb.bin (8192 bytes)!
html/ (directory)
--- output omitted ---
 [OK - 2946560 bytes]

Switch#
Switch#dir
Directory of flash:/

    2  -rwx      1811599  Mar 01 1993 00:07:37  c2900xl-c3h2s-mz.120-5.WC14.bin
    3  -rwx       105970  Jul 18 2000 01:26:29  c2900XL-diag-mz-120.5.2-XU
    4  drwx          704  Mar 01 1993 00:08:32  html
   18  -rwx          994  Mar 01 1993 00:00:46  config.text
   20  -rwx          329  Mar 01 1993 00:00:50  env_vars
    5  -rwx         8192  Mar 01 1993 00:07:38  e2rb.bin
   17  -rwx          109  Mar 01 1993 00:08:33  info
   19  -rwx          109  Mar 01 1993 00:08:33  info.ver

3612672 bytes total (565760 bytes free)
Switch#
Switch#conf t
Enter configuration commands, one per line.  End with CNTL/Z.
Switch(config)#boot system flash:c2900xl-c3h2s-mz.120-5.WC14.bin
Switch(config)#^Z
Switch#
Switch#sh boot
BOOT path-list:           flash:c2900xl-c3h2s-mz.120-5.WC14.bin
Config file:              flash:config.text
Enable Break:             no
Manual Boot:              no
HELPER path-list:
NVRAM/Config file
     buffer size:         32768
Switch#
Switch#reload

System configuration has been modified. Save? [yes/no]: no
Proceed with reload? [confirm]
```

Catalyst Switch IOS Upgrade Procedure (Cisco IOS Release 12.1 and later)

```
Switch>
Switch>en
Switch#conf t
Enter configuration commands, one per line.  End with CNTL/Z.
Switch(config)#int vlan 1
Switch(config-if)#ip add 172.16.0.1 255.255.255.0
Switch(config-if)#no shut
Switch(config-if)#^Z
Switch#
Switch#ping 172.16.0.2

Type escape sequence to abort.
Sending 5, 100-byte ICMP Echos to 172.16.0.2, timeout is 2 seconds:
!!!!!
Success rate is 100 percent (5/5), round-trip min/avg/max = 1/200/1000 ms
Switch#
Switch#dir
Directory of flash:/

    2  -rwx        2126   Mar 1 1993 00:01:15 +00:00  config.text
    4  -rwx          24   Mar 1 1993 00:01:15 +00:00  private-config.text
    7  drwx         192   Mar 1 1993 00:13:41 +00:00  c3550-i5k9l2q3-
mz.122-25.SE
    8  drwx         192   Mar 1 1993 00:04:27 +00:00  c3550-i9q3l2-mz.121-
19.EA1c
  420  -rwx         350   Mar 1 1993 00:13:41 +00:00  system_env_vars
  419  -rwx           0   Mar 1 1993 00:13:41 +00:00  env_vars

15998976 bytes total (1409024 bytes free)
Switch#
Switch#delete /force /recursive flash:c3550-i5k9l2q3-mz.122-25.SE
Delete filename [c3550-i5k9l2q3-mz.122-25.SE]?
Switch#
Switch#archive download-sw tftp://172.16.0.2/c3550-ipservicesk9-tar.122-
25.SEE.tar
Loading c3550-ipservicesk9-tar.122-25.SEE.tar from 172.16.0.2 (via Vlan1): !
!!!!!!!!!!!!!!!!!!!!!!!!!!!!!!!!!!!!!!!!!!!!!!!!!!!!!!!!!!!!!!!!!!!!!!!!!!!!!!
!!!!!!!!!!!!!!!!!!!!!!!!!!!!!!!!!!!!!!!!!!!!!!!!!!!!!!!!!!!!!!!!!!!!!!!!!!!!!!
!!!!!!!!!!!!!!!!!!!!!!!!!!!!!!!!!!!!!!!!!!!!!!!!!!!!!!!!!!!!!!!!!!!!!!!!!!!!!!
[OK - 8878080 bytes]
examining image...
extracting info (287 bytes)
Image info:
    Version Suffix: ipservicesk9-122-25.SEE
    Image Name: c3550-ipservicesk9-mz.122-25.SEE.bin
    Version Directory: c3550-ipservicesk9-mz.122-25.SEE
    Ios Image Size: 7137792
    Total Image Size: 8878592
    Image Feature: IP|LAYER_3|PLUS|SSH|3DES|MIN_DRAM_MEG=64
    Image Family: C3550
```

```
Extracting files...
extracting info (287 bytes)
extracting c3550-ipservicesk9-mz.122-25.SEE/c3550-ipservicesk9-mz.122-
25.SEE.bin (7131928 bytes)
c3550-ipservicesk9-mz.122-25.SEE/html/ (directory)
extracting c3550-ipservicesk9-mz.122-25.SEE/html/layers.js (1616 bytes)
--- output omitted ---
extracting info.ver (287 bytes)
New software image installed in flash:c3550-ipservicesk9-mz.122-25.SEE
Configuring system to use new image...done.
Switch#
Switch#sh boot
BOOT path-list:          flash:c3550-ipservicesk9-mz.122-25.SEE/c3550-
ipservicesk9-mz.122-25.SEE.bin
Config file:             flash:/config.text
Private Config file:     flash:/private-config.text
Enable Break:            no
Manual Boot:             no
HELPER path-list:
NVRAM/Config file
      buffer size:       393216
Switch#
Switch#reload

System configuration has been modified. Save? [yes/no]: no
Proceed with reload? [confirm]
```

Cisco Router Password Recovery Procedure

- Power on the router, and then send a **break sequence** (**Ctrl-Break**) to enter ROMmon.

```
System Bootstrap, Version 5.2(11a), RELEASE SOFTWARE
Copyright (c) 1986-1995 by cisco Systems
4000 processor with 16384 Kbytes of main memory

Abort at 0x10fb602 (PC)
>o
Configuration register = 0xffff2102 at last boot
Bit#    Configuration register option settings:
15      Diagnostic mode disabled
14      IP broadcasts do not have network numbers
13      Boot default ROM software if network boot fails
12-11   Console speed is 9600 baud
10      IP broadcasts with ones
08      Break disabled
07      OEM disabled
06      Ignore configuration disabled
03-00   Boot file is cisco2-4000 (or 'boot system' command)

>
>o/r 0x2142 [1]
>i [2]


System Bootstrap, Version 5.2(11a), RELEASE SOFTWARE
Copyright (c) 1986-1995 by cisco Systems
4000 processor with 16384 Kbytes of main memory
F3: 9248+6029511+165008 at 0x12000
Self decompressing the image :
################################################################
################################################################
######################################################## [OK]


                 Restricted Rights Legend

Use, duplication, or disclosure by the Government is
subject to restrictions as set forth in subparagraph
(c) of the Commercial Computer Software - Restricted
Rights clause at FAR sec. 52.227-19 and subparagraph
(c) (1) (ii) of the Rights in Technical Data and Computer
Software clause at DFARS sec. 252.227-7013.


            cisco Systems, Inc.
            170 West Tasman Drive
            San Jose, California 95134-1706




Cisco Internetwork Operating System Software
IOS (tm) 4000 Software (C4000-JS-M), Version 12.1(27b), RELEASE SOFTWARE
(fc1)
Copyright (c) 1986-2005 by cisco Systems, Inc.
Compiled Tue 16-Aug-05 16:53 by pwade
Image text-base: 0x00012000, data-base: 0x00C19718
```

[1] – Change the configuration register to ignore the contents of NVRAM.
    Issue the **confreg** command instead on Cisco 2600 Series and later.
[2] – Issue the **reset** command instead on Cisco 2600 Series and later.

```
cisco 4000 (68030) processor (revision 0xA0) with 16384K/4096K bytes of
memory.
Processor board ID 5079453
G.703/E1 software, Version 1.0.
Bridging software.
X.25 software, Version 3.0.0.
SuperLAT software (copyright 1990 by Meridian Technology Corp).
TN3270 Emulation software.
2 Ethernet/IEEE 802.3 interface(s)
2 Serial network interface(s)
128K bytes of non-volatile configuration memory.
8192K bytes of processor board System flash (Read/Write)


        --- System Configuration Dialog ---

Would you like to enter the initial configuration dialog? [yes/no]: no


Press RETURN to get started!


Router>
Router>en
Router#copy startup-config running-config
Router#
Router#conf t
Enter configuration commands, one per line.  End with CNTL/Z.
Router(config)#no enable secret
Router(config)#enable secret cisco
Router(config)#
Router(config)#config-register 0x2102
Router(config)#^Z
Router#
Router#sh ver
Cisco Internetwork Operating System Software
IOS (tm) 4000 Software (C4000-JS-M), Version 12.1(27b), RELEASE SOFTWARE
(fc1)
Copyright (c) 1986-2005 by cisco Systems, Inc.
Compiled Tue 16-Aug-05 16:53 by pwade
Image text-base: 0x00012000, data-base: 0x00C19718

--- output omitted ---

Configuration register is 0x2142 (will be 0x2102 at next reload)

Router#
Router#copy running-config startup-config
Building configuration...
[OK]
Router#
```

Catalyst Switch Password Recovery Procedure

- Hold down the **Mode** button located on the left side of the front panel while powering the switch. Release the **Mode** button after the Port 1 LED goes out (older models, or the SYST LED stables (recent models).

```
C2900XL Boot Loader (C2900-HBOOT-M) Version 12.0(5.2)XU, MAINTENANCE INTERIM
SOFTWARE
Compiled Mon 17-Jul-00 18:19 by ayounes
 starting...
Base ethernet MAC Address: 00:04:27:c1:d3:c0
Xmodem file system is available.

The system has been interrupted prior to initializing the
flash filesystem.  The following commands will initialize
the flash filesystem, and finish loading the operating
system software:

    flash_init
    load_helper
    boot

switch: flash_init
Initializing Flash...
flashfs[0]: 18 files, 2 directories
flashfs[0]: 0 orphaned files, 0 orphaned directories
flashfs[0]: Total bytes: 3612672
flashfs[0]: Bytes used: 3046912
flashfs[0]: Bytes available: 565760
flashfs[0]: flashfs fsck took 6 seconds.
...done Initializing Flash.
Boot Sector Filesystem (bs:) installed, fsid: 3
Parameter Block Filesystem (pb:) installed, fsid: 4
switch: load_helper
switch: rename flash:config.text flash:config.old
switch: boot
Loading "flash:c2900xl-c3h2s-mz.120-5.WC14.bin"...##########################
#############################################################################
#############################################################################

File "flash:c2900xl-c3h2s-mz.120-5.WC14.bin" uncompressed and installed,
entry point: 0x3000
executing...


            Restricted Rights Legend

Use, duplication, or disclosure by the Government is
subject to restrictions as set forth in subparagraph
(c) of the Commercial Computer Software - Restricted
Rights clause at FAR sec. 52.227-19 and subparagraph
(c) (1) (ii) of the Rights in Technical Data and Computer
Software clause at DFARS sec. 252.227-7013.

            cisco Systems, Inc.
            170 West Tasman Drive
            San Jose, California 95134-1706
```

```
Cisco Internetwork Operating System Software
IOS (tm) C2900XL Software (C2900XL-C3H2S-M), Version 12.0(5)WC14, RELEASE
SOFTWARE (fc1)
Copyright (c) 1986-2006 by cisco Systems, Inc.
Compiled Thu 16-Feb-06 14:39 by antonino
Image text-base: 0x00003000, data-base: 0x00352454


Initializing C2900XL flash...
flashfs[1]: 18 files, 2 directories
flashfs[1]: 0 orphaned files, 0 orphaned directories
flashfs[1]: Total bytes: 3612672
flashfs[1]: Bytes used: 3046912
flashfs[1]: Bytes available: 565760
flashfs[1]: flashfs fsck took 8 seconds.
flashfs[1]: Initialization complete.
...done Initializing C2900XL flash.
C2900XL POST: System Board Test: Passed
--- output omitted ---
cisco WS-C2924-XL (PowerPC403GA) processor (revision 0x11) with 8192K/1024K
bytes of memory.
Processor board ID FAB0444S155, with hardware revision 0x01
Last reset from power-on

Processor is running Enterprise Edition Software
Cluster command switch capable
Cluster member switch capable
24 FastEthernet/IEEE 802.3 interface(s)

32K bytes of flash-simulated non-volatile configuration memory.
Base ethernet MAC Address: 00:04:27:C1:D3:C0
Motherboard assembly number: 73-3382-08
Power supply part number: 34-0834-01
Motherboard serial number: FAB044313HR
Power supply serial number: DAB04232RDQ
Model revision number: A0
Motherboard revision number: C0
Model number: WS-C2924-XL-EN
System serial number: FAB0444S155
C2900XL INIT: Complete

00:00:30: %SYS-5-RESTART: System restarted --
Cisco Internetwork Operating System Software
IOS (tm) C2900XL Software (C2900XL-C3H2S-M), Version 12.0(5)WC14, RELEASE
SOFTWARE (fc1)
Copyright (c) 1986-2006 by cisco Systems, Inc.
Compiled Thu 16-Feb-06 14:39 by antonino

         --- System Configuration Dialog ---

At any point you may enter a question mark '?' for help.
Use ctrl-c to abort configuration dialog at any prompt.
Default settings are in square brackets '[]'.


Continue with configuration dialog? [yes/no]: no
Press RETURN to get started.
```

```
Switch>
Switch>en
Switch#rename config.old config.text
Destination filename [config.text]?
Switch#
Switch#copy config.text running-config
Destination filename [running-config]?
994 bytes copied in 2.301 secs (497 bytes/sec)
Switch#
Switch#conf t
Enter configuration commands, one per line.  End with CNTL/Z.
Switch(config)#no enable secret
Switch(config)#enable secret cisco
Switch(config)#^Z
Switch#
Switch#copy running-config startup-config
Building configuration...
[OK]
Switch#
```

Appendix 2
Frame Relay Switch Configuration

Basic Frame Relay Switching Network with 3 Cisco Routers

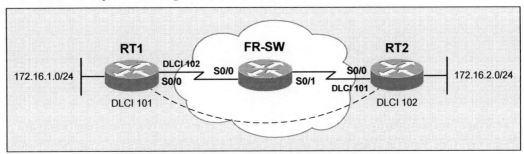

Figure A2-1: Sample Frame Relay Switching Network I

- Frame Relay Switching configuration on FR-SW:

```
!
hostname FR-SW
!
frame-relay switching
!
interface Serial0/0
 no ip address
 encapsulation frame-relay
 clockrate 1000000
 frame-relay intf-type dce
 frame-relay route 102 interface Serial0/1 101
!
interface Serial0/1
 no ip address
 encapsulation frame-relay
 clockrate 1000000
 frame-relay intf-type dce
 frame-relay route 101 interface Serial0/0 102
!
```

- The **frame-relay switching** global configuration command enables FR switching on a router.

- The **frame-relay route** {*input dlci*} **interface** {*outgoing interface*} {*output dlci*} interface subcommand defines a static entry in the Frame Relay switching table.

- No IP address configuration is required on the Frame Relay switch interfaces (L3 function). It only requires mapping of DLCIs to interfaces (L2 function).

- The **show frame-relay route** EXEC command verifies the configuration of a FR switch:

```
FR-SW#show frame-relay route
Input Intf      Input Dlci      Output Intf     Output Dlci     Status
Serial0/0       102             Serial0/1       101             active
Serial0/1       101             Serial0/0       102             active
FR-SW#
```

- The 3 possible Frame Relay PVC states in the output of the **show frame-relay pvc** EXEC command in a DTE router are **ACTIVE**, **INACTIVE**, and **DELECTED**. An **INACTIVE** PVC indicates that there is a problem between the remote router and the remote Frame Relay switch.

- Frame Relay configuration on RT1:

```
!
hostname RT1
!
interface Serial0/0
 ip address 200.1.1.1 255.255.255.0
 encapsulation frame-relay
!
interface FastEthernet1/0
 ip address 172.16.1.1 255.255.255.0
!
router eigrp 1
 network 172.16.0.0
 network 200.1.1.0
 no auto-summary
!
```

- Frame Relay configuration on RT2:

```
!
hostname RT2
!
interface Serial0/0
 ip address 200.1.1.2 255.255.255.0
 encapsulation frame-relay
!
interface FastEthernet1/0
 ip address 172.16.2.1 255.255.255.0
!
router eigrp 1
 network 172.16.0.0
 network 200.1.1.0
 no auto-summary
!
```

- Below shows the output of the **show frame-relay map** EXEC command on RT1:

```
RT1#show frame-relay map
Serial0/0 (up): ip 200.1.1.2 dlci 102(0x66,0x1860), dynamic,
           broadcast,, status defined, active
RT1#
```

- Below shows the output of the **show frame-relay map** EXEC command on RT2:

```
RT2#sh frame-relay map
Serial0/0 (up): ip 200.1.1.1 dlci 101(0x65,0x1850), dynamic,
           broadcast,, status defined, active
RT2#
```

- The dynamic keyword represents DLCI address mapping that is **dynamically learned** via the Inverse ARP process.

Routers Back-to-Back Connection Through AUX Ports

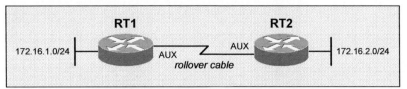

Figure A2-2: Back to Back AUX Connection

- Back-to-Back AUX Connection configuration on RT1:

```
!
interface Async1
 ip address 10.10.10.1 255.255.255.0
 async mode dedicated
!
ip route 0.0.0.0 0.0.0.0 Async1
!
line aux 0
 speed 38400
!
```

- Back-to-Back AUX Connection configuration on RT2:

```
!
interface Async1
 ip address 10.10.10.2 255.255.255.0
 async mode dedicated
!
ip route 0.0.0.0 0.0.0.0 Async1
!
line aux 0
 speed 38400
!
```

- The Async1 interfaces above use SLIP encapsulation (by default). PPP encapsulation can also be used to provide other additional features, eg: authentication.

- Static routes are being used, as routers could not send routing updates across AUX connections.

Constructing a Compound Frame Relay Switch

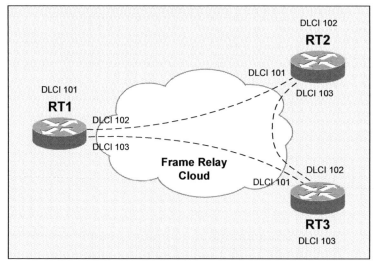

Figure A2-3: Sample Frame Relay Switching Network II

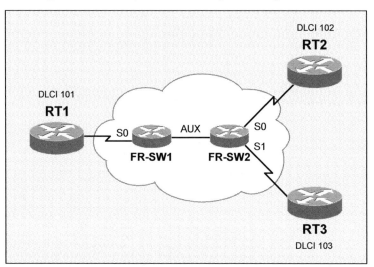

Figure A2-4: Physical Connections with a Compound Frame Relay Switch

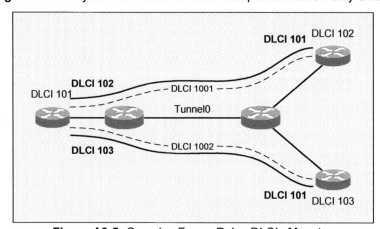

Figure A2-5: Complex Frame Relay DLCIs Mapping

- **Frame Relay Switch configuration on FR-SW1:**

```
!
frame-relay switching
!
interface Tunnel0
 no ip address
 tunnel source Async1
 tunnel destination 10.10.10.2
!
interface Serial0
 no ip address
 encapsulation frame-relay
 clockrate 1000000
 frame-relay intf-type dce
 frame-relay route 102 interface Tunnel0 1001
 frame-relay route 103 interface Tunnel0 1002
!
interface Async1
 ip address 10.10.10.1 255.255.255.0
 async mode dedicated
!
line aux 0
 speed 38400
!
```

- **Frame Relay Switch configuration on FR-SW2:**

```
!
frame-relay switching
!
interface Tunnel0
 no ip address
 tunnel source Async1
 tunnel destination 10.10.10.1
!
interface Serial0
 no ip address
 encapsulation frame-relay
 clockrate 1000000
 frame-relay intf-type dce
 frame-relay route 101 interface Tunnel0 1001
 frame-relay route 103 interface Serial1 102
!
interface Serial1
 no ip address
 encapsulation frame-relay
 clockrate 1000000
 frame-relay intf-type dce
 frame-relay route 101 interface Tunnel0 1002
 frame-relay route 102 interface Serial0 103
!
interface Async1
 ip address 10.10.10.2 255.255.255.0
 async mode dedicated
!
line aux 0
 speed 38400
!
```

This page is intentionally left blank

Appendix 3
The IP Routing Process

The IP routing process is fairly simple and doesn't change, regardless of the size network you have. For an example, we'll use Figure A3-1 to describe step by step what happens when PC1 wants to communicate with PC2 on a different network.

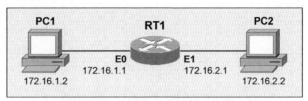

Figure A3-1: The IP Routing Process

In this example, a user on PC1 pings PC2's IP address. Routing doesn't get simpler than this, but it still involves a lot of steps. Let's work through them:

1. Internet Control Message Protocol (ICMP) creates an Echo Request payload (which is just the alphabet in the data field).
2. ICMP hands that payload to Internet Protocol (IP), which then creates a packet. At a minimum, this packet contains an IP source address, an IP destination address, and a Protocol field with 01h (remember that Cisco likes to use 0x in front of hex characters, so this could look like 0x01). All of that tells the receiving host to whom it should hand the payload when the destination is reached – in this example, ICMP.
3. Once the packet is created, IP determines whether the destination IP address is on the local network or a remote one.
4. Since IP determines this is a remote request, the packet needs to be sent to the default gateway so the packet can be routed to the remote network. The Registry in Windows is parsed to find the configured default gateway.
5. The default gateway of host 172.16.1.2 (PC1) is configured to 172.16.1.1. To be able to send this packet to the default gateway, the hardware address of the router's interface Ethernet0 (configured with the IP address of 172.16.1.1) must be known. Why? So the packet can be handled down to the Data Link layer, framed, and sent to the router's interface connected to the 172.16.1.0 network. Hosts communicate only via hardware address on the local LAN. It is important to understand that PC1, in order to communicate to PC2, must send the packets to the MAC address of the default gateway on the local network.
6. Next, the ARP cache is checked to see if the IP address of the default gateway has already been resolved to a hardware address:
    - If it has, the packet is then free to be handed to the Data Link layer for framing. (The hardware destination address is also handed down with that packet.)
    - If the hardware address isn't already in the ARP cache of the host, an ARP broadcast is sent out onto the local network to search for the hardware address of 172.16.1.1. The router responds to the request and provides the hardware address of Ethernet0, and the host caches this address. The router also caches the hardware address of PC1 in its ARP cache.
7. Once the packet and destination hardware address are handed to the Data Link layer, the LAN driver is used to provide media access via the type of LAN being used (in this example, Ethernet). A frame is then generated, encapsulating the packet with control information. Within that frame are the hardware destination and source addresses, plus in this case, an Ether-Type field that describes the Network layer protocol that handed the packet to the Data Link layer – in this case, IP. At the end of the frame is something called a Frame Check Sequence (FCS) field that houses the result of the Cyclic Redundancy Check (CRC).

8. Once the frame is completed, it's handed down to the Physical layer to be put on the physical medium (in this example, twisted-pair wire) one bit at a time.

9. Every device in the collision domain receives these bits and builds the frame. They each run a CRC and check the answer in the FCS field. If the answers don't match, the frame is discarded.
   - If the CRC matches, then the hardware destination address is checked to see if it matches too (which, in this example, is the router's interface Ethernet0).
   - If it's a match, then the Ether-Type field is checked to find the protocol used at the Network layer.

10. The packet is pulled from the frame, and what is left of the frame is discarded. The packet is handed to the protocol listed in the Ether-Type field – it's given to IP.

11. IP receives the packet and checks the IP destination address. Since the packet's destination address doesn't match any of the address configured on the receiving router itself, the router will look up the destination IP network address in its routing table.

12. The routing table must have an entry for the network 172.16.2.0, or the packet will be discarded immediately and an ICMP message will be sent back to the originating device with a "destination network unreachable" message.

13. If the router does find an entry for the destination network in its table, the packet is switched to the exit interface – in this example, interface Ethernet1.

14. The router packet-switches the packet to the Ethernet1 buffer.

15. The Ethernet buffer needs to know the hardware address of the destination host and first check the ARP cache.
   - If the hardware address of PC2 has already been resolved, then the packet and the hardware address are handed down to the Data Link layer to be framed.
   - If the hardware address has not already been resolved, the router sends an ARP request out E1 looking for the hardware address of 172.16.2.2.
     PC2 responds with its hardware address, and the packet and destination hardware address are both sent to the Data Link layer for framing.

16. The Data Link layer creates a frame with the destination and source hardware addresses, Ether-Type field, and FCS field at the end of the frame. The frame is handed to the Physical layer to be sent out on the physical medium one bit at a time.

17. PC2 receives the frame and immediately runs a CRC. If the result matches what's in the FCS field, the hardware destination address is then checked. If the host finds a match, the Ether-Type field is then checked to determine the protocol that the packet should be handed to at athe Network layer – IP, in this example.

18. At the Network layer, IP receives the packet and checks the IP destination address. Since there's finally a match made, the Protocol field is checked to find out to whom the payload should be given.

19. The payload is handed to ICMP, which understands that this is an Echo Request. ICMP responds to this by immediately discarding the packet and generating a new payload as an Echo Reply.

20. A packet is then created including the source and destination IP addresses, Protocol field, and payload. The destination device is now PC1.

21. IP then checks to see whether the destination IP address is a device on the local LAN or on a remote network. Since the destination device is on a remote network, the packet needs to be sent to the default gateway.

22. The default gateway IP address is found in the Registry of the Windows device, and the ARP cache is checked to see if the hardware address has already been resolved from an IP address.

23. Once the hardware address of the default gateway is found, the packet and destination hardware address are handed down to the Data Link layer for framing.

24. The Data Link layer frames the packet of information and includes the following in the header:
    - The destination and source hardware addresses
    - The Ether-Type field with 0x0800 (IP) in it
    - The FCS field with the CRC result in row
25. The frame in now handed down to the Physical layer to be sent out over the network medium one bit at a time.
26. The router's Ethernet1 interface receives the bits and builds a frame. The CRC is run, and the FCS field is checked to make sure the answers match.
27. Once the CRC is found to be okay, the hardware destination address is checked. Since the router's interface is a match, the packet is pulled from the frame and the Ether-Type field is checked to see what protocol at the Network layer the packet should be delivered to.
28. The protocol is determined to be IP, so it gets the packet. IP runs a CRC check on the IP header first, and then checks the destination IP address. (IP does not run a complete CRC as the Data Link layer does, it only checks the header for errors)
29. Since the router does know how to get to network 172.16.1.0 – the exit interface is Ethernet0, so the packet is switched to interface Ethernet0.
30. The router checks the ARP cache to determine whether the hardware address for 172.16.1.2 has already been resolved.
31. Since he hardware address to 172.16.1.2 is already cached from the originating trip to PC2, the packet and destination hardware address are handed t the Data Link layer.
32. The Data Link layer builds a frame with the destination hardware address and source hardware address, and then puts IP in the Ether-Type field (0x0800). A CRC is run on the frame, and the result is placed in the FCS field.
33. The frame is then handed to the Physical layer to be sent out onto the local network one bit at a time.
34. The destination host receives the frame, runs a CRC, checks the destination hardware address, and looks in the Ether-Type field to find out whom to hand the packet to.
35. IP is the designated receiver, and after the packet is handed to IP at the Network layer, it checks the Protocol field for further direction. IP finds instructions to give the payload to ICMP, and ICMP determines the packet to be an ICMP Echo Reply.
36. ICMP acknowledges that is has received the reply by sending an exclamation point (!) to the user interface. ICMP then attempts to send 4 more Echo Requests to the destination host.
    Note: PC1 is assumed to be a device running Cisco IOS, which sending 5 ICMP Echo Requests by default, and display an exclamation mark upon each successful ping.

This page is intentionally left blank

Dissecting the Windows Routing Table

```
C:\>ipconfig

Windows IP Configuration


Ethernet adapter Local Area Connection:

        Connection-specific DNS Suffix  . :
        IP Address. . . . . . . . . . . : 172.16.0.2
        Subnet Mask . . . . . . . . . . : 255.255.255.0
        Default Gateway . . . . . . . . : 172.16.0.1

C:\>route print or netstat -r
===========================================================================
Network Destination        Netmask          Gateway       Interface  Metric
1        0.0.0.0          0.0.0.0       172.16.0.1     172.16.0.2      1
2      127.0.0.0        255.0.0.0       127.0.0.1      127.0.0.1       1
3     172.16.0.0    255.255.255.0       172.16.0.2     172.16.0.2     20
4     172.16.0.2  255.255.255.255       127.0.0.1      127.0.0.1      20
5 172.16.255.255  255.255.255.255       172.16.0.2     172.16.0.2     20
6       224.0.0.0      240.0.0.0        172.16.0.2     172.16.0.2     20
7 255.255.255.255  255.255.255.255      172.16.0.2     172.16.0.2      1
Default Gateway:       172.16.0.1
===========================================================================
```

- **Gateway** is the IP address of the next-hop router inbound interface.
  Interface is the IP address of the local router outbound interface.
  Metric is the distance to a remote (or destination) network. If there are multiple routes to a same network, the route with the **lowest metric** will be used to forward packets to the network.

- Generally, gateway and interface reside in the same subnet.

- Below describes all the routes displayed in the routing table above:
  1) Default route or default gateway.
  2) Loopback network – destine all packets to the 127.0.0.0/8 network to itself (127.0.0.1).
  3) Route to local network – the directly attached network.
  4) Route to local host (127.0.0.1), which is identified as a host route.
  5) Route to **directed broadcast**, the broadcast which is sent to all hosts of a particular subnet or a group of subnets. It is identified as a host route. May be forwarded by a router (normally the default gateway) configured with the **ip directed-broadcast** interface subcommand.
  6) Route to multicast networks.
  7) Route to **flooded / limited broadcast**, the local broadcast within a subnet. It is identified as a host route. Normally sent by hosts that do not know their network numbers and addresses and are querying some servers for those information (eg: DHCP). May be forwarded by routers with the **ip helper-address** {ip-addr} interface subcommand.
  Note: Host routes are destinations with the subnet mask of 255.255.255.255.

- Below shows the command syntax for adding a [persistent] route:
  route [-p] add {dest-net-addr} **mask** {netmask} {gw-ip-addr} [**metric** {metric}]

- Below shows the command syntax for deleting or removing an existing [persistent] route:
  route delete {dest-net-addr} [**mask** {netmask} [gw-ip-addr]]

This page is intentionally left blank

Appendix 5
Decimal-Hex-Binary Conversion Chart

Decimal	Hex	Binary	Decimal	Hex	Binary	Decimal	Hex	Binary
0	00	00000000	32	20	00100000	64	40	01000000
1	01	00000001	33	21	00100001	65	41	01000001
2	02	00000010	34	22	00100010	66	42	01000010
3	03	00000011	35	23	00100011	67	43	01000011
4	04	00000100	36	24	00100100	68	44	01000100
5	05	00000101	37	25	00100101	69	45	01000101
6	06	00000110	38	26	00100110	70	46	01000110
7	07	00000111	39	27	00100111	71	47	01000111
8	08	00001000	40	28	00101000	72	48	01001000
9	09	00001001	41	29	00101001	73	49	01001001
10	0A	00001010	42	2A	00101010	74	4A	01001010
11	0B	00001011	43	2B	00101011	75	4B	01001011
12	0C	00001100	44	2C	00101100	76	4C	01001100
13	0D	00001101	45	2D	00101101	77	4D	01001101
14	0E	00001110	46	2E	00101110	78	4E	01001110
15	0F	00001111	47	2F	00101111	79	4F	01001111
16	10	00010000	48	30	00110000	80	50	01010000
17	11	00010001	49	31	00110001	81	51	01010001
18	12	00010010	50	32	00110010	82	52	01010010
19	13	00010011	51	33	00110011	83	53	01010011
20	14	00010100	52	34	00110100	84	54	01010100
21	15	00010101	53	35	00110101	85	55	01010101
22	16	00010110	54	36	00110110	86	56	01010110
23	17	00010111	55	37	00110111	87	57	01010111
24	18	00011000	56	38	00111000	88	58	01011000
25	19	00011001	57	39	00111001	89	59	01011001
26	1A	00011010	58	3A	00111010	90	5A	01011010
27	1B	00011011	59	3B	00111011	91	5B	01011011
28	1C	00011100	60	3C	00111100	92	5C	01011100
29	1D	00011101	61	3D	00111101	93	5D	01011101
30	1E	00011110	62	3E	00111110	94	5E	01011110
31	1F	00011111	63	3F	00111111	95	5F	01011111

Decimal	Hex	Binary	Decimal	Hex	Binary	Decimal	Hex	Binary
96	60	01100000	128	80	10000000	160	A0	10100000
97	61	01100001	129	81	10000001	161	A1	10100001
98	62	01100010	130	82	10000010	162	A2	10100010
99	63	01100011	131	83	10000011	163	A3	10100011
100	64	01100100	132	84	10000100	164	A4	10100100
101	65	01100101	133	85	10000101	165	A5	10100101
102	66	01100110	134	86	10000110	166	A6	10100110
103	67	01100111	135	87	10000111	167	A7	10100111
104	68	01101000	136	88	10001000	168	A8	10101000
105	69	01101001	137	89	10001001	169	A9	10101001
106	6A	01101010	138	8A	10001010	170	AA	10101010
107	6B	01101011	139	8B	10001011	171	AB	10101011
108	6C	01101100	140	8C	10001100	172	AC	10101100
109	6D	01101101	141	8D	10001101	173	AD	10101101
110	6E	01101110	142	8E	10001110	174	AE	10101110
111	6F	01101111	143	8F	10001111	175	AF	10101111
112	70	01110000	144	90	10010000	176	B0	10110000
113	71	01110001	145	91	10010001	177	B1	10110001
114	72	01110010	146	92	10010010	178	B2	10110010
115	73	01110011	147	93	10010011	179	B3	10110011
116	74	01110100	148	94	10010100	180	B4	10110100
117	75	01110101	149	95	10010101	181	B5	10110101
118	76	01110110	150	96	10010110	182	B6	10110110
119	77	01110111	151	97	10010111	183	B7	10110111
120	78	01111000	152	98	10011000	184	B8	10111000
121	79	01111001	153	99	10011001	185	B9	10111001
122	7A	01111010	154	9A	10011010	186	BA	10111010
123	7B	01111011	155	9B	10011011	187	BB	10111011
124	7C	01111100	156	9C	10011100	188	BC	10111100
125	7D	01111101	157	9D	10011101	189	BD	10111101
126	7E	01111110	158	9E	10011110	190	BE	10111110
127	7F	01111111	159	9F	10011111	191	BF	10111111

Decimal	Hex	Binary	Decimal	Hex	Binary
192	C0	11000000	224	E0	11100000
193	C1	11000001	225	E1	11100001
194	C2	11000010	226	E2	11100010
195	C3	11000011	227	E3	11100011
196	C4	11000100	228	E4	11100100
197	C5	11000101	229	E5	11100101
198	C6	11000110	230	E6	11100110
199	C7	11000111	231	E7	11100111
200	C8	11001000	232	E8	11101000
201	C9	11001001	233	E9	11101001
202	CA	11001010	234	EA	11101010
203	CB	11001011	235	EB	11101011
204	CC	11001100	236	EC	11101100
205	CD	11001101	237	ED	11101101
206	CE	11001110	238	EE	11101110
207	CF	11001111	239	EF	11101111
208	D0	11010000	240	F0	11110000
209	D1	11010001	241	F1	11110001
210	D2	11010010	242	F2	11110010
211	D3	11010011	243	F3	11110011
212	D4	11010100	244	F4	11110100
213	D5	11010101	245	F5	11110101
214	D6	11010110	246	F6	11110110
215	D7	11010111	247	F7	11110111
216	D8	11011000	248	F8	11111000
217	D9	11011001	249	F9	11111001
218	DA	11011010	250	FA	11111010
219	DB	11011011	251	FB	11111011
220	DC	11011100	252	FC	11111100
221	DD	11011101	253	FD	11111101
222	DE	11011110	254	FE	11111110
223	DF	11011111	255	FF	11111111

This page is intentionally left blank

CCNA Extra Knowledge

MISC Basic Networking Notes

- The most common network user applications on today's networks are **email**, **web browsers**, **instant messaging**, **collaboration**, and **databases**.

- Below are the 3 categories of network applications:
    i)   **Batch applications** are started by a human complete with no other interaction, eg: FTP and TFTP.
    ii) **Interactive applications** include database updates and queries. A person requests data from the server and waits for a reply. Response time depends more on the server than the network.
    iii) **Real-time applications** include VoIP and video. Network bandwidth is critical as these applications are time critical. Quality of Service (QoS) and sufficient network bandwidth are mandatory for these applications.

The LLC – Logical Link Control (IEEE 802.2)

- LLC was originated from the **High-Level Data Link Control** (HDLC) and uses a subset of the HDLC specification. It is the upper data link sublayer that provides an interface for upper layers to deal with any type of MAC lower sublayer, eg: 802.3 Ethernet and 802.5 Token Ring in order to achieve **physical media independence**. It is used for managing the data link communication, defining **Service Access Points** (SAPs) to identify and encapsulate network layer protocols. **Note:** LLC is the same for various physical media, eg: Ethernet, Token Ring, and WLAN.

- LLC defines 3 types of operations (or services) for data communication:

LLC Type 1	**Connectionless and unreliable**. Allows network layer protocols to run on it. Generally used by network layer protocols that using a transport layer.
LLC Type 2	**Connection-oriented and reliable**. Allows the LLC sublayer to provide connection establishment, data acknowledgement, error recovery, and flow control (windowing or sliding window). A retransmission timer is started when an endpoint sends frames to its peer. The frames will be retransmitted if an acknowledgment is not received within the timeout interval. Generally used in LAN environments where network and transport layer protocols are not involved.
LLC Type 3	**Connectionless and reliable**.

- Connection-oriented LLC (**LLC2**) uses a 2-byte Control field (in the 802.2 LLC header).

Late Collision

- Late collision is a type of collisions found in the CSMA/CD environment where a collision error is detected after the first 64 bytes of the frame have been sent. It occurs when 2 end systems encounter a collision upon frame transmission even they have performed collision detection. This condition can occur when the network is so large that the frame propagation from one end to another takes longer than the time used to perform collision detection.

- Late collisions are not retransmitted by the NIC (Layer 2). They are left for the upper layers (eg: TCP) to detect and recover the loss of data.

Duplex VS Simplex Communications

Duplex	2 directly connected devices can communicate with another **in both directions**.
Half-Duplex	Allows communication in both directions, but only 1 direction at a time. 1 way (lane) with 2 directions. Ex: walkie-talkie – both speakers cannot speak and be heard at the same time. One must use "Over" to indicate the end of a speech before another one can speak.
Full-Duplex	Allows communication in both directions at the same time. 2 ways (lanes) with 2 directions (a two-lane road with one lane for each direction). Ex: Telephone – it allows both callers to speak and be heard at the same time.
Simplex	2 directly connected devices can communicate with another **only in 1 direction**. 1 way (lane) and 1 direction. Ex: Fiber optic strands (a pair of TX and RX strands is used to connect 2 devices).

Manually Configured (Static) MAC Address

- A **static address** for a device can be restricted to a specific port, with a specific VLAN. A static address will not be removed from the MAC address table when an interface link is down – it is bound to the assigned interface and non-movable. When a static address is seen on another interface, the address will be ignored and will not be written to the address table. A static address cannot be (dynamically) learnt on another port until it is being removed from the running-config.

- The syntax for configuring a static MAC address is
  mac-address-table static {*mac-addr*} **vlan** {*vlan-id*} **interface** {*intf-type intf-num*}
  mac-address-table static {*mac-addr*} {*intf-type intf-num*} **vlan** {*vlan-id*}
  (Cisco IOS Release 12.0)

- The example below configures a static MAC entry for the NIC with 1111.1111.1111. Connection of the NIC to interfaces other than Fa0/1 will have connectivity but no accessibility.

```
Switch(config)#mac-address-table static 1111.1111.1111 vlan 1 int Fa0/1
```

MISC Data Link Layer Notes

- Ethernet is an example of **connectionless** networks, which means that the destination end systems are not contacted prior to communication, nor is there any mechanism for the sender to know whether a frame has reached its intended destination.

- Every time a transparent bridge learns a MAC address, it would timestamp the entry. When the bridge sees a frame from this MAC address, it refreshes the timestamp. If the bridge does not hear from this source for a specific amount of time (aging timer), the bridge deletes the entry from its bridging table. The default MAC address table aging timer is 5 minutes or 300 seconds.

- **Content-Addressable Memory** (CAM) is a special type of computer memory that implements the lookup-table function in a single clock cycle (single operation) using dedicated comparison circuitry. CAMs are hardware-based search engines that are much faster than algorithmic approaches for search-intensive applications. CAMs are especially popular in network devices, which require high-speed table lookup for packet switching and forwarding.

- The default ARP table aging time is 4 hours (14400 seconds); while the default MAC address table aging time is 5 minutes (300 seconds). Aging time is the period that an entry is being kept.

- The **arp timeout** {*seconds*} interface subcommand and **mac-address-table aging-time** {*seconds*} global configuration command modify the ARP table aging timer and MAC address table aging timer respectively.

- A **balanced** line is a transmission line that consists of 2 connectors of the same type which there is no master-slave relationship – the DTE and DCE are treated as equals. Each station may initialize, supervise, recovery from errors, and send frames at any time.

- A **balun** can be used to convert balanced signal to unbalanced signal.

- **Alignment error** is an error that occurs in Ethernet networks, where a received frame has extra bits – a number that is not divisible by 8. Alignment errors are generally caused by collisions and eventually frame damage.

- **Bit-oriented protocols** are data link layer protocols that transmit frames regardless of the frame content. **Byte-oriented protocols** use a specific character from the user character set to mark the boundaries of frames. As compared with byte-oriented protocols, bit-oriented protocols are more efficient and support full-duplex operation. As a result, byte-oriented protocols have been superceded or replaced by bit-oriented protocols.

- Broadcasts and IP networks are not limited to VLANs, even though it is very tempting to think so. If 2 switches are connected with a crossover cable, with one configured with VLAN 10 on all ports, and another configured with VLAN 20 on all ports; hosts that connected to the switches are able to communicate as they as on the same IP network!

- **Media** is the plural for **medium**; just like **data** is the plural of **datum**.

- **Switch Buffering** – Switches have the same cabling and signal regeneration benefits as hubs, and reducing or even eliminating collisions by buffering frames. When switches receive multiple frames on different switch ports, they store the frames in memory buffers to prevent collisions.

MISC Physical Layer Notes

- The maximum point-to-point transmitting distance for a full-duplex mode 100BaseTX/FX multimode fiber converter is 2KM; under half-duplex mode, this is limited to 412m.

- The maximum point-to-point transmitting distance for a full-duplex mode 100BaseTX/FX single-mode fiber converter is 120KM. It is not recommended for a 100BaseTX/FX single-mode fiber converter to run under cable half-duplex mode with single-mode fiber.

- To fully utilize the advantage of long-distance transmission with fiber optics, the 100BaseTX/FX converters should be deployed together with switches instead of hubs, as switches support full-duplex mode, which allows point-to-point connection up to 2KM for multimode fiber and up to 120KM for single-mode fiber.

- 1000BaseSX Gigabit ports on 10/100 and Gigabit switches only support point-to-point connections of up to 280m. Gigabit multimode-SX-to-single-mode-LX converters have the potential to extend the distance to 10KM (the maximum point-to-point transmitting distance is 10KM + 280m = 10280m).

- Below describes the differences between stacking and cascading:

Stacking	Connecting multiple switches or hubs together with an SCSI cable. The cable plugs into the rear port of each switch or hub. The physical switches form a single logical switch.
Cascading	Connecting multiple switches or hubs together with UTP cables. The cables plugs into the front port of each switch or hub.

Stacking is the better solution when the devices are near to each other; while cascading is more suitable for linking devices that are further apart or differing makes (vendor, model, etc).

- **Note:** The backplane speed of a stack is limited to 32Gbps. For comparison, some larger modular switches can support 720Gbps on their backplanes.

- 2 pairs of wires (1 pair for **transmission**, another pair for collision detection and **reception**) in 100BaseTX UTP 8-pin connector are used for full-duplex transmission:

Pin Number	Signal
1	TX+
2	TX-
3	RX+
4	-
5	-
6	RX-
7	-
8	-

- **DOCSIS** – Data over Cable Service Interface Specification.

- The **5-4-3** repeater deployment rule – There can be a maximum of 5 physical segments between any 2 hosts, with 4 repeaters between the hosts, and only 3 physical segments can have hosts connected upon them. The other 2 physical segments can be used only to link the segments to extend the network length. This rule only applicable to bus topologies that use repeaters or hubs, and not applicable to extended start topologies that use switches. This rule which is no longer applicable for the context of today's networks, was the source of pain for those who didn't ever notice or understand it.

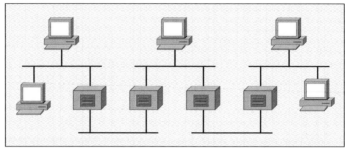

Figure A6-1: The 5-4-3 Repeater Deployment Topology

- **Signal Quality Error** (SQE) is designed to fix the problem in earlier versions of Ethernet where a NIC does not know if a transceiver is connected. The SQE test is used to test the collision detection circuit between a transceiver and a NIC. After data is successfully transmitted, the Ethernet transceiver would assert the SQE signal on the collision detection circuit of the NIC. The NIC treats this as a verification that the transceiver will inform it when a collision occurs.

- The SQE test is no longer being used in modern Ethernet networks, as most NICs already have an integrated transceiver and hence the test for the collision detection circuit is unnecessary.

- NRZ and NRZI encoding schemes are used for transmitting digital data. Both signals are not self-clocking.

- **Non-Return to Zero** (NRZ) encoding is used in low speed synchronous and asynchronous links. With NRZ, a binary 1 bit signal is sent as a high voltage value and a binary 0 signal is sent as a low voltage value – there is no encoding at all! The receiver may lose synchronization when using NRZ due to long runs of consecutive bits with the same value (no changes in voltage).

- With **Non-Return to Zero Inverted** (NRZI) encoding, a 0 is encoded as no change or transition in the voltage level, while a 1 is encoded when there is a change or transition in the voltage level – either **from low to high** or **from high to low**.

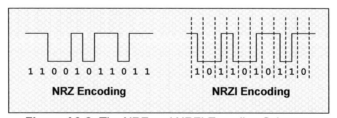

Figure A6-2: The NRZ and NRZI Encoding Schemes

- Parity checking is a method of error checking in data transmission. An extra bit – the parity bit is added to each character or data word so that the sum of the bits will be either an odd number (**odd parity**) or an even number (**even parity**).

Multiplexing Methods

- Multiplexing is a technology that is used to combine and send multiple digital signals simultaneously across a single physical transmission channel (wire, fiber, or link).

- Multiplexing occurs on the physical layer, as it combines multiple signals across a single physical channel.

- **Time-Division Multiplexing** (TDM) is a technique for assigning bandwidth on a single wire to data from several channels based on pre-assigned time slots. Bandwidth is allocated to each channel based on time slots, regardless of whether there is data to be transferred. Bandwidth will be wasted when there is no data to transfer. The SDH/SONET is an example application of TDM. **Note: Statistical Time-Division Multiplexing** (STDM) is an advanced version of TDM.

- **Frequency-Division Multiplexing** (FDM) is a form of signal multiplexing where multiplex baseband signals are modulated on different frequency carrier waves and combined together to create a composite signal. Data channels are allocated bandwidth based on the signal frequency of the traffic. Ex: FM radio.

- The concept corresponding to FDM in the optical domain is known as **Wavelength-Division Multiplexing** (WDM). **Wavelength-Division Multiplexing** (WDM) and **Dense WDM** (DWDM) are technologies that are being used in fiber-optic communications which multiplex multiple optical carrier signals of a single fiber optic by using different wavelengths (colours) of laser light to carry different signals. Data channels are allocated bandwidth based on wavelength (inverse of frequency).

- With **Statistical-Division Multiplexing** (SDM), the link sharing is adapted to the instantaneous traffic demands of the data streams that are translated over each channel (bandwidth is dynamically allocated to data channels). SDM is an alternative to multiplexing methods that create a fixed sharing of a link, eg: TDM and FDM.

- **Asynchronous Time-Division Multiplexing** (ATDM) is differs from normal TDM in which the time slots are assigned when necessary rather than pre-assigned to certain transmitters.

Ethernet Autonegotiation and Duplex Mismatch

- Ethernet autonegotiation uses FLPs (**Fast Link Pulses**) and NLPs (**Normal Link Pulses**) bursts (or signals) to negotiate the speed and duplex settings as well as other autonegotiation parameters between 2 NICs to allow them to operate at the highest possible performance mode.

- Autonegotiation is an **active** method that negotiates the speed and duplex settings; while auto-sensing is a rather **passive** method that only detects the speed of operation – **it is impossible to passively determine the duplex mode**.

- Autonegotiation is a protocol; hence it only works if it is running on both sides of a link. Setting a switch port to a specific speed and duplex disables autonegotiation for duplex mode. As a result, the end system connecting to the switch port is not able to see autonegotiation parameters, and hence connects only at half-duplex – **duplex mismatch** is occurred.

- Duplex mismatch normally produce poor performance and data link errors (eg: runt errors [1], input errors, CRC errors). Always remember to hardcode the speed and duplex settings at both ends or configure autonegotiation at both ends in order to avoid duplex mismatch!
Note: The end system performs auto-sensing when the autonegotiation process fails.
[1] Runts are Ethernet frames that are less than the IEEE 802.3 minimum frame size of 64 bytes and are truncated before they were fully received. Possible causes are collision, buffer underrun, and malfunction network card or software.
In computing, **buffer underrun** is a state occurring when a buffer used to communicate between 2 devices or processes is fed with data at a lower speed than the data is being read from it.

- In half-duplex operation, the RX line is being monitored for frames. If the RX line is receiving a frame, no frames are sent until the RX line is clear. A collision would occur when a frame is received on the RX line while a frame is being sent on the TX line.

- In full-duplex operation, the RX line is not being monitored, and the TX line is always considered available. Collisions do not occur as the TX and RX lines are completely independent.

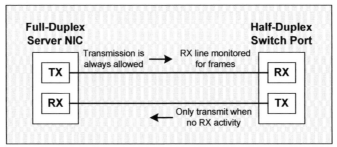

Figure A6-3: Common Autonegotiation Failure Scenario

- When one side of a link operates in full-duplex, and another side operates in half-duplex, a large number of collisions will occur on the half-duplex side; due to the full-duplex side transmits frames without checking its RX line, and chances are it will be sending frames constantly. The **chances of collision is high**, as when the half-duplex side transmit a frame after it sees the RX line is not receiving any frame, the full-duplex side also transmit a frame as it never check its RX line. The half-duplex side does not expect a frame to be received when it is sending a frame – a collision occurs. Additionally, the half-duplex side would have a hard-time for getting a chance to transmit, resulting in **poor performance** for communication with the device.

- A 10Mbps Ethernet link (fixed speed) defaults to half-duplex, whereas a 100Mbps Fast Ethernet link (dual speed 10/100) defaults to full-duplex. Multispeed links (10/100/1000) default to autonegotiate the duplex mode.

- Gigabit Ethernet uses a more robust autonegotiation mechanism and has low chances to fail. Therefore Gigabit Ethernet interfaces should always be set to autonegotiation.

ISO-TP: OSI Transport Layer Protocols

- The OSI suite defines the following 5 transport layers protocols:

TP0 (Transport Protocol Class 0)	Performs **segmentation** and **reassembly** functions.
TP1 (Transport Protocol Class 1)	Performs **segmentation**, **reassembly**, and **error recovery**. It segments and sequences PDUs and retransmits them or reinitiates the connection if an excessive number of PDUs are unacknowledged.
TP2 (Transport Protocol Class 2)	Performs **segmentation**, **reassembly**, and **multiplexing**.
TP3 (Transport Protocol Class 3)	Performs **segmentation**, **reassembly**, **error recovery**, and **multiplexing**. It segments and sequences PDUs and retransmits them or reinitiates the connection if an excessive number of PDUs are unacknowledged.
TP4 (Transport Protocol Class 4)	Same with TP3. It is the most **commonly used** among OSI transport protocols. **Similar to TCP** in the TCP/IP suite.

- The protocols **increase in complexity** from Class 0 to 4.

The TCP Connection States

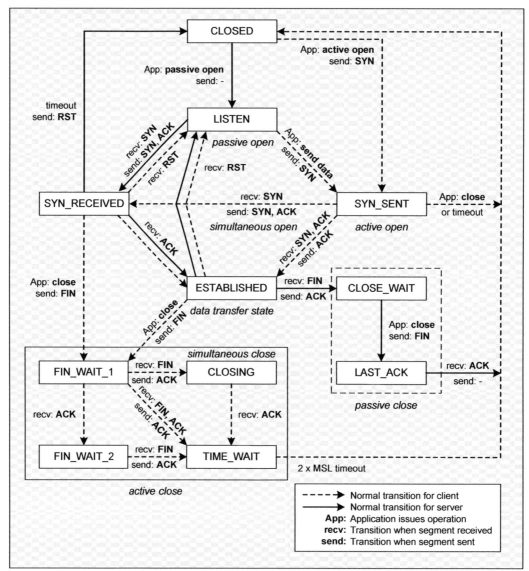

Figure A6-4: The TCP Finite State Machine

- In this context of discussion, a **client** is the peer that requests a connection; and a **server** is the peer that accepts a connection.

- **Handshake** is a series of information exchanged between devices to ensure both ends are synchronized for data transmission and operation.

Active open	A client socket initiates a connection by sending a SYN segment which contains the server's port number and the client's **Initial Sequence Number** (ISN). The client socket enters into the SYN_SENT state.
Passive open	Indicates a server socket is opened and listening or waiting for incoming SYN.
Active close	Initiated by the client socket when it finished receiving data. The client socket sends a FIN segment and enters into the FIN_WAIT_1 or FIN_WAIT_2 state. The connection is now a half-closed connection, where the client no longer sends data but still able to receive data from the server. The server socket enters into the passive close state upon receiving the FIN segment from the client.
Passive close	Occurs when the server socket receives the FIN segment from the client active close. The server socket enters into the CLOSE_WAIT state. The server socket is waiting for the server application to close. The server sends its FIN when the server application is closed.
Simultaneous open	Occurs when both client and server applications send a SYN to each other to establish a TCP connection. However, the possibly is small, as the server required to know the port of the client host that the SYN should destined to. TCP simultaneous open is normally found in **P2P applications**.
Simul. close	Occurs when both client and server applications perform active close.

- A connection goes through the following states during its lifetime:

State	Description
LISTEN	The server socket waits for a connection request from any remote client host.
SYN_SENT	The client socket waits for an acknowledgment after a connection request is sent.
SYN_RECEIVED	The server socket receives a connection request and pending to reply an acknowledgment to the client. The SYN Flood DoS attack would typically cause a lot of TCP connections in this state.
ESTABLISHED	Represents an established connection. Data communication is allowed. The normal state for the data transfer phase of a connection.
FIN_WAIT_1	The client socket has initiated active close and wait for an acknowledgment from the server after a connection termination request (FIN segment) is sent.
FIN_WAIT_2	The client socket has received an acknowledgment for its connection termination request but is still waiting for the connection termination request (FIN segment) from the server.
CLOSE_WAIT	The remote client socket is closed. The server socket enters into passive close state and waits for a connection termination request from the server application.
CLOSING	The client socket waiting for a connection termination acknowledgment from the remote server socket.
LAST_ACK	The server application and socket are closed. Waiting for the **final ACK** for the connection termination request from the remote client socket.
TIME_WAIT	The client socket waiting for enough time to pass to make sure the stray packets destined to the closed socket are flushed out from the network.

Note: Application layer protocol (eg: HTTP and Telnet) servers tend to initiates active close than clients, which reverse the client and server roles in TCP. TCP assumes that clients tend to initiate active close (by first sending a segment with the FIN bit set).

- **Q:** How does a client application enter the ESTABLISHED state from the CLOSED state?
  A: The client application calls the connect() socket function, which causes TCP to send an empty segment with the SYN bit set and enters into the SYN_SENT state. The server then replies with an empty segment with the SYN and ACK bits set. When the client receives the SYN/ACK segment, it replies with and ACK segment, and reports a successful connection establishment to the client application.

- **Q:** What is the normal TCP shutdown sequence?
  A: TCP is a bidirectional protocol – the connection is shutdown in 2 identical phases, one for each direction. When the server finished sending data (the application protocol has finished using the connection, but TCP still has some works to perform), it sends a segment with the FIN bit set, which the client replies with a segment with ACK bit set. This sequence happens again when the server waits for the FIN segment from the client, and replies with an ACK segment to the client.
  Note: This is the normal TCP shutdown sequence observed in application layer protocols (eg: HTTP and Telnet), which reverse the client and server roles in TCP, as TCP assumes that clients tend to initiate active close (by first sending a segment with the FIN bit set).

- **Q:** What is the usage of the RST bit?
  A: It represents an abnormal close, which happens under several circumstances. The 2 common TCP reset occurrences are "connection refused" and "connection terminated by remote host". The 1st case happens when trying to connect to a non-open port on a remote host, while the 2nd case happens when the remote host interrupts the connection, the application crashes, or there is a malicious insertion of a segment with the correct IP and TCP information (eg: source and destination IP addresses, source and destination port numbers, sequence number) and RST bit set. A TCP session that ends with a TCP reset may not indicate a problem. Sometimes TCP resets indicate a network problem (misconfigured IPS), but there are cases in which a TCP reset is OK. Application developers may elect to issue a TCP reset instead of the exchange of FIN-ACK packets to free up resources more quickly when tearing down a connection-oriented TCP session.

- **Q:** What's wrong when connections keep getting into the FIN_WAIT_x state?
  A: Either the application or remote host is not closing the connection properly. Since FIN_WAIT states often last up to 10 minutes, it is well worth the effort to find and fix the root cause.

- **Q:** What's wrong when there are many connections in the TIME_WAIT state?
  A: Nothing wrong. TIME_WAIT is absolutely normal. Every socket that gets closed normally goes through this state after it is closed. This state is a safety mechanism that catches stray packets that are destined for a closed connection. Since the maximum time that such stray packets can exist is 2 times the **maximum segment lifetime**, hence the TIME_WAIT state lasts for 2 x MSL. However, there is no easy way to estimate MSL on the fly, so protocol stacks normally hard-code a value (15 – 60 sec) for it. Hence, TIME_WAIT usually lasts 30 – 120 sec.
  Glossary:

Stray packets	Duplicate packets that are still in the network when a connection is closed.
MSL	The maximum length of time a TCP segment can exist (or alive) in a network.
Stack	The software implementation of a network protocol suite (eg: TCP/IP).

HTTP and TCP TIME_WAIT State

- Due to the nature of TCP/IP, it is possible that after an active close has commenced, there are duplicate packets that traversing around the network and trying to reach their destination sockets. If a new socket binds to the same port before these old packets are flushed out from the network, old and new data could be mixed up.

- In HTTP, active close always initiated by the server. A server socket enters the TIME_WAIT state when it receives the last FIN from the client and replies with an ACK.

- Application protocol (eg: HTTP and Telnet) servers tend to initiates active close than clients, which reversed the client and server roles in TCP, as TCP assumes that clients tend to initiate active close. If that is the case, TIME_WAITs won't be existed in a busy web server as they do. When the active close is initiated by clients, the TIME_WAIT state and the responsibility of keeping old and new data from intermixing would tend to be on the client sockets.

Dissecting TCP and IP Header Fields

4-bit	Nibble
8-bit	Byte / Octet
32-bit	Word

- **Header Length** or **Data Offset** (4 bits) specifies the number of 32-bit words in the TCP header, which indirectly indicates where the application data begins.

- **Unused** or **Reserved** (6 bits) bits are reserved for future use. All must be 0s.

- **Flags** or **Control Bits** (6 bits):

URG	Indicates that the Urgent Data Pointer field is significant – data is sent out-of-band.
ACK	Indicates that the Acknowledgment Number field is significant. The receiver will send an ACK that equals to the sender's sequence number plus the length (amount of data), which is also the sequence number of the next octet the receiver expects to receive.
PSH	The Push function forces data delivery without waiting for buffers to fill. The data will also be delivered to the user-level application on the receiving end without buffering.
RST	Reset – instantaneous abort a connection in both directions – an abnormal session close.
SYN	Synchronize the initial sequence numbers during the session establishment process.
FIN	Used by a graceful session close which shows that the sender has no more data to send.

- Whenever a receiving TCP sees the PSH flag, it will pass the data to the receiving process without waiting for more data – the receiving buffer that contains data associated with a PSH flag will be passed to application for processing even if the buffer is not fully filled.

- **Checksum** (16 bits) is the 16-bit one's complement of the one's complement sum of the header, options, and application data. This field is filled with 0s when computing the checksum.
  Note: The Header Checksum field in the IPv4 header is a checksum that is calculated based on all the fields in the IPv4 header **only**; hence only the IPv4 header is being checked for errors. The Header Checksum field is filled with 0s when computing the checksum.

- **Urgent Data Pointer** (16 bits) indicates a positive offset from the current sequence number in the segment. It points to the sequence number of the octet following the urgent data (the end of the urgent data). This field is only being interpreted when the URG control bit in a segment is set. TCP must inform the application layer how much urgent data remains to be read from the connection whenever it receives a segment with an urgent data pointer.

- **Options** (variable) may exist at the end of the TCP header. Their lengths are multiple of 8 bits. The TCP checksum covers all the TCP options.

- Below lists some common TCP options:

Kind (8-bit)	Length (8-bit)	Description
0	-	**EOL** – End of Option List. Indicates the end of the option list. Used at the end of all options, not the end of each option.
1	-	**NOP** – No Operation. May be used between options to align the beginning of a subsequent option to a word boundary.
2	4	**MSS** – Maximum Segment Size. Indicates the maximum receive segment size at the TCP that sent out this segment. This option must only be sent in the initial connection request – connection request segments with SYN control bit set. Any segment size is allowed if this option is not used.
4	2	**SACK permitted**. The **Selective Acknowledgment** (SACK) extension uses 2 forms of TCP options: an enabling option – **SACK permitted**, that may be sent in a SYN segment to indicate the use of SACK option in an established connection; and the **SACK option**, which may be sent over an established connection after the SACK permitted is granted operation.
5	Variable	**SACK options.** They are used to convey extended acknowledgment information over an established connection. It is normally sent by a receiver to inform the sender about the **non-contiguous blocks of received data**, which mostly caused by the lost of a TCP segment. The receiver will wait for the retransmissions of the missing block of data to fill in the gap. A TCP client includes the SACK options along with the ACK segment to the TCP server whenever there is queued and unacknowledged data. SACK optimizes **TCP retransmissions with selective retransmission**, which skips the retransmission of selectively acknowledged segments. The SACK option can be sent only when the TCP client has received the SACK permitted option in the SYN segment from the TCP server, which indicates that the server supports SACK.

- The SACK option fields:

Left Edge	The first sequence number of this queued and unacknowledged data block.
Right Edge	The last sequence number of this queued and unacknowledged data block.

Reference: RFC 2018 – TCP Selective Acknowledgment Options.

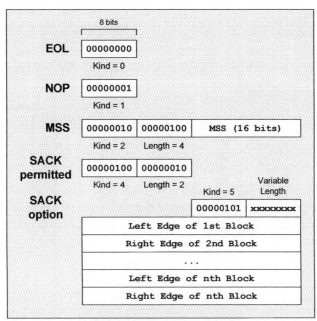

Figure A6-5: TCP Options

- **Padding** (variable) which is comprised of 0s is used to ensure the TCP header is 32-bit aligned.

- The **Type of Service** (TOS) field in the IP header was intended to use for **TOS routing**, in which a router would have separate routing tables for different TOS values. When forwarding a packet, the router would first choose a routing table based on the packet's TOS, followed by normal routing table lookup. TOS routing has rarely been implemented in the Internet. Only 2 routing protocols – OSPF and IS-IS have ever supported the calculation of separate paths based on TOS.

- The first 3 bits in the TOS field in the IP header were being used for IP Precedence, in which values from 0 – 7 can be used to specify the transmission priority of packets at each router hop. IP Precedence does not affect the path of a packet as with TOS. IP Precedence is being phased out in favor of DSCP, but is supported by many applications and routers.

- **Differentiated Services Code Point** (DSCP) is a modification of the TOS field. 6 bits of the field are being reallocated for use as the DSCP field. DSCP is not compatible with IP Precedence.

- An application can modify the handling of IP packets by extending the IP header with IP options. IP options are rarely used for regular IP packets, as most routers are heavily optimized for forwarding IP packets without IP options. The use of IP options introduces a potential DoS vulnerability against routers due to the additional processing workload of packets with IP options.

- Most IP options (eg: the *record-route* and *timestamp* options) are used for statistics collection and do not affect the forwarding path of packets. However, the *strict-source route* and *loose-source route* options can be utilized by the originator of a packet to control the forwarding path the packet.

- **IP source routing** is often considered as a security hole, as even with security is being provided through address filtering, the final destination of a packet might buried in the IP options field. As a result, most routers are configured to discard packets containing source routing options with the **no ip source-route** global configuration command.

TCP Selective Acknowledgment (SACK) and Fast Retransmission

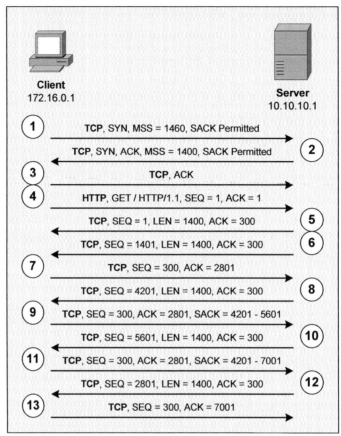

Figure A6-6: TCP Selection Acknowledgment (SACK)

- In the above scenario, there are total of 5 segments to be sent from 10.0.0.1 to 172.16.0.1:
  1) 1 – 1400, **2)** 1401 – 2800, **3)** 2801 – 4200, **4)** 4201 – 5600, and **5)** 5601 – 7000.

- Below describes the steps involved in the scenario:
  i)   Steps 1, 2, and 3 show the TCP three-way handshake connection establishment phase. Both end systems agree to use SACK. The agreed MSS is 1460 bytes.
  ii) 10.10.10.1 transmits the 1st and 2nd segments to 172.16.0.1 (Steps 5 and 6). 172.16.0.1 acknowledges the segments (Step 7).
  iii) 10.10.10.1 transmits the 4th and 5th segments to 172.16.0.1 (Step 8 and 10). The 3rd segment is lost. With **selective acknowledgment**, 172.16.0.1 selectively acknowledges the out-of-order segments, instead of cumulatively acknowledging the last in-order segment received (Step 9 and 11).
  iv) With **fast retransmission**, which skips the retransmission of selectively acknowledged segments, 10.10.10.1 retransmits the 3rd segment to 172.16.0.1 (Step 12).
  v)   Finally, 172.16.0.1 cumulatively acknowledges the receipt of all segments (Step 13).

Dive into Proxy ARP

- Proxy ARP allows a host with not routing capability to reach remote subnets without the default gateway configuration. The hosts assume the network they reside as a flat network in which they can reach any hosts after the ARP resolution process. Proxy ARP is defined in RFC 1027.

- Below are some of the disadvantages of using Proxy ARP:
  - i) It increases the amount of ARP traffic on the network.
  - ii) A host requires larger ARP table for handling IP-to-MAC address mappings.
  - iii) Security threat – spoofing, where a host claims to be another for intercepting packets.

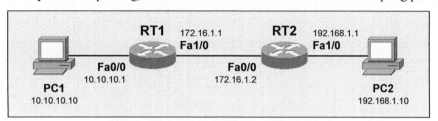

Figure A6-7: Sample Proxy ARP Network

- Below shows the ARP table on PC1 when RT1 providing Proxy ARP service and PC1 is not configured with any default gateway:

```
PC1#sh arp
Protocol   Address          Age (min)   Hardware Addr   Type   Interface
Internet   10.10.10.10          -       cc00.0f28.0000  ARPA   FastEthernet0/0
Internet   10.10.10.1           0       cc01.0f28.0000  ARPA   FastEthernet0/0
Internet   192.168.1.10         0       cc01.0f28.0000  ARPA   FastEthernet0/0
Internet   172.16.1.2           0       cc01.0f28.0000  ARPA   FastEthernet0/0
PC1#
RT1#sh ip redirects
Default gateway is not set

Host                Gateway          Last Use   Total Uses   Interface
ICMP redirect cache is empty
RT1#
```

Local Proxy ARP

- Below shows the output of the **show ip interface** {*intf-type intf-num*} command which shows that local proxy ARP is disabled. This section discusses what Local Proxy ARP is and its usage.

```
Router#sh ip int fa1/0
FastEthernet1/0 is up, line protocol is up
  Internet address is 10.10.10.1/24
  Broadcast address is 255.255.255.255
  Address determined by setup command
  MTU is 1500 bytes
  Helper address is not set
  Directed broadcast forwarding is disabled
  Outgoing access list is not set
  Inbound  access list is not set
  Proxy ARP is enabled
  Local Proxy ARP is disabled
--- output omitted ---
```

- Local Proxy ARP is used when there is a need to perform proxy ARP for hosts in local network. Normally network devices do not perform local proxy ARP as they would assume the host with the requested IP address would answer the ARP request itself.

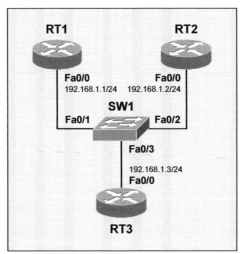

Figure A6-8: Sample Local Proxy ARP Network

- The **switchport protected** interface subcommand is configured on SW1 Fa0/1 and Fa0/2. The **ip local-proxy-arp** interface subcommand is configured on RT3 Fa0/0.

- Below shows that RT3 is performing proxy ARP for RT2:

```
RT1#ping 192.168.1.2
Type escape sequence to abort.
Sending 5, 100-byte ICMP Echos to 17.0.0.2, timeout is 2 seconds:
!!!!!
Success rate is 100 percent (5/5), round-trip min/avg/max = 1/3/4 ms
RT1#sh arp
Protocol  Address          Age (min)  Hardware Addr   Type   Interface
Internet  192.168.1.1           -     1111.1111.1111  ARPA   FastEthernet0/0
Internet  192.168.1.2           6     3333.3333.3333  ARPA   FastEthernet0/0
Internet  192.168.1.3           5     3333.3333.3333  ARPA   FastEthernet0/0
```

- The **switchport protected** interface subcommand configures a switch port as a protected port. **Protected ports** have the following characteristics:
  i) A protected port does not forward any traffic (including unicast, multicast, and broadcast) to other protected ports – traffic cannot be forwarded between protected ports at Layer 2; all traffic between protected ports must be forwarded through a Layer 3 device.
  ii) Traffic between a protected port and a non-protected port is forwarded as usual.
  Note: This feature applies upon a single switch, and cannot be extended across multiple switches.

- Protected ports are being used in environments where traffic must not be forwarded between ports on the same switch so that an end system does not see the traffic from another end system. Below are some other sample usages of protected ports:
  i) A hotel environment where the ports for each room should not be able to communicate with each other, but they need to communicate with the gateway.
  ii) A DMZ zone where the ports for each server should not be able to communicate with each other in order to prevent further damages of other servers when a server is owned.
  iii) A collocation environment where servers from different customers should not be able to communicate with each other.

Determining Cisco Router Memory Size

- The **show version** EXEC command is able to tell how much **Dynamic RAM** (DRAM) and **packet memory** (separate SRAM or shared memory) are installed in a Cisco router.

- The Cisco 4000, 4500, 4700, and 7500 series routers have separate DRAM and packet memory. The example below shows a router with **64M** of DRAM and **2M** of SRAM (packet memory):
  ```
  cisco RSP4 (R5000) processor with 65536K/2072K bytes of memory.
  ```
  The example below shows a router with **256M** of DRAM and **8M** of SRAM (packet memory):
  ```
  cisco RSP8 (R7000) processor with 262144K/8216K bytes of memory.
  ```

- The Cisco 1600, 2500, 2600, 3600, and 7200 series routers use a fraction of their DRAM as packet memory. Hence both numbers need to be added to find out the real amount of DRAM. The example below shows a router with 29696K + 3072K = 32768K = **32M** of DRAM.
  ```
  cisco 2611 (MPC860) processor (revision x) with 29696K/3072K bytes of memory.
  ```
  The example below shows a router with 93184K + 5120K = 98304K = **98M** of DRAM.
  ```
  cisco 2621XM (MPC860P) processor (revision) with 93184K/5120K bytes of memory.
  ```

- DRAM is mainly used for system processing, eg: storing routing tables, routing protocols data, network accounting information, and running the Cisco IOS software; while packet memory is used for packet buffering of the router network interfaces and CPU cache memory functions. The packet memory on Cisco 4000, 4500, 4700, and 7500 series routers is the total physical I/O memory (also known as **SRAM** or **Fast Memory**); while the packet memory on Cisco 1600, 2500, 2600, 3600, and 7200 series routers is the amount of **shared memory**, which is a portion of the DRAM.

- The terms I/O memory (iomem), shared memory, Fast Memory, and PCI memory are all refer to **Packet Memory**, which is either a separate physical RAM stick or module, or shared DRAM.

- **Static RAM** (SRAM) is a type of semiconductor memory that does not need to be periodically refreshed as **Dynamic RAM** (DRAM). Memory refresh is the process of periodically reading information from an area of computer memory, and rewriting the read information back to the same area immediately without any modification. SRAM is still volatile, as the data stored in it is eventually lost when the memory is not powered.

- SRAM is more expensive, but faster and far less power hungry when idle (no periodical refresh) compared to DRAM. Additionally, due to a more complex internal structure, SRAM is less dense that DRAM and hence not used for high-capacity, low-cost applications, eg: PC main memory.

The Myth of the Running Configuration file

- The **reload** privileged command is the only way to restore the configuration of a device into its last reboot state. Replacing the running-config with the startup-config or a configuration file from a TFTP server will be **unsuccessful** – configuration is **merged** instead of being overwritten.

- The Configuration Replace and Configuration Rollback feature which introduced in Cisco IOS Release 12.3(7)T and 12.2(25)S provides the capability to replace the current running configuration with any configuration file. The **configure replace** privileged command can be used to overwrite the running configuration.

Spanning Tree Protocol Port ID

- When 2 switches are interconnected with multiple cross cables, the root port of the non-root bridge switch (SW2) is the port that connects to the **lowest Port ID** of the root bridge (SW1).

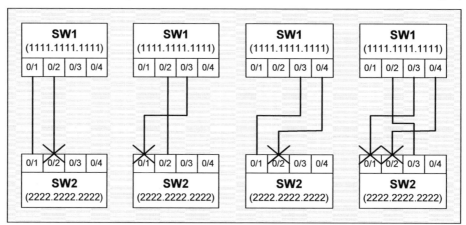

Figure A6-8: Spanning Tree Protocol Port ID

Router-on-a-Stick VLAN Trunking Encapsulation and IP Address Configuration

- Below shows the configuration sequence of VLAN trunking encapsulation and IP address on a router subinterface in Router-on-a-Stick setup. The VLAN trunking encapsulation must be configured prior to configuring an IP address.

```
RT1#conf t
Enter configuration commands, one per line.  End with CNTL/Z.
RT1(config)#int fa0/0.1
RT1(config-subif)#ip add 192.168.1.1 255.255.255.0

% Configuring IP routing on a LAN subinterface is only allowed if that
subinterface is already configured as part of an IEEE 802.10, IEEE 802.1Q,
or ISL VLAN.

RT1(config-subif)#
RT1(config-subif)#encapsulation ?
  dot1Q  IEEE 802.1Q Virtual LAN
  isl    Inter Switch Link - Virtual LAN encapsulation
  sde    IEEE 802.10 Virtual LAN - Secure Data Exchange

RT1(config-subif)#encapsulation dot1Q 1
RT1(config-subif)#ip add 192.168.1.1 255.255.255.0
RT1(config-subif)#^Z
RT1#
RT1#sh int fa0/0.1
FastEthernet0/0.1 is up, line protocol is up
  Hardware is AmdFE, address is cc01.0520.0000 (bia cc01.0520.0000)
  Internet address is 192.168.1.1/24
  MTU 1500 bytes, BW 100000 Kbit, DLY 100 usec,
    reliability 255/255, txload 1/255, rxload 1/255
  Encapsulation 802.1Q Virtual LAN, Vlan ID 1.
  ARP type: ARPA, ARP Timeout 04:00:00
RT1#
```

switchport trunk encapsulation and switchport mode trunk Configuration

- Below shows the configuration sequence of VLAN trunking on a Fast Ethernet interface. The VLAN trunking encapsulation must be configured (with the **switchport trunk encapsulation** interface subcommand) prior to configuring a trunking interface with the **switchport mode trunk** interface subcommand.

```
Switch#sh run int fa0/1
Building configuration...

Current configuration : 68 bytes
!
interface FastEthernet0/1
 switchport mode dynamic desirable
end

Switch#
Switch#sh int fa0/1 trunk

Port        Mode         Encapsulation  Status       Native vlan
Fa0/12      desirable    negotiate      other        1

Port        Vlans allowed on trunk
Fa0/12      none

Port        Vlans allowed and active in management domain
Fa0/12      none

Port        Vlans in spanning tree forwarding state and not pruned
Fa0/12      none
Switch#
Switch#conf t
Enter configuration commands, one per line.  End with CNTL/Z.
Switch(config)#int fa0/1
Switch(config-if)#switchport mode trunk
Command rejected: An interface whose trunk encapsulation is "Auto" can not
be configured to "trunk" mode.
Switch(config-if)#
Switch(config-if)#switchport trunk encapsulation ?
  dot1q     Interface uses only 802.1q trunking encapsulation when trunking
  isl       Interface uses only ISL trunking encapsulation when trunking
  negotiate Device will negotiate trunking encapsulation with peer on
            interface

Switch(config-if)#switchport trunk encapsulation dot1q
Switch(config-if)#switchport mode trunk
Switch(config-if)#^Z
Switch#
```

The Problem of Router-on-a-Stick Configuration on Ethernet Interface

- RT1 with router-on-a-stick configuration on an Ethernet interface was unable to communicate with PC1 resides in **Native VLAN** due to confusion of using the main interface and subinterface. **Note:** This problem does not happen on Fast Ethernet interfaces.

- Below shows the configuration on RT1 which experienced the above describe problem scenario:

```
!
interface Ethernet0/0
 no ip address
 full-duplex
!
interface Ethernet0/0.1
 encapsulation dot1Q 1 native
 ip address 192.168.1.1 255.255.255.0
!
interface Ethernet0/0.2
 encapsulation dot1Q 2
 ip address 192.168.2.1 255.255.255.0
!
interface Ethernet0/0.3
 encapsulation dot1Q 3
 ip address 192.168.3.1 255.255.255.0
!
```

- Below shows the root cause of the problem – RT1 unable to communicate with PC1:

```
RT1#debug arp
ARP packet debugging is on
RT1#
RT1#ping 192.168.1.2 rep 1

Type escape sequence to abort.
Sending 1, 100-byte ICMP Echos to 192.168.1.2, timeout is 2 seconds:
.
Success rate is 0 percent (0/1)
RT1#
RT1#sh arp
Protocol  Address          Age (min)  Hardware Addr   Type   Interface
Internet  192.168.1.1            -     cc01.01c4.0000  ARPA   Ethernet0/0.1
Internet  192.168.1.2            0     Incomplete      ARPA
RT1#
RT1#sh log | in ARP
00:07:31: IP ARP: sent req src 192.168.1.1 cc01.01c4.0000,
00:07:31: IP ARP rep filtered src 192.168.1.2 cc02.01c4.0000, dst
192.168.1.1 cc01.01c4.0000 wrong cable, interface Ethernet0/0
RT1#
```

- Below shows the output of the **show arp** command after implemented a workaround – configure the native VLAN IP address on the main interface instead of the subinterface:

```
RT1#sh arp
Protocol  Address          Age (min)  Hardware Addr   Type   Interface
Internet  192.168.1.1            -     cc01.01c4.0000  ARPA   Ethernet0/0
Internet  192.168.1.2            0     cc02.01c4.0000  ARPA   Ethernet0/0
```

Switching Technologies

- The load balancing method chosen for packet forwarding depends on the type of switching performed by a router. Cisco IOS supports the following 2 common switching methods:

Process Switching	Performs **packet-by-packet** load balancing. Utilizes CPU resource for looking up the next hop in the routing table for every packet that needs to be forwarded.
Fast Switching	Performs **destination-by-destination** or **session-by-session** load balancing. Uses a route cache for determining the destination IP address and the next hop IP address, which is **less CPU intensive** than process switching.

- The first packet to any host is always process switched. If fast switching is enabled on the outbound interface, the router would create a **cache entry** for the destination host after it forwarded the first packet. The cache entry is then used to forward all subsequent packets destined to the same host. Route cache lookup is much faster than routing table lookup.

- Cisco IOS offers **other technologies and methods of switching** IP packets depend on the hardware platform and IOS version.

Dissecting Subnet Zero

- Traditionally, it was strongly recommended not to use subnet zero (all-0s) and broadcast subnet for addressing (RFC 950 – Internet Standard Subnetting Procedure). This is to avoid the confusion of having a network and a subnet with indistinguishable addresses.

- Below shows a Class B network – 172.16.0.0/16 is subnetted with /18 subnet mask:

Subnet Address	Subnet Mask	Broadcast Address	Valid Host Range
172.16.0.0	255.255.192.0	172.16.63.255	172.16.0.1 – 172.16.63.254
172.16.64.0	255.255.192.0	172.16.127.255	172.16.64.1 – 172.16.127.254
172.16.128.0	255.255.192.0	172.16.191.255	172.16.128.1 – 172.16.191.254
172.16.192.0	255.255.192.0	172.16.255.255	172.16.192.1 – 172.16.255.254

- As shown in the example above, 172.16.16.16 is resides in the 172.16.0.0 subnet (subnet zero). This subnet address is same with the network address – a network and subnet with indistinguishable addresses.

- **RFC 1878 – Variable Length Subnet Table For IPv4** states that the practice of excluding all-0s and all-1s subnets is **obsolete**.

- **MISC Note:** Broadcast address is used in both logical (L3) and hardware (L2) addressing. With logical addressing, the host address will be all 1s. With hardware addressing, the hardware address will be all 1s in binary (all Fs in hexadecimal).

- Sample Subnet Zero configuration:

```
Router(config)#no ip subnet-zero
Router(config)#int fa0/0
Router(config-if)#ip address 10.0.0.1 255.255.255.0              (1)
Bad mask /24 for address 10.0.0.1
Router(config-if)#ip address 10.1.0.1 255.255.255.0              (2)
Router(config-if)#ip address 172.16.0.1 255.255.255.0           (3)
Bad mask /24 for address 172.16.0.1
Router(config-if)#ip address 172.16.1.1 255.255.255.0           (4)
Router(config-if)#ip address 192.168.0.1 255.255.255.192        (5)
Bad mask /26 for address 192.168.0.1
Router(config-if)#ip address 192.168.0.65 255.255.255.192       (6)
Router(config-if)#exit
Router(config)#
Router(config)#ip subnet-zero
Router(config)#int fa0/0
Router(config-if)#ip address 10.0.0.1 255.255.255.0
Router(config-if)#ip address 172.16.0.1 255.255.255.0
Router(config-if)#ip address 192.168.0.1 255.255.255.192
Router(config-if)#
```

- Subnet Zero explanation:

1	10.0.0.1/24. Class A. Default subnet mask is /8.				
	10	0	0	1	
	00000000	00000000	00000000	00000001	Subnet Zero

2	10.1.0.1/24. Class A. Default subnet mask is /8.				
	10	1	0	1	
	00000000	00000001	00000000	00000001	Not Subnet Zero

3	172.16.0.1/24. Class B. Default subnet mask is /16.				
	172	16	0	1	
	10101100	00010000	00000000	00000001	Subnet Zero

4	172.16.1.1/24. Class B. Default subnet mask is /16.				
	172	16	1	1	
	10101100	00010000	00000001	00000001	Not Subnet Zero

5	192.168.0.1/26. Class C. Default subnet mask is /24.				
	192	168	0	1	
	11000000	10101000	00000000	00000001	Subnet Zero

6	192.168.0.65/26. Class C. Default subnet mask is /24.				
	192	168	0	65	
	11000000	10101000	00000000	01000001	Not Subnet Zero

- **Note:** The **no ip subnet-zero** global configuration command only affects the subnet zero; it does not affect the broadcast (all-1s) subnet.

Default Route (Gateway of Last Resort) Configurations

- The **ip default-gateway** {*ip-addr*} command should only be used when **ip routing is disabled** on the Cisco device (eg: switch); or used to reach the TFTP server during IOS upgrade, as a limited-function IOS (RXBOOT) with **no routing capability** will be loaded.

- The **ip default-network** {*classful-net-addr*} and **ip route 0.0.0.0 0.0.0.0** {*classful-net-addr | ip-addr*} commands can be used when **ip routing is enabled** on the Cisco device. The major difference between these 2 commands is that configuring a static default route only defines a default route for a single router, while **ip default-network** {*classful-net-addr*} is able to propagate the default route to other routers via a routing protocol.

The **passive-interface** Router Subcommand

- The **passive-interface** router subcommand on most routing protocols (eg: RIP) would restrict outgoing routing updates only. The router would still receive and process incoming routing updates from other routers which reside on the passive interface subnet of the router.

- In EIGRP, the **passive-interface** {*intf-type intf-num*} router subcommand suppresses the exchange of Hello packets between 2 routers, resulting in their neighbor relationship will never be formed and hence will never exchange routing updates. This suppresses not only outgoing routing updates, but also incoming routing updates.

The **permanent** keyword in the Static Route Configuration

- Without the **permanent** keyword in a static route statement, an inactive interface will cause the directly connected network and all the associated static routes removed from the routing table.

- Adding the **permanent** keyword to a static route statement will keep the static route remains in the routing table no matter what happens, even if the interface associated with the static route goes down (or shutdown) or the directly-connected network is removed from the routing table.

- The advantage of this option is that static routes do not need to be processed for insertion into / removal from the routing table upon interface status change, hence saving processing resources. The processing time for static routing insertion into / removal from the routing table is 1 second. Prior to Cisco IOS Release 12.0, this processing time was 5 seconds.

- **Note:** Configuring static routes with the **permanent** keyword could make a subnet that doesn't even exist to be shown in the routing table!

- Below shows the behavior of the routing table before and after using the **permanent** keyword:

```
Router#sh run | in ip route
ip route 172.16.1.0 255.255.255.0 10.10.10.2
Router#
Router#sh ip route

Gateway of last resort is not set

     172.16.0.0/24 is subnetted, 1 subnets
S       172.16.1.0 [1/0] via 10.10.10.2
     10.0.0.0/30 is subnetted, 1 subnets
C       10.10.10.0 is directly connected, Serial1/0
Router#
Router#debug ip routing
IP routing debugging is on
Router#
00:03:34: is_up: 1 state: 4 sub state: 1 line: 0
00:03:42: %LINEPROTO-5-UPDOWN: Line protocol on Interface Serial1/0, changed
state to down
00:03:42: is_up: 0 state: 4 sub state: 1 line: 0
00:03:42: RT: interface Serial1/0 removed from routing table
00:03:42: RT: del 10.10.10.0/30 via 0.0.0.0, connected metric [0/0]
00:03:42: RT: delete subnet route to 10.10.10.0/30
00:03:42: RT: delete network route to 10.0.0.0
00:03:43: RT: del 172.16.1.0/24 via 10.10.10.2, static metric [1/0]
00:03:43: RT: delete subnet route to 172.16.1.0/24
00:03:43: RT: delete network route to 172.16.0.0
Router#
Router#sh ip route

Gateway of last resort is not set

Router#
```

```
Router#conf t
Enter configuration commands, one per line.  End with CNTL/Z.
Router(config)#no ip route 172.16.1.0 255.255.255.0
Router(config)#ip route 172.16.1.0 255.255.255.0 10.10.10.2 permanent
Router(config)#^Z
Router#
00:05:22: %LINEPROTO-5-UPDOWN: Line protocol on Interface Serial1/0, changed
state to up
00:05:22: is_up: 1 state: 4 sub state: 1 line: 0
00:05:22: RT: add 10.10.10.0/30 via 0.0.0.0, connected metric [0/0]
00:05:22: RT: interface Serial1/0 added to routing table
00:05:23: RT: add 172.16.1.0/24 via 10.10.10.2, static metric [1/0]
Router#
Router#sh ip route

Gateway of last resort is not set

     172.16.0.0/24 is subnetted, 1 subnets
S        172.16.1.0 [1/0] via 10.10.10.2
     10.0.0.0/30 is subnetted, 1 subnets
C        10.10.10.0 is directly connected, Serial1/0
Router#
Router#
00:06:04: is_up: 1 state: 4 sub state: 1 line: 0
00:06:12: %LINEPROTO-5-UPDOWN: Line protocol on Interface Serial1/0, changed
state to down
00:06:12: is_up: 0 state: 4 sub state: 1 line: 0
00:06:12: RT: interface Serial1/0 removed from routing table
00:06:12: RT: del 10.10.10.0/30 via 0.0.0.0, connected metric [0/0]
00:06:12: RT: delete subnet route to 10.10.10.0/30
00:06:12: RT: delete network route to 10.0.0.0
Router#
Router#sh ip route

Gateway of last resort is not set

     172.16.0.0/24 is subnetted, 1 subnets
S        172.16.1.0 [1/0] via 10.10.10.2
Router#
Router#conf t
Enter configuration commands, one per line.  End with CNTL/Z.
Router(config)#int s1/0
Router(config-if)#shut
Router(config-if)#^Z
Router#
00:06:35: is_up: 0 state: 6 sub state: 1 line: 0
00:06:37: %LINK-5-CHANGED: Interface Serial1/0, changed state to
administratively down
00:06:37: is_up: 0 state: 6 sub state: 1 line: 0
Router#
Router#sh ip route

Gateway of last resort is not set

     172.16.0.0/24 is subnetted, 1 subnets
S        172.16.1.0 [1/0] via 10.10.10.2
Router#
```

RIPv1 and VLSM

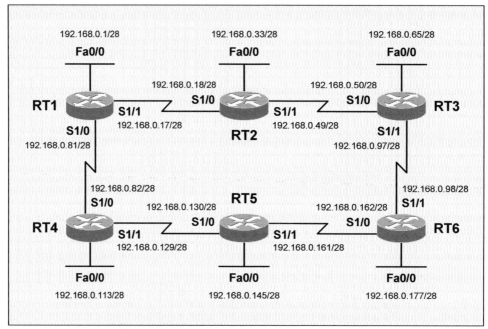

Figure A6-9: Sample RIPv1 and VLSM Network

- The network above is subnetted using a Class C address block. In the network above, there are a total of 12 networks (6 LANs and 6 point-to-point WANs). The 255.255.255.240 (/28) subnet mask is used to support a maximum of 16 networks with 14 usable IP addresses on each LAN.

- RIPv1 does not support VLSM information, so all networks must have the same subnet mask.

- This sample setup shows that even RIP does not support VLSM, such networks can be setup when all subnets are using the same subnet mask.

- Below shows the routing table on RT1:

```
RT1#sh ip route

     192.168.0.0/28 is subnetted, 12 subnets
C       192.168.0.0 is directly connected, FastEthernet0/0
C       192.168.0.16 is directly connected, Serial1/1
R       192.168.0.32 [120/1] via 192.168.0.18, 00:00:01, Serial1/1
R       192.168.0.48 [120/1] via 192.168.0.18, 00:00:01, Serial1/1
R       192.168.0.64 [120/2] via 192.168.0.18, 00:00:01, Serial1/1
C       192.168.0.80 is directly connected, Serial1/0
R       192.168.0.96 [120/2] via 192.168.0.18, 00:00:01, Serial1/1
R       192.168.0.112 [120/1] via 192.168.0.82, 00:00:12, Serial1/0
R       192.168.0.128 [120/1] via 192.168.0.82, 00:00:12, Serial1/0
R       192.168.0.144 [120/2] via 192.168.0.82, 00:00:13, Serial1/0
R       192.168.0.160 [120/2] via 192.168.0.82, 00:00:12, Serial1/0
R       192.168.0.176 [120/3] via 192.168.0.18, 00:00:01, Serial1/1
                      [120/3] via 192.168.0.82, 00:00:12, Serial1/0
RT1#
```

Fun with NATs and ACLs (Firewalls)

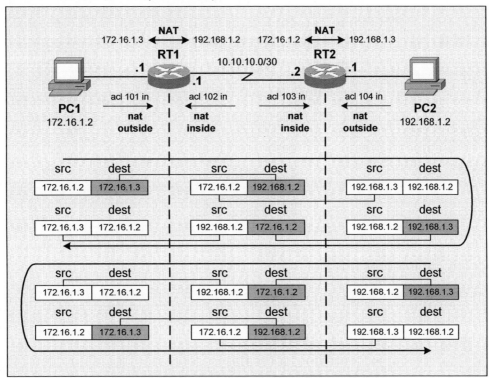

Figure A6-10: Network Setup for NATs and ACLs

- NAT configuration on RT1 for PC1 to remote access PC2 192.168.1.2 via NAT IP 172.16.1.3:
  `RT1(config)#`**ip nat inside source static 192.168.1.2 172.16.1.3**

- NAT configuration on RT2 for PC2 to remote access PC1 172.16.1.2 via NAT IP 192.168.1.3:
  `RT2(config)#`**ip nat inside source static tcp 172.16.1.2 23 192.168.1.3 23**

- Extended IP Access Lists configuration on RT1 and RT2 for PC1 to remote access (Telnet) PC2:

PC1 to PC2:
`RT1(config)#`**access-list 101 permit tcp host 172.16.1.2 host 172.16.1.3 eq 23**
`RT2(config)#`**access-list 103 permit tcp host 172.16.1.2 host 192.168.1.2 eq 23**

PC2 back to PC1:
`RT2(config)#`**access-list 104 permit tcp host 192.168.1.2 eq 23 host 192.168.1.3**
`RT1(config)#`**access-list 102 permit tcp host 192.168.1.2 eq 23 host 172.16.1.2**

- Extended IP Access Lists configuration on RT1 and RT2 for PC2 to remote access (Telnet) PC1:

PC2 to PC1:
`RT2(config)#`**access-list 104 permit tcp host 192.168.1.2 host 192.168.1.3 eq 23**
`RT1(config)#`**access-list 102 permit tcp host 192.168.1.2 host 172.16.1.2 eq 23**

PC1 back to PC2:
`RT1(config)#`**access-list 101 permit tcp host 172.16.1.2 eq 23 host 172.16.1.3**
`RT2(config)#`**access-list 103 permit tcp host 172.16.1.2 eq 23 host 192.168.1.2**

- Below shows the NAT operations on RT1 and RT2 and ACL hit counts when PC1 accesses PC2:

```
RT1#debug ip nat
IP NAT debugging is on
RT1#
00:02:30: NAT: s=172.16.1.2, d=172.16.1.3->192.168.1.2 [14748]
00:02:32: NAT: s=172.16.1.2, d=172.16.1.3->192.168.1.2 [14748]
00:02:36: NAT: s=172.16.1.2, d=172.16.1.3->192.168.1.2 [14748]
00:02:38: NAT*: s=192.168.1.2->172.16.1.3, d=172.16.1.2 [19343]
00:02:38: NAT*: s=172.16.1.2, d=172.16.1.3->192.168.1.2 [14749]
00:02:38: NAT*: s=172.16.1.2, d=172.16.1.3->192.168.1.2 [14750]
--- output omitted ---
RT1#
RT1#sh access-list
Extended IP access list 101
    10 permit tcp host 172.16.1.2 host 172.16.1.3 eq telnet (28 matches)
    20 permit tcp host 172.16.1.2 eq telnet host 172.16.1.3
Extended IP access list 102
    10 permit tcp host 192.168.1.2 eq telnet host 172.16.1.2 (14 matches)
    20 permit tcp host 192.168.1.2 host 172.16.1.2 eq telnet
RT1#
RT1#sh ip nat statistics
Total active translations: 1 (1 static, 0 dynamic; 0 extended)
Outside interfaces:
  FastEthernet0/0
Inside interfaces:
  FastEthernet1/0
Hits: 36  Misses: 0
Expired translations: 0
Dynamic mappings:
RT1#
-----------------------------------------------------------------
RT2#
00:02:31: NAT: s=172.16.1.2->192.168.1.3, d=192.168.1.2 [14748]
00:02:37: NAT*: s=192.168.1.2, d=192.168.1.3->172.16.1.2 [19343]
00:02:37: NAT*: s=172.16.1.2->192.168.1.3, d=192.168.1.2 [14749]
--- output omitted ---
RT2#sh access-list
Extended IP access list 103
    10 permit tcp host 172.16.1.2 host 192.168.1.2 eq telnet (25 matches)
    20 permit tcp host 172.16.1.2 eq telnet host 192.168.1.2
Extended IP access list 104
    10 permit tcp host 192.168.1.2 eq telnet host 192.168.1.3 (14 matches)
    20 permit tcp host 192.168.1.2 host 192.168.1.3 eq telnet
RT2#
-----------------------------------------------------------------
PC1#telnet 172.16.1.3
Trying 172.16.1.3 ... Open


User Access Verification

Password:
PC2>who
    Line       User        Host(s)              Idle      Location
   0 con 0                 idle              00:00:56
*  66 vty 0                idle              00:00:00  192.168.1.3

   Interface   User              Mode         Idle      Peer Address

PC2>
```

- Below shows the NAT operations on RT2 and RT1 and ACL hit counts when PC2 accesses PC1:

```
RT2#debug ip nat
IP NAT debugging is on
RT2#
00:04:42: NAT: s=192.168.1.2, d=192.168.1.3->172.16.1.2 [50878]
00:04:42: NAT*: s=172.16.1.2->192.168.1.3, d=192.168.1.2 [2634]
00:04:42: NAT*: s=192.168.1.2, d=192.168.1.3->172.16.1.2 [50879]
00:04:42: NAT*: s=192.168.1.2, d=192.168.1.3->172.16.1.2 [50880]
--- output omitted ---
RT2#
RT2#sh access-list
Extended IP access list 103
    10 permit tcp host 172.16.1.2 host 192.168.1.2 eq telnet
    20 permit tcp host 172.16.1.2 eq telnet host 192.168.1.2 (17 matches)
Extended IP access list 104
    10 permit tcp host 192.168.1.2 eq telnet host 192.168.1.3
    20 permit tcp host 192.168.1.2 host 192.168.1.3 eq telnet (25 matches)
RT2#
RT2#sh ip nat statistics
Total active translations: 1 (1 static, 0 dynamic; 0 extended)
Outside interfaces:
  FastEthernet0/0
Inside interfaces:
  FastEthernet1/0
Hits: 40  Misses: 0
Expired translations: 0
Dynamic mappings:
RT2#
-----------------------------------------------------------------
RT1#
00:04:43: NAT: s=192.168.1.2->172.16.1.3, d=172.16.1.2 [50878]
00:04:43: NAT*: s=172.16.1.2, d=172.16.1.3->192.168.1.2 [2634]
00:04:43: NAT*: s=192.168.1.2->172.16.1.3, d=172.16.1.2 [50879]
00:04:43: NAT*: s=172.16.1.2, d=172.16.1.3->192.168.1.2 [2635]
--- output omitted ---
RT1#sh access-list
Extended IP access list 101
    10 permit tcp host 172.16.1.2 host 172.16.1.3 eq telnet
    20 permit tcp host 172.16.1.2 eq telnet host 172.16.1.3 (17 matches)
Extended IP access list 102
    10 permit tcp host 192.168.1.2 eq telnet host 172.16.1.2
    20 permit tcp host 192.168.1.2 host 172.16.1.2 eq telnet (25 matches)
RT1#
-----------------------------------------------------------------
PC2#telnet 192.168.1.3
Trying 192.168.1.3 ... Open


User Access Verification

Password:
PC1>
PC1>who
    Line       User        Host(s)              Idle       Location
   0 con 0                 idle                 00:00:35
*  66 vty 0                idle                 00:00:00   172.16.1.3

  Interface  User                 Mode         Idle    Peer Address

PC1>
```

Bidirectional (2-Way) NAT

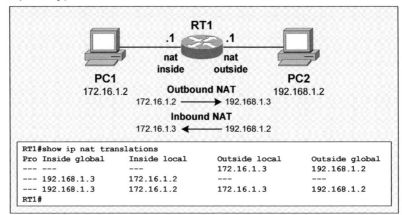

Figure A6-11: Network Setup for Bidirectional (2-Way) NAT

- Traditional Outbound NAT is designed to handle outbound connections, in which clients of the inside local network initiate requests to outside global Internet hosts. Bidirectional NAT, 2-Way NAT, or Inbound NAT is an enhancement upon NAT to handle connections initiated from the outside network.

- The network setup on Figure A6-10 can be achieved using a single router. PC1 accesses PC2 using 172.16.1.3 outside local; while PC2 accesses PC1 using 192.168.1.3 inside global.

- Bidirectional NAT configuration on RT1:

```
!
interface FastEthernet0/0
 ip address 172.16.1.1 255.255.255.0
 ip nat inside
!
interface FastEthernet1/0
 ip address 192.168.1.1 255.255.255.0
 ip nat outside
!
ip nat inside source static 172.16.1.2 192.168.1.3
ip nat outside source static 192.168.1.2 172.16.1.3 add-route
!
```

- The **add-route** keyword adds a static /32 host route for the outside local address. This route is used for routing and translating packets that travel from the inside to the outside of the network.

```
RT1#sh ip route

Gateway of last resort is not set

     172.16.0.0/16 is variably subnetted, 2 subnets, 2 masks
C       172.16.1.0/24 is directly connected, FastEthernet0/0
S       172.16.1.3/32 [1/0] via 192.168.1.2
C    192.168.1.0/24 is directly connected, FastEthernet1/0
RT1#
```

NAT Attack Session – ip nat inside source and ip nat outside source

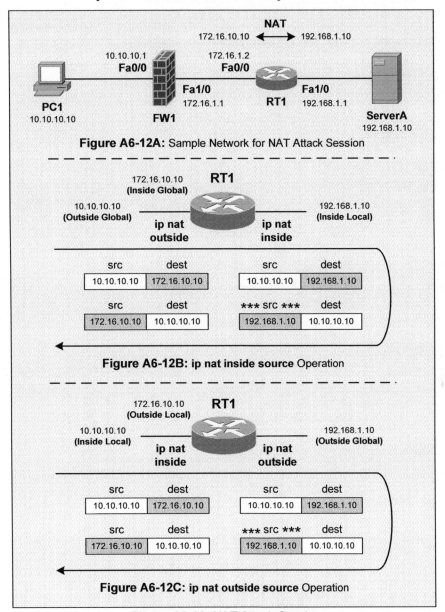

Figure A6-12A: Sample Network for NAT Attack Session

Figure A6-12B: ip nat inside source Operation

Figure A6-12C: ip nat outside source Operation

Figure A6-12: NAT Attack Session

- This section shows how to achieve the same result – ServerA communicates with PC1 using 172.16.10.10 NAT IP instead of 192.168.1.10 real IP with **inside source** and **outside source** NAT configurations. This is a knowledge attack session which strengthens the understanding of NAT terminologies and operations.

- The ******* indicates where the NAT operations are initiated according to the **ip nat** commands.

- **Note:** A router does not require a physical nor logical interface to reside in the NAT IP address subnet for the operation of NAT – 172.16.10.0/24 in this case. As compared to the previous section – NAT with Virtual Interface, which the router has a logical loopback interface and advertising the NAT IP subnet (10.2.2.0/24) using EIGRP.

- RT1 configuration for **ip nat inside source** operation:

```
!
interface FastEthernet0/0
 ip address 172.16.1.2 255.255.255.0
 ip nat outside
!
interface FastEthernet1/0
 ip address 192.168.1.1 255.255.255.0
 ip nat inside
!
ip nat inside source static 192.168.1.10 172.16.10.10
!
```

- Below shows the NAT debug messages on RT1 for the configuration above:

```
RT1#debug ip nat
IP NAT debugging is on
RT1#
00:04:29: NAT*: s=10.10.10.10, d=172.16.10.10->192.168.1.10 [15]
00:04:29: NAT*: s=192.168.1.10->172.16.10.10, d=10.10.10.10 [15]
00:04:29: NAT*: s=10.10.10.10, d=172.16.10.10->192.168.1.10 [16]
00:04:29: NAT*: s=192.168.1.10->172.16.10.10, d=10.10.10.10 [16]
00:04:29: NAT*: s=10.10.10.10, d=172.16.10.10->192.168.1.10 [17]
00:04:29: NAT*: s=192.168.1.10->172.16.10.10, d=10.10.10.10 [17]
```

- RT1 configuration for **ip nat outside source** operation:

```
!
interface FastEthernet0/0
 ip address 172.16.1.2 255.255.255.0
 ip nat inside
!
interface FastEthernet1/0
 ip address 192.168.1.1 255.255.255.0
 ip nat outside
!
! Option #1
ip nat outside source static 192.168.1.10 172.16.10.10
ip route 172.16.10.10 255.255.255.255 FastEthernet1/0
!
! Option #2
ip nat outside source static 192.168.1.10 172.16.10.10 add-route
=====================================================================
RT1#sh ip route

Gateway of last resort is not set

     172.16.0.0/16 is variably subnetted, 2 subnets, 2 masks
S       172.16.10.10/32 [1/0] via 192.168.1.10
C       172.16.1.0/24 is directly connected, FastEthernet0/0
     10.0.0.0/24 is subnetted, 1 subnets
S       10.10.10.0 [1/0] via 172.16.1.1
C    192.168.1.0/24 is directly connected, FastEthernet1/0
RT1#
```

Complex ACL

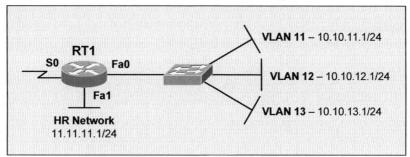

Figure A6-13: Sample Complex ACL Network

- The user requirement for the sample network above is to deny all access (Microsoft file sharing, Remote Desktop, ICMP ping, etc) from PCs in VLAN 11, 12, and 13 to the PCs in HR Network.

- Below shows a sample solution by applying an inbound access list to RT1 Fa1 interface:

```
access-list 101 deny tcp 11.11.11.0 0.0.0.255 eq 135 10.10.11.0 0.0.0.255
access-list 101 deny tcp 11.11.11.0 0.0.0.255 eq 139 10.10.11.0 0.0.0.255
access-list 101 deny tcp 11.11.11.0 0.0.0.255 eq 445 10.10.11.0 0.0.0.255
access-list 101 deny udp 11.11.11.0 0.0.0.255 eq 137 10.10.11.0 0.0.0.255
access-list 101 deny udp 11.11.11.0 0.0.0.255 eq 138 10.10.11.0 0.0.0.255
access-list 101 deny tcp 11.11.11.0 0.0.0.255 eq 3389 10.10.11.0 0.0.0.255
access-list 101 deny icmp 11.11.11.0 0.0.0.255 10.10.11.0 0.0.0.255 echo-reply
! -----------------------------------------------
access-list 101 deny tcp 11.11.11.0 0.0.0.255 eq 135 10.10.12.0 0.0.0.255
access-list 101 deny tcp 11.11.11.0 0.0.0.255 eq 139 10.10.12.0 0.0.0.255
access-list 101 deny tcp 11.11.11.0 0.0.0.255 eq 445 10.10.12.0 0.0.0.255
access-list 101 deny udp 11.11.11.0 0.0.0.255 eq 137 10.10.12.0 0.0.0.255
access-list 101 deny udp 11.11.11.0 0.0.0.255 eq 138 10.10.12.0 0.0.0.255
access-list 101 deny tcp 11.11.11.0 0.0.0.255 eq 3389 10.10.12.0 0.0.0.255
access-list 101 deny icmp 11.11.11.0 0.0.0.255 10.10.12.0 0.0.0.255 echo-reply
! -----------------------------------------------
access-list 101 deny tcp 11.11.11.0 0.0.0.255 eq 135 10.10.13.0 0.0.0.255
access-list 101 deny tcp 11.11.11.0 0.0.0.255 eq 139 10.10.13.0 0.0.0.255
access-list 101 deny tcp 11.11.11.0 0.0.0.255 eq 445 10.10.13.0 0.0.0.255
access-list 101 deny udp 11.11.11.0 0.0.0.255 eq 137 10.10.13.0 0.0.0.255
access-list 101 deny udp 11.11.11.0 0.0.0.255 eq 138 10.10.13.0 0.0.0.255
access-list 101 deny tcp 11.11.11.0 0.0.0.255 eq 3389 10.10.13.0 0.0.0.255
access-list 101 deny icmp 11.11.11.0 0.0.0.255 10.10.13.0 0.0.0.255 echo-reply
! -----------------------------------------------
access-list 101 permit ip any any
!
interface FastEthernet1
 ip address 11.11.11.1 255.255.255.0
 ip access-group 101 in
!
```

The Access Control List **established** Keyword

- The **established** keyword is only applicable to TCP access list entries to match TCP segments that have the ACK **and / or** RST control bit set (regardless of the source and destination ports), which assumes that a TCP connection has already been established in one direction only. **Non-matching** cases are initial TCP connection-establishment segments with only the SYN bit set.

- A typically usage is to differentiate the connections originating inside from connections originating elsewhere. Figure below shows a scenario which allowing internal systems to initiate Telnet connections to any Internet site (outside network), but not the other way around. A simple solution is to block incoming packets that don't have the ACK or RST bits set by using the **established** keyword, which permitting return traffic for connections that are established and initiated from the inside, and denying connections initiated from outside to inside.

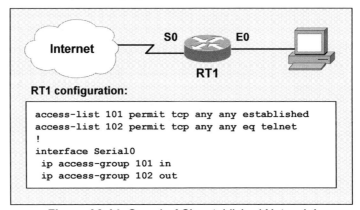

RT1 configuration:

```
access-list 101 permit tcp any any established
access-list 102 permit tcp any any eq telnet
!
interface Serial0
 ip access-group 101 in
 ip access-group 102 out
```

Figure A6-14: Sample ACL established Network I

- **Note:** This method of blocking unwanted traffic originating from the outside network can be circumvented – it is possible to forge a packet with the appropriate bits set – spoofing TCP flags. However, a proper **stateful packet-filtering firewall** will not fall to such an attack.
- Another usage is to allow connections to be initiated from client systems only, but not from the server to the others. This can prevent abuse from the server and tighten the server to offer only the necessary services.

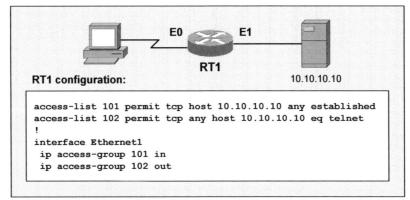

RT1 configuration:

```
access-list 101 permit tcp host 10.10.10.10 any established
access-list 102 permit tcp any host 10.10.10.10 eq telnet
!
interface Ethernet1
 ip access-group 101 in
 ip access-group 102 out
```

Figure A6-15: Sample ACL established Network II

- The **access-list 101 permit tcp any any established** is equivalent to **access-list 101 permit tcp any any ack rst**. When configuring the latter command, it will be appeared as the former command in the running configuration.

The Access Control List fragments Keyword

- The **fragments** keyword indicates that an access list entry is **only** applied to **non-initial packet fragments** (L3). The fragment is either permitted or denied accordingly. The default behavior is without the **fragments** keyword.

- The **fragments** keyword cannot be configured for an access list entry that contains any L4 information. Ex: **access-list 101 permit tcp host 1.1.1.1 host 2.2.2.2 eq 80 fragments** is invalid.

- Without the **fragments** keyword (default), an access list entry that contains only L3 information (eg: **access-list 101 permit ip host 10.10.10.1 host 10.10.10.2**) is matched with all types of packets – non-fragmented packets, initial and non-initial packet fragments.
  Note: The **fragments** keyword indicates that an access list entry will be matched with non-initial fragments.

- Without the **fragments** keyword (default), an access list entry that contains L3 and L4 information (eg: **access-list 101 permit tcp host 10.10.10.1 host 10.10.10.2 eq telnet**) is matched with non-fragmented packets and initial packet fragments and is either permitted or denied accordingly.
    o When a **permit** statement (without the **fragments** keyword) is matched with non-initial packet fragments, the non-initial fragments are permitted.
    o When a **deny** statement (without the **fragments** keyword) is matched with non-initial packet fragments, the next access list entry is processed, and the fragments are not being denied!
  Summary: The **deny** statements (without the **fragments** keyword) are handled differently for non-initial packet fragments than the **permit** statements (without the **fragments** keyword).

- Do not simply add the **fragments** keyword to every access list entry, as the 1st fragment (initial fragment) will not be matched with an access list **permit** or **deny** entry that contains the **fragments** keyword – the packet is compared to the next access list entry, until it is either permitted or denied by an access list entry that does not contain the **fragments** keyword. Therefore, 2 **deny** access list entries are needed for every **deny** entry. The 1st **deny** entry of the pair will not include the **fragments** keyword to be applied for initial fragments; the 2nd **deny** entry of the pair will include the **fragments** keyword to be applied for non-initial fragments.

- **Note:** Packet fragments are considered individual packets and each is counted individually as a packet in access list accounting.

- When there are multiple **deny** access list entries for a particular host with different L4 ports, only a single **deny** access list entry with the **fragments** keyword for the host is required. All the packet fragments are handled in the same manner by the access list.

- The fragment control feature affect policy routing if the policy routing is based on the **match ip address** command and the access list has entries that match L4 through L7 information. It is possible for non-initial fragments to be matched with the access list and are policy routed, even if the 1st fragment was not policy routed (or the reverse).

- This feature provides a better match capability between initial and non-initial fragments and hence allows the configuration of advanced policy routing.

Switch Port Access Control Lists

- Switch port ACLs can only be applied as **inbound** lists with **extended named access lists** upon **L2 switch interfaces**.

- MAC extended access lists perform filtering based on the source and destination MAC addresses, as well as the optional EtherType information.

```
Switch#conf t
Enter configuration commands, one per line.  End with CNTL/Z.
Switch(config)#mac access-list ?
  extended  Extended Access List

Switch(config)#mac access-list extended ?
  WORD  access-list name

Switch(config)#mac access-list extended example01
Switch(config-ext-macl)#deny any host ?
  H.H.H  48-bit destination MAC address

Switch(config-ext-macl)#deny any host 1111.1111.1111
Switch(config-ext-macl)#permit any any
Switch(config-ext-macl)#^Z
Switch#
Switch#sh access-list
Extended MAC access list example01
    deny    any host 1111.1111.1111
    permit any any
Switch#
Switch#conf t
Enter configuration commands, one per line.  End with CNTL/Z.
Switch(config)#int fa0/1
Switch(config-if)#mac access-group example01 ?
  in  Apply to Ingress

Switch(config-if)#mac access-group example01 in
Switch(config-if)#^Z
Switch#
Switch#sh mac access-group int fa0/1
Interface FastEthernet0/1:
    Inbound access-list is example01
Switch#
```

- The question is do we really want to deny MAC addresses? Deny access based on the EtherType field in the Ethernet frame header is usually the better option.

- Blocking 0x0800 would mean blocking all IP traffic, which could be handy in the future when forcing everyone to run IPv6!

- MAC access lists can filter traffic based on various EtherType:

```
Switch(config-ext-macl)#deny any any ?
  <0-65535>     An arbitrary EtherType in decimal, hex, or octal
  aarp          EtherType: AppleTalk ARP
  amber         EtherType: DEC-Amber
  appletalk     EtherType: AppleTalk/EtherTalk
  cos           CoS value
  dec-spanning  EtherType: DEC-Spanning-Tree
  decnet-iv     EtherType: DECnet Phase IV
  diagnostic    EtherType: DEC-Diagnostic
  dsm           EtherType: DEC-DSM
  etype-6000    EtherType: 0x6000
  etype-8042    EtherType: 0x8042
  lat           EtherType: DEC-LAT
  lavc-sca      EtherType: DEC-LAVC-SCA
  lsap          LSAP value
  mop-console   EtherType: DEC-MOP Remote Console
  mop-dump      EtherType: DEC-MOP Dump
  msdos         EtherType: DEC-MSDOS
  mumps         EtherType: DEC-MUMPS
  netbios       EtherType: DEC-NETBIOS
  vines-echo    EtherType: VINES Echo
  vines-ip      EtherType: VINES IP
  xns-idp       EtherType: XNS IDP
  <cr>
```

Advanced Access Control List Configurations

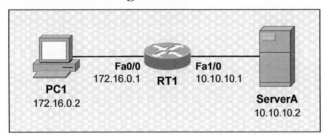

Figure A6-16: Network Setup for Advanced Access Control List Configurations

- **Dynamic access lists** or **Lock-and-Key Security** is a type of ACL traffic filtering security feature that dynamically filters IP protocol traffic. Users that would like to traverse through the router are normally blocked by the extended ACL until they authenticates themselves to the router through a Telnet session with a username and password. After the user is authenticated, the Telnet connection is dropped, and a dynamic ACL entry is appended to the existing extended ACL to temporary allow the user to access resources that are blocked behind the router for certain duration until the specified timeout expires.

- Below shows a sample Dynamic Access Lists configuration on RT1:

```
[1]  Router(config)#username remote password cisco123
[1]  Router(config)#username remote autocommand access-enable host timeout 10
[2]  Router(config)#access-list 101 permit tcp any host 172.16.0.1 eq telnet log
[3]  Router(config)#access-list 101 dynamic remote-access01 timeout 15 permit ip
     172.16.0.0 0.0.0.255 10.10.10.0 0.0.0.255 log
     Router(config)#int fa0/0
     Router(config-if)#ip access-group 101 in
     Router(config-if)#exit
     Router(config)#line vty 0 4
[4]  Router(config-line)#login local
```

Note: Configuring the **autocommand access-enable host timeout 10** line command under **line vty 0 4** which is normally found in other configuration examples is not as flexible as configuring the **autocommand** for particular users with the **username** privileged commands.

- Below describes the configuration steps for the sample dynamic access list configuration:
  1) Create a user authentication method on the router. This can either be local authentication or remote security database using RADIUS or TACACS+ server. This sample configuration defines a user named **remote** with a password of **cisco123** and a line of command (**access-enable host timeout 10** in this case) which will be issued automatically (due to the **autocommand** keyword) after the user is authenticated via the Telnet session to the router.
  Note: The **access-enable** EXEC command creates a temporary access-list entry.
  2) Define an extended ACL to allow only Telnet access to the router (for authentication), but block all other traffic.
  3) Create a dynamic extended ACL that applies to the extended access list 101 after the user is authenticated via the Telnet session to the router.
  4) Since this sample configuration is using local authentication, the router needs to be configured to locally authenticate when a user connects to its VTY ports.

- **Reflexive access lists** are dynamic access lists that allow traffic based on the detection of traffic in the opposite direction as well as upper-layer session information. They often permit outbound traffic which originated from an inside network but deny inbound traffic which originated from an outside network.

- Reflexive ACLs cannot be defined with standard or numbered ACLs; they can only be defined with **extended named ACLs** and can be used along with other standard or extended ACLs. They are temporary entries that are created when a new IP session begins and are removed when the session ends (when the last segment with FIN or RST is seen or the idle timeout expires). Reflexive ACLs are not applied directly to an interface, but are "nested" within an extended named IP ACL that is applied to an interface.

- Below shows a sample Reflexive Access Lists configuration on RT1 as well as the output of the **show access-list** EXEC command on RT1:

```
!
ip access-list extended Telnet-In
 evaluate RACL-1
 deny   ip any any
ip access-list extended Telnet-Out
 permit tcp host 172.16.0.2 host 10.10.10.2 eq telnet reflect RACL-1
 deny   ip any any
!
interface FastEthernet1/0
 ip address 10.10.10.1 255.255.255.0
 ip access-group Telnet-In in
 ip access-group Telnet-Out out
!
--------------------------------------------------------------------
RT1#sh access-list
Reflexive IP access list RACL-1
Extended IP access list Telnet-In
    10 evaluate RACL-1
    20 deny ip any any
Extended IP access list Telnet-Out
    10 permit tcp host 172.16.0.2 host 10.10.10.2 eq telnet reflect RACL-1
    20 deny ip any any
RT1#
```

- **Time-based access lists** provide time-oriented access control. A certain time of day and week is specified and the period is often identified with a **time range reference name**. The time range name will be used as a reference in extended ACL configuration.

- Below shows a sample Time-based Access Lists configuration that defines **no Internet access during office hours** – Monday to Friday, 9am to 6pm.

```
Router#conf t
Enter configuration commands, one per line.  End with CNTL/Z.
Router(config)#time-range no-http
Router(config-time-range)#?
Time range configuration commands:
  absolute  absolute time and date
  default   Set a command to its defaults
  exit      Exit from time-range configuration mode
  no        Negate a command or set its defaults
  periodic  periodic time and date

Router(config-time-range)#periodic ?
  Friday     Friday
  Monday     Monday
  Saturday   Saturday
  Sunday     Sunday
  Thursday   Thursday
  Tuesday    Tuesday
  Wednesday  Wednesday
  daily      Every day of the week
  weekdays   Monday thru Friday
  weekend    Saturday and Sunday

Router(config-time-range)#periodic weekdays 09:00 to 18:00
Router(config-time-range)#exit
```

```
Router(config)#ip access-list extended Time_no-http
Router(config-ext-nacl)#deny tcp any any eq www time-range no-http
Router(config-ext-nacl)#permit tcp any any
Router(config-ext-nacl)#exit
Router(config)#int fa0/0
Router(config-if)#ip access-group Time_no-http in
Router(config-if)#^Z
Router#
Router#sh clock
10:00:01.835 UTC Sun Jan 6 2008
Router#sh time-range
time-range entry: no-http (inactive)
   periodic weekdays 9:00 to 18:00
   used in: IP ACL entry
Router#sh access-list
Extended IP access list Time_no-http
    deny tcp any any eq www time-range no-http (inactive)
    permit tcp any any
Router#
-----------------------------------------------------------------------
Router#sh clock
10:00:01.139 UTC Mon Jan 7 2008
Router#sh time-range
time-range entry: no-http (active)
   periodic weekdays 9:00 to 18:00
   used in: IP ACL entry
Router#sh access-list
Extended IP access list Time_no-http
    deny tcp any any eq www time-range no-http (active)
    permit tcp any any
Router#
```

- **Context-Based Access Control** (CBAC) is a Cisco IOS Firewall feature which provides advanced traffic filtering functionality and secure access control on a per-application basis. CBAC is often referred to as **Stateful IOS Firewall Inspection**.

- CBAC provides multiple levels of network protection with the following functions:

Traffic Filtering	Intelligently filters TCP and UDP segments based on application layer protocol information (eg: FTP connection information). Without CBAC, traffic filtering is limited to access list implementations which only able to examine the information at the network and transport layers. Due to the capability of learning the state information of the sessions and control them, CBAC supports filtering for application layer protocols that involve multiple channels created as a result of negotiations in the control channel. Many multimedia protocols and other protocols (eg: FTP, RPC, SQL*Net) involve multiple channels in their communications. CBAC can be configured to inspect application layer traffic for sessions and connections that are originated from either side of a firewall and permit the specified traffic through it; hence it can be used for intranet, extranet, and Internet perimeters of a network.

Traffic Inspection	Inspects traffic that passes through a firewall to discover and manage state information for TCP and UDP sessions. The state information is used to create temporary openings in the access lists to allow return traffic for permissible sessions. With the capabilities of inspecting and maintaining TCP and UDP session information, CBAC is able to detect and prevent certain types of network attacks, eg: SYN Flooding. CBAC helps to protect against DoS attacks with the following approaches: i) Inspects TCP sequence numbers in to see if they are within expected ranges and drops the suspicious packets. ii) Drops half-open connections, which require firewall processing and memory resources to maintain. iii) Detects unusually high rates of new connections and issue alert messages. Besides that, CBAC can also help to protect against certain DoS attacks which involve fragmented IP packets. Even though the firewall prevents an attacker from establishing actual connections to an end system, the attacker can disrupt services on the end system by sending many non-initial IP fragments, which can eventually tie up resources on the target end system as it tries to reassemble the incomplete packets.
Alerts and Audit Trails	Generates real-time alerts and audit trails for tracking suspicious activities and network transactions (eg: time stamps, source and destination hosts, ports, total number of transmitted bytes, etc). With CBAC inspection rules, alerts and audit trail information can be configured on a per-application protocol basis.
Intrusion Prevention	Provides a limited amount of intrusion detection to protect against specific SMTP attacks. With intrusion detection, SYSLOG messages are reviewed and monitored for specific attack signatures. When CBAC detects an attack, it resets the offending connections and generates a SYSLOG message to a SYSLOG server.

- CBAC only effective for the specified protocols. If a particular is not specified for CBAC, the existing access lists will determine how the traffic for the particular protocol is being processed. No temporary openings will be created for protocols that are not specified for CBAC inspection.

- CBAC can only provide protection against certain types of attacks, but not all types of attacks. CBAC should not be considered as a perfect defense; there is no such thing as a perfect defense. CBAC detects and prevents most types of popular network attacks.

- **Authentication Proxy** requires the Cisco IOS Firewall feature set as well. It is able to authenticate inbound and/or outbound users and grant the access to the resources that are blocked behind a firewall. By launching a browser to access resources behind the firewall, the firewall would respond to the HTTP session and redirect the user to an authentication page which a valid username and password must be supplied for authentication purpose. An authentication entry will be created for the user. There is no intervention by the authentication proxy for subsequent HTTP sessions through the firewall as long as a valid authentication entry exists for the user.

Optional PPP Commands

- The **compress predictor** interface subcommand enables the PPP Predictor compression algorithm; while the **compress stac** interface subcommand enables the PPP Stacker compression algorithm.

- The **ppp quality** {*percent*} interface subcommand ensures a PPP link meets a percentage of quality during the optional link-quality determination phase in the PPP link establishment phase. This is to determine whether the link quality is sufficient to bring up any Layer 3 protocols. The link will not be established if it does not meet the percentage level.
  Note: PPP link establishment is handled by Link Control Protocol (LCP).

- The **ppp authentication** {**pap** | **chap**} {**chap** | **pap**} interface subcommand defines a PPP link to use the 1st authentication protocol, but will try 2nd authentication protocol if the 1st authentication protocol fails or rejected by the other side.

- The **ppp sent-username** {*username*} **password** {*password*} interface subcommand is mandate in PAP configuration.

- In PPP authentication configuration, passwords are case sensitive but usernames are **not** case-sensitive.

Unidirectional PPP PAP Authentication

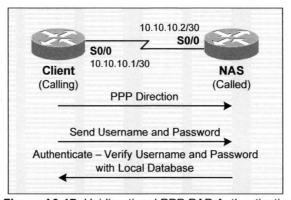

Figure A6-17: Unidirectional PPP PAP Authentication

- Unidirectional PPP PAP authentication configuration on Client:

```
interface Serial0/0
 ip address 10.10.10.1 255.255.255.252
 encapsulation ppp
 ppp direction callout
 ppp pap sent-username Client password 0 cisco
```

Note: The **ppp authentication pap** interface subcommand is not required on Client.

- Unidirectional PPP PAP authentication configuration on NAS:

```
username Client password 0 cisco
!
interface Serial0/0
 ip address 10.10.10.2 255.255.255.252
 encapsulation ppp
 ppp authentication pap [callin]
 ppp direction callin
```

Note: The **callin** keyword of the **ppp authentication pap** interface subcommand is optional

- A router configured with the **ppp authentication pap** interface subcommand will use PAP to verify the identity of the peer, which means that the peer must present its username and password to the local device for verification. The local device would use the local username-based authentication system to verify and authenticate its peer.

- The function of the **username** {*remote-username*} **password** {*passwd*} statement is different for PAP and CHAP. With PAP, it is only used to verify that an incoming username and password are valid; whereas CHAP uses it to generate the response to a challenge and verify a response.

- For one-way PAP authentication, the **username** {*remote-hostname*} **password** {*passwd*} statement is only required on the called device to verify the username and password sent by the calling device; whereas for two-way PAP authentication, it is required on both devices.

- A router configured with the **ppp authentication pap callin** interface subcommand configured will only authenticate the peer during incoming calls – it will not authenticate the peer for outgoing calls.

- The **ppp pap sent-username** {*local-username*} **password** {*passwd*} interface subcommand is configured on the calling device to authenticate itself to a remote called device. The remote device must have the same set of **username – password** statement configured.

- The **ppp direction** {**callin** | **callout** | **dedicated**} interface subcommand is introduced in Cisco IOS Release 12.2T. This command is useful when a router is connected to an interface type where there is no inherent call direction, eg: a back-to-back or leased-line connection.

- Below shows the output of the PPP authentication debug messages for a successful unidirectional PAP authentication on Client:

```
Client#sh debug
PPP:
  PPP authentication debugging is on
  PPP protocol negotiation debugging is on

Client#conf t
Enter configuration commands, one per line.  End with CNTL/Z.
Client(config)#int s1/0
Client(config-if)#no shut
Client(config-if)#
00:07:14: %LINK-3-UPDOWN: Interface Serial0/0, changed state to up
00:07:14: Sc0/0 PPP: Using configured call direction
00:07:14: Se0/0 PPP: Treating connection as a callout
00:07:14: Se0/0 PPP: Session handle[5A000003] Session id[25]
00:07:14: Se0/0 PPP: Phase is ESTABLISHING, Active Open
00:07:14: Se0/0 PPP: Authorization required
00:07:14: Se0/0 PPP: No remote authentication for call-out
00:07:14: Se0/0 LCP: O CONFREQ [Closed] id 25 len 10
00:07:14: Se0/0 LCP:    MagicNumber 0x0013D707 (0x05060013D707)
00:07:14: Se0/0 LCP: I CONFREQ [REQsent] id 83 len 14
00:07:14: Se0/0 LCP:    AuthProto PAP (0x0304C023)
00:07:14: Se0/0 LCP:    MagicNumber 0x0113BFC6 (0x05060113BFC6)
00:07:14: Se0/0 LCP: O CONFACK [REQsent] id 83 len 14
00:07:14: Se0/0 LCP:    AuthProto PAP (0x0304C023)
00:07:14: Se0/0 LCP:    MagicNumber 0x0113BFC6 (0x05060113BFC6)
00:07:14: Se0/0 LCP: I CONFACK [ACKsent] id 25 len 10
00:07:14: Se0/0 LCP:    MagicNumber 0x0013D707 (0x05060013D707)
00:07:14: Se0/0 LCP: State is Open
00:07:14: Se0/0 PPP: No authorization without authentication
00:07:15: Se0/0 PPP: Phase is AUTHENTICATING, by the peer
00:07:15: Se0/0 PAP: Using hostname from interface PAP
00:07:15: Se0/0 PAP: Using password from interface PAP
00:07:15: Se0/0 PAP: O AUTH-REQ id 25 len 17 from "Client"
00:07:15: Se0/0 PAP: I AUTH-ACK id 25 len 5
00:07:15: Se0/0 PPP: Phase is FORWARDING, Attempting Forward
00:07:15: Se0/0 PPP: Queue IPCP code[1] id[1]
00:07:15: Se0/0 PPP: Phase is ESTABLISHING, Finish LCP
00:07:15: Se0/0 PPP: Phase is UP
00:07:15: Se0/0 IPCP: O CONFREQ [Closed] id 1 len 10
00:07:15: Se0/0 IPCP:    Address 10.10.10.1 (0x03060A0A0A01)
00:07:15: Se0/0 CDPCP: O CONFREQ [Closed] id 1 len 4
00:07:15: Se0/0 PPP: Process pending ncp packets
00:07:15: Se0/0 IPCP: Redirect packet to Se1/0
00:07:15: Se0/0 IPCP: I CONFREQ [REQsent] id 1 len 10
00:07:15: Se0/0 IPCP:    Address 10.10.10.2 (0x03060A0A0A02)
00:07:15: Se0/0 IPCP: O CONFACK [REQsent] id 1 len 10
00:07:15: Se0/0 IPCP:    Address 10.10.10.2 (0x03060A0A0A02)
00:07:15: Se0/0 CDPCP: I CONFREQ [REQsent] id 1 len 4
00:07:15: Se0/0 CDPCP: O CONFACK [REQsent] id 1 len 4
00:07:15: Se0/0 IPCP: I CONFACK [ACKsent] id 1 len 10
00:07:15: Se0/0 IPCP:    Address 10.10.10.1 (0x03060A0A0A01)
00:07:15: Se0/0 IPCP: State is Open
00:07:15: Se0/0 IPCP: Add link info for cef entry 10.1.1.2
00:07:15: Se0/0 IPCP: Install route to 10.1.1.2
00:07:15: Se0/0 CDPCP: I CONFACK [ACKsent] id 1 len 4
00:07:15: Se0/0 CDPCP: State is Open
00:07:16: %LINEPROTO-5-UPDOWN: Line protocol on Interface Serial0/0, changed
state to up
Client(config-if)#
```

- Below shows the output of the PPP authentication debug messages for a successful unidirectional PAP authentication on NAS:

```
NAS#
00:07:08: Se0/0 LCP: I CONFREQ [Listen] id 25 len 10
00:07:08: Se0/0 LCP:    MagicNumber 0x0013D707 (0x05060013D707)
00:07:08: Se0/0 PPP: Authorization required
00:07:08: Se0/0 LCP: O CONFREQ [Listen] id 83 len 14
00:07:08: Se0/0 LCP:    AuthProto PAP (0x0304C023)
00:07:08: Se0/0 LCP:    MagicNumber 0x0113BFC6 (0x05060113BFC6)
00:07:08: Se0/0 LCP: O CONFACK [Listen] id 25 len 10
00:07:08: Se0/0 LCP:    MagicNumber 0x0013D707 (0x05060013D707)
00:07:09: Se0/0 LCP: I CONFACK [ACKsent] id 83 len 14
00:07:09: Se0/0 LCP:    AuthProto PAP (0x0304C023)
00:07:09: Se0/0 LCP:    MagicNumber 0x0113BFC6 (0x05060113BFC6)
00:07:09: Se0/0 LCP: State is Open
00:07:09: Se0/0 PPP: Phase is AUTHENTICATING, by this end
00:07:09: Se0/0 PAP: I AUTH-REQ id 25 len 17 from "Client"
00:07:09: Se0/0 PAP: Authenticating peer Client
00:07:09: Se0/0 PPP: Phase is FORWARDING, Attempting Forward
00:07:09: Se0/0 PPP: Phase is AUTHENTICATING, Unauthenticated User
00:07:09: Se0/0 PPP: Sent PAP LOGIN Request
00:07:09: Se0/0 PPP: Received LOGIN Response PASS
00:07:09: Se0/0 PPP: Phase is FORWARDING, Attempting Forward
00:07:09: Se0/0 PPP: Phase is AUTHENTICATING, Authenticated User
00:07:09: Se0/0 PPP: Sent LCP AUTHOR Request
00:07:09: Se0/0 PPP: Sent IPCP AUTHOR Request
00:07:09: Se0/0 LCP: Received AAA AUTHOR Response PASS
00:07:09: Se0/0 IPCP: Received AAA AUTHOR Response PASS
00:07:09: Se0/0 PAP: O AUTH-ACK id 25 len 5
00:07:09: Se0/0 PPP: Phase is UP
00:07:09: Se0/0 IPCP: O CONFREQ [Closed] id 1 len 10
00:07:09: Se0/0 IPCP:    Address 10.10.10.2 (0x03060A0A0A02)
00:07:09: Se0/0 PPP: Sent CDPCP AUTHOR Request
00:07:09: Se0/0 PPP: Process pending ncp packets
00:07:09: Se0/0 CDPCP: Received AAA AUTHOR Response PASS
00:07:09: Se0/0 CDPCP: O CONFREQ [Closed] id 1 len 4
00:07:09: Se0/0 IPCP: I CONFREQ [REQsent] id 1 len 10
00:07:09: Se0/0 IPCP:    Address 10.10.10.1 (0x03060A0A0A01)
00:07:09: Se0/0 AAA/AUTHOR/IPCP: Start.  Her address 10.1.1.1, we want
0.0.0.0
00:07:09: Se0/0 PPP: Sent IPCP AUTHOR Request
00:07:09: Se0/0 AAA/AUTHOR/IPCP: Reject 10.1.1.1, using 0.0.0.0
00:07:09: Se0/0 AAA/AUTHOR/IPCP: Done.  Her address 10.1.1.1, we want
0.0.0.0
00:07:09: Se0/0 IPCP: O CONFACK [REQsent] id 1 len 10
00:07:09: Se0/0 IPCP:    Address 10.10.10.1 (0x03060A0A0A01)
00:07:09: Se0/0 CDPCP: I CONFREQ [REQsent] id 1 len 4
00:07:09: Se0/0 CDPCP: O CONFACK [REQsent] id 1 len 4
00:07:09: Se0/0 IPCP: I CONFACK [ACKsent] id 1 len 10
00:07:09: Se0/0 IPCP:    Address 10.10.10.2 (0x03060A0A0A02)
00:07:09: Se0/0 IPCP: State is Open
00:07:09: Se0/0 CDPCP: I CONFACK [ACKsent] id 1 len 4
00:07:09: Se0/0 CDPCP: State is Open
00:07:09: Se0/0 IPCP: Add link info for cef entry 10.1.1.1
00:07:09: Se0/0 IPCP: Install route to 10.1.1.1
00:07:10: %LINEPROTO-5-UPDOWN: Line protocol on Interface Serial0/0, changed
state to up
NAS#
```

- Below shows the output of the PPP authentication debug messages for a failed unidirection PAP authentication (wrong **username - password** statement configured on NAS) on Client and NAS:

```
Client(config-if)#no shut
Client(config-if)#
00:12:38: Se0/0 PPP: Phase is ESTABLISHING, Passive Open
00:12:38: Se0/0 LCP: State is Listen
00:12:38: Se0/0 LCP: State is Open
00:12:38: Se0/0 PPP: No authorization without authentication
00:12:38: Se0/0 PPP: Phase is AUTHENTICATING, by the peer
00:12:38: Se0/0 PAP: Using hostname from interface PAP
00:12:38: Se0/0 PAP: Using password from interface PAP
00:12:38: Se0/0 PAP: O AUTH-REQ id 40 len 17 from "Client"
00:12:39: Se0/0 PAP: I AUTH-NAK id 40 len 26 msg is "Authentication failed"
00:12:39: Se0/0 LCP: I TERMREQ [Open] id 134 len 4
00:12:39: Se0/0 LCP: O TERMACK [Open] id 134 len 4
00:12:39: Se0/0 PPP: Sending Acct Event[Down] id[29]
00:12:39: Se0/0 PPP: Phase is TERMINATING
00:12:41: Se0/0 LCP: TIMEout: State TERMsent
00:12:41: Se0/0 LCP: State is Closed
00:12:41: Se0/0 PPP: Phase is DOWN
-------------------------------------------------
NAS#
00:12:30: Se0/0 PPP: Phase is ESTABLISHING, Passive Open
00:12:30: Se0/0 LCP: State is Listen
00:12:32: Se0/0 LCP: TIMEout: State Listen
00:12:32: Se0/0 PPP: Authorization required
00:12:32: Se0/0 LCP: State is Open
00:12:32: Se0/0 PPP: Phase is AUTHENTICATING, by this end
00:12:32: Se0/0 PAP: I AUTH-REQ id 40 len 17 from "Client"
00:12:32: Se0/0 PAP: Authenticating peer Client
00:12:32: Se0/0 PPP: Phase is FORWARDING, Attempting Forward
00:12:32: Se0/0 PPP: Phase is AUTHENTICATING, Unauthenticated User
00:12:32: Se0/0 PPP: Sent PAP LOGIN Request
00:12:32: Se0/0 PPP: Received LOGIN Response FAIL
00:12:32: Se0/0 PAP: O AUTH-NAK id 40 len 26 msg is "Authentication failed"
00:12:32: Se0/0 PPP: Sending Acct Event[Down] id[28]
00:12:32: Se0/0 PPP: Phase is TERMINATING
00:12:32: Se0/0 LCP: O TERMREQ [Open] id 134 len 4
00:12:33: Se0/0 LCP: I TERMACK [TERMsent] id 134 len 4
00:12:33: Se0/0 LCP: State is Closed
00:12:33: Se0/0 PPP: Phase is DOWN
```

Unidirectional PPP CHAP Authentication

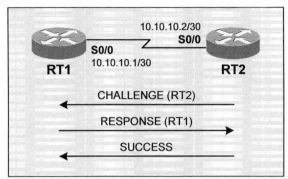

Figure A6-18: Unidirectional PPP CHAP Authentication

- This lab demonstrates the mechanisms of unidirectional (one-way) PPP CHAP authentication. Below describes the situation of the initial lab setup:
  - i)   Both routers have no username and PPP authentication configurations.
  - ii)   Both routers can ping each other.
  - iii) Both routers have enabled PPP authentication debugging with **debug ppp authentication**.

- The **username - password** statement is required on **both devices** for both unidirectional and bidirectional CHAP authentication. In unidirectional CHAP authentication (a local device authenticating a remote device), it is first used by the remote device (RT1) to response to the challenge generated by the local device (RT2), and then used by the local device (RT2) to verify the response from the remote device (RT1).

- Below enable PPP CHAP authentication on RT2. The debugging messages show RT2 challenges RT1 but RT1 is unable to response to RT2's challenge.

```
RT2(config)#int s0/0
RT2(config-if)#ppp authentication chap
RT2(config-if)#
00:15:52: Se0/0 CHAP: O CHALLENGE id 1 len 24 from "RT2"
00:15:53: %LINEPROTO-5-UPDOWN: Line protocol on Interface Serial0/0, changed
state to down
00:15:54: Se0/0 CHAP: O CHALLENGE id 2 len 24 from "RT2"
00:15:56: Se0/0 CHAP: O CHALLENGE id 3 len 24 from "RT2"
-----------------------------------------------------------------
RT1#
00:15:52: Se0/0 CHAP: I CHALLENGE id 1 len 24 from "RT2"
00:15:52: Se0/0 CHAP: Username RT2 not found
00:15:52: Se0/0 CHAP: Unable to authenticate for peer
00:15:52: %LINEPROTO-5-UPDOWN: Line protocol on Interface Serial0/0, changed
state to down
00:15:54: Se0/0 PPP: Using default call direction
00:15:54: Se0/0 PPP: Treating connection as a dedicated line
00:15:54: Se0/0 CHAP: I CHALLENGE id 2 len 24 from "RT2"
00:15:54: Se0/0 CHAP: Username RT1 not found
00:15:54: Se0/0 CHAP: Unable to authenticate for peer
00:15:56: Se0/0 CHAP: I CHALLENGE id 3 len 24 from "RT2"
00:15:56: Se0/0 CHAP: Username RT1 not found
00:15:56: Se0/0 CHAP: Unable to authenticate for peer
```

- Below configure the username and password on RT1. The debugging message show RT1 is able to response to RT2's challenge but RT2 is unable to validate RT1's response.

```
RT1(config)#username RT2 password cisco123
RT1(config)#
00:18:24: Se0/0 CHAP: I CHALLENGE id 67 len 24 from "RT2"
00:18:24: Se0/0 CHAP: O RESPONSE id 67 len 24 from "RT1"
00:18:24: Se0/0 CHAP: I FAILURE id 67 len 26 msg is "Authentication failure"
00:18:26: Se0/0 CHAP: I CHALLENGE id 68 len 24 from "RT2"
00:18:26: Se0/0 CHAP: O RESPONSE id 68 len 24 from "RT1"
00:18:26: Se0/0 CHAP: I FAILURE id 68 len 26 msg is "Authentication failure"
-----------------------------------------------------------------
RT2#
00:18:24: Se0/0 CHAP: O CHALLENGE id 67 len 24 from "RT2"
00:18:24: Se0/0 CHAP: I RESPONSE id 67 len 24 from "RT1"
00:18:24: Se0/0 CHAP: Unable to validate Response.  Username RT1 not found
00:18:24: Se0/0 CHAP: O FAILURE id 67 len 26 msg is "Authentication failure"
00:18:26: Se0/0 CHAP: O CHALLENGE id 68 len 24 from "RT2"
00:18:26: Se0/0 CHAP: I RESPONSE id 68 len 24 from "RT1"
00:18:26: Se0/0 CHAP: Unable to validate Response.  Username RT1 not found
00:18:26: Se0/0 CHAP: O FAILURE id 68 len 26 msg is "Authentication failure"
```

Note: The alternative configuration on RT1 is the **ppp chap hostname RT1** and **ppp chap password cisco123** interface subcommands.

- Below configure the username and password on RT2 for RT2 to validate RT1's response.
  Finally the unidirectional (one-way) PPP CHAP authentication is successful.

```
RT2(config)#username RT1 password cisco123
RT2(config)#
00:20:54: Se0/0 CHAP: O CHALLENGE id 127 len 24 from "RT2"
00:20:54: Se0/0 CHAP: I RESPONSE id 127 len 24 from "RT1"
00:20:54: Se0/0 CHAP: O SUCCESS id 127 len 4
00:20:54: %LINEPROTO-5-UPDOWN: Line protocol on Interface Serial0/0, changed
state to up
-----------------------------------------------------------------
RT1#
00:20:48: Se0/0 CHAP: I CHALLENGE id 127 len 24 from "RT2"
00:20:48: Se0/0 CHAP: O RESPONSE id 127 len 24 from "RT1"
00:20:48: Se0/0 CHAP: I SUCCESS id 127 len 4
00:20:49: %LINEPROTO-5-UPDOWN: Line protocol on Interface Serial0/0, changed
state to up
00:20:50: Se0/0 PPP: Using default call direction
00:20:50: Se0/0 PPP: Treating connection as a dedicated line
```

- LCP packets are sent during the PPP link establishment phase. These packets contain several Configuration Option fields that allow PPP devices to negotiate how they want the link to be established – the maximum datagram size the link can carry, authentication, quality monitoring, and compression. If no Configuration Option field is present, the default configurations are used.

Frame Relay DLCIs

- DLCIs are 10 bits long. Below shows the range of Frame Relay DLCI. Practically, it allows up to 992 PVCs per Frame Relay physical link.

DLCI Range	Usage
0	LMI for ANSI Annex D or CCITT/ITU-T Q.933A type LMIs
1 – 15	Reserved for future use
16 – 1007	User traffic
1008 – 1022	Reserved for future use
1023	Reserved for LMI or and CLLM messages for Cisco-type LMI

Note: CLLM is referred to as **Consolidated Link Layer Management**.

- The LMI DLCI in the **show interface** EXEC command defines the type of LMI being used.

ANSI	LMI DLCI 0 LMI type is ANSI Annex D frame relay DTE
Cisco	LMI DLCI 1023 LMI type is CISCO frame relay DTE
CCITT/ITU-T Q.933A	LMI DLCI 0 LMI type is CCITT frame relay DTE

```
Router#sh int s0/0
Serial0/0 is up, line protocol is up
  Hardware is M4T
  Internet address is 10.10.10.10/24
  MTU 1500 bytes, BW 1544 Kbit, DLY 20000 usec,
     reliability 255/255, txload 1/255, rxload 1/255
  Encapsulation FRAME-RELAY, crc 16, loopback not set
  Keepalive set (10 sec)
  LMI enq sent  75, LMI stat recvd 76, LMI upd recvd 0, DTE LMI up
  LMI enq recvd 0, LMI stat sent  0, LMI upd sent  0
  LMI DLCI 0  LMI type is ANSI Annex D  frame relay DTE
--- output omitted ---
```

- The **ITU Telecommunication Standardization Sector** (ITU-T) coordinates standards for telecommunications on behalf of **International Telecommunication Union** (ITU). The **Comité Consultatif International Téléphonique et Télégraphique** (CCITT) or International Telegraph and Telephone Consultative Committee was created in 1956. It was renamed to ITU-T in 1993.

- Multicasting support is an extension of the LMI specification that allows efficient distribution of routing information and ARP requests across a Frame Relay network. Multicasting uses the reserved DLCIs from 1019 to 1022.

IEEE 802.11 Standards and Specifications

- Below lists the IEEE 802.11 Standards / Specifications as well as their purpose:

IEEE 802.11a	54Mbps 5GHz standard.
IEEE 802.11b	Enhancements to 802.11 to support 5.5Mbps and 11Mbps.
IEEE 802.11c	Bridge operation procedures. Included in the IEEE 802.1d standard.
IEEE 802.11d	International (country-to-country) roaming extensions.
IEEE 802.11e	Enhancements to 802.11 – Quality of Service. Including packet bursting.
IEEE 802.11F	Inter-Access Point Protocol.
IEEE 802.11g	54Mbps 2.4GHz standard. Backward compatible with 802.11b.
IEEE 802.11h	Spectrum Managed 5GHz 802.11a – **Dynamic Frequency Selection** (DFS) and **Transmit Power Control** (TPC).
IEEE 802.11i	**Wi-Fi Protected Access 2** (WPA2) for enhanced security (authentication and encryption). Also referred to as **Robust Security Network** (RSN).
IEEE 802.11j	Extensions for Japan and US public safety.
IEEE 802.11k	Enhancements to 802.11 – Radio Resource Management (RRM).
IEEE 802.11m	Maintenance of the standard, odds and ends.
IEEE 802.11n	Higher throughput improvements using **Multiple Input, Multiple Output** (MIMO) antennas.
IEEE 802.11p	**Wireless Access for the Vehicular Environment** (WAVE) for vehicular environments, eg: ambulances and passenger cars.
IEEE 802.11r	Fast roaming.
IEEE 802.11s	**Extended Service Set** (ESS) Mesh Networking.
IEEE 802.11T	**Wireless Performance Prediction** (WPP).
IEEE 802.11u	Internetworking with non-802 networks, *eg:* cellular networks.
IEEE 802.11v	Wireless network management.
IEEE 802.11w	Protected Management Frames.
IEEE 802.11y	3650–3700 operation in the US.
IEEE 802.11z	Extensions to **Direct Link Setup** (DLS).

- The IEEE project naming convention uses upper-case letters (eg: 802.1Q) to identify **standalone** standards, and lower-case letters to identify **amendments** (previously known as supplements) to existing standards. There should never be 2 projects differing only in the case of letters!

- The REV notation (eg: 802.1Q-REV) is used to identify a revision of an existing standard, which has more extensive changes to the existing standard than an amendment. Previously, revisions also had their own project names.

IEEE 802.11 Frame Types

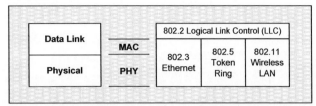

Figure A6-19: IEEE 802.11 in the OSI Reference Model

- The IEEE 802.11 architecture resides in the Data Link **Media Access Control** (MAC) sublayer and the Physical layer in the OSI reference model.

- The **Basic Service Set** (BSS) and **Extended Services Set** (ESS) are the 2 available **infrastructure** modes of WLAN. Another mode of WLAN is **ad-hoc** mode.

- **Basic Service Set** (BSS) is the basic building block of a WLAN. It is often being referred to as the coverage area of an access point. An access point acts as a master to control the wireless stations within a BSS. A BSS is identified by an SSID. The most basic BSS is **Independent Basic Service Set** (IBSS) or **ad-hoc mode BSS**, which comprised of 2 wireless clients; whereas the most basic **infrastructure mode BSS** is comprised of an access point and a wireless client.

- The IEEE 802.11 WLAN specification defines various frame types than Ethernet for wireless communications, as well as managing and controlling wireless connections. The types of frames in the IEEE 802.11 specification are **management, control, and data frames**. Understanding the different IEEE 802.11 frame types is essential for analyzing and troubleshooting the operation of WLANs.

- Every IEEE 802.11 WLAN frame contains the MAC addresses of the source and destination wireless stations, a Frame Control field that indicates the 802.11 protocol version, frame type, and various indicators (eg: whether WEP is enabled, power management is active, etc), a Sequence Control field, the frame body, and the Frame Check Sequence for error detection.

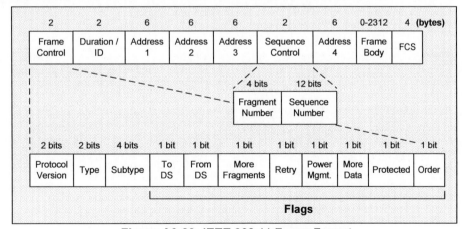

Figure A6-20: IEEE 802.11 Frame Format

- Figure A6-20 shows the frame format of the IEEE 802.11 WLAN specification.
  Below describes the subfields and flags in the Frame Control field:

Protocol Version	Indicates the version of the 802.11 protocol. A receiving station uses this value to determine whether it supports the version of the protocol of the received frame.
Type and Subtype	Determine the function of the frame – management, control, or data. The type and subtype fields for each frame type determine the specific function to perform.
To DS and From DS	Indicates whether the frame is destined to or exiting from the distributed system (DS). All frames of wireless stations that are associated with an access point (infrastructure mode) will have one of the DS bits set. The interpretation of the Address fields depends on the setting of these bits.
More Fragments	Indicates whether there are more subsequent fragments for a particular management or data frame are to follow. Control frames are not fragmented, hence this bit is always set to 0 for control frames.
Retry	Indicates whether the management or data frame is being retransmitted.
Power Management	Indicates whether the sending wireless station is in active or power-saving mode.
More Data	Used to inform a wireless station which is in power-saving mode that the access point has more frames to send to it. Also used by an access points to indicate that additional broadcast or multicast frames are to follow. This bit is only being used in management and data frames; hence this bit is always set to 0 for control frames.
Protected	Indicates whether encryption and authentication are used for the frame. Control frames may not be encrypted; hence this bit is always set to 0 for control frames.
Order	Indicates that all received data frames must be processed in sequence.

- Below shows how to interpret the **To DS** and **From DS** bits:

	From DS = 0	From DS = 1
To DS = 0	All management, control, and data frames within an IBSS (ad-hoc).	Data frames arrived at a wireless station (from AP) in an infra. WLAN.
To DS = 1	Data frames transmitted from a wireless station (to AP) in an infra. WLAN.	Data frames on a wireless bridge (WDS, **Wireless Distribution System**).

- The Duration/ID field is used in all control frames (except with the subtype of PS-Poll) to indicate the remaining duration needed to receive the next frame transmission.

- Wireless stations may want to save battery power by turning off antennas. When the subtype is PS-Poll, it contains the **association identity** (AID) of the waking transmitting station, which indicates which BSS the station belongs to. **Note:** PS is referred to as **Power Save**.

- An 802.11 frame may contain up to 4 Address fields. The general rule is that Address 1 indicates the receiver of a frame, Address 2 as the transmitter, and Address 3 for filtering by the receiver. Depends upon the type of frame, the 4 Address fields will contain a combination of the following address types:

BSS Identifier (BSSID)	Used to uniquely identify each BSS (WLAN). When the frame is from a wireless station in an infrastructure BSS, the BSSID is the MAC address of the access point; when the frame is from a wireless station in an IBSS (ad-hoc) mode, the BSSID is a locally administered MAC address generated with a 46-bit random number, and is generated by the wireless station that initiated the IBSS.
Source Address (SA)	Indicates the 48-bit MAC address of the source station that created and transmitted the frame (source of the transmission). Only 1 station can be the source of a frame.
Destination Address (DA)	Indicates the 48-bit MAC address of the destination station to receive the frame (recipient).
Transmitter Address (TA)	Indicates the 48-bit MAC address of the wireless interface that transmitted the frame onto the wireless medium. The TA is only being used in **wireless bridging**.
Receiver Address (RA)	Indicates the 48-bit MAC address of the (immediate) wireless station which should receive and process the frame. If it is a wireless station, the RA is the DA. For frames destined to a node on an Ethernet network connected to an access point, the RA is the wireless interface of the access point, and the DA may be a node attached to the Ethernet.

- Below shows the usage of the Address fields in data frames:

Function	To DS	From DS	Address 1 (RX)	Address 2 (TX)	Address 3	Address 4
IBSS	0	0	DA	SA	BSSID	-
From AP	0	1	DA	BSSID	SA	-
To AP	1	0	BSSID	SA	DA	-
WDS	1	1	RA	TA	DA	SA

Note: Address 1 indicates the receiver; while Address 2 indicates the transmitter.

- The Sequence Control field contains the following 2 subfields:

Fragment Number	Indicates the number of each frame of a fragmented upper-layer packet. The 1st fragment will have a fragment number of 0, and each subsequent fragment of a fragmented packet increments the fragment number incremented by one.
Sequence Number	Indicates the sequence number of each frame. It begins at 0 and incremented by 1 until 4095 and rollovers to zero and begins again (**modulo-4096**). All fragments of a fragmented packet as well as retransmitted frames will have the same sequence number.

- Below lists the IEEE 802.11 **management frames** that allow wireless stations to establish and maintain communications:

Association Request	The 802.11 association process allows an access point to synchronize and allocate resources for a wireless adapter. A wireless adapter begins the process by sending an Association Request frame to an access point. Upon receiving the Association Request frame, the access point is considered associated with the wireless adapter and would allocate an association ID and resources for the wireless adapter. An Association Request frame contains information such as the SSID of the WLAN the wireless client wishes to associate with and the supported data rates.
Association Response	An access point would send an Association Response frame containing an acceptance or rejection notice to the wireless adapter requesting association. An Association Response frame contains information, eg: the association ID and the supported data rates.
Reassociation Request	When a wireless adapter roams away from its currently associated access point after found another access point with a stronger beacon signal, the wireless adapter would send a Reassociation Request frame to the new access point. The new access point would then coordinate with the previous access point to forward the data frames meant for the wireless adapter that may still be in the buffer of the previous access point.
Reassociation Response	An access point sends a Reassociation Response frame containing an acceptance or rejection notice to a wireless adapter requesting reassociation. Similar to the Association Response frame, the Reassociation Response frame contains information regarding an association – the association ID and the supported data rates.
Probe Request	A wireless station sends a Probe Request frame when it would like to obtain information of another wireless station. Ex: A wireless adapter sends a Probe Request frame to determine the access points that are within range.
Probe Response	A wireless station receives a Probe Request frame would respond with a Probe Response frame that contains capability information, eg: the supported data rates.
Beacon	An access point sends Beacon frames periodically to announce its presence and the services if offers using SSID, timestamp, and other access point parameters to wireless adapters that are within range. Wireless adapters continuously scan all 802.11 radio channels for beacon frames to choose the best access point to associate with. Beacon frames are also used to logically separate WLANs.
Disassociation	A wireless station sends a Disassociation frame to another wireless station when it would like to terminate the association. Ex: A wireless adapter that is shutting down gracefully can send a Disassociation frame to notify its associated access point that it is powering off. The access point can then remove the wireless adapter from the association table and release the allocated memory resources.

Authentication	The 802.11 authentication process is where an access point accepts or rejects the identity of a wireless adapter. A wireless adapter begins the process by sending an Authentication frame that contains its identity to the access point. For open authentication, the access point responds with an Authentication frame as a response to indicate the acceptance or rejection; while for shared-key authentication, the access point responds with an Authentication frame containing challenge text, which the wireless client must response with an Authentication frame containing the encrypted version of the challenge text using the shared-key for the access point to verify its identity. WLAN authentication occurs at L2 and is authenticating devices instead of users. The authentication and association processes are occurred in sequence. **Note:** Authentication occurs first and then followed by association.
Deauthentication	A wireless station sends a Deauthentication frame to another wireless station in order to terminate a secure connection.

- Below lists the IEEE 802.11 **control frames** that assist the delivery of data frames between wireless stations:

Request to Send (RTS)	A station sends a RTS frame to another station as the 1st phase of the necessary 2-way handshake before transmitting a data frame.
Clear to Send (CTS)	A station response to a RTS frame with the CTS frame to provide the clearance for the source station to transmit a data frame. The CTS frame contains a time value which would cause all nearby stations (including hidden stations) to hold off data transmission for a certain period of time necessary for the source station to transmit its frames.
Acknowledgement (ACK)	A destination station would run an error checking process to detect the presence of errors upon received a data frame. The destination station would send an ACK frame to the source station if no errors are found. The source station will retransmit the frame if it doesn't receive an ACK for the frame for a certain period of time.

Note: Kindly refer to Page 174 for the discussion of the CSMA/CA and RTS/CTS mechanisms.

- Finally, **data frames** are used to carry upper layers data – packets.

- Below shows the wireless client association process:
    i)   Access points send out beacons announcing the SSID and supported data rates.
    ii)   A wireless client scans all changes and sends out Probe Request frames to all access points within range.
    iii)   All access points within range reply with a Probe Response frame, and the wireless client listens for the responses from the access points.
    iv)   The wireless client associates with the access point with the strongest signal. Authentication and other security information are sent to the access point.
    v)   The access point accepts the association request and associated with the wireless client.
    Note: 802.1X authentication could occur straight after the association process is completed.

- The maximum Ethernet frame size is 1518 bytes whereas a wireless frame could be as large as 2346 bytes. Usually the WLAN frame size is limited to 1518 bytes as WLANs are often connected to and communicating with wired Ethernet networks.

IEEE 802.11 Types and Subtypes

Type Value b3 b2	Type Description	Subtype Value B7 b6 b5 b4	Subtype Description
00	Management	0000	Association Request
00	Management	0001	Association Response
00	Management	0010	Reassociation Request
00	Management	0011	Reassociation Response
00	Management	0100	Probe Request
00	Management	0101	Probe Response
00	Management	0110–0111	Reserved
00	Management	1000	Beacon
00	Management	1001	ATIM
00	Management	1010	Disassociation
00	Management	1011	Authentication
00	Management	1100	Deauthentication
00	Management	1101–1111	Reserved
01	Control	0000–1001	Reserved
01	Control	1010	PS-Poll
01	Control	1011	RTS
01	Control	1100	CTS
01	Control	1101	ACK
01	Control	1110	CF End
01	Control	1111	CF End + CF-ACK
10	Data	0000	Data
10	Data	0001	Data + CF-ACK
10	Data	0010	Data + CF-Poll
10	Data	0011	Data + CF-ACK + CF-Poll
10	Data	0100	Null function (no data)
10	Data	0101	CF-ACK (no data)
10	Data	0110	CF-Poll (no data)
10	Data	0111	CF-ACK + CF-Poll (no data)
10	Data	1000–1111	Reserved
11	Reserved	0000–1111	Reserved

IEEE 802.1X Port-Based Authentication

- The IEEE 802.1X standard defines a client-server-based access control and authentication protocol that restricts unauthorized devices from gaining access to a network through publicly accessible ports. The authentication server authenticates a client connects to a switch port before granting the available network services to the client.

- 802.1X allows only **Extensible Authentication Protocol over LAN** (EAPOL) traffic through the switch port which an unauthenticated client is connected to. Normal traffic can pass through the switch port after authentication is completed successfully.

- With 802.1X port-based authentication, network devices have the following **device roles**:

Client (Supplicant)	The device (workstation) that requires access to the LAN. Responds to the requests from the switch. Must be running 802.1X-compliant client software.
Switch or **Access Point** (Authenticator)	Controls the physical access to the network based on the authentication status of the client. Acts as a proxy between the client and authentication server, which requests identity information from the client, verify the information with the authentication server, and relays the response to the client. It is responsible for the **re-encapsulation** of the EAP and RADIUS frames for communication with a client and an authentication server respectively.
Authentication Server	Performs the authentication of the client. It validates the identity of the client and notifies the switch or access point whether the client is authorized to access the network. Currently, the RADIUS security system with EAP extensions is the only supported authentication server.

Note: RADIUS is referred to as **Remote Authentication Dial-In User Service**.

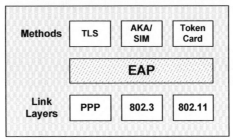

Figure A6-21: The EAP Architecture

- EAP is designed to run over any link layer and use any number of authentication methods.

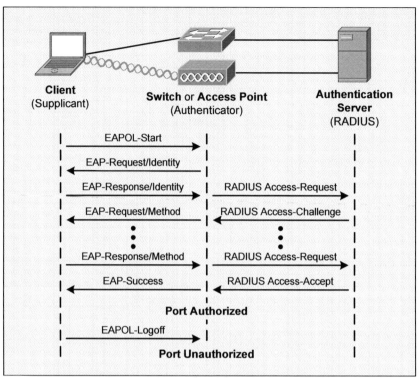

App06-22: IEEE 802.1X Authentication Message Exchange

- Below describes a typical WLAN 802.1X authentication process:
  1) A wireless client becomes active on the medium. After the IEEE 802.11 WLAN Probe Request/Response, Authentication, and Association processes, the access point forces the port into an unauthorized state, which only 802.1X traffic is forwarded.
  2) The access point replies with an EAP-Request Identity message to the wireless client to obtain the client's identity. The wireless client's EAP-Response Identity message, which contains the client's identity, is forwarded to the authentication server.
  3) The authentication server authenticates the wireless client and sends an Access Accept (or Access Reject) message to the access point.
  4) Upon receiving the Access Accept message, the access point relays the EAP-Success message to the wireless client and transitions the client's port to an authorized state and normal traffic is forwarded.

- **Note:** Below lists the sequence of establishing WLAN connectivity with 802.1X authentication: **Probe Request, Probe Response, Authentication, Association, 802.1X authentication...**

- When 802.1X is enabled, ports are authenticated before any other L2 or L3 features are enabled.

- **Note:** 802.1X is also considered as an efficient and effective alternative solution to port security.

VPN and IPsec Basics

- Virtual Private Networks (VPNs) allow the creation of private networks across a public domain (eg: Internet) for private and secured data transmission.

- VPNs are secure and inexpensive. There are 2 types of VPN implementation – using IPsec to create authentication and encryption services; and establishing tunnels via tunneling protocols.

- Tunneling is method of overcoming protocol restrictions by encapsulating or wrapping packets from a protocol in another protocol and transmits the encapsulated packet over a network that supports the encapsulating protocol.

- Below describes the most common tunneling protocols:

Layer 2 Forwarding (L2F)	A Cisco-proprietary tunneling protocol created for **Virtual Private Dial-Up Networks** (VPDNs), where devices create secure connections to a corporate network using dial-up connections. L2F was later replaced by L2TP (backward compatible with L2F).
Point-to-Point Tunneling Protocol (PPTP)	Created by Microsoft for secure data transmission between remote networks and corporate network.
Layer 2 Tunneling Protocol (L2TP)	Created by Cisco and Microsoft to replace L2F and PPTP. L2TP merged both L2F and PPTP capabilities into one tunneling protocol.
Generic Routing Encapsulation (GRE)	Another Cisco-proprietary tunneling protocol. It forms (unencrypted) virtual point-to-point links which are able to encapsulate a variety of protocols inside IP packets. It can also be used to protect the private address space from being advertised to any public domain.

Note: There are many types of tunnels. VPNs are tunnels; GRE creates tunnels; Secure Shell (SSH) is also a form of tunnel. Tunnels can encrypt data so that only the other side can see it, as with SSH; they can make a remote network appears local, as with GRE; or they can do both, as with VPN.

- IPsec is a suite of industry standard network layer (L3) protocols and algorithms for securing communications over the IP-based networks by authenticating and/or encrypting IP packets. IPsec also includes the IKE protocol for establishing shared security information (**Security Association**, SA) between 2 network devices or end systems to support secure communication.
Note: Other Internet security protocols, eg: SSL and SSH, are operate from the Transport layer up to the Application layer (L4 – L7).
Note: The official term of "**IPsec**" as defined by the IETF is often wrongly addressed as "**IPSec**".

- IPsec secures a path between a pair of gateways, a pair of hosts, or a gateway and a host.

- IPsec unable to encrypt non-IP traffic. For such a situation, a GRE tunnel would first be created to encrypt the non-IP traffic and followed by using IPsec to encrypt the GRE tunnel. Additionally, multicast can only be passed on GRE tunnels.
Note: A tunnel is a software interface on a Cisco router that is used to transport non-IP and non-routable protocols (eg: AppleTalk, SNA, IPX, etc) across an IP network.

- IPsec-based VPN is comprised of 2 parts – **Internet Key Exchange** (IKE) protocol and IPsec security protocols – **Authentication Header** (AH) and **Encapsulating Security Payload** (ESP). Below describes the flow of IPsec events:
    i) **IKE Phase 1: IKE Security Negotiation** – IKE negotiates how to protect IKE by establishing an authenticated and secure channel between 2 IKE peers called the **IKE Security Association**. IKE Phase 1 is consists of **Main Mode** or **Aggressive Mode**. The peer that initiates the session will propose or offer at least one or more configured ISAKMP policies which specify a combination of encryption algorithm, hash algorithm, authentication type, Diffie-Hellman group, and the lifetime. The remote peer will then try to find a matching configured policy that has the same parameters as the one being sent by its peer. If no matching policy is found, IKE will terminate the negotiation. If a policy is mutually agreed upon, IKE will complete the negotiation process and an **ISAKMP SA** will be created. Additionally, peers in an IPsec session must authenticate themselves among each other during IKE Phase 1 Main Mode exchange before IKE can proceed.
    ii) **IKE Phase 2: IPsec Security Negotiation** – IKE negotiates how to protect IPsec by negotiating the IPsec security associations (SAs) and generating the keys for IPsec. IKE Phase 2 negotiation is done in only 1 mode – **Quick Mode**. The peer that initiates the session will propose or offer at least one or more configured transforms which specify a combination of authentication and/or encryption algorithm. The remote peer will then try to find a matching configured transform that has the same parameters as the one being sent by its peer. If no matching transform is found, IKE will terminate negotiation and an IPsec VPN will not be established. If a policy is mutually agreed upon, IKE will complete the negotiation process and an **IPsec SA** will be created.
    iii) IPsec transfers the actual data in the VPN tunnel using the authentication and encryption methods agreed upon the IKE negotiation process.

- **Internet Key Exchange** (IKE) allows 2 VPN endpoints verify the identity of each other (using pre-shared keys or RSA) in IKE Phase 1, and negotiate the methods (security policies) for secured data transmission in IKE Phase 2. IKE manages VPN connections by defining a set of **Security Associations** (SAs) for each connection. Each SA has its own SAID.

- In a VPN, before a communication path is considered secure, the VPN endpoints must be authenticated. IPsec uses the following authentication methods to authenticate peers:

Pre-Shared Keys	Secret key values that are manually configured on each peer.
RSA signatures	Use the exchange of digital certificates to authenticate the peers.

- IKE is a hybrid protocol that uses part of Oakley and part of SKEME inside the ISAKMP framework; hence IKE is formerly known as ISAKMP/Oakley. IKE typically uses ISAKMP for **key exchange** and **establishment of SAs**, although other methods can be used.

- IKE establishes both ISAKMP and IPsec SAs for an IPsec VPN session. IKE first negotiates an ISAKMP SA with the peer. It is possible to configure multiple policy statements with different parameters, and then allow the peers to negotiate and establish a mutual agreement.

- An IPsec SA defines the security algorithms or parameters associated with particular connection – the IPsec protocol (AH, ESP, or both), the session keys used for data encryption, etc. IPsec SAs are unidirectional (simplex); hence there is always more than 1 IPsec SA per IPsec connection. In cases where only either AH or ESP is used, 2 SAs will be created for each connection – one for each the incoming and outgoing traffic. In cases where AH and ESP are used in conjunction, 4 SAs will be created.

- The **Internet Security Association and Key Management Protocol** (ISAKMP) defines the procedures for authenticating peers, IKASAMP and IPsec SAs establishment, negotiation, modification, and deletion; key generation, and threat mitigation (eg: DoS and replay attacks).

- Instead of ISAKMP (the use of **ipsec-isakmp** keyword along with the **crypto map** global configuration command), **manual keying** (the use of **ipsec-manual** keyword along with the **crypto map** global configuration command) which require manual entry of the shared secret session keys (used for hashing and encryption) on both crypto endpoints is also possible.

- IPsec operation requires both ends to be configured with the same **transform set**, which specifies the methods for encrypt and decrypt the data. IPsec uses 2 primary security protocols – **Authentication Header** (AH) and **Encapsulating Security Payload** (ESP). These protocols are used for secured data transmission through an IPsec-based VPN tunnel. IPsec-based VPNs can be established using AH only, ESP only, or both AH and ESP.

- The **Authentication Header** (AH) protocol provides authentication for both the IP header and data of a packet using a one-way hash function. The sender first generates a one-way hash, and then the receiver generates the same one-way hash. If the packet has changed in any way, it won't be authenticated and will be dropped. IPsec relies upon AH to guarantee authenticity. AH provides integrity check on the entire packet, but it doesn't provide any encryption services.

- ESP only provides integrity check (and encrypts) on the data of a packet (and the ESP header); while AH checks the entire packet – both header and data. AH is used for authentication only, while ESP can be used for either encryption or authentication only; or both.

- Although AH and ESP are typically used independently, they are often being used together to provide data encryption service. **Note:** It is important to use authentication even if encryption is used, as encrypt-only implementations are subject to some forms of effective attacks.

- ESP provides the following 4 functionalities or capabilities:

Confidentiality (Encryption)	Provided through the use of symmetric encryption algorithms, eg: DES, 3DES. Confidentiality can be selected separately from all other services, but the confidentiality selected must be the same on all VPN endpoints.
Data Origin Authentication and Connectionless Integrity	Joint services offered as an option in conjunction with the confidentiality option. Authentication ensures that the connection is established with the desired system.
Anti-Replay Protection	This service works only if data origin authentication is selected. It is based upon the receiver – it is effective only if the receiver checks the sequence number of the received packets with a sliding window of the destination gateway or host to prevent replay attacks.
Traffic Flow Confidentiality	This service works only when tunnel mode is selected. It is most effective if implemented at a security gateway, where the source-destination patterns of attacks is visible.

- The degree of security of IPsec VPN is based on the encryption algorithm used and the length of the pre-shared key. The longer the key, the harder it is to be broken.

- IPsec is not bound to any specific encryption or authentication algorithm, keying or technology, or security algorithms, which allows IPsec to support newer and better algorithms.

- IPsec supports the following 3 types of encryption algorithms:

Data Encryption Standard (DES)	Uses a 56-bit key that ensures high performance encryption. Uses a symmetric key cryptosystem.
Triple DES (3DES)	A variant of DES that breaks data into 64-bit blocks. 3DES then processes each block 3 times, each time with an independent 56-bit key, hence providing significant improvement in encryption strength over DES. Uses a symmetric key cryptosystem.
Advanced Encryption Standard (AES)	Provides stronger encryption than DES and is more efficient than 3DES. Key lengths can be 128-, 192-, and 256-bit keys.

- Encryption algorithms (eg: DES, 3DES, and AES) require a symmetric shared secret key to perform encryption and decryption. The **Diffie-Hellman Key Exchange (D-H)** is a public key exchange process that allows 2 parties that have no prior knowledge of each other to negotiate symmetric shared secret keys used for encryption and decryption over an insecure channel. The shared secret keys are negotiated between crypto endpoints dynamically, which only the prime modulus size for use in the D-H exchange is needed to be specified. IKE uses the D-H keys to encrypt the ISAKMP SA when establishing the IPsec SAs. Additionally, D-H is also used to generate shared secret keys to be used in the ciphers specified in the IPsec transforms, which are then used in conjunction with the D-H keys by the IPsec to encrypt and decrypt the data passes through the IPsec VPN tunnel.

- IPsec uses a data integrity algorithm called **Hash-based Message Authentication Code** (HMAC) that adds a hash to the message to ensure data integrity. The hash guarantees the integrity of the original message. If the transmitted hash matches the received hash, the message is considered has not been tampered.

- IPsec uses the following 2 HMAC algorithms:

Message Digest Algorithm 5 (MD5)	Uses a 128-bit shared secret key. The message and 128-bit shared secret key are combined and run through the MD5 hash algorithm, producing a 128-bit hash. This hash is then added to the original message and sent to the destination host.
Secure Hash Algorithm 1 (SHA-1)	Uses a 160-bit shared secret key. The message and 160-bit shared secret key are combined and run through the SHA-1 hash algorithm, producing a 160-bit hash. This hash is then added to the original message and sent to the destination host.

- Below lists the 2 modes of IPsec operation:

Transport	Only the payload of the IP packet is encrypted and/or authenticated. The routing is intact, as the IP header is neither modified nor encrypted. It is used for host-to-host or end-to-end communications (end systems perform the security processing).
Tunnel	The entire IP packet is encrypted and/or authenticated. The original packet is encapsulated entirely into a new packet with a new set of source and destination IP addresses for routing to work. It is used for network-to-network or portal-to-portal communications (gateways or routers perform the security processing). It is the traditional and **default** mode of IPsec VPNs.

- The Tunnel mode is most commonly used to secure existing IP traffic for communication between end systems on networks connected to IPsec-enabled routers. With routers or VPN endpoints performing the IPsec encryption, no changes are required to the software and drivers on the end systems – the IPsec implementation is **transparent** to end systems.

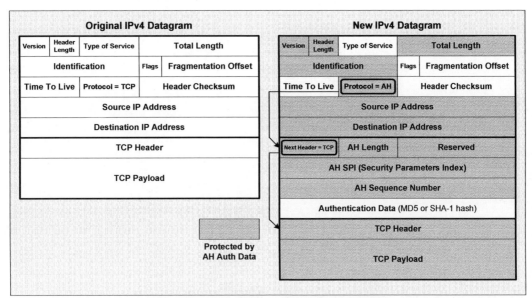

Figure A6-23: IPsec in AH Transport Mode

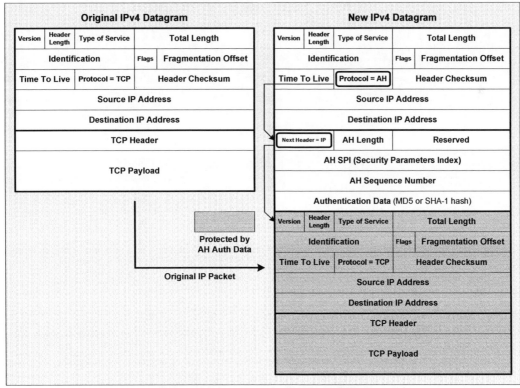

Figure A6-24: IPsec in AH Tunnel Mode

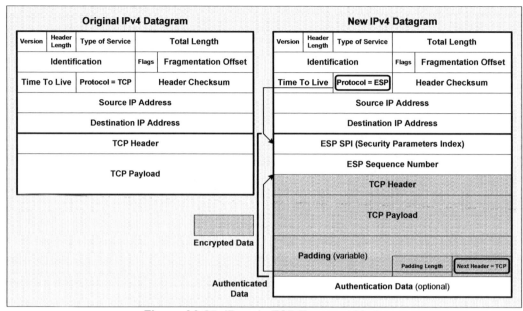

Figure A6-25: IPsec in ESP Transport Mode

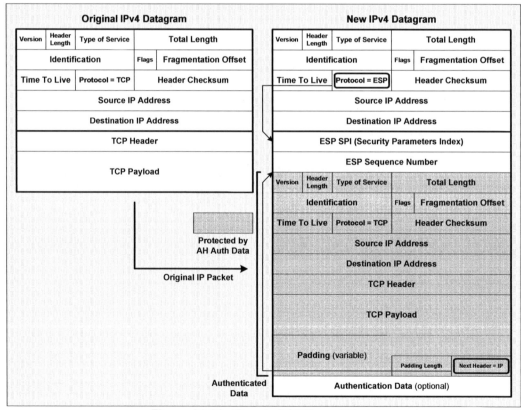

Figure A6-26: IPsec in ESP Tunnel Mode

- The main challenge and problem faced by IKE and IPsec is NAT, as both protocols were not designed to work through NAT. **NAT Traversal** (NAT-T) has evolved as a method of enabling IPsec-protected IP packets to work well in NAT environments by encapsulating ISAKMP and ESP packets into UDP Port 4500 packets.
  The IPsec NAT Transparency feature was introduced in Cisco IOS Release 12.2T.
  The access control list configuration named UDP Port 4500 as "non500-isakmp". 😊

IPsec Configuration

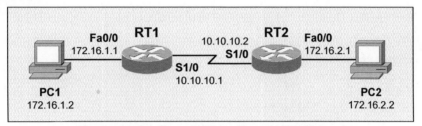

Figure A6-27: Sample IPsec-Based VPN Network

- IPsec configuration on RT1:

```
hostname RT1
!
crypto isakmp policy 1
 encr 3des
 authentication pre-share
 group 2
crypto isakmp key CISCO-1234 address 10.10.10.2
!
!
crypto ipsec transform-set ESP-3DES-SHA esp-3des esp-sha-hmac
!
crypto map CMAP-Site2 1 ipsec-isakmp
 description *** IPsec Tunnel to RT2 ***
 set peer 10.10.10.2
 set transform-set ESP-3DES-SHA
 match address 102
!
interface Serial1/0
 crypto map CMAP-Site2
!
ip route 172.16.2.0 255.255.255.0 10.10.10.2
!
access-list 102 permit ip 172.16.1.0 0.0.0.255 172.16.2.0 0.0.0.255
```

- IPsec configuration starts with configuring the **ISAKMP protection suite**. The **crypto isakmp policy** global configuration command first defines an ISAKMP policy. It is possible to define multiple policies; the **priorities** of the policies determine the sequence of the policies during the IKE negotiation phase (IKE Phase 1).

- The **authentication pre-share** ISAKMP subcommand tells IKE to use the manual key configured with the **crypto isakmp key** global configuration command for authentication. **Note:** The other 2 options beside the **pre-share** keyword are **rsa-encr** and **rsa-sig**, which configures RSA Encryption and RSA Signature respectively. These keywords are used when configuring ISAKMP using a CA (**Certification Authority**) instead of pre-shared keys.
Note: CA is a 3rd-party entity which is responsible for issuing and revoking digital certificates. Each device that has its own certificate and public key of the CA can authenticate other devices within a particular CA domain.

- The **group** {*Diffie-Hellman group*} ISAKMP subcommand defines the size of the modulus to use for Diffie-Hellman calculation. Group 1 is 768-bit long, group 2 is 1024-bit long, and group 5 is 1536-bit long. The higher-number groups are significantly more CPU intensive but are more secure than other lower-number groups. The default is group 1.

- It is possible to specify up to **6** transform sets for a particular crypto map and allow the peers to negotiate a mutually agreed transform.

```
!
crypto ipsec transform-set ESP-DES-MD5 esp-des esp-md5-hmac
crypto ipsec transform-set ESP-3DES-SHA esp-3des esp-sha-hmac
!
crypto map CMAP-Site2 1 ipsec-isakmp
 description *** IPsec Tunnel to RT2 ***
 set peer 10.10.10.2
 set transform-set ESP-DES-MD5 ESP-3DES-SHA
 match address 102
!
```

Troubleshooting ISDN

Troubleshooting ISDN BRI Layer 1

- This section is only applicable to troubleshooting ISDN BRI Layer 1 deactivated status. If the ISDN BRI Layer 1 is up and active as shown in the **show isdn status** EXEC command, kindly proceed to **Troubleshooting ISDN BRI Layer 2**.

- Detailed information on ISDN Layer 1 states and signals are defined in the ITU-T I.430 standard.

- The **show controller bri** {*num*} EXEC command is used for advanced ISDN Layer 1 troubleshooting by displaying the information about the ISDN Layer 1 activation status.

```
Router>sh controllers bri0/0
BRI unit 0:
Layer 1 is ACTIVATED. (ISDN L1 State F7)
--- output omitted ---
```

- Use the following table to interpret the ISDN Layer 1 states:

L1 State	L1 State Name	L1 State Description
F1	Inactive	In this inactive (powered off) state, the terminal equipment (TE) is not transmitting and cannot detect the presence of any input signal.
F2	Sensing	This state is entered after the TE has been powered on but has not determined the type of signal (if any) that the TE is receiving. When in this state, a TE may go into a lower power consumption state.
F3	Deactivated	This is the deactivated state of the physical protocol. Neither the network termination (NT) nor the TE is transmitting. When in this state, a TE may go to a low power consumption mode.
F4	Awaiting Signal	When the TE wishes to initiate activation, it sends an Activation signal to the NT and awaits a response.
F5	Identifying Input	At the first receipt of any signal from the NT, the TE stops sending Activation signals and awaits the activation signal or synchronized frame from the NT.
F6	Synchronized	When the TE has received an Activation signal from the NT, it responds with a synchronized frame and is awaiting a synchronized frame from the NT.
F7	Activated	This is the normal active state, with the protocol activated in both directions. Both the NT and the TE are transmitting normal frames. State F7 is the only state where the B and D channels contain operational data.
F8	Lost Framing	This is the condition when the TE has lost frame synchronization and is awaiting re-synchronization.

- **Note:** Most of the ISDN Layer 1 states are temporary and can be cleared with the **clear interface bri** {*num*} privileged command or a router reboot. Contact the Telco for further troubleshooting if those states persist for a long period.

Troubleshooting ISDN E1/T1 Physical Layer Alarms and Error Events

-   This section explains the common alarm types and error events that may appear during the operations of ISDN E1/T1 as well as the troubleshooting techniques.

-   The **show controller e1 | t1** {*num*} EXEC command displays the controller status specific to the controller hardware, error statistics about the E1/T1 link, local or remote alarm information, and information for identifying and troubleshooting ISDN physical and data link layer problems.

-   Issue the **show controller e1 | t1** {*num*} EXEC command repeatedly to see if the counters for the frame loss, line code, and slip seconds errors and various alarms are increasing for a particular duration of time, eg: 1 minute, 5 minutes.

-   Below shows the sample output of the **show controller e1 | t1** {*num*} EXEC command. The output comprises of the alarm and error event sections.

```
Router>sh controller e1
E1 1/0 is up.
  Applique type is Channelized E1 - balanced
  No alarms detected.
  alarm-trigger is not set
  Framing is CRC4, Line Code is HDB3, Clock Source is Line.
  Module type is Channelized E1/T1 PRI
  Version info Firmware: 0000001D, FPGA: C
  Hardware revision is 0.0        , Software revision is 29
  Protocol revision is 1
  number of CLI resets is 16
  Last clearing of alarm counters 1d22h
    receive remote alarm   :    0,
    transmit remote alarm  :    0,
    receive AIS alarm      :    0,
    transmit AIS alarm     :    0,
    loss of frame          :    0,
    loss of signal         :    0,
    Loopback test          :    0,
    transmit AIS in TS 16  :    0,
    receive LOMF alarm     :    0,
    transmit LOMF alarm    :    0,
  MIB data updated every 10 seconds.
  Data in current interval (443 seconds elapsed):
    0 Line Code Violations, 0 Path Code Violations
    0 Slip Secs, 0 Fr Loss Secs, 0 Line Err Secs, 0 Degraded Mins
    0 Errored Secs, 0 Bursty Err Secs, 0 Severely Err Secs, 0 Unavail Secs
  Total Data (last 24 hours)
    0 Line Code Violations, 0 Path Code Violations,
    0 Slip Secs, 0 Fr Loss Secs, 0 Line Err Secs, 0 Degraded Mins,
    0 Errored Secs, 0 Bursty Err Secs, 0 Severely Err Secs, 0 Unavail Secs
Router>
```

-   Contact the Telco for encoding and framing settings. HDB3 is the only defined encoding scheme for E1 links, while CRC4 framing format is most widely used. Look for `Clock Source is Line` in the output of the **show controller e1 | t1** {*num*} EXEC command to verify that the clocking is derived from the Telco.

- Alarms are serious conditions that require attentions. Excessive errors, hardware problems, and signal disruption can trigger alarms. The alarms are coded as **colors**. Different vendors define alarm differently, and finding the details descriptions of the alarms can be challenging. RFC 1232 describes most alarms; however, they are defined for use in SNMP and are not intended to become a standard for hardware implementation.

- A **Red Alarm** is triggered when a Loss of Signal (LoS) or Loss of Frame (LoF) error is detected. After a local device has a red alarm, it would send a yellow alarm to the far-end. When the far-end receives the yellow alarm, it would trigger a yellow alarm.
  Note: A red alarm is usually indicated on the opposite end of the yellow alarm, and vice versa.

- **Loss of Signal** (LoS) is the state where no electrical pulses have been detected – the line is dead, there is no alarm and signal. LoS is equivalent to not connecting any cable to the interface.
  Loss of Frame (LoF) indicates that a certain number of frames have been received with framing bits in error. The data is considered garbage as the synchronization between both ends is invalid.

- A sample scenario of red alarm is when something has failed on an ISDN switch, the switch would trigger a local red alarm and sends out yellow alarm signal to alert the neighboring router regarding the problem. Another sample scenario is when an ISDN switch is sending garbled frame to the neighboring router, which sees consecutive LoF errors and declares a red alarm. When the router declares a red alarm, a yellow alarm is sent back out across the link.

- Interpreting the behaviors of red alarms can be challenging and confusing. Generally, a red alarm indicates that there is a problem happening on the local device. However, the router in the 2nd scenario above was receiving too much LoF errors until it is unable to recognize the signals and frames from the ISDN switch.

- A **Yellow Alarm** is also known as a **Remote Alarm Indication** (RAI). A yellow alarm is declared when a yellow alarm signal is received from the far-end. A yellow alarm does not necessarily indicate a problem on the local device; rather there is a problem at the far-end device, which has declared a red alarm and notifies the local device. Generally, a yellow alarm indicates that the far-end receiver is in a LoS or LoF state. When the receiver experiences LoS or LoF, the transmitter sends a yellow alarm. The circuit is considered as a **one-way link** – the transmitting line towards the far-end device is experiencing problem while the transmitting line towards the local device is functioning as it is able to receive the Yellow Alarm signal.
  Note: A yellow alarm is usually indicated on the opposite end of the red alarm, and vice versa.

- A **Blue Alarm** is also known as an **Alarm Indication Signal** (AIS). RFC 1232 does not define about this condition. A blue alarm is triggered when the receiver receives an AIS. Generally, a blue alarm indicates that there is a problem upstream. An AIS in a framed or unframed all-1s signal which is transmitted to maintain transmission continuity. It typically occurs when the far-end CSU has lost its terminal side equipment or a cable is disconnected.

- The blue alarm is often sent from the service provider to both ends of the circuit to notify them that there is a problem within the service provider's network.

- Below addresses ISDN E1/T1 controller alarms along with the procedures to correct them:

Receive Alarm Indication Signal (rxAIS)	Indicates that a stream of framed or unframed all-1s signal is received. This problem should be cleared when the LoF error is rectified. Change the framing format with the **framing {esf | sf | crc4 | no-crc4}** interface subcommand.
Receive Remote Alarm Indication (rxRAI)	Indicates that the far-end device has a problem with the signal which is receiving from the local device. Perform hard plug loopback tests to verify the ISDN controller hardware is OK. Check or replace cables to isolate cabling problems.
Transmit Remote Alarm Indication (txRAI)	Indicates that the ISDN interface has a problem with the signal it receives from the far-end equipment. Check the settings at the remote end to ensure that they match the local port settings.
Transmit Alarm Indication Signal (txAIS)	Indicates that the ISDN controller is shut down. Issue the **show controller e1 | t1** {*num*} EXEC command to verify that the ISDN controller is up. If the ISDN controller is down, issue the **no shutdown** interface subcommand to bring it up.

- Below describes the various error events that occur on ISDN E1/T1 lines along with the troubleshooting guidelines for them:

Linecode Violations	Indicates that either a Bipolar Violation (BPV) or excessive zero error event is present. BPVs are inserted upon the synchronization of circuits with B8ZS linecoding. Linecode errors occur when BPVs that are used for synchronization are received. Excessive zero errors occur when 8 or more 0s in sequence are received on circuits with AMI linecoding. These errors normally occur due to an AMI/B8ZS linecoding misconfiguration on the intermediate devices along the transmission path.
Pathcode Violations	Examples are frame synchronization errors for SF and cyclic redundancy check (CRC) errors for ESF. Both linecode and pathcode violations are often present at the same time; hence always verify the linecoding configuration. Note that some errors can occur due to impulse noise, in which the errors might appear only a few times a day and the impact or interrupt is minimal.
Slip Seconds	Indicates a clocking problem. The ISDN network would provide the clocking in which the CPE must synchronize. Look for `Clock Source is Line` in the output of the **show controller e1 | t1** {*num*} EXEC command to verify that the clocking is derived from the Telco.
Loss of Frame	Triggered when the receiver detects multiple framing-bit errors. The data is considered garbage as the synchronization between both ends is invalid. When this state is triggered, the framer starts searching for a correct framing pattern. The LoS state ends when reframe occurs. Ensure the framing format is configured correctly. Change the framing format with the **framing {esf | sf | crc4 | no-crc4}** interface subcommand.

Loss of Signal	Triggered upon observing 175 +/- 75 contiguous pulse positions with no pulses of either positive or negative polarity for T1 lines; or when more than 10 consecutive 0s are detected for E1 lines.
Code Violation Error	The CRC value in the received frame does not match with the corresponding locally calculated CRC value.
Bipolar Violation	Occurs when 2 mark signals (1s) occur in sequence with the same polarity (when not part of a B8ZS substitution). T1 signaling specifies that each mark must be the opposite polarity of the one preceding it. It also includes other error patterns such as 8 or more consecutive 0s and incorrect parity.
Errored Second	A second with one or more Code Violation Error or Loss of Frame events have occurred. The presence of Bipolar Violations also triggers an Errored Second. Some errored seconds may occur on a normal circuit.
Severely Errored Second	A second with 320 or more Code Violation Error or Loss of Frame events have occurred. Also known as Extreme Errored Second (EES).
Unavailable Second	A second that the CSU is in the Unavailable Signal state, including the initial 10 seconds to enter the state, but excluding the 10 seconds to exit the state.

Troubleshooting ISDN Layer 2

- Understanding the output messages of the **debug isdn q921** command is vital in troubleshooting ISDN Layer 2 Firstly, issue the **debug isdn q921** to enable the ISDN Layer 2 debugging which provides the details of ISDN Layer 2 transactions between the router and the Telco ISDN switch. Subsequently, issue the **clear interface bri** {*num*} or **clear interface serial** {*num*:**15**} privileged command to reset the ISDN interface which forces the router to renegotiate ISDN Layer 2 information with the Telco ISDN switch.

- Below shows the sample output messages of the **debug isdn q921** command:

```
Router#debug isdn q921
debug isdn q921 is             ON.
Router#
Router#sh isdn status
Global ISDN Switchtype = basic-net3
ISDN BRI0/0 interface
        dsl 0, interface ISDN Switchtype = basic-net3
    Layer 1 Status:
        ACTIVE
    Layer 2 Status:
        TEI = 76, Ces = 1, SAPI = 0, State = TEI_ASSIGNED
    Layer 3 Status:
        0 Active Layer 3 Call(s)
    Active dsl 0 CCBs = 0
    The Free Channel Mask:  0x80000003
    Total Allocated ISDN CCBs = 0
Router#
Router#clear int bri0/0
Router#
23:20:28: ISDN BR0/0 Q921: User TX -> IDREQ ri=24872 ai=127
23:20:28: ISDN BR0/0 Q921: User RX <- IDASSN ri=24872 ai=75
23:20:28: ISDN BR0/0 Q921: L2_EstablishDataLink: sending SABME
23:20:28: ISDN BR0/0 Q921: User TX -> SABMEp sapi=0 tei=75
23:20:28: ISDN BR0/0 Q921: User RX <- UAf sapi=0 tei=75
23:20:28: %ISDN-6-LAYER2UP: Layer 2 for Interface BR0/0, TEI 75 changed to
up
23:20:38: ISDN BR0/0 Q921: User RX <- RRp sapi=0 tei=75 nr=0
23:20:38: ISDN BR0/0 Q921: User TX -> RRf sapi=0 t    Total Allocated ISDN
CCBs = 0
23:20:48: ISDN BR0/0 Q921: User RX <- RRp sapi=0 tei=75 nr=0
23:20:48: ISDN BR0/0 Q921: User TX -> RRp sapi=0 tei=75 nr=0
23:20:48: ISDN BR0/0 Q921: User TX -> RRf sapi=0 tei=75 nr=0
23:20:48: ISDN BR0/0 Q921: User RX <- RRf sapi=0 tei=75 nr=0
Router#
Router#sh isdn status
Global ISDN Switchtype = basic-net3
ISDN BRI0/0 interface
        dsl 0, interface ISDN Switchtype = basic-net3
    Layer 1 Status:
        ACTIVE
    Layer 2 Status:
        TEI = 75, Ces = 1, SAPI = 0, State = MULTIPLE_FRAME_ESTABLISHED
    Layer 3 Status:
        0 Active Layer 3 Call(s)
    Active dsl 0 CCBs = 0
    The Free Channel Mask:  0x80000003
    Total Allocated ISDN CCBs = 0
Router#
```

```
--- output omitted ---
23:23:05: ISDN BR0/0 Q921: User RX <- DISCp sapi=0 tei=75
23:23:05: %ISDN-6-LAYER2DOWN: Layer 2 for Interface BR0/0, TEI 75 changed to
down
23:23:05: ISDN BR0/0 Q921: User TX -> UAf sapi=0 tei=75
Router#sh isdn status
Global ISDN Switchtype = basic-net3
ISDN BRI0/0 interface
        dsl 0, interface ISDN Switchtype = basic-net3
    Layer 1 Status:
        ACTIVE
    Layer 2 Status:
        TEI = 75, Ces = 1, SAPI = 0, State = TEI_ASSIGNED
    Layer 3 Status:
        0 Active Layer 3 Call(s)
    Active dsl 0 CCBs = 0
    The Free Channel Mask:  0x80000003
    Total Allocated ISDN CCBs = 0
```

IDREQ	Identity Request transmitted from the router to the ISDN switch requesting a Terminal Endpoint Identifier (TEI). All IDREQ messages have an AI value of 127 which indicates that the ISDN switch can assign any available TEI value.
IDASSN	Identity Assigned message with the TEI value of 75 assigned by ISDN switch is received from the ISDN switch.
SABMEp	Request the connection to be in Multiple Frame Established state. **SABME** → Set Asynchronous Balanced Mode Extended.
UAf	Unnumbered Acknowledgment (UA) of the SABME message. The ISDN Layer 2 is now in Multiple Frame Established state.

- An operational and functioning ISDN circuit (Multiple Frame Established) should have periodic exchanges of RRp sapi = 0 and RRf sapi = 0 messages between the router and ISDN switch. The interval between **Receiver Ready poll** (RRp) and **Receiver Ready final** (RRf) messages is usually 10 or 30 seconds.
  Note: TX -> indicates that a message is generated by the router while RX <- indicates that a message is received by the router.

- Below shows the **debug isdn q921** messages originated from the ISDN switch which indicate various ISDN Layer 2 problems:

Message	Description
ID-Denied	The ISDN switch cannot assign the requested TEI. If this message has an AI value of 127, it indicates that the ISDN switch has no TEI available.
IDREM	The ISDN switch has removed the TEI from the connection. The router must terminate all existing communication using the particular TEI.
DISC	The sending side of the DISConnect message has terminated the operation of ISDN Layer 3 for the connection. It may be unnumbered acknowledged by the other side. The router should then send a SABME message to reestablish the link.
DM	Indicates the Acknowledged Disconnect mode. The ISDN switch does not wish to enter the Multiple Frame Established state, and hence the router will remain in Layer 2 TEI_ASSIGNED state. The router will continuously send SABME messages until the ISDN switch responds with a UA instead of DM.
FRMR	The Frame Reject Response indicates an error that cannot be recovered by retransmission. The router will initiate a Layer 2 reset and transmit a SABME message to request to enter into Multiple Frame Established state.

Troubleshooting ISDN Layer 3

- Only proceed to this section after ISDN Layers 1 and 2 on both ends of a circuit are verified OK.

- ISDN call failures could be due to any of the following:
  i)   Dial-on-Demand Routing (DDR) related issues.
  ii)   ISDN Layer 1, 2, or 3 problems.
  iii)   Point-to-Point Protocol (PPP), including authentication, Link Control Protocol (LCP), or IP Control Protocol (IPCP) related issues.

- Figure A6-28 illustrates common Q.931 transactions during a successful ISDN call setup and teardown.

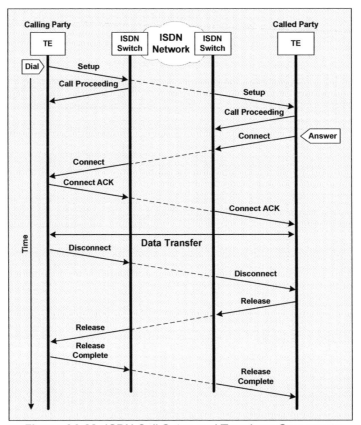

Figure A6-28: ISDN Call Setup and Teardown Sequences

- Pay attention to the direction of the output messages from the **debug isdn q931** privileged command. The TX -> indicates that a message is generated by the router while the RX <- indicates that a message is received by the router.

- The source of a problem can be identified by following the direction of a particular message and the response. Ex: If the local router unexpectedly receives a RELEASE message from the ISDN switch, then it will reset its end of the call as well. This indicates that there is an issue in the ISDN switch or the remote router.

- Verify that the message received or sent is the expected one. Ex: If the called party receives a SETUP message but responses with a DISCONNET message instead of a CONNECT message, then troubleshoot the called router and not the ISDN network.

- Below lists all the possible Q.931 messages during call establishment and termination:

Message	Description
SETUP	Indicates that a device would like to establish an ISDN Layer 3 call.
CALL_PROC	The SETUP message is received and is being processed by the network and/or the remote device.
ALERTING	Informs the network that the router is alerting the user, which would normally be the case for a telephone and the alert would ring the handset. This message is normally associated with equipment using a handset, eg: an ISDN telephone or TA and is not usually seen for data calls.
CONNECT	Call is accepted.
CONNECT_ACK	**Connect Acknowledge**. The device has received the CONNECT message. Higher layer protocols (eg: PPP) should now begin the negotiation process.
DISCONNECT	A router initiates a DISCONNECT message, which usually indicates that an operational ISDN call is disconnected due to some higher layer issues (eg: DDR, PPP, etc). The 3-way Disconnect Handshake will be accompanied by a RELEASE message, a Disconnect Cause Code, and a RELEASE_COMP message.
RELEASE	A router acknowledges the DISCONNECT message and continues the circuit termination process. The RELEASE message is sent between the DISCONNECT and RELEASE_COMP messages.
RELEASE_COMP	**Release Complete**. The call termination is completed. This message is often seen during a normal call termination initiated by one of the routers; in response to a SETUP message from the calling party when there is a mismatch of bearer capability between the ISDN switch and the router; or due to protocol error if the coding of the SETUP message does not comply with the Q.931 standard or the ISDN switch configuration.

- If the calling router does not send a SETUP message to the ISDN switch, the problem is likely related to ISDN Layer 1, 2, or DDR issues, and is not ISDN Layer 3 related.
  Perform the following troubleshooting tasks on the calling and called routers:
  i)   Verify that the ISDN switch types on both routers are configured correctly.
  ii)   Verify that the ISDN Layers 1 and 2 on both routers are functioning.
  iii)   Perform ISDN loopback test calls on both routers to verify they are able to initiate and accept calls.
  iv)   Verify the ISDN network of the called side is functioning by making a test call to the called router with a regular analog phone, in which the router should receive a SETUP message, although the call would eventually fail as it is not an ISDN call.
  v)   Verify that the calling router has a route to the destination with the **show ip route** EXEC command.
  vi)   Verify that the interesting traffic on the calling router is identified correctly.
  vii)   Verify that the appropriate **dialer string** or **dialer map** interface subcommand on the calling router refers to the correct number to the called router.
  viii) Check the DDR configuration and use the **debug dialer** privileged command to verify that the calling router is able to initiate calls.
  ix)   If the called router does not send a CONNECT message, check if the call is rejected due to the misconfiguration of the **isdn caller** {*incoming-number*} interface subcommand.
  x)   Contact the Telco and determine whether the long distance call service is activated.

ISDN Loopback Test Call

- In a loopback call, a router dials the ISDN number of its own BRI. The call is proceed to the ISDN switch, which then being switched to the 2nd BRI channel. The call is seen by the router as an incoming call on the 2nd channel. Therefore, the router both sends and receives an ISDN call on different B channels and act as both the **called** and **calling** routers.

- Loopback call tests the ability of a router to initiate and accept ISDN calls. It can also provide an indication that the physical links to the ISDN switch along with the ISDN switch are functioning.

Q.931 ISDN Layer 3 Disconnect Cause Codes

- This section explains how to interpret the ISDN disconnect cause codes which appear in the output of the **debug isdn q931** privileged command to indicate the reason for ISDN call disconnection or failure.

- The ISDN Layer 3 disconnect cause code the has the following format:
  Cause i = 0x*AABBCC* - *reason.*

AA	Cause Code Origination Point
BB	Disconnect Cause Code
CC	Optional Diagnostics Field

- Below lists all the Cause Code Origination Points:

80	Router
81	Private network near the local router (possibly a local private branch exchange – PBX)
82	Public network near the local router (local Telco switch)
83	Transit network in the ISDN cloud
84	Public network near the remote router (remote Telco switch)
85	Private network near the remote router (possibly a remote private branch exchange – PBX)
87	International network
8A	Network beyond the internetworking point

- Below lists all the standard ITU-T Q.931 Disconnect Cause Codes:

80	**Normal Disconnect**. The ISDN call disconnects normally.
81	**Unallocated or unassigned number**. The ISDN switch receives the ISDN number in the correct format. However, the number is not in the ISDN switch's routing table or it has no path across the ISDN network. Check the routing table to see whether the number is available; and check the correct digits were dialed and it is a valid number.
82	**No route to specified transit network**. The ISDN switch receives a request to route the call through an unrecognized intermediate (or transit) network – the ISDN switch has no route to the transit network. This problem can be due to either the transit network does not exist, or the transit network exists but does not serve the ISDN switch. This cause is supported on a network-dependent basis.
83	**No route to destination**. The dialed number is in the ISDN switch's routing plan, but there is no physical route to the destination and hence the called party is not reachable. This problem can be due to either the D channel is down at either end, or the span or WAN is not connected correctly. This cause is supported on a network-dependent basis.

84	**Send special information tone**. The called party is not reachable and a special information tone should be returned from the calling party. Check the dialing number and verify whether any prefix is required to access the network, eg: a 9 might need to be dialed for outbound calls through a PBX. Contact the Telco or PBX administrator for details.
85	**Misdialed trunk prefix**. There is erroneous inclusion of a trunk prefix in the dialed number. Check the dialing number and verify whether any prefix is required to access the network, eg: a 9 might need to be dialed for outbound calls through a PBX. Contact the Telco or PBX administrator for details.
86	**Channel unacceptable**. The service quality of the specified channel is insufficient to accept the connection. The call fails due to the channel is not acceptable (unusable) for the call. If a PBX is in used, check the configuration of the PBX. If a PRI is used, find out how many channels are provided by the Telco.
87	**Call awarded and being delivered in an established channel**. The called party receives an incoming call, but the call is being connected to a channel already established for similar calls (eg: packet-mode virtual calls).
88	**Preemption**. The call is being preempted or blocked. Sometimes calls are blocked if another call has a higher priority than the current call, which is common with voice calls. Wait and call again later. If a local or remote PBX is in used, check the configuration of the PBX. Contact the Telco if the problem persists.
89	**Preemption, circuit reserved for re-use**. The call is being cleared as one of the routers involved in the call has requested to terminate and clear the call.
90	**Normal call clearing**. The call disconnects and normal call clearing occurs due to one of the routers involved in the call requested to terminate and clear the call. This is one of the most common cause codes and is received for many reasons. Most of the time, the ISDN network is not the source of this cause. If a call fails with this cause, it is most likely fails with a higher layer protocol, eg: PPP, authentication, or idle timeout related issues. Verify the router configuration to resolve such problems. Additionally, if callback is configured on the local router, the remote router will disconnect the calls, generates this code, and calls the local router back.
91	**User busy**. The called party acknowledges the connection request. However, it is unable to accept the call due to all B channels are in use (the dialed number is busy). The routers are compatible with the call in this situation. **Note:** If there are multiple ISDN circuits, the Telco can configure them in a hunt-group, which calls are switched to next available circuit.
92	**No user response**. The called party does not respond to the call establishment message within a prescribed duration, or it does not wish to answer the call. The called party must respond with either an alert or connect indication according to ITU-T Q.931, when either timer T303 or T310 expires.
93	**No answer from user**. The called party is alerted to the connection request but does not respond with a connect indication to establish the connection within a prescribed duration. This cause is not necessary generated by Q.931 procedures; it may be generated by internal network timers. The problem is at the remote router.
94	**Subscriber absent**. The remote router is unavailable or disconnected from the ISDN network. Contact the person responsible for the remote router.
95	**Call rejected**. The remote router rejects the call due to an unknown reason. **Note:** The remote router is able to accept the call as it is able to respond with this cause, it is neither busy nor incompatible. This cause may also be generated by the ISDN network indicating that the call was cleared due to a supplementary service constraint.

96	**Number changed**. The called number is no longer assigned to any device. The new called number may optionally be included in the diagnostic field. If the network does not support this cause, the caller receives disconnect cause code 81 – unallocated or unassigned number.
97	**Redirection to new destination**. The call is routed to a different number. Check the called number and verify the configuration of the PBX if PBX is in used.
99	**Exchange routing error**. The call cannot be successfully routed to the remote router. Check the called number and verify the configuration of the PBX if a PBX is in used.
9A	**Non-selected user clearing**. The remote router is able to accept the call. However, it rejects the call due to the call is not assigned to any user.
9B	**Destination out of order**. The remote router is not reachable as there is a problem sending the signaling message to the remote router. This condition is often temporary, but can also last for an extended period in some cases. Possible causes are ISDN layer 1 or 2 fails at the remote end, or the remote router is powered off.
9C	**Invalid number format**. The call fails due to the called number is not in a valid format or is incomplete. This can also happen when the local router calling out using network-specific ISDN Type of Number (TON) when it should be calling out using National or Unknown for the ISDN Type of Number (TON). Verify whether the format of the number is correct, which includes any necessary digits for a PBX or long distance.
9D	**Facility rejected**. The ISDN network is unable to provide a requested supplementary service.
9E	**Response to STATUS ENQUIRY**. This cause code is included in a STATUS message when the STATUS message is generated upon the receipt of a STATUS ENQUIRY message.
9F	**Normal, unspecified**. This is a very common cause code and happens when the network is not able to determine the next course of action for the call. No action is required.
A1	**Circuit out of order**. The call fails due to some problems in the ISDN network.
A2	**No circuit / channel available**. The call fails due to no B channel is available to answer the call.
A3	**Destination unattainable**. The destination is not reachable through the ISDN network. Contact the Telco.
A4	**Out of order**. Some parts of the ISDN network necessary to route the call is out of order. The destination is not reachable due to a network malfunction. This condition can last for a relatively long period. An immediate attempt to reconnect will probably fail. Try to use a Presubscribed Inter-exchange Carrier (PIC) if a long distance carrier is being used. A PIC allows us to verify whether the problem lies with the long distance carrier.
A6	**Network out of order**. The destination is not reachable due to a network malfunction. This condition can last for a relatively long period. An immediate attempt to reconnect will probably fail. Try to use a Presubscribed Inter-exchange Carrier (PIC) if a long distance carrier is being used. A PIC allows us to verify whether the problem lies with the long distance carrier.
A7	**Permanent frame mode connection out of service**. This cause code is included in a STATUS message to indicate that a permanently established frame mode connection is terminated. Contact the Telco if the problem persists.
A8	**Permanent frame mode connection operational**. This cause code is included in a STATUS message to indicate that a permanently established frame mode connection is fully operational again and capable of carrying user information after a termination. The connection is probably terminated by a faulty equipment previously.
A9	**Temporary failure**. The call is disconnected due to a network malfunction. This condition is not likely to last a long period of time; another call attempt can be tried immediately. Contact the Telco if the problem persists.

AA	**Switching equipment congestion**. The destination is unreachable due to a temporary high traffic load on the network switching equipment. Try again later.
AB	**Access information discarded**. The ISDN network is unable to provide the requested access information. **Note:** The diagnostics field may indicate the particular type of discarded access information, eg: user-to-user information, low layer compatibility, high layer compatibility, and sub-address.
AC	**Requested circuit / channel not available**. The remote router is unable to provide the requested channel due to an unknown reason. This may happen when there is a glare condition, in which both sides are selected top-down or bottom-up channel hunting. This problem is usually temporary.
AF	**Resources unavailable, unspecified**. This cause code is used to report a resource unavailable event only when no other cause in the resource unavailable class applies. This problem is usually temporary.
B1	**Quality of service (QoS) unavailable**. The ISDN network unable to provide the requested Quality of Service as defined in Recommendation X.213. This problem can occur due to a subscription problem, or the ISDN network does not support throughput or transit delay.
B2	**Requested facility not subscribed**. The local router is not authorized to use a requested supplementary service which is implemented by the ISDN switch. The administrator has probably not completed the necessary administrative arrangements with the service provider. The ISDN network can also return this cause code if a call is made without supplying the SPIDs, or the SPIDs are entered wrongly. Ensure that the SPIDs are correct, or contact the Telco for verification.
B4	**Outgoing calls barred**. There are some restrictions on outgoing calls. The ISDN network does not allow the local router to make outgoing calls.
B5	**Outgoing calls barred within CUG**. There are some restrictions on outgoing calls. The ISDN network does not allow the local router to make outgoing calls although the calling party is a member of the CUG for the outgoing CUG call. Outgoing calls are not allowed for this member of the CUG. Contact the Telco.
B6	**Incoming calls barred**. The ISDN network does not allow the local router to receive calls. Contact the Telco.
B7	**Incoming calls barred within CUG**. The ISDN network does not allow the local router to receive calls although the called party is a member of the CUG for the incoming CUG call. Incoming calls are not allowed for this member of the CUG. Contact the Telco.
B9	**Bearer capability not authorized**. The local router requests a bearer capability that the ISDN switch implements, however the local router is not authorized to use the capability. A subscription problem usually causes this problem.
BA	**Bearer capability not presently available**. The ISDN network normally provides the requested bearer capability. However, the capability is unavailable at the particular moment. Normally caused by a temporary ISDN network problem or a subscription problem.
BE	**Inconsistency in designated outgoing access information and subscriber class**. There is an inconsistency in the designated outgoing access information and subscriber class.
BF	**Service or option not available, unspecified**. This cause code is used to report a service or option is unavailable event only when no other cause in the service or option not available class applies. Normally caused by a subscription problem.
C1	**Bearer capability not implemented**. The ISDN network is unable to provide the requested bearer capability, eg: requesting 64kb data when only speech is supported. Contact the Telco for further troubleshooting.

C2	**Channel type not implemented**. The equipment sending this cause does not support the requested channel type.
C5	**Requested facility not implemented**. The equipment sending this cause does not support the requested supplementary service.
C6	**Only restricted digital info bearer capability available**. The equipment sending this cause does not support and hence unable to provide unrestricted digital information bearer service (64kb). It only supports the restricted version of the requested bearer capability.
CF	**Service or option not implemented, unspecified**. This cause code is used to report a service or option not implemented event only when no other cause in the service or option not implemented class applies. Normally caused by a subscription problem.
D1	**Invalid call reference value**. The equipment sending this cause receives a call with a call reference that is not currently in use or assigned on the user-network interface. Ex: The call that is being referenced by the call reference value does not exist on the system.
D2	**Identified channel does not exist**. The equipment sending this cause receives a request to use an inactive channel for a call. Ex: When a PRI is subscribed to use channels 1 to 12 and the router or the ISDN network attempts to assign a call to channels 13 to 25.
D3	**A suspended call exists, but this call identity does not**. The ISDN switch receives a call resume request which contains a Call Identify (ID) information element that differs from the ID in use for any currently suspended call.
D4	**Call identity in use**. The ISDN switch receives a call suspend request which contains a call ID that is already in use for a suspended call which the call can be resumed instead of suspended again.
D5	**No call suspended**. The ISDN switch receives a call resume request when there is no currently suspended call. This transient error can be resolved through successive call retries.
D6	**Call having the requested call identity has been cleared**. The ISDN switch receives a call resume request which contains a call ID that indicates a suspended call. However, either a network timeout or the remote router has cleared the call while the call was suspended.
D7	**User not member of CUG**. The called party for the incoming CUG call is not a member of the specified CUG; or the calling party is an ordinary subscriber calling a CUG subscriber.
D8	**Incompatible destination**. Indicates an attempt to connect to non-ISDN device (eg: an analog line), in which the equipment sending this cause is not capable of answering a particular type of call – it is unable to accommodate a low layer compatibility, high layer compatibility, or other compatibility attributes. This cause code often appears when the calling device dials a wrong number and reaches a non-ISDN device; a data call is made to a voice number; a voice call is made to a number that only supports data; calling a restricted line in unrestricted mode; or calling a POTS phone using unrestricted mode. Check that the correct number is dialed. If the dialed number is correct, contact the Telco to verify that the ISDN switch configuration.
DA	**Non-existent CUG**. The specified CUG does not exist. Contact the Telco if the problem persists.
DB	**Invalid transit network selection**. The ISDN switch is requested to route the call through an unrecognized intermediate network – it receives a transit network identification which is in an incorrect format as defined in Annex C of ITU-T Q.931.
DF	**Invalid message, unspecified**. This cause code is used to report an invalid message event only when no other cause in the invalid message class applies. This problem usually occurs due to a D channel error. Contact the Telco if the problem occurs systematically.

E0	**Mandatory information element missing**. The equipment sending this cause receives a message is missing an information element that is necessary for it to process the message. This problem usually occurs due to a D channel error. Upgrade the Cisco IOS software on the router to resolve this problem. Contact the Telco if the problem occurs systematically.
E1	**Message type non-existent or not implemented**. The equipment sending this cause receives an unrecognized message due to either the message type is invalid, or it does not support or implement the message type. The problem usually occurs due to the D channel of the local router or the configuration of the remote router.
E2	**Message not compatible with call state or message type non-existent or not implemented**. The equipment sending this cause receives a message that is not permissible in the call state according to the procedures, or it receives a STATUS message which indicates an incompatible call state. This problem usually occurs due to a D channel error. Contact the Telco if the problem occurs.
E3	**Information element non-existent or not implemented**. The equipment sending this cause receives a message that contains an unrecognized information element which it does not support or implement. However, the message does not need to contain the information element in order for the equipment sending this cause to process the message. This problem usually occurs due to a D channel error. Contact the Telco if the problem occurs.
E4	**Invalid information element contents.** The ISDN switch receives a message that contains invalid contents in the information element – the information element is implemented, but one or more of the fields in the information element are coded differently. This cause is usually followed by the information element that is causing the problem.
E5	**Message not compatible with call state**. The ISDN switch receives a message that does not correspond to the current call state for the call.
E6	**Recovery on timer expired**. Occurs when ISDN messages do not arrive in specified time according to the Q.931 specification. This cause if sometimes followed by the expired timer. Wait and try again later. Contact the Telco if the problem persists.
E7	**Parameter not implemented**. The equipment sending this cause receives a message which contains an unrecognized parameter which it does not support or implement. Contact the Telco if the problem occurs.
EE	**Message with unrecognized parameter discarded**. The equipment sending this cause has discarded a received message which contains an unrecognized parameter.
EF	**Protocol error, unspecified**. This cause code is used to report a protocol error event only when no other cause in the protocol error class applies. This problem usually occurs due to a D channel error.
FF	**Interworking, unspecified**. The ISDN network is interworking with another network which does not provide the next course of action. The precise problem is unknown.

Note: Closed User Group (CUG) is a facility in X.25 and ISDN networks that allows a called number to be available only to a limited number of users in a virtual private network.

This page is intentionally left blank

Index

I

ICMP (Internet Control Message Protocol), 15, 72 - 74
  Can't Fragment code, 72
  Destination Unreachable messages, 72
  Echo Request / Reply messages, 15, 72
  Host Unreachable, 72
  Network Unreachable code, 72
  Protocol Unreachable code, 72
  Redirect messages, 72, 74
  Source Quench messages, 73
  Time Exceeded messages, 15, 72, 73
  Unreachable codes, 72
icons, 1
identifying
  data link layer encapsulated data, 17, 23
  subnet broadcast address, 63
  IP addresses in a subnet, 63
idle frames (synchronous data link protocols), 152
IETF encapsulation, Frame Relay, 159
IGMP (Internet Group Management Protocol), 20
IGRP (Interior Gateway Routing Protocol), 79, 80
  configuration, 87 - 89
  metric, 79
  variance, 79, 90
inbound access list, 135
inside global addresses, 125, 129
inside local addresses, 125, 129
interaction
  adjacent-layer interaction, 3
  same-layer interaction, 3
interesting traffic, ISDN, 193, 194
interior gateway protocols, 75
interior routing protocols
  classifying, 75
  EIGRP, 95 - 98, 107 - 110
  IGRP, 79, 80, 87 - 89
  OSPF, 91 - 95, 99 - 106
  RIP, 79, 80, 85 - 87
interoperability, 1
interworking, Frame Relay, 162, 163
invalid timer, 80
IOR (Index of Refraction), 27
IOS
  boot sequence, 37
  CLI error messages, 32
  configuration register, 37
  copy operation, 36
  image name decode, 37
  modes, 37
  ROMmon, 37
  RXBOOT, 37
  upgrade process, 36
IP
  address classes, 61
  IP addresses, 12
  IPv4 datagram format, 13
  private addressing, 62
  subnetting, 12, 62, 63
IPCP (IP Control Protocol), 150
IPv6, 64
IPX (Internetwork Packet Exchange), 12
IPXCP (IPX Control Protocol), 150
ISDN (Integrated Services Digital Networks)
  BRI, 196, 197
  call setup, 197
  CHAP, 195
  circuit establishment, 189
  configuration, 193 - 202
  DDR, 193 - 196
  dialer groups, 200
  dialer profiles, 200 - 202
  displaying status information, 197, 198
  encoding (PRI), 192, 199
  framing (PRI), 192, 199
  function groups, 190
  idle timers, 193, 196
  Layer 2 messages, 197, 198
  Layer 3 messages, 197, 198
  legacy DDR, 193 - 196
  modems, 187, 191
  Multilink PPP, 202
  out-of-band signaling, 189
  PRI
    configuration, 199
    E1 / T1 controllers, 199
    encoding, 192, 199
    framing, 192, 199
  reference points, 191
  signaling, 194, 195
  SPIDs, 189, 196
ISL (Inter-Switch Link) trunking, 51, 52
ISM (Industrial, Scientific, and Medical) bands, 173
ITU (International Telecommunications Union), 147, 188

J

jamming signal, 18

Printed in Great Britain
by Amazon.co.uk, Ltd.,
Marston Gate.